ORAL
COMMUNICATION

DONALD C. BRYANT
University of Iowa

KARL R. WALLACE
University of Illinois

New York

APPLETON-CENTURY-CROFTS, INC.

ORAL COMMUNICATION

A Short Course in Speaking

Third Edition

ACKNOWLEDGMENTS

Fig. 1, p. 49: Courtesy of *Reader's Guide to Periodical Literature* and *Engineering Index*.
Fig. 2, p. 49: Courtesy of *The Public Affairs Information Service*.
Fig. 3, p. 54: First table, courtesy of *Survey of Current Business;* Second table, courtesy of *Statistical Abstract of the United States*.
Fig. 6, p. 95: Courtesy of Time, Inc.
Fig. 7, p. 96: Courtesy of *The New York Times*.
Fig. 8, p. 98: Courtesy of *The New York Times*.
Fig. 9, p. 98: Courtesy of *The Wall Street Journal*.
Fig. 10, p. 99: Courtesy of the University of Illinois.
Fig. 11, p. 99: Courtesy of *The New York Times*.
Fig. 12, p. 100: Courtesy of the University of Illinois.
Fig. 13, p. 100: Courtesy of *The Chicago Sun-Times*.

Preface:

for Student and Teacher

THIS THIRD, revised edition, like its predecessors, is intended for students in those courses that demand ample coverage of essential precept, but do not permit time for extended study of theory and principles. We have retained our plan, therefore, of giving full coverage to such matters as getting started right, finding subjects and materials, amplifying and organizing ideas, and developing good style and delivery. At the same time we reduce to a minimum the theoretical background in rhetoric and the psychology of communication and the philosophical discussion of speech in the social and political fabric. Thus we have attempted to write a relatively brief book without the expository inadequacies of handbook or manual.

Again like its predecessors, this edition is abridged and adapted from the corresponding revised edition (third) of our *Fundamentals of Public Speaking* (1960). Hence we think it, like that one, better than the earlier editions. We think that the organization and handling of precepts and methods, especially in treating the use of expository materials, the organization of ideas, style, and the problems of persuasion, are clearer, sharper, and pedagogically firmer than they were in former editions. New generations of students and growing circles of professional colleagues inevitably leave upon the teacher and writer the salutary marks of their stimulation and counsel. We know that they have both guided and goaded us into new clarity and precision in the organization of the book; and no doubt they have had a share also in the gain we think we have made in extent and depth of materials.

This edition, like the others, we think, follows progressively the needs of the student in a beginning course in public speaking, where he is asked to make speeches almost from the outset, before he has had time or opportunity to go far in the textbook. Accordingly, after introducing him to the implications of the study which he is undertaking (Chapter 1), we present to him a minimum of operating principle and method for his speeches (Chapter 2). Hence he may begin his systematic speech-making upon a basis which will be extended and amplified later but will not have to be unlearned or essentially modified. We believe that we have dealt with first things first, and we have found the procedure effective and useful in the classroom.

Much of the book is actually new in conception and development, and we have thoroughly rewritten about half of it. Nevertheless, we still pay more attention to the two subjects of organization and delivery than perhaps is common. For our continued emphasis upon knowledge and thought as fundamental to good speaking and upon the "gentleman conversing" as the norm of delivery, we feel no need to offer special justification. Among the pedagogical improvements which we think that we have achieved in this edition is the association of interest with style, with methods and techniques of amplifying and developing statements, and with motivation. To handle interest thus, instead of treating it as a separate topic, seems both psychologically and linguistically sound, for attention and interest may accompany the content and style of any statement and be bound into the development of any kind of discourse.

In both of our books our purpose, of course, is the same as it has been from the first: to provide college students and other mature learners with a firm foundation and sound principles for the study and practice of public speaking. Although the principles and precepts, interpreted by the alert and resourceful teacher, may not necessarily lead students to speak more often or more volubly than their less tutored fellows, we hope that students will learn to speak more appropriately and usefully, in short, *better,* than the uninstructed. Modern society, we might well agree, does not need more public speaking, but it certainly needs and deserves better public address and discussion. Since improvement in speaking may be stimulated by the study of good speeches, we include again a brief selection of speeches for study and reading aloud. Some, such as Bruce Barton's *Which Knew Not Joseph,* we retain from the previous edition, and others, such as President Kennedy's *Inaugural Address,* are new to this edition.

Our pedagogical purpose has led us to write primarily for the student. We have attempted, wherever possible, to supply him with how-to-do-it directions. Nevertheless, we have steadily endeavored to bring to him some understanding of the principles necessary to intelligent practice. Even the novice should *understand* as well as *do.*

We assume that the student who makes the most profitable use of this book, or of any textbook in public speaking, will consider himself a learner and will read to understand and to apply its teachings. Some of those teachings, perhaps many of them, will seem obvious, even commonplace—what every sensible person knows. They seem so to us also. We know, however—what the student will realize upon consideration—that many such principles are too often accepted in theory but ignored in practice. They seem like the essence of common sense; but like common sense in other areas, they seldom work unless the learner tries consciously to make them work.

Some of the methods and procedures we advise may seem at times unduly thorough for the simple speeches being undertaken. The student must realize, however, that he should be gaining knowledge and developing reliable methods and habits of work and thought which will be adequate to large occasions as well as small, to difficult problems as well as easy ones. In the establishing of habits of orderly procedure—for example, in organizing ideas into a workable pattern for easy recall during delivery—the student must go through the whole process, no matter how obvious much of it may seem, and the instructor who would serve him best should see that he does. He must be required to think in detail about the way to go about thinking.

Like most authors, we find it impossible to acknowledge properly our debts to the persons, both students and colleagues, who have influenced us. They have been many and we are grateful to them. For special counsel on parts of this book, we here thank Professors Marie Hochmuth Nichols, Richard Murphy, and King Broadrick of the University of Illinois, Dean Earnest S. Brandenburg of Washington University, and Professors H. Clay Harshbarger and Orville A. Hitchcock of the University of Iowa. Very helpful in checking the material in Chapter 4 and in supplying the photographs for that chapter have been Professor Richard Smith and Mr. L. W. Dunning of the University of Illinois Library.

Acknowledgments of permission to reproduce certain materials are made elsewhere.

D. C. B.

K. R. W.

Contents

ORAL
COMMUNICATION

CHAPTER ONE

Introduction:
The Study of Public Speaking

PUBLIC SPEAKING is systematic, practical communication which aims, through speech and gesture, to add to the knowledge and understanding of listeners or to influence their attitudes and conduct. The study of public speaking is directed toward principles and practice, knowledge and experience. The principles of public address were first formulated and organized into a textbook over 2400 years ago. They were drawn from the practice and experience of hundreds of speechmakers in the ancient Greek world. They have been transmitted down through the centuries to us, sometimes remaining unchanged, sometimes being altered and added to. Political and social conditions, changing from age to age, have created different roles and values for public address and have prompted new styles and habits of public speaking. The conditions of modern society likewise affect standards of communication. Modern speechmakers, through their accumulated experience, add to our knowledge; and students of public address, employing the methods of history, criticism, and scientific experiment, add information year by year.

The roll of those who have written on the principles of public speaking includes the names of some of the most prominent men in history: Plato and Aristotle, the greatest philosophers and teachers of ancient Greece; Cicero, one of the two foremost public speakers of the ancient world; Quintilian, the Roman teacher, whose treatise on the education of the public speaker (*Institutes of Oratory*) is one of the basic educational works of all time; Tacitus, the Roman historian; St. Augustine, one of the fathers of the Church; Erasmus, the eminent Renaissance scholar; Thomas Hobbes and Francis Bacon, two of the great English philosophers; Fénelon, the French bishop; and John Quincy Adams, the American scholar, teacher, and President. Each age has had many good teachers and writers on the subject, and in every age the study of public speaking has had a place in education—often a prominent place.

This is not to say that the teachers and the doctrines in the textbooks have always been much the same in kind and quality. Like all other so-

1

cial phenomena, public speaking has changed with fashion and with the needs and interests of times and countries. The theory and the practice of public speaking have been good and they have been bad, like the theory and practice of politics, and medicine, and ethics, and poetry. The greatest of the textbook writers, Aristotle, however, early established the principle that the best public speaking is not founded, as Plato had accused his contemporaries of founding theirs, on glibness of tongue and baseless appeal to ignorance and emotion. It is founded on knowledge and sound thinking, though it is supported by eloquence and emotion for its greater effectiveness. It is practical, popular discourse directed toward adjusting ideas to people and people to ideas through words and gesture.

VALUES OF PUBLIC SPEAKING

As the study of public speaking has enjoyed dignity and importance in all the ages of Western civilization, so it thrives today when the demands upon the spoken word and the facilities for transmitting it are much greater than they ever were before. Today, of course, to aid in the running of our complicated society, we have as well tremendous quantities of all sorts of printed matter. But because of the extent and the increased complexity of our social, economic, and political life, there is not less but more demand for oral communication.

The student will want to recognize for himself the values which modern society associates with public speaking. Some are personal; some are social. Some are self-evident, because they are linked to such motives as self-improvement, personal success, and confidence. Others are less evident, because they are connected with such values as social responsibility, the welfare of others, and the health of democratic society. Perhaps these values are obvious and are generally accepted. At any rate, the student who is enrolled in a course in public speaking is convinced that there are significant advantages to be gained. In Chapter 1 of our *Fundamentals of Public Speaking* (3rd edition, 1960), we have discussed the personal and social values at some length. In this chapter, however, we wish to point especially to one of those values which is, perhaps, more likely to be overlooked than the rest—the ability to listen critically.

The Habit of Critical Listening

Training in public speaking should not only help one become a better speaker; it should also make one a better *listener* and should facilitate a more critical and intelligent understanding of those social processes in which public speaking plays a prominent role. In former times the art of listening was widespread and necessary. In the earlier stages of our society, public speaking was practically the only means available for the large scale dissemination of news, information, ideas, and opinions. But with the invention of printing, the rise of literacy, the appearance of the newspaper, and the simultaneous growth in the size and complexity of our social and political organization, the printed word became the chief means of reaching great masses of people. As a result, skill in listening seemed less essential than skill in reading. Since the rise of radio and the development of television, however, the spoken word competes with the newspaper in reaching great audiences. We get our news now as much by radio and TV as by newspaper; our political leaders address us as much by radio and TV as by newspaper; our advertisers sell us goods by TV and radio in greater quantities than they ever did through the press or mail solicitation.

Under this modern barrage of words which deluges every home, we have not as a people acquired the attitude of the judicious critic. We do not *habitually* weigh and consider; rather, we respond in a blanket fashion. If a speaker can interest and entertain us, we listen with approval; if we like a speaker because of his reputation or his political allegiance, we approve of what he says without much resistance; if we dislike a speaker, we indiscriminately condemn his message. Extremely valuable in modern society, then, is the ability to listen with discrimination. As you become a more skilled, a more accomplished, in short, a better speaker, you should also become a more critical listener—less gullible, more stable, wiser, and clearer-minded, better able to distinguish the solid from the hollow, the forthright from the dishonest, the real from the fake. The audience is as vital a part of public speaking as the speaker. The analytical and critical study of public speaking, such as that undertaken in this book and conducted in public speaking classrooms, will usually result in an individual's becoming a better listener, a better member of an audience.

SOME MISCONCEPTIONS ABOUT PUBLIC SPEAKING

Recognizing the values of oral communication often provides the incentives needed to sustain the earnest study of public speaking. Goals and motives are always important. Yet our experience as teachers reveals that some persons have picked up attitudes and misconceptions which hinder wholehearted study. Their attitudes are most often expressed in statements like these: "I'm not cut out to be a speaker." "I distrust glib speakers, and I don't want to be one." "Some speakers, like the advertisers and hucksters, sound affected and insincere." "A lot of speakers today, like the politicians, aren't saying anything worth saying." "Yes, I'd like to speak well, but I don't think I can discover the secret which will make *me* a good speaker." Underlying such statements are at least four misconceptions. They are misconceptions because they confuse good public speaking with bad and because they confuse a "talent" or "gift" with what may be achieved through well-directed hard work.

The Born Speaker

The first misconception is the belief that public speaking is only a natural ability or a knack. You either have it or you don't, and if you don't, there's nothing much you can do about it. Here we have the age-old argument: Which is more important, art or nature—training or native ability?

As Quintilian asserted long ago, the question has little meaning, for it is obvious that a person with no ability at all cannot be given ability by study. On the other hand, there is abundant evidence that the study of public speaking can make poor speakers good and good speakers better. It is doing so all the time, in every public speaking class in the country, and it has done so throughout history. Demosthenes, the greatest orator of Greece, had to learn to speak, and he learned the hard way. Cicero, the greatest of the Roman speakers, was also, as we have seen, a thorough student of rhetoric. The Earl of Chesterfield, one of the most polished and effective speakers ever to sit in the House of Lords, was thoroughly familiar with the classical principles of public speaking, which he recommended earnestly to his young son whom he hoped to make into a good public speaker.

True, some exceptional persons do *seem* to become satisfactory speakers through native ability and unconscious imitation alone. So, too, there seem to be born singers, born baseball players, and born cooks. On the other hand, given a reasonable portion of brains, almost anyone can learn to be an acceptable public speaker if he is willing to work intelligently and persistently. Few persons in any generation have the mind, soul, physical endowments, talents, genius, and opportunity to become such public speakers as Cicero, Burke, Churchill, or Franklin Roosevelt; and few people have the need for such ability. The mechanical engineer or the physician or the shop foreman or the college student who will for a few months devote the same energy to the study of public speaking that he gives to his specialty can learn to speak acceptably.

Distrust of Skill in Speech

A second common misconception—that skillful speakers are less trustworthy than unskillful speakers—seems to come from the mistaken value many persons put upon inarticulateness, from the common distrust of anyone who *seems* to do anything too well or too easily. "He sounded too good; he was too smooth; he must be a scoundrel" is a criticism as basically unsound as it is frequent. Somewhere in our development we have become victims of the feeling that only the evil or false can be pleasant, that the greater the truth and the sounder the teaching, the more unpleasant must be their expression! If powerful, pleasant, or fluent speaking can make falsehood, deceit, and intellectual emptiness seem to the unwary like truth, honesty, and solid sense, how much more attractive may not the same qualities of utterance make the good, the desirable, the real? If Hitler rose to power through his speeches, so did Paul, St. Augustine, Samuel Adams, Lincoln, and Churchill. A halting, embarrassed, garbled inarticulateness never was a guarantee of excellence in any profession. In a society which is supported as substantially as ours is by speech, the most lamentable fact is not that audiences are gullible and easily led and that many speakers and commercial and political hucksters play upon emotion without sound ideas and make the "worse appear the better reason." The sadder fact is that more of the intelligent, able, and honest people do not take the trouble to equip themselves to be critical members of audiences and better speakers. Virtue and goodness of themselves may be sufficient for the successful maintenance of the Kingdom of Heaven, but they apparently need mighty support if they are to govern the nations on earth. Educated men may well ponder Francis Bacon's advice that "the business of rhetoric is to make pictures of virtue and goodness, so that they may be seen."

Affectation

A third misconception of public speaking is that the speaker must adopt a studied, somewhat "affected" delivery, insincere sentiment, and elegant, inflated language. Every thoughtful person is opposed to the absurd exhibitionism of so-called "elocution," to the hollow bombast and the slick effrontery and falsehood of high-pressure salesmanship. The terms *elocution* and *oratory* have been badly victimized by being popularly attached to oral monstrosities. At their best, these currently unacceptable kinds of public speaking once satisfied the fashions and tastes of a day that is gone. At their worst, they were spectacular nonsense. It is a mistake to suppose that public speaking should be damned because some of its manifestations are strange or outmoded. Good public speaking does not demand a special manner and vocabulary which set it apart and make it different from ordinary talk. It is ineffective and useless so far as it seems to be engaged in for itself. It must be communication fitted to the manners and fashions of the persons talked to, and it must not be out of harmony with the ideas and feelings the speaker is trying to communicate. "Elocution," "oratory," or for that matter, much of the advertising talk we hear on the air, is not bad because it is public speaking; it is bad because its language, content, and manner of delivery are ridiculously out of harmony with the nature and worth of the thing being talked about and the person doing the talking.

Content Unrelated to Skill

Another misconception is that it is possible to learn to "make speeches" quite apart from learning to say anything in particular. This false notion sometimes may have a certain plausibility about it. One who has learned well the principles of public speaking and has mastered the practice of them will be able to use them for speeches on a great many subjects. Learning to make speeches, however, is not like learning to make tin cans, which may be made well without the maker's knowing whether the cans are to hold peas or beans. The principles of good speaking are never entirely separate from the materials to which they are being applied. Needless to say, lots of nonsense is talked in the world, lots of words are uttered in public—even harmoniously to the ear—when no idea, information, or worthy sentiment is conveyed; and doubtless these performances may be called public speaking. They cannot, however, be said to be *good* public speaking, and good public speaking is what we seek to achieve. For purposes of analysis and criticism we break the total process of public speaking into the subsidiary processes which make it up. This we do in order to be able to study and learn one thing at a time. We must always remember, however, that a speech is an organic whole. It must be judged as a whole, not as expression only, or delivery only, or as thought only. It is unwise, therefore, for the learner to think of a speech as something in and for itself. He had better think of a speech on a specific subject, for a specific purpose, delivered by a specific person, before a specific audience, at a specific time and place. Hence, the content or materials of a speech, as well as its form, language, and delivery, are inseparable from the speaker's purpose and the occasion.

It is inevitable, accordingly, that the public speaker or the student of public speaking must have something of consequence to say. This means that the man who knows most about most things and most people —he who has thought most, has read most, has experienced most, has observed most, has become most familiar with the minds and hearts and manners of his fellow men, and has retained most completely the knowledge and insight thus gained—this man, if he has also learned the principles of public speaking and has cultivated the will to communicate, will be the best speaker. Of course, most good speakers, even college professors, fall somewhat short of these ideals. Nevertheless, no matter how restricted the area of subject matter within which we may choose to speak, it is our duty as speakers to know our subjects well and, in addition, to acquire a store of knowledge of human beings and a store of available ideas by which we can make our subjects clear, interesting, and convincing. Only thus can we have something worth saying and the means of communicating it successfully to others who do not know it or have not thought it already.

All except the dullest of us gain some knowledge and some experience from the mere process of living, and the more we are subjected to education, the greater our knowledge and experience become. Much of what we acquire is common to others like us, but each of us has some store, however meager, of knowledge and experience more or less peculiar to himself. This stock of common and special material serves very well as a start for most beginning speakers and students of public speaking, but unless it is rapidly and deliberately augmented it soon begins to get thin and shopworn. Subjects upon which we want to talk and can talk become hard to find, and our reserve of the common ingredients of good speaking becomes sadly depleted. If you want to speak well, then, the answer, and the only answer, is: *learn more, observe more, think more,* not only when you have a speech to make, but between times. Pumping a dry well is an unrewarding occupation except in the mere bodily exercise which it provides for the man on the handle of the pump. If your time and effort in your study of public speaking are well expended, you will learn not only to speak but to speak *about something.* You will learn how to discover and use the resources which you already have; and you will learn to increase those resources and keep on increasing them.

The Magic Push Button

One last misconception standing in the way of profitable study of public speaking perhaps needs attention, though by implication we have considered it already. That is the very popular idea that teachers of public speaking, and good speakers, could reveal if they would the "secret" of success on the platform. Somehow the idea dies hard that there is a miracle-making formula which needs only to be grasped by a man to turn him into an effective, eloquent fellow, full of excellent thoughts which he manages to impose upon an audience without effort or pain to himself or to his hearers. This is nonsense, and the whole of education exposes the emptiness of the "secret" theory, however attractive it may be. True, the best speakers do the right thing at the right time largely *by habit,* and hence they may be no more aware of their basic process than they are in any other *habitual* act. Furthermore, some persons acquire habits more easily than others do. But the ultimate fact is that a habit is learned—learned through work that is guided by self-criticism and by the criticism of others.

THE ESSENTIAL PROBLEM

Now, if we have disposed of the principal misconceptions which tend to distort a student's view of speechmaking, we can consider certain implications of the definition of public speaking with which we began this chapter. The student then can guide his study and practice accordingly. The essential consideration is that public address seeks to produce effect-on-listeners. An audience-to-be-affected gives rise to the speech, and the kind of effect intended determines the type of speech which will be made. And the audience strongly affects the behavior of the speaker. It gives to him and to his speaking a sense of directness: a speaker not only recognizes the presence of his hearers but *feels* their presence. Even in radio-TV, speaker and listener sense some immediacy. Factors of time and place and subject combine to give a concrete character and personality to an audience; and the speaker plans for this specific audience and occasion.

The Classroom Audience

As a student of public speaking you will gradually discover the best example of a specific audience—an audience whose interests, abilities, and opinions you will learn much about. It is, of course, your classroom audience, ever present and ever real. Do not be misled into thinking that the class situation is either solely, or primarily, artificial. It is a contrived situation only in part. Both listener and speaker are studying and practicing the art of oral communication and are self-consciously aware of that fact. And in the classroom, as a rule, listeners don't invite their fellows to speak to them—the instructor does that. But in all other respects, you are in a real communicative environment. You face real persons. You face the same audience often enough to know much about its "personality." (Indeed, unless you become a clergyman or a trial lawyer, you may never again as a speaker know an audience so well.) By accepting your classmates as they are, by speaking to them rather than to some remote, imaginary group, by trying to make them understand, to interest them, or otherwise to influence them, you can help yourself acquire a lively sense of *direct* communication.

Effect and Response

In directing attention to the effect of a speech upon its hearers, we are talking about *response*. To consider the effect of a speech, accordingly, is to think of the response to the speech as a whole. The proper response to a speech is not *at* the speech or *to* the speaker, but is in line with what the speech is trying to do. The correct response is well illustrated by the Athenian audience who after hearing Demosthenes urge war against Philip went away saying, "Let's fight the Macedonians." The wrong response is represented by the Athenians' reaction to Aeschines' oratory, when they exclaimed, "What a wonderful speech!"

The kinds of responses to a speech correspond to three kinds of effects.

The effect may be that of knowledge and understanding. The listener is able to say, "I see," "I know," or "I understand." His knowledge has gained breadth or depth.

The effect may be some change in the listener's opinions or attitudes, and the shift may be in different directions. This fact was well illustrated by a classroom audience which heard a speech contending that alimony in divorce cases was justified only when the wife or the children needed support. Some listeners who already held the view found their beliefs reinforced and intensified. Some who had held no opinion on the subject said that they had accepted the speaker's belief. Still others, in disagreement with the speaker, reported that they were less strongly opposed, even uncertain.

The effect may be action of one kind or another, ranging from polite hand clapping to enthusiastic applause to doing what the speech suggests or directs.

These are the main kinds of responses to speeches (and to any practical discourse), although on rare occasions there are speeches to which we respond only with interest, pleasure, or amusement. It is important only to recognize that there is always some kind of response to a communication, and that the response consists in whatever the audience thinks and does. Sometimes the response is immediate and can be observed, as when a man buys insurance after the sales talk. More often it is remote and unrecognized, as when we find one day that we have a new attitude toward Latin Americans, not knowing that past information and argument, absorbed through forgotten speeches, articles, and discussions about Latin-American problems, have brought about the change. Talk, anybody's talk, anywhere and anytime, may be responsible for shifts of belief.

Kinds of Speeches

The classification of speeches is based on the listener and the kinds of response he makes to speechmaking and to practical discourse in general. In keeping with the responses we have just discussed, we can group speeches into two fundamental types, the informative and the persuasive.

The informative speech seeks to impart knowledge or illumination to an audience. Its materials consist of facts and data, on the one hand,

and principles, laws, and explanations of the facts, on the other. They are the materials which form the basis of any field of study—engineering, home economics, physics, accounting, medicine. Hence a common type of informative speech is the lecture. The listener is a learner and the result of his learning is knowledge.

The persuasive speech aims at influencing the opinion and conduct of an audience. Its materials are drawn from those problems about which men hold different beliefs and opinions—controversial matters which call for decision and action from time to time. The problems may be very general: In what ways can we improve public school education? They may be quite specific: Should the high school graduate be able to speak a foreign language? Technically, the materials of persuasion are the opinions, arguments, and facts surrounding a problem which is calling for decision. A persuasive speech is always telling hearers what they *ought* to believe or to do. A persuasive speech says: Accept this view, or act in ways consistent with it. The listener is the judge. He accepts or rejects the view, or he may doubt the view. He acts on the view, or he does not, when he has the chance.

Speaker and Audience

In no other communicative endeavor does the personality of the communicator register so directly upon the audience and so immediately influence the effect as in oral communication. Whenever a speech is made to listeners, a speaker is delivering it. He cannot, like a painter, complete his object, hang it in a gallery, and go away. Nor can he, like a writer, finish off his composition and send it abroad for whatever audience may find it. In oral communication, the speaker as a person wields direct influence.

We know that some qualities of personality and character, critically important in communication, are revealed through our ideas and opinions. These reflect such values as truthfulness, humor, knowledge and competence, accuracy of statement, sincerity and consistency of belief, respect and sympathy for others. Such qualities or their opposites are evident in most communications, particularly in writing and speaking. Some, however, are signaled most directly by the inflections, intonations, and qualities of the voice. Our ears, for example, instantly recognize the notes of friendliness, sympathy, humor, modesty, and respect. They at once sense the ring of conviction and truth and detect as readily the tones of insecurity, sarcasm, and falsity. Our eyes, observing the gestures of face and body, take in at a glance the signs of friendliness, liveliness, and directness. They also derive impressions from appearance and dress. Thus does the speaker, as do any of us in our everyday conversation, draw his own portrait swiftly and surely. The personality and character of the novelist are usually in the background and must be searched for; the personality of the speaker is in the foreground, revealed in everything he says and does.

As a student of speaking you can begin at once to develop or confirm in yourself those qualities of character and personality which will themselves speak on your behalf as you address your audiences. You can undertake to master those fundamental processes, to which this book is devoted, which underlie good oral communication. You can learn, moreover, to handle them methodically, for you can look ahead to your speaking date, take early stock of your resources, add to them as soon as possible, set aside time for organizing and outlining your materials, and reserve definite periods for oral rehearsal. Intelligent planning and work bring gratifying results; you don't need to be a genius to build a good speech. Recognizing these facts, you can rapidly develop a great deal of confidence in your own abilities. Furthermore, through your speeches you can win respect and influence as a person. You can offer useful knowledge and information to your classroom listeners. You can present opinions that are well reasoned and well grounded on evidence. You can prepare thoroughly and speak clearly and accurately. You can respect the interests of your hearers and treat them in a direct and friendly manner. By having their welfare at heart, you create the right impression.

We now turn at once to the methodical business of constructing and presenting speeches.

FURTHER READING

BERELSON, B., "Democratic Theory and Public Opinion," *Public Opinion Quarterly*, 16 (Fall 1952), 311–330.

BRYANT, Donald C., "Rhetoric: Its Functions and Its Scope," *Quarterly Journal of Speech*, 39 (December 1953), 401–424.

BRYANT, Donald C., and Karl R. WALLACE, *Fundamentals of Public Speaking*, 3rd ed. (New York, Appleton-Century-Crofts, Inc., 1960), Chs. 1 & 2.

BRYSON, Lyman, ed., *The Communication of Ideas* (New York, 1948).

HAYAKAWA, S. J., *Language in Action*, rev. ed. (New York, 1949).

HUNT, Everett L., "Rhetoric as a Humane Study," *Quarterly Journal of Speech*, 41 (April 1955), 114–117.

LANGER, Susanne K., *Philosophy in a New Key* (Baltimore, Md., 1948), Ch. 4, "Discursive and Presentational Forms."

NILSEN, T. R., "Free Speech, Persuasion, and the Democratic Process," *Quarterly Journal of Speech*, 44 (October 1958), 235–243.

O'NEILL, J. M., and A. T. WEAVER, *The Elements of Speech* (New York, 1938), Chs. 1–3.

CHAPTER TWO

The First Speeches

Getting Started Right

Long before the beginning student of public speaking has had time to study the substance of the textbook and to advance far in his mastery of the principles of speechmaking, he will already have begun gaining experience in speaking. Soon after the introduction, therefore, firm guidance in the application of some few fundamentals seems needed. If he grasps those fundamentals, the student, even in his first speeches, will be prepared to proceed systematically in the use of principles which he will later study more fully. He will avoid the hazard of having to unlearn faulty procedures and to break bad habits which he had begun to fix through random practice.

In his earliest speeches a learner's principal problems may appear to be breaking the ice and getting a little experience in talking on his feet. Our experience indicates, however, that almost from the first the student may overcome the worst of his initial hesitancy and timidity and may progress toward some confidence before an audience at the same time that he learns to crystallize, clarify, and develop ideas according to sound and systematic principles.

In order to establish at once, therefore, certain operating procedures and fundamental patterns for the first speeches, we offer this chapter on introductory principles. The important matter from the start is the conscious application—the use—of sound principles, patterns, and procedures. They should become the speaker's *habitual* ways of thinking for speaking. Then, many of the problems which plague beginning speakers will have disappeared.

Establishing good habits of behavior before an audience involves also the systematic study of delivery, which we will present in a later chapter. Since, however, some novice speakers may encounter certain emotional problems at the outset of their experience in speechmaking, we offer in this early chapter, along with the basic methods of developing ideas, brief but fundamental suggestions for coping with problems of confidence, nervousness, and stage fright.

There are times, of course, when one has the impulse to speak or the obligation to speak but has nothing particular to say. Then the first problem is finding a subject and material. Most students, after very little consideration, will find their accumulated resources quite equal to the demands of their initial, short speeches. Besides, in school and college they have usually had considerable experience in finding subjects and materials for written exercises in English composition. They have learned something about utilizing their reading and a good deal about taking stock of their own knowledge and experience in order to write interestingly. Those same resources will enable them initially to find the substance for speaking interestingly to others. The problem of finding a subject and finding materials, therefore, we will defer for the time being. (See Chapters 3 & 4.)

Managing Ideas

The problems of managing the substance of speeches to good advantage, however—the problems of stating and filling out ideas—may properly occupy attention at this point. Most college students and educated adults are more experienced and better prepared in this phase of speechmaking than at first they may be aware. There are few who, in school or in conversation or controversy outside of school, have not many times produced answers to questions and demands like these:

> I think I get what you mean, but say it again another way so I can be sure.
> That sounds like a sensible statement. Can you back it up with facts and information?
> What do you mean by saying that people seldom do anything much better than they have to? Are there such people? Give me an example or two.
> I wouldn't be surprised that you have something which may be useful in your new method of determining public opinion, but I don't really understand it. What is it like?
> I believe that you mean what you say, and I respect your opinion, but it's only your opinion. Who else says so?

THE BASIC PATTERN

Each of the preceding situations points up the prime principle of communication. Each involves crystallizing an idea, an opinion, a judgment, or a matter of inquiry into a statement and points to filling out, clarifying, enriching, supporting, amplifying—in short, developing it.

Each situation illustrates the basic operating pattern of thinking for speaking and of organizing speeches—an arrangement of *statement* and *development* for the statement. Anyone whose study of written composition has included the concept of *topic sentence* has encountered something resembling the underlying pattern of good speeches. And anyone who has considered the various common methods of developing a topic sentence into an effective paragraph will have begun his initiation into the methods of giving form and development to ideas in the first speeches. The problems of theme writing and speechmaking are by no means the same, but their methods of giving order and movement to their materials are certainly comparable.

As Aristotle asserted long ago, and as practice still demonstrates, a good speech, and each of the basic units which together make up a good speech, consist essentially of two elements: (1) a *statement* and (2) a *development* which explains or reinforces the statement.

The Statement

For our present purposes a *statement* is a declarative sentence formulating an idea, a feeling, a judgment, an opinion, a matter of inquiry, which needs *development* through particularization, illustration, concretion, interpretation, reinforcement, or support of some sort if it is to convey its intended meaning to the audience to whom it is addressed. Each of the demands and queries above occurs because some declarative statement has been made or implied, the meaning of which appears not to be clear enough or full enough for the listener. The speaker, in replying to the query, would probably make the statement again and then would satisfy his listener with the kind of developing material asked for.

Development

By *development* we mean the sum of such methods, materials, and language as should serve with a particular group of listeners to make particular, to make concrete, to reinforce, to enliven, to support, or otherwise to fill out the meaning and significance of the *statement.* Anything a speaker says, then, which tends to prove his point, explain his idea, or make his statement clear, vivid, or attractive to his audience is considered development.

There are many possible sources and methods of development. We will discuss most of them in the later chapters. In his first speeches, however, the student should try consciously to become aware of perhaps four or five obvious means of development and should concentrate on using them. These means are indicated by the queries on page 13. In answer to query (1) what is needed is a *restatement* of the same thing which has been said; in answer to (2) the speaker will give *factual information;* in replying to (3) *examples* should clear up the uncertainty; in order to satisfy the inquirer in (4) the speaker will have to make *comparisons;* and for (5) the speaker will offer *testimony.*

Kinds of Developing Material

For first speeches the most common and most useful kinds of development may be identified thus:

RESTATEMENT

Restatement is largely a matter of language. By expressing an idea over again in other language or other form or both, a speaker not only adds emphasis but may often hit upon terminology and phrasing which will strike his listeners as clearer, fuller, more familiar, or in some other way more understandable or more forceful than the language of the original statement.

FACTUAL INFORMATION

When we say that a speaker knows what he is talking about, that he has the facts on his subject, we usually mean that he has filled out and supported his ideas with plenty of information—with factual data, with figures and statistical material, with observation, all of which may be verified independently of the speaker.

EXAMPLE

Whether as the short, undeveloped *specific instance* or as the longer, fully developed *illustration*, example is the detailing, sketching, narrating, describing, or otherwise setting before the audience of typical circumstances, of characteristic cases, of particular instances which help to make clear, vivid, or credible the statement which the speaker wants his audience to accept.

COMPARISON AND CONTRAST

Comparison and contrast are closely related to example. They are concerned with showing likenesses and differences among objects, ideas, and situations. The former puts stress upon illuminating similarities; the latter on dissimilarities.

TESTIMONY

Simply described, testimony is the say-so of someone other than the speaker, in support of a point or in explanation of an idea. One very common form of testimony is *quotation,* including quotation from men and books of the past.

Such, in brief, are the five most common and useful methods and materials of *development* which the student should begin using at once in his first speeches. We will discuss each of them more fully in later chapters—under the general topic of *amplification* in the informative speech in Chapter 5, and under the topic of *support* in the persuasive speech in Chapter 11. Now we will proceed to illustrate the use of these materials of development in characteristic patterns of the short speech.

PUTTING THE SPEECH TOGETHER—PATTERN

On page 13 we remarked that some arrangement of *statement* with *development* of the statement comprises the basic operating pattern for a speaker's thinking and for organizing speeches. That is, when one thinks most efficiently for speaking, one habitually thinks of ideas one wishes to communicate, and one thinks of them in connection with material with which one might fill out those ideas. These elements may come to mind as idea first, followed by developing matter; or as concrete facts and examples first, leading to the idea; or as some of the potential material first, then a version of the idea, followed by more developing matter. The order is largely dependent on habit and circumstances and will vary with the speaker and with the occasion. The important factor for the speaker is the habit of joining the two basic elements into regular patterns of movement. The formulation of an idea should result at once in the movement toward material with which to develop it; and the apprehension of facts, events, similarities, and so forth, should lead to an idea of what they signify—to a relevant *statement.*

These patterns in the speaker's own thinking serve him as patterns for organizing his material into speeches, or units of speeches. The three common patterns may be represented schematically as follows:

Pattern 1

> Statement to be Developed

> Developing Material

Pattern 2

| Developing Material |

| Statement to Which It Leads |

Pattern 3

| Developing Material |

| Statement Being Developed |

| Developing Material |

The diagrammatic arrangement above is intended to illustrate two facts: (1) Development materials may precede the statement they support, or they may succeed the statement, or they may both precede and follow. (2) No matter what the time order of the statement and its developing ideas, the development is always logically subordinate to the statement, and the statement is always logically superior to the development. In the diagrams this relationship is suggested by extending the statement to the left of its developing materials.

We observe in passing that these patterns also illustrate possible nucleii for the speech outline, which is the plan, or blueprint, for the construction of the speech. Like the blueprint for a house or a jet-bomber, it is most useful if it is prepared before final construction is begun. Full consideration of the speech outline will be given later, in Chapter 7. At the present time we will concern ourselves only with the basic patterns in their simplest forms. We will employ the several kinds of development and the three patterns of statement-development.

Patterns of the Short Speech

1. The most usual pattern of the short speech on a simple, expository theme may be illustrated by the scheme on page 18. The governing *statement* is made at the beginning and is developed through information, example, testimony, and restatement. No doubt, in such a speech comparison or contrast also might profitably have been used. Observe that in the brief speech of this sort, restatement may serve as conclusion as well as additional development.

The development of the transistor has opened new vistas for the portable radio receiver.

DEVELOPMENT

The transistor has eliminated the heaviest and the most fragile parts of the radio. (*Information*)

The transistor requires only small flashlight batteries for power. (*Information*)

The transistor replaced the vacuum tube. (*Information*)

It has made really tiny radios practicable. (*Information*)

Radios with strong, clear tone and wide range may measure no more than 3″ x 4″ x 1″. (*Information*)

Our postman says that his transistor radio, which he carries in his shirt pocket, has taken most of the monotony out of walking his rounds each day. (*Testimony*)

The radio we use while hiking and boating we keep in the glove compartment of the car along with the camera. (*Example*)

In a world of TV, the transistor radio has established a secure place of its own. (*Restatement*)

STATEMENT

The summer weather in this city is neither excessively hot nor excessively humid.

DEVELOPMENT

The average mean summer temperature is 75°.

The average number of days from June 1 to October 1 when the temperature rises above 85° is 14.

The average number of days during the same period when the temperature does not rise above 75° is 50.

The normal humidity in summer is 50%.

The average number of days in summer when the humidity rises above 70% is 15.

The "discomfort index" shows fewer than 10 days in the "very uncomfortable" range.

(*Information*)

The preceding figures are provided by the United States Weather Bureau. (*Testimony*)

2. A brief, simple speech may be developed through the use of information chiefly. This pattern and development is more likely to appear as one unit of a complex speech, but it is sometimes effective for the simple, short, informative speech. See the lower chart on the facing page.

3. The pattern for the short speech in which the development precedes and leads up to the statement is illustrated in the scheme below for a speech employing example exclusively. The speaker plans to cite briefly several specific instances, then to clinch his idea with extended *illustration*. With this speech the audience would probably get

DEVELOPMENT

As we begin our college year, we have to stand in line (*Specific Instances*):

at the registrar's to get our cards,

at each department's table in the field house to register for our courses,

at the treasurer's to pay our fees,

at the health center for our physical examinations,

at the bookstore to buy our supplies,

at the cafeteria counter to get our dinner.

Let us follow Jack Waller from 6:00 a. m. to 7:00 p. m. of registration day of his freshman year. (*Illustration*)

STATEMENT

Obviously, getting into college, and staying in college, are largely matters of standing in line.

a special satisfaction out of the explicit appearance of the *statement* at the end, where the statement would serve as a neat conclusion as well.

As we have sketched it, this speech would be intended principally for entertainment through a kind of ironic humor. If the speaker's purpose were more serious, if he were addressing the university administration and advocating some improvement at registration time, he would probably want to use additional kinds of materials for development, especially *information* and *comparison*. He might give figures, perhaps collected by the student newspaper, showing just how long the average student spends in getting registered, at which department's table he has to wait the longest, and at what times of day the congestion is worst. The speaker might also wish to offer some comparison with registration in other universities, and some testimony from individual students and faculty.

4. A special kind of short speech developing an idea (stated or implied) by offering one extended example, or *illustration,* usually of the narrative

or story sort, may be most interesting and effective in pointing a moral or enlivening an idea. Such, for example, is Jesus' parable of the Good Samaritan (*Luke* 10:30–37).

STATEMENT

> (*Your neighbor is he who needs your help.*)

DEVELOPMENT

> The story of the man who went down from Jerusalem to Jericho illustrates what it is to be a neighbor.

Observe that the *statement* in this little speech is not the question which was asked of Jesus, "Who is my neighbor?" It is the *answer* to that question. That answer does not appear as a formulated statement in this speech. Hence it is placed in parentheses in the scheme above. Nevertheless it is the governing *idea*, implicit in the story, and must be included in the scheme.

The many *details* of examples need not be included in the scheme or outline, but there should be a separate descriptive heading for each example. The student might consider how one would phrase the statement for the parable of the Prodigal Son (*Luke* 15:11–32), and for the parable of the Talents (*Matthew* 25:14–30).

In a speech about registration, like the one already sketched, the speaker might well limit himself to one narrative example of his own experience, such as the one concerning Jack Waller, including all the appalling (or amusing) episodes and either formulating the statement explicitly at the end or suggesting to the listeners that they form their own conclusions. This also would be a speech of one extended *illustration*.

5. *Testimony* by itself seldom provides adequate development when an idea of any consequence is to be explained or supported. Even the writers of advertising, who are the most flagrant users of testimony, do not regularly rely on it exclusively, except for very brief, quick impact: "Buy Kleen Kine Milk. Babe Ruth approved of milk; the Bible associates milk with honey; and we all know the phrase, 'the milk of human kindness.' " Advertisers usually couple testimony with something which is intended to seem like information: "Kleen Kine Milk is up to three times more nourishing for up to 15% less." (More and less than *what* is seldom indicated.) Though easily abused, testimony may be very well and effectively used in conjunction with other kinds of supporting material, especially example and information.

The following scheme illustrates development by testimony. It also serves as an example of the pattern in which the statement is both preceded and followed by development.

DEVELOPMENT

> "A man's a man for a' that," said Robert Burns. (*Testimony*)
>
> Edmund Burke said that he did not know how to draw up an indictment against a whole people. (*Testimony*)

STATEMENT

> *A man is best judged for himself, not for his race, class, nationality, or religion.*

DEVELOPMENT

> The Constitution of the United States recognizes no qualitative categories for judging men. (*Information*)
>
> Records of crime show that native-born Americans commit as serious crimes as do immigrants. (*Information*)
>
> There is no reliable evidence of inherent intellectual or moral superiority between the white man and the Negro. (*Information*)
>
> "The fault, dear Brutus, is not in our stars but in ourselves. . . ." (*Testimony, serving as conclusion*)

6. The following scheme suggests the development of a statement through the use of comparison and analogy.

STATEMENT

> *The government of the U.S.S.R. is based on an ascending concentration of power, from the local soviets to the Supreme Soviet.*

DEVELOPMENT

> It may be called a pyramid of power. (*Metaphor*)
>
> It is like a large business organization, where each of the minor executives has several supervisors reporting to him, and he in turn reports to a superior who reports to a superior, and so on. (*Comparison*)
>
> It is like the English system of privy councils under Elizabeth I. (*Analogy—to be extended*)
>
> "Every flea has little fleas
>   Upon his back to bite 'im,
> And little fleas have lesser fleas—
>   So on *ad infinitum*." (*Testimony, as illustrative comparison*)

The sample schemes just given illustrate the kinds of speeches simplest in form and plan: speeches in which only a single statement requires development. Most speeches are not so simple. Nevertheless, the best speeches, however long and complex, consist of basic units of statement-and-development such as we have been examining, combined into larger patterns. The structure and outlines of such speeches, as we have said, will be the business of Chapter 7. Until the student has studied that chapter, he will do well to concentrate on developing his skill with *statement* and *development* in the simple structure of one or two units.

Introductions and Conclusions

We have said little or nothing in this chapter about introductions, conclusions, connective and transitional material, and the sort of filling-in with words and sentences, which go to make the bare structure into the neat, shapely speech. These elements deserve full consideration. Later chapters will be devoted to them. All we wish to say now is: Keep introductions and conclusions in the first speeches brief and simple. An introduction need consist only of a statement or two which will get the attention of listeners and at the same time will lead into the ideas which follow it. The conclusion of a short speech, as we have suggested in the scheme on pages 17–18, often consists simply of *restating* the idea expressed in the statement.

STAGE FRIGHT

Some consideration, as we have said, must be given early to the kinds of experience which more or less inhibit the mental processes of the speaker—the experiences which distract his attention from ideas, prevent him from concentrating on meanings and communication, and block his impulses to gesture. The experiences are mixtures of emotion and feeling, recognized as degrees of fear and anxiety and loosely referred to in popular terms as "stage fright" and "nervousness."

Through experience in public speaking one learns to overcome such irrelevant emotions or at least so to live with them that they do little damage. They are not major problems for most college students of public speaking, especially if the high school has given those students some experience in speaking, because the college-age person is well on the way to maturity. The person who may most directly encounter emotional problems in delivery is usually one to whom public speaking is a completely new experience. Often he magnifies the problems out of all proportion to their real significance. He unwisely turns the proverbial molehill into a mountain. The novice speaker will do well to let the molehill be a molehill, to regard any emotional impediments as rationally and as objectively as possible, and to discipline himself intelligently.

The Fear Response

The person who feels wrought up before and during the delivery of his speech must avoid confusing what is normal with what may be abnormal. Much of the feeling that is labeled "nervousness" and "worry" is as normal as roses in June. It is always evoked by any new situation to which we want to respond appropriately and successfully. The delivery of a speech presents that kind of situation. So we stew and worry, fuss and fidget, just as we do over any task we really care about.

Nervousness and worry are often accompanied by tension. Unless tension is so extreme as to freeze one into a state of immobility, it is as desirable and useful to the speaker as it is to the toned-up athlete. The man who takes public speaking as a routine job will make a routine speech. The person who encounters the responsibility of speech-making without feeling some apprehension and strain is either exceedingly stupid or exceedingly vain. Hence, welcome the toned-up tensity of feeling. It will help you speak better than you think you can.

True stage fright, on the other hand, is a special kind of fear response that will inhibit the speaker. The following analysis will distinguish stage fright from ordinary fear and desirable tension. First, it is a withdrawal or retreat response. Although the everyday fear experience may be marked by running away or otherwise avoiding the object of fright, stage fright is often marked by trembling, knee shaking, rigidity and immobility, and fast, irregular breathing prior to the speech or during delivery. Furthermore, the suffering speaker finds himself in a situation where he cannot run away without publicly admitting failure and thus damaging his pride. Consequently, his response on the platform is not ordinary avoidance-behavior, such as running away or simply avoiding speaking, but tautness, rigidity, and immobility of both body and mind. Second, the cause of such behavior, as in any case of fear, is twofold: (1) the situation means harm and danger, and (2) danger can be avoided by flight or withdrawal. To the speaker, danger means failure, failure to remember, to do well, to say the acceptable thing, to behave acceptably.

It should be clear, therefore, that if stage fright is this kind of experience it can be attacked in three ways: (1) by minimizing the appearance of danger in the situation, (2) by dispelling the idea that danger can be met only by withdrawing and running away, and (3) by not running away. A speaker may be able to attack at all these points, but if he can attack at only one point he will experience less fear and apprehension. What he should do is to analyze the experience as pro-

foundly as he can (here his instructor may be of great help) and try
to discover what point to assault and what tactics to employ.

Minimizing the Hazard

For the novice speaker, there are effective ways of coping with emotional problems in a rational and objective manner. First, he recognizes
that speaking to an audience does not differ greatly from speaking in
private; public speaking is but an enlarged conversation. Thus public
speaking may become less formidable and be associated with what he
may already do well.

Second, he can rapidly build up a feeling of familiarity about public
speaking. This is done through experience, an unsurpassed teacher. It is
accomplished, also, through the study of principles and through listening to speeches and reading them. Knowledge of what makes a good
speech and of what is expected of speakers in the way of information
and interest, composition and organization, presentation and behavior,
in both informative and persuasive speeches, does much to take the
danger out of the situation. It is the new and strange that may cause
harm, and once the situation is experienced and understood one possible cause of harm is removed.

Third, the classroom speaker should realize that his fellows are with
him, not against him. Since all are engaged in the same enterprise, the
classroom audience is not so critical of his endeavors as he may think;
it is as sympathetic and as helpful an audience as exists anywhere.
It is quick to praise and admire good work because it appreciates,
infinitely more than does the casual, outside audience, the sweat and
labor behind a good speech.

Finally, he can capitalize upon the advantages of beginning speech
preparation early and of preparing *thoroughly*. Thorough preparation
brings with it four psychological aids: (1) A speaker knows that he is
ready to meet the situation; (2) he knows that he is better equipped to
cope with any last-minute adjustments to his audience than if he were
not well prepared; (3) he knows that good preparation means less
chance of forgetting; and (4) he gains confidence.

Confronting the Hazard

The starting point of the fear experience, as we have seen, is perceiving
that a situation is harmful and that harm can be escaped by retreating.
It is possible to perceive danger and not size it up as something to run
from. Indeed, we do this when we experience anger, for the stimulus
of anger is *danger* plus awareness that there is something to be attacked
and to be destroyed. It should be evident, then, that what we see or

think of as dangerous need not cause fear. This fact has important application for the anxious speaker. He can deliberately interpret the hazardous situation as something to be confronted squarely, to be faced positively and directly. It is like a foe to be conquered, not to be fled from. Thus, he induces or adopts the attitude of *determination* toward his task. In effect, he says to himself, "I will speak; I will continue to speak; I will welcome every opportunity to speak; I will keep at it." He knows full well, moreover, that if he quits but *once* and runs, he has let fear get the better of him, and his job is that much harder.

Replacing Fear by Another Emotion

If one regards the hazards of speaking as something to be overcome by positive attack, he stands an excellent chance of replacing fear with some other emotion. We cannot experience two emotions simultaneously. Accordingly, acute stage fright can sometimes be overcome if the speaker can work on a subject he feels keenly about. Perhaps the most serviceable subjects are those which will rouse *indignation, humor, pity,* and *sympathy.*

If you would experience indignation, look for situations which you regard as unjust and unfair, and try to make your hearers see them as such. Select a subject which will give some opportunity for a humorous story or two, and if possible start out the speech with an anecdote or a funny story. Or present evils where people are suffering undeserved calamity and hardship; thus you will stimulate pity and sympathy in yourself.

Sometimes the emotion of pride can overcome, partially if not entirely, the fear of speaking publicly. Most students want to make good speeches and to be recognized by their classmates as good speakers. The reward they seek is not merely a grade, but pride, prestige, and reputation. Accordingly, pride may be definitely felt by the speaker during the stages of his preparation, and if felt it can be nursed along and encouraged. As he works he may find himself reacting like this: "I certainly have some good material here; it's real news"; "This is an argument that will make them stop and think"; "This is a good illustration"; "The structure of this speech is so clear that nobody can miss it"; "That rehearsal went so well I can come pretty close to doing the same thing tomorrow." When he can pat himself on the back, there isn't much room left for extreme worry.

Avoiding Withdrawal Movements and Bodily "Sets"

Besides attacking the stimulus-situation that is characteristic of fear, one can also mitigate fear by attacking the response itself. Instead of permitting avoidance-behavior and withdrawal movements, one moves forward and into the situation. Indeed, approach-behavior can yield a bonus. It is in part the physiological basis of feelings of assurance and confidence.

The suggestions below are little things, yet they help some persons tremendously because emotion and bodily activity are inseparable.

Behavior Just Before Speaking

Sit upright and lean forward a little; thus the bodily set is that of advancement.

Breathe rather deeply and *regularly*. Rhythmical breathing accompanies poise.

Let the shoulders sag a little and try to *feel* relaxed in the region of the shoulders and chest.

Walk briskly to the platform. Don't drag and shuffle along. Be positive in movement.

When you reach your speaking position, take time to settle down before utterance. Ease off bodily, allowing the arms to hang comfortably or to *rest* on the stand or lectern.

Behavior During Speaking

As you start speaking, take a step or two toward the audience. During the introduction move about more than may be appropriate to the rest of the speech. Gesture more than you might otherwise.

If you get stuck during the speech and can't remember what comes next, you can gain control over the blank moment by proceeding as follows: (1) Try to remember, but don't struggle long lest you tighten up unduly and begin to panic. (2) *Summarize aloud* what you have already said. The act of summarizing breaks up the onset of panic, and in addition, nine times out of ten, suggests the next idea or calls to mind a principal idea. (The summary will almost invariably prompt recall if the speech has been well organized beforehand.) This tactic keeps the mind working.

The reason for the procedure is that any emotional experience feeds upon itself. Once started, it becomes its own stimulus. The emotion of fear pyramids and becomes increasingly intense, until in extreme cases the body trembles or goes rigid. To control the emotion, one breaks into its pattern as early as possible and thus doesn't let it pyramid.

If after two or three speeches, a person still feels unduly disturbed, he may select a subject that will let him use diagrams on the blackboard. He will then have to be active—drawing the sketch, moving to and from the board at intervals, and pointing out special features. Or he may select a subject that will require handling a model, perhaps to take apart and assemble as he talks. Even the expedient of taking two or three books to the platform and quoting briefly from them gives hands and arms something to do.

The person who is emotionally upset because public speaking is new to him will soon discover that he has no cause for fear. He should look at the problem rationally, reduce its newness to familiar terms through study and experience, and along the way test out any positive measures of control which seem applicable to him. He should not, however, expect or desire to be rid of all nervousness, worry, and tension. In the proper degree, these aspects of the speaking experience work for him, rather than against him. Perhaps, after all, the wisest advice comes from a veteran teacher: "One can't be abnormally self-conscious if he gives first place to the welfare of others. So put your audience first. Plan everything you do for your hearers. Interest them. Their welfare is the thing, not your ego."

CONCLUSION

The attentive student will find himself prepared to proceed now to the full, detailed study of the several principal aspects of public speaking, at the same time that, following the guidance of this chapter, he begins to get profitable experience in speaking. He will be establishing the habit (1) of stating and developing ideas according to a few basic patterns, (2) of bringing to bear on his main ideas the force of factual information, examples, comparisons and contrasts, and testimony, and (3) of concentrating on his audience and his message rather than on himself as he is talking. In his subsequent study he will find elaboration, refinement, and re-enforcement of the habits which he has begun to establish in his first speeches.

CHAPTER THREE

Subjects for Speeches

"IF I CAN only get a subject, I'm all set; the worst is over!" That perennial cry of the student in the course in public speaking suggests that any speaker, even the novice, recognizes the value inherent in a good subject: a subject which (1) is worth the trouble and time and energy that must go into the preparation and presentation of a speech and (2) is appropriate to speaker, audience, and occasion. Important as a good subject is, however, a speaker should not expect to find the perfect subject that will automatically turn into a good speech. There isn't any such. The novice speaker who sets out to make himself understand a consequential subject and to make his audience understand it too, will go a long way toward making a satisfactory speech.

A SUBJECT WORTH THE TROUBLE

In Chapter 1 we argued that there is probably no such thing as good speaking apart from what is said. Most speaking involves matters of common concern on which men seek to inform or instruct each other, and questions of public consequence about which men dispute and contend with each other. The learner of speechmaking will use his time and energy wisely if from the start he chooses subjects of those sorts which are likely to be more rather than less interesting and valuable to his audiences, and subjects which will encourage him to equip himself for the kind of speaking which as a citizen he is likely to be called upon to do.

Each individual has a vocational life and a public or civic or social life which will provide him with occasions for speechmaking. If when he is taking his course in public speaking the student knows what his vocation is to be and has some knowledge of it—if, for example, he is a student of engineering or of dentistry—he will reasonably choose some of the time to practice his speaking on special subjects drawn from his vocation. Even so, he will do well to begin to accustom himself to handling publicly those subjects and problems of broader and more general ignorance and controversy which come under the general notions of the social, economic, cultural, and political. The class in public speaking is one of the few places where he has much opportunity to prepare for the more general speaking of the active citizen. In the following pages we will offer guidance in finding such subjects, under considerations of appropriateness to speaker, audience, and occasion. As we proceed, we suggest strongly that even in his first, short speeches, the student should assume that part of his function is to advance his own education in human affairs, and his audience's as well.

APPROPRIATENESS TO SPEAKER

In looking for a subject, think first of what you yourself know and what your past experience has given you. Look for subjects in these sources:

In your mind, life, and experiences

In your work

In the work of persons with whom you are associated or acquainted

In your reading or in listening to radio, TV, or public speeches

In the movies, plays, exhibitions, sporting events you see

In the clubs, organizations which you know about

In the current affairs, events, and problems of your locality, your city, your state, the nation, the world—personal, social, domestic, religious, educational, as well as political and economic.

Let us now discuss these sources more fully.

Knowledge and Experience

Abolish the common idea (much more prevalent in public speaking classes than in ordinary social intercourse) that nothing that *you* know, that *you* believe, that *you* want, that *you* have done, can be of interest to other people. We all, to be sure, have many of the same experiences and the same thoughts. Even so we also have many of the same interests, and we often enjoy nothing more than proving to each other that we have common experiences. Witness any gathering where people talk about their ailments and operations. Your own mind and your own experience are your first good sources of subjects; and no subject is really good until, in the broadest sense, it has become your own. You may not be a real-estate operator or a builder, but you have just gone through the experience of buying property and building a house. The information you gathered and the problems you faced are full and fresh in your mind and will prove interesting to your audience, whose experiences and information are at best scantier and more remote than yours. In short, what do you know more about, what do you under-stand more fully, what have you thought through more completely than most people? The answers to these questions will provide sub-jects for speeches. You have a head start in these subjects. If you don't know enough, though you know more than most people, you can learn more.

A portion of your experience which should prove lucrative in finding subjects for speeches is the *conversation* you engage in or overhear. What do you and your friends talk about? What questions do you ask? What do other people talk about and ask about? Answers to these questions give fairly good notions of what people are interested in. Use these leads to remind yourself of what you know or of what people are apparently curious about.

Occupation and Profession

Everyone is to some extent a specialist. He knows his own job more intimately than other people know it, and he is better acquainted with the jobs which go on about him—in his shop, in his department, in his plant, in his industry, in his neighborhood, or in his home town—than are strangers. We all, of course, know a little something about the work of a secretary, a bookkeeper, a file clerk, a salesman, a crane operator, a head usher, a filling-station attendant; and if you tell us, in general terms, *only what everyone knows,* you will not interest us. If, however, from your own concrete experience, you distinguish your job as a sec-retary to the vice-president of the Chow-Chow Mills, or as file clerk in the U.S. Inspector's Office from other such jobs, we will be interested. What does it take to be editor of the campus newspaper, manager of the basketball team, server of hot foods in the cafeteria, assistant tele-phone operator, laboratory assistant in zoology? What does one do? What does one have to know?

What do you know or can you find out about the qualifications for some occupation or profession and the advantages and disadvantages of that kind of work—your own, your father's, your friend's, or the job which you wish you had? Most of us, for example, have vague and general ideas of what abilities are needed in an accountant, a labor organizer, a student of chemistry. But if you know accurately, personally, and in detail, consider telling us.

Reading and Listening

Have you read a book, an article, a piece in the paper lately which seemed informative, interesting, provocative of ideas? Have you thus run across a fresher or newer or better outlook on something that stirs your interest anew? Perhaps it is worth explanation or interpretation. Perhaps you can recommend that your hearers read it. Of course your job will be to explain the book or article to the audience, not merely to indicate that you have read it; to show your audience that they will enjoy the book, not merely to tell them so. To these ends you will use much vivid, specific detail.

What have you heard said on the radio or television which provoked ideas or gave you interesting or valuable information which your audience may have missed? If you are listening for subjects, you will find many possibilities.

Courses of Study

For students in school or college, reading and listening are likely to be largely connected with courses of study. Do not neglect that natural and obvious source of subjects for speeches. What courses are you taking which are not being taken by most of the students in your public speaking classes? What ideas or information from those courses can you make clear to other people? What phases of the courses which your classmates are taking have you gone into more fully than they have? And there will be valuable by-products of the use of such subjects in speeches, for there is no surer way of making yourself master of any subject matter than by preparing to explain it to one who does not know.

You can hardly overestimate the value of the courses you are studying, or have studied, as sources of subjects. Consider the student who explained what a chemical solution is. He drew his subject from his chemistry course in quantitative analysis. One-third of his listeners were taking the same course from the same instructor; yet he did not bore them, nor did he speak over the heads of the rest of his audience. All found the speech intensely interesting. Why? Because he was wise enough (1) to take a subject that all knew at least something about and thus was to a greater or lesser degree familiar; (2) to amplify the information he had heard in class and had read in the textbook by consulting other books on the nature of chemical solutions and by asking his instructor for further information on one matter that was not clear to him, thus gaining and presenting information that was new to his audience; and (3) to present the results of his thinking so clearly and systematically that the order and structure of his ideas made listening easy and pleasant. One of his classmates paid him this compliment: "Ted, you were 200 per cent better than the professor himself." (That is sometimes possible.)

What this student speaker did, you can do—if you have the wisdom, the imagination, and the energy to add new information to the old, to find a new "slant" or point of view, and to work over the ideas until you can deliver them clearly. What are the potentialities for subjects in your courses in science (physics, chemistry, geology, biology), in English literature and language, in the social studies (psychology, economics, sociology, history, political science, and philosophy), in engineering, in law, and in medicine? One of the most practical steps you can take toward finding subjects is to thumb through your notes and textbooks, with these questions in mind: What topics need further clarification and illustration? What ones might be especially interesting and timely? If you make a list, its length will surprise you! If there is a neat formula for a short speech, perhaps this is it: Add new information to the old, include new illustrations for the old information, and present it all so clearly that it cannot be misunderstood.

Clubs and Organizations

Most people have heard of many clubs and organizations to which you belong, but that is as far as common knowledge goes. What these organizations are, what they do, what their importance in the community is, are matters upon which we are ignorant and about which we will be glad to be informed if you will make it pleasant for us to listen. We know, of course, that most clubs have officers, meetings, dues, and elections, and if that is all you tell us about your organization, we will not care much. If, on the other hand, you assume our familiarity with most of these routine facts and spend your time telling us what social, civic, business, or other activities really distinguish the Junior Women's Chamber of Commerce, the Rotary Club, the Classical Club, or the Quarterback Club from other clubs, we will be interested and informed. In any thriving community, there are scores, and on an average campus dozens, of such subjects for speeches.

Current Affairs and Problems

Current affairs, problems, and events constitute a source of subjects for speeches which is most often, and rightly, turned to by students of public speaking. The dangers are, however, that students will turn to them too exclusively and will conceive of them too generally. There are many small subjects as well as large ones in these areas. It is not necessary to discuss a public question in all its aspects in order to speak on it. One does not have to tackle the whole subject of equality of the races in order to discuss profitably the joint use of municipal recreational facilities. Nor does one need to be a national authority on state governments in order to make himself well enough informed on the legislative article of the proposed new state constitution to talk profitably upon it to a general audience.

People are often poorly informed on current affairs and problems, except those few which strike them immediately, personally, and deeply. We all, however, are eager to be told. Otherwise there would be far fewer analysts and commentators on the radio, on TV, and in the press. Any speaker who will inform himself with reasonable thoroughness on a public question, or even on any phase of such a question, will have several good subjects for speeches, both now and for some time to come. Engineers, as well as other specialists, may find subjects adapted to their special knowledge in current events. For example, one engineer noticed in the newspaper the account of the collapse of a new Mississippi river bridge in a high wind. The event prompted him to look into the history of similar accidents, and his investigations resulted in a very good speech on the current collapse, others like it, and the probable cause.

Current problems and questions are often only the immediate versions of problems and questions that are always with us, the discussion of which is always pertinent and potentially interesting. Religion, love and marriage, divorce, education, taxation, war and peace, race relations, good government, health—all these are subjects which are unlikely to be exhausted for many years to come. Though they are old subjects, phases of them may at any time be made new by a speaker who will restate them in a new way, give them fresh illustration, adapt them to current conditions.

The Speaker as Learner

Many students have made excellent speeches simply by following up subjects about which they were curious and wanted to learn more. Engineering students frequently say that they like their public speaking class because it provides them with the opportunity, which their full schedules would not otherwise permit, of reading in materials outside their field. They often pick subjects on which they have little knowledge but a lot of curiosity. Two years ago a young lady was first in a university-wide speech contest, speaking on the plight of the ignored American Indian. Her curiosity had been piqued by a plane conversation with a lawyer who represented an Indian reservation. Later she made her speech class the occasion for informing herself fully. She specialized in the subject and made one of the best speeches in the class. So if you have a bent of curiosity about a subject, pursue it.

If you follow your curiosity, you can be confident that your interest in a subject will develop fast. You will be learning something new, and novelty is always attractive. Furthermore, you will illustrate for yourself an old principle: interest grows with knowledge.

In the final analysis, the apparent worth of the subject is usually of less importance than what you make of the subject—what you do with it. A usable subject chosen early, therefore, is better than a very good subject chosen too late for you to do it justice in preparation.

APPROPRIATENESS TO THE AUDIENCE

What are audiences interested in? First, more often than not, they are interested in what you know about and are interested in. Especially is this true of the classroom audience, and many of these possibilities we have pointed to already.

Second, they are interested in what all human beings are fundamentally interested in. They are attracted by *new light on what is already familiar to them.* Can you supply "news"—news about the campus hero or some public figure; about the latest thing in airplanes, automobiles, medical techniques, engineering procedures, styles in clothes, accident insurance, radio? Or, can you present the old and familiar in a new and unusual way? Can you offer a fresh point of view or a new interpretation? Not only do new facts and data claim attention; new ways of looking at the established, familiar facts also are often effective. Detective stories almost always illustrate this truth. The facts are put before the district attorney, the slow-witted police sergeant, the smart detective, and the reader, and each supplies his own interpretation. Each interpretation usually produces a different murderer, and each is interesting, although eventually there is but one correct solution. What is *your* reaction to the subjects which students argue about? If you have a different view or an especially strong view, you have a potentially good subject.

Third, people are interested in familiar ideas and facts presented systematically and clearly. We often enjoy seeing familiar facts brought together and given structure and continuity, so that we recognize the whole and its parts all in neat order. You might discover, for example, that after your class had read this chapter you could hold their interest on the topic "How to Find Speech Subjects" if you did nothing more than present an orderly, concise review.

APPROPRIATENESS TO THE OCCASION

The specific occasion that brings speaker and audience together frequently suggests subjects. Ask yourself: Under what circumstances of time and of place will my speech be given?

Specific Time and Occasion

Is the occasion a regular quarterly meeting of an employee's association of a department store? And does the meeting fall early in January? If you were the president of the association and knew you had to speak, what might you talk on? Might the occasion suggest both your subject and your purpose? Would you, for example, want to entertain your hearers with an account of incidents of the recent Christmas shopping madhouse? The audience might well be in a mood to respond favorably to humor. On the other hand, if the company had just announced a lay-off of 10 per cent of the employees, the audience might be in no mood to hear an entertaining speech. Would you explain what they must do about completing their income tax returns? Or would you try to persuade them to attend meetings more regularly and to bring in other members? In brief, an audience meeting at a particular time has ideas and feelings about recent or coming events; if a speaker is aware of these, they may influence his choice of subject and general purpose.

Aspects of the Classroom Occasion

Even in the public speaking class, a speaker cannot escape considerations of time and place in choosing his subject. True, you are confronting the same audience day after day; you speak under the same general conditions and often your general purpose to inform, to amuse, to persuade is prescribed by your instructor, and the circumstances are taken for granted. But the circumstances of the classroom, unfortunately, are what many beginning speakers really overlook. Because the same general situation recurs, they forget two important aspects of the occasion. The first is the specific time at which the student speaks. You may be scheduled, for example, to be the first speaker of the morning. You should not forget that your hearers have just come from other classes, and their minds may still be turning over ideas derived from these classes. They may be still thinking about what they were reading or studying in the library the hour before. Some may be set to carry on some sly preparation for their next class while you speak, and others may want to read the newspaper they have just picked up. Some may still be in the throes of a brief bull session, and some may be thinking primarily about the free afternoon ahead, or the evening date. On the other hand, if you are to speak after your class has heard a speaker, you should not forget that your hearers' minds are turning over what he has said and what has been said by the class in discussing and criticizing his speech. As you step to the platform your hearers' attention is not on the ideas of your speech; their interest is elsewhere. If you recognize this inevitable aspect of the classroom audience in choosing your subject, you will want to pick a subject so interesting that you can drive out such competing ideas, and the "so interesting" subject will probably be directly concerned with their interests as students or with subjects that you can readily associate with their interests.

Students Are Real

The second aspect of the classroom situation which beginning speakers often fail to face squarely is that the class itself—the audience—is actually a real, flesh-and-blood group that can be readily interested in what a speaker has to say, as well as in how he says it. True it is that in a public speaking class students have the impression that practice in speaking is the main thing, that the audience merely furnishes a chance for practice, and that the set-up, in short, is an artificial, learning situation. Let us grant that the circumstances are somewhat artificial, and then let us not make the situation any more artificial than it is. Avoid the error of supposing that by imagining your class to be the Young Men's Business Club and selecting a subject appropriate to that group you can make your speech more genuine. If you fancy the class to be something other than it really is, you virtually ignore your listeners. They are quick to realize this and rightly conclude that if they are to be interested at all they must be concerned with your skill, technique, and presentation. If in selecting a subject you sidestep your audience in the classroom, you cannot expect to secure attention for your ideas. Long observation of classroom audiences has shown over and over again that they do become interested in what is said. After all, both students and instructors are human beings to be dealt with as an audience or as a series of audiences. We have our interests, our feelings, our experiences, our enthusiasms, our share of ignorance, our prejudices, and our wrong ideas. We can stay awake or go to sleep. We can be interested or bored. Our ignorance can be removed, our opinions changed. And we are probably as sympathetic an audience as you will ever address. Therefore, speak to us in *our* own persons and speak in *your* own person. We are various enough in our natures that your problems will be sufficiently real as long as you will be with us. Interest *us,* inform *us,* persuade *us.* Never try just to "make a speech"; it can't be done. Consider your audience in the *classroom* as you would anywhere else.

Influence of Time Limit on Subject and Purpose

In the occasion and circumstances of any speech, the time allotted to the speaker must greatly influence the choice of specific subject and purpose. The time factor is especially important in the short speech. Once you have a subject that you think will interest your hearers, that you are informed about (or can become informed about), and that is appropriate to the current mood and thought of your listeners, you inevitably confront this question: How can I limit and restrict my subject so as to leave a single impression with my audience?

If you are a *personage* and are asked to speak before the East End Kiwanis Club or the students of Central High School because they want to hear *you,* regardless of what you speak about, you have the whole responsibility of choosing your subject—both the general subject, "Education," for example, and the particular delimitation of that subject, for instance, courses in safety on the highway. If you are an authority on South America and are asked to speak before the St. Andrew's Men's Club but are not given a subject, the supposition is, of course, that you will speak on South America, but you will have to decide what limited corner of the subject, South America, you will explore in the twenty minutes you will occupy in speaking. Perhaps you will choose the Christian Men's Club in Natal, Brazil, as most proper for audience, occasion, and time available. Even if you are asked to speak to the Chapter of Sigma Beta on the founders of the fraternity, you still have the problem of defining just what part of that subject you will try to cover. Whenever you speak, unless you are merely delivering a canned speech written and arranged for by someone else (as sometimes happens in political campaigns), you will have the problem, if not of choosing your general subject, at least of defining it—often both.

The delimiting of the general subject you are to use into a specific subject of such size and simplicity that you can handle it fully enough in the time at your disposal is not always easy, but it must be carried through if you are to avoid the skimming speech, the speech of too-little-about-too-much. No speaker, for example, no matter how "full of his subject," could say anything adequate on all the phases of the subject of television, in from five to ten minutes. He must, therefore, select some unified phase or segment of the subject which will meet the knowledge and interests of his particular audience, and *limit* himself to that. Instead of casually dipping into the subject of bullfighting for five minutes, he might better stick to explaining fully some of the terms used in describing bullfights; or instead of trying to present hurriedly all the reasons why shippers should prefer railroads to trucks, he might well concentrate on the one or two reasons which will touch his present audience most closely.

Limiting the subject must be a process of *cutting down*, not *thinning out*. Strange as the advice may seem, experience shows that most student speakers need to say *more about less, not less about more.* They need to say *enough about something rather than too little about everything.*

Since the mistake most often made by speakers in settling upon specific subjects is saying too little about too much, we shall suggest two expedients that should help you in choosing a limited view of your subject and of making a single impression upon your hearers. We shall assume that you are to speak briefly—from four to seven minutes. We shall assume, too, that you believe your hearers will be interested in "Collective Bargaining" as a subject and that they have a good deal of information about it.

Determining and phrasing concisely your specific purpose will often limit your subject satisfactorily. Do you want your audience to be firm in their support of collective bargaining? But for whom? Public employees? A particular class of public employees such as firemen? Or teachers? Or policemen, if the right to strike is not included? In particular kinds of situations? Consequently, you may be led to phrase your specific purpose accordingly: To show that people are right to support collective bargaining for industrial workers; or to show that it is right to exclude domestic help from collective bargaining. Observe that to state your purpose in a general way is not enough. "To explain why collective bargaining exists," "To argue against collective bargaining"—these are far too broad in scope, even for a ten-minute speech.

In developing the ideas that will accomplish your purpose, *plan to use at least two one-minute illustrations.* If you cannot use two detailed illustrations, the chances are that you have not limited your purpose and subject to the point where you can make a single, vivid impression on your hearers.

Subjects Too Difficult for Oral Presentation

Though there are many more kinds of subjects available to them than some student speakers realize, it is true that certain kinds of subjects are unadaptable to successful oral presentation and still others require facilities usually not available to a speaker. In one phase of the instruction intended to improve the effectiveness of employees in an industrial plant, the leader of a group of foremen first described fully and carefully how to tie the fire underwriters' knot. He then asked members of the audience to tie the knot—but no one ever could. Next he explained and demonstrated, but still no one could tie the knot. Until he guided an individual several times through the actual performance, the instruction proved ineffective. Here was a subject unadapted to effective oral presentation. The audience learned from the speaker's words that there was a knot to be tied. He might also successfully have informed them of the uses of the knot, and possibly why the knot was better than others for certain purposes. He could not make them understand the knot itself.

Subjects of the following kinds are likely to be very difficult or impossible for unaided oral presentation:

Subtle or complicated processes, the explanation of which requires the accurate visualization by the listener of a long series of actions and the correct remembering of them.

Technical subjects requiring the mastery of specialized concepts and vocabulary, and the pursuit of close reasoning which demands reviewing and slow working out through study. Many papers read at scientific and learned gatherings, even before specialists, result only in the audience's realizing that some investigation has been done and some conclusions reached by the speaker, the account of which it will be necessary to read over and study carefully later on.

Subjects requiring the detailed understanding of large quantities of figures and statistics. (If, of course, only the conclusions and the fact that statistics have been used to derive the conclusions are important, then these subjects are quite usable.)

Subjects which involve the discussion of intimate or personal material which people would read alone without embarrassment or discomfort but which they will be reluctant to listen to in a group.

There follow classified samples of usable subjects for classroom speeches, subjects which may also fit many occasions and audiences outside. Study them carefully each time you have a subject to choose. Don't merely glance through them and go on fretting. They will usually provide a subject for you or suggest one to you.

SUBJECTS TO THINK ABOUT

Public Questions (Small phases of which should be used for short speeches.)

Juvenile delinquency	Aid for dependent children
Farm legislation	A labor party
Federal highway program	Liquor control
Local health problems	Regulation of radio and television

Traffic problems
Unemployment insurance
Conservation
Personal property tax
Sales tax
The Electoral College
Government by bureaus
Race relations
Minority problems
Women in business
Women in industry
Socialized medicine
Old age benefits

Interstate trade barriers
Federal aid to education
Discriminatory legislation
Desegregation in education
Military training
Fair trade laws
Quality controls
Government in business
Public utilities
Treatment of criminals
Divorce
Marriage laws
Urban redevelopment

What Is It?

Withholding tax
Community Chest
Rotary Club
Y.M.C.A.
Women's Chamber of Commerce
Mortar Board
Phi Beta Kappa
High fidelity
Speech disorders
Geology of the Great Lakes
Grade-point system
Short ballot
Regimentation
Honor system
Savings and loan association
Subcontracting
Reciprocal trade agreement
Modern music
World of the atom
Delta Sigma Rho
Optimists Club

Lions Club
F.C.C.
Junior Red Cross
Collective bargaining
Photoelectric cell
Photoelasticity
Radioactive isotopes
Grade labelling
Group hospitalization insurance
Single tax
Deficit spending
League of Women Voters
Check-off
Closed shop
Balanced diet
Time and motion study
Vitamins
Octane rating
Group insurance
Nurse's aid
Space capsule

How to Do It

Making hunting knives
Studying for examinations
Making fish flies
Planning a garden
Caring for a garden
Writing good letters
    Business letters
    Personal letters
Designing a dress
Making up for a play
Using the slide rule

Caring for indoor plants
Using and caring for a microscope
Getting elected
Thinking for oneself
Operating a tractor
Organizing a local political campaign
Selling a car
Refinishing a table
Building a house
    Site
    Design

Using the comptometer
Using the microfilm viewer
Mixing drinks
Buying a house
Buying a car

Plumbing layout
Electrical layout
Interior decoration
Insurance

Description or Explanation of a Process—How It Works

Separating cream
Filling a silo
Laying a concrete pavement
Vulcanizing inner tubes
Fractional distillation
Pressure cooking
Mining sulphur
The forward pass
Refining bauxite
An electric clock
Vacuum coffee-maker
A slot machine
Helicopter
Deep freeze unit
Rumor
Gossip
Jet engine
Gas turbine engine
Improving reading

Taking inventory
Making up the payroll
Running a student publication
  Editing
  Managing business
  Reporting
Amending the constitution
Grading beef
Making pottery
Making glass
The "numbers" racket
Youth camps
Youth hostels
Induction heating
Radiation heating
Blowing glass
TV picture tube
Improving photography
Constructing a theater set

Jobs or Professions, Businesses

File clerk
Timekeeper
Rewrite man
Welder
Machinist
Floor walker
Accountant
Private secretary
Teller
Broker
Librarian
Bond salesman
Public relations man
Buyer
Radio announcer
Radio actor

Dentist
Personnel director
Case worker
Investigator
Construction foreman
Copyreader
Proofreader
Advertising
Selling
Medicine
Service station operator
Teaching
Banking
Manufacturing
Test pilot
Bus driver

Practical Applications or Uses of Special Studies or Scientific Principles

Boyle's law
The lever

Centrifugal force
Magnetic field

Bernoulli's theorem
Logarithms
Calculus
Physical geography
Friction
The pendulum

Vector analysis
Phonetics
Anatomy
Physical chemistry
Radiation
Fission

Personal and Miscellaneous

"Read this book"
"See this movie"
"Visit this vacation spot"
"Take up this sport"
"Take up this hobby"
"Listen to this radio program"
"Watch this TV program"
"Take this college course"
"Learn this game"
"Read this magazine"
"Listen to this opera, this symphony"
"Study this subject"
"See this art exhibit"
"Read this newspaper"

The country and the city
Religion
Churchgoing
Family relations
Campus activities
Values of college
Athletic scholarships
Accelerated education
Mexican churches
Student life in the U.S.S.R.
This college and the one I used to attend

CHAPTER FOUR

Sources of Materials

WHEN A SPEAKER has chosen his subject, or at least has a possible subject in mind, he can proceed to work efficiently. Conscious of his subject and beginning to live with it, he finds it attracting ideas to itself from many sources and often at unexpected times. Awareness of subject seems to prime his brain, put him on the alert, and sharpen his perceptions.

One who really gets interested in a subject will encounter no great trouble in picking up ideas, bits of fact, examples and illustrations, from his normal reading and from his conversation with others. The greater trouble will come in remembering them. Our memories are woefully weak, and the easiest way of helping them is by pencil and paper. Make no mistake about this: If you want to prepare speeches efficiently, write down the idea the moment you get it. If you merely resolve to record it later, or if you say, "I surely won't forget *that*," the chances are ten to one that you won't have the idea when you finally set to work building up your speech. In conferring with students on speech subjects, dozens of times each semester an instructor hears, "I had a grand idea for my speech the other day, but now I can't think of it." When you get that grand idea, no matter where you are, *jot it down*—on a card, an envelope, anything.

METHOD IN COLLECTING MATERIALS

If you want to achieve economy of effort in preparing your speeches, you will have to discipline yourself to work methodically. Because no two minds work exactly alike, there is of course no single method of working which is equally effective for everyone. So each person has to take himself in hand and develop procedures that are economical for him. Yet simply because there is no rigid formula for everybody, the young speaker in particular must not ignore method and must avoid jumping about aimlessly and frantically. Such activity is sheer waste, that way madness lies.

A few general conditions underlie creative activity. Being aware of them should help you work out your own procedures and come up with a speech that is characteristically yours and nobody else's.

Much out of Much

The mind is like a storehouse. If there is much in it, much can come out; if there is little in it, little will come out. Ten items of information can be combined in a hundred different ways. Three items can be combined in only nine different ways. What we call "inspiration" seems to be directly proportional to the amount of our information and to the extent and depth of our experience. The preparation of a speech is basically a matter of rapidly extending one's experience with his subject, of working it over, of keeping it alive, until a satisfying product has jelled.

Like Attracts Like

Unlike the elementary law of electricity that like charges repel each other, an idea supported by a motive attracts similar ideas and repels dissimilar ones. We see what we want to see and don't see what we don't want to see—unless someone forces it on us. Similarly, when you have a subject and know you are going to make a speech, you have a combination of idea and motive which serves as an effective stimulus condition to prompt related responses. The trick lies in keeping subject and motive in the forefront of consciousness. If you can train yourself to do this, you will find yourself picking up related ideas out of your past experience and out of your current studies and conversation with others. The popping up of such ideas may seem mysterious and wonderful. But it isn't. You have simply stacked the cards intelligently in your favor.

Listening and Talking

These activities, and the two described below, are the most direct methods of extending knowledge and experience about one's subject.

You may find some ideas and information through casual conversation and discussion with your friends. But don't depend upon casual contacts solely—don't play your cards idly. Play them with finesse, by *seeking* talk with others on your subject. Steer the conversation in your direction and plan interviews with persons who are informed. Especially in college circles you can find such persons—both students and instructors. The great virtue of conversation is not only that it tells you what you do not know and what you need to verify and clarify, but that it also strengthens and intensifies what you do know. Furthermore, the questions other people ask, as well as the information they disclose, tell you what *they* do not know and would find interesting. So conversation provides clues which may reveal the state of information and interest of your audience. Political speakers know this. When they go into a strange community for a speech, they like to talk first with the local newspapermen.

Observing and Investigating

If your subject makes it possible, go look as well as talk. If you were speaking on the functions or the problems of the local school board, you could well go and observe a session of the board. If you were condemning the tactics of the justices of the peace, you could easily go look at the local justice in action.

The special boon of observation is that it makes experience vivid and intense. Because it registers sharp impressions, it lengthens memory.

Reading

Conversation, observation, and direct investigation are the preferred ways of knowing what you are talking about. But for most young speakers at most times, they are extremely limited ways. Students especially haven't the time and opportunity to travel about, and being young they have little solid experience behind them. So reading remains the fastest and most practicable avenue for the extension of knowledge.

You can read up on a speech subject efficiently if you will distinguish between focus and perspective. The focus is your specific subject. With that in mind you can read with a purpose and go directly to the relevant source materials in the library or elsewhere. Indeed, you may have a number of foci—those parts of your subject which you have previously acquired through conversation and other ways. These you may need to extend or verify. At any rate, you can read as a hound hunts, with nose on the trail. Believe us, you can have no more frustrating experience than entering a library with no subject, your speech due in a few days, and starting to read about wildly. It is like being dropped into a maze and seeing no discernible way out.

Getting perspective on your subject entails reading not only on the subject, but around it. The more you can learn about the history and background of the subject, the better. You will rapidly become aware that your special subject is closely related to more general ones—it has parents and brothers, so to speak. For example, if you planned to talk on the best method of reviewing for examinations, you would soon be led to the principles of learning and of memory. You should be especially sure to read anything on your subject which your audience is very likely to have read or to know about. Otherwise your listeners may well react, "Doesn't he know that we know so-and-so and are thinking about this-and-that?" Finally, if you are working on a controversial subject, don't firmly make up your mind what side you are on until you have read widely. Don't become so channeled that you cannot consider fairly the best arguments on all sides. In short, getting the perspective on a subject gives you the same effect as perspective in a picture: it provides depth for the foreground.

How much should you read? No one can say for sure. But a few trusted rules of thumb may help you to decide. In general, read all that you can digest in the time you have available—and then read a little more. The extra article adds to the confidence. If you are preparing an informative speech, read enough to have the feeling that no one in your audience can ask a relevant question you cannot answer. If you are working up a persuasive speech, read until you find the arguments repeating themselves. Then you can be reasonably sure you have not missed the important ones.

Enough has been said of the general methods of collecting ideas and materials by which a person, in anticipation of speaking on a subject, can put much into himself and consequently be able to give much out. What comes out may well reveal thorough and extensive preparation, yet the product will not represent the best efforts of the speaker unless his reading has been dominated by two fundamental attitudes.

Read Critically

The person who is determined to disbelieve everything he reads is usually as badly off as he who swallows everything whole. Read to learn and to understand, or as Bacon said, "to weigh and consider," not to approve or disapprove. Make up your mind to approval or disapproval, if either is involved, *after* you know the subject. Read suspiciously, also, concerning the source and authority of the material. When you are reading opinion and argument, and even when you are reading primarily informative, factual material, determine, if you can, who wrote what you are reading, and why it was written. Be careful to notice when and where it was published. Who a writer is, what his basic beliefs and assumptions are, and the purpose for which he is presenting his explanation or his argument may tell you much about the value of the material for your purposes. You can learn a good deal about an author by consulting the sources of biographical information listed later in this chapter.

Read Accurately

There is enough misunderstanding, misinformation, and misrepresentation everywhere already. A careful investigator and accurate communicator guards against creating more. So be sure you *understand* not only what your source says, but what it means. Perhaps read swiftly the first time you read a book or article to get the general drift. But thereafter read only as fast as you can understand. Moreover, consider statements, ideas, and information with relation to the context in which they occur. A statement often means one thing in its context and something very different when it stands by itself.

FINDING INFORMATION IN PRINT

The library is to the speechmaker what the laboratory is to the scientist. It is the place of search and research.

A full discussion of sources for reading material is ordinarily found in any good book on composition and rhetoric. Furthermore, the reference librarians in any school or public library will gladly introduce a student to the many guides to reading matter. We shall do no more than mention briefly some of the most important bibliographical aids.

Books and General Articles

In searching for material in print, give attention first to the experts and specialists all about you. This saves time. If you want a modern biologist's view on evolution, for example, ask a teacher of biology to recommend a book or article. He will be delighted to have you show an interest. If you have had a college course related to your subject, consult your notes and reference lists. Then when you enter the library you can look directly for this recommended material. Later you can resort to the sources below to amplify your information.

The Card Catalogue

Doubtless you know that the card catalogue in a library lists all the books in the library alphabetically. Each book usually has cards in three places in the catalogue, one filed under author, another by title, and a third by subject matter. Knowing either of the first two, you can turn up the specific book. If you have only a subject in mind, say *plastics, nursing, Russian education,* start with it, and after the card bearing the subject name, you will find the books related to it.

Don't fail to take a long look at a card. Remember that it not only lists the date of the book and its contents, but it helps spot related books. It will note whether the book contains a bibliography or reference list. At the bottom of the card will appear two or three *subjects,* under which you can look for other books.

In general, prefer the latest book on your subject. You can learn what it is by consulting the *Cumulative Book Index.* This work lists all books printed in the United States since 1928 and is kept up to the month.

Having located the book in the *Index,* you can then turn to the card catalogue to see whether your library has it.

Encyclopedias

Collier's Encyclopedia

Encyclopædia Britannica

Encyclopedia Americana

These sources try to keep their materials up to date by regularly publishing supplements, some of them appearing annually. See *Britannica Book of the Year,* 1938 to date. The encyclopedias are valuable not only for their general articles on a variety of subjects, but also for the short reference lists which usually conclude the principal articles.

Specific Articles and Pamphlets

Indexes General in Scope

The *Readers' Guide to Periodical Literature,* subscribed to by all libraries, is an up-to-date listing of practically all popular and semi-popular magazines and periodicals in America. In it, all articles are listed alphabetically as to author, title, and subject, as books are listed in the card catalogue. In looking for articles on a subject, don't limit yourself to looking only under the name that you happen to have in mind for that subject, for example, *taxes.* Look also under other possible names for the same general subject, such as *taxation, revenue, finance.* The *Readers' Guide* is published monthly and the monthly installments are assembled into quarterly and yearly volumes. *Poole's Index* to periodicals is useful similarly, especially for articles published before the *Readers' Guide* was begun (1900). The *19th Century Readers' Guide,* 1890–1899, published in 1944, covers some of the same material within *Poole's Index* but arranges the entries according to the same system used in the current *Readers' Guide.*

To find articles in periodicals published *outside* (and within) the

United States, consult *The International Index to Periodicals,* which indexes scholarly journals as well as popular periodicals.

HIGHWAY engineering

Building of a turnpike; Connecticut turnpike. il map Fortune 56:162–9 N '57
Hooking into the interstate highway system. maps Am City 72:132–3 Ap '57
Local street plan is a must. H. K. Evans. maps Am City 72:159+ D '57
St Louis Park establishes uniform street construction practices. T. Chenoweth. il Am City 72:164–5 D '57
Saving highway bumps, and cash. il Bsns W p59+ Je 1 '57
Steel for roads. Bsns W p52 My 11 '57

INDUSTRIAL PLANTS—Automation

Automation in Europe, T. W. BLACK. Tool Engr v 39 n 3 Sept 1957 p 73–7. Review of current status of automation in Europe, based on discussions at recent Paris Automation Conference.

Automation—Verbal Fiction, Psychological Reality, EARL OF HALSBURY. Instn Production Engrs—J v 36 n 5 May 1957 p 333–43. Definition· of automation as including transfer processing, automatic assembly, control engineering and communications engineering; progress achieved in these fields and future trends; industries where automation is unlikely; social and economic consequences; ways of integrating progress of technology with social change. Reprint from Impact, Dec 1956.

Fig. 1. Sample Index Entries: Specific Subject Headings and References to Specific Articles

LABOR

Man and industry: the impact on human well-being of a rapidly evolving industrialization. Charles E. Hendry and others. Univ Toronto Q 26:191–267 Ja '57
   Addresses before a round table, University of Toronto, Toronto, Ont., Oct. 22, 1956.
   See also

Absentee.sm (labor)	Leave of absence
Agricultural labor	Lockouts
Anti-unionism	Migrant labor
Apprenticeship	Part-time employment
Child labor	Piece work
Church and labor	Professional workers
Convict labor	
Domestic service	Recruiting of labor
Employees	Restrictive labor
Employees, Dismissal of	practices
	Right to work
Employees' representation in management	Seasonal labor
	Skilled labor
	Slowdown strikes
Employment	Strikes
Featherbedding	Technical workers
Government and labor-management relations	Trade unions
	Unemployment
Hours of labor	Unfair labor practices
Industrial relations	Work
Injunctions	

Bibliography

Bibliography [selected list of publications on economics, social and labor conditions]. bibl Internat Labour R 76:311–23 S '57 (cont. mo.)
Book reviews and notes [publications of labor interests]. bibl Mo Labor R 80:1112–17 S '57 (cont. mo.)
Books, articles, current literature in the labor field. bibl Labor Law J 8:628–33 S '57 (cont. mo.)
Publications recently received in Department of labour library [Canada]. bibl Labour Gaz (Can) 57:1115–19 S '57 (cont. mo.)·
Recent publications [selected list of articles and publications on many aspects of labor conditions and industrial relations]. Bernard G. Naas and Curtis W. Stucki. bibl Ind Labor Relations R 11:105–14 O '57 (cont. q.)

Fig. 2. Sample Index Entries: Topics Related to a Specific Subject Heading, and Related Bibliography

The Public Affairs Information Service, similar to the *Readers' Guide* in form and method of listing, includes not only periodical articles but books, pamphlets, and documents related to all subjects connected with public affairs.

The New York Times Index lists by subject (and author, if any) all articles that have appeared in *The New York Times.* The *Index* will also help you to locate material in other newspapers your library may have and to which there is no index. In the *Times Index* note the *date* of the event or material you are interested in. With the date as a guide you can find what you want in other newspapers.

The Vertical File Index is especially useful for locating pamphlet material published by a variety of organizations. It is issued monthly. Users should realize that most libraries cannot acquire all the pamphlets listed in this catalogue. The General Reference Room in a library usually keeps the *current* pamphlets on hand, and the quickest way to find out what may be available on your subject is to ask the reference room attendant. Large colleges maintain departmental libraries housed in special rooms in the main library building or elsewhere on the campus; these

include collections of materials devoted to journalism, engineering, social sciences, education, and the like. Inquire at such places for pamphlet material. Consult also the Card Catalogue, for libraries keep the most important pamphlets permanently.

The Monthly Catalog—United States Government Publications lists all publications issued by the various departments and agencies of the government. The entries are arranged by subject and title. The *Catalog* is extensive and rather complicated, but it is probably the best single source of authoritative government information. When one uses it for the first time, he may need to ask the librarian for guidance.

Indexes Restricted in Scope

The range of the specialized indexes is indicated fairly accurately by their titles. They concentrate on materials appearing in publications dealing with particular fields. Each aims to cover everything in its field. Hence one discovers more articles related to farming in the *Agricultural Index* than he does in the *Readers' Guide*. Similarly, the *Readers' Guide* lists fewer articles on education than the *Education Index* does. The more specialized the subject of your speech is, the more useful is the appropriate special index.

Agricultural Index

Applied Science and Technology Index

Art Index

Biographical Index

Business Periodicals Index

Dramatic Index

Education Index

Engineering Index

Speech Index

The last named source is an index to collections of famous speeches, by subject and speaker.

Most of the more specialized encyclopedias are out of date. Nevertheless, attention should be called to two of them, for students still find their short historical articles useful:

Encyclopedia of the Social Sciences (1930–1935)

Encyclopedia of Religion and Ethics (1908–1927)

Statistical Information

The sources below collect a vast amount of miscellaneous information concerning business, labor, industry, and social welfare. They are mines of facts.

World Almanac and Book of Facts (1868 to date)

Information Please Almanac (1947 to date)

Statistical Abstract of the United States (1878 to date)

Statesman's Yearbook: Statistical and Historical Annual of the States of the World (1867 to date)

Monthly Labor Review (Reports on employment, payrolls, industrial disputes, retail prices, cost of living)

Survey of Current Business (Statistics on domestic and foreign trade, exports and imports, etc.)

Fig. 3. Entries Illustrating the Kinds of Factual Information to Be Found

**Table 2.—Per Cent Change in Plant and Equipment
Expenditures, 1957 Actual to 1958 Anticipated**

	As reported in—	
	Late April and May	Late January and February
Manufacturing	−25	−17
Durable-goods industries	−29	−22
Nondurable-goods industries	−20	−12
Mining	−25	−15
Railroads	−47	−38
Transportation, other than rail	−17	−19
Public utilities	2	4
Commercial and other	−11	−13
Total	−17	−13

Sources: U.S. Department of Commerce, Office of Business Economics, and Securities and Exchange Commission.

No. 700. RESEARCH AND DEVELOPMENT IN THE NATURAL SCIENCES: 1954

[For accounting years coinciding with calendar 1953 or ending during 1954. Estimates constructed on different basis from those in table 696 and therefore not comparable. Refers in general only to the natural sciences; however, some funds utilized for research in the social sciences are included, due to the difficulty of separately identifying such funds. Although detailed figures are not yet available for a later year, the national total for 1956 is estimated at about $9 billion]

MAJOR SECTORS	AS SOURCES OF FUNDS ($1,000,000)		AS PERFORMERS OF RESEARCH		
			Funds used ($1,000,000)		
	For research and development	For basic research	For research and development	For basic research	Scientists and engineers employed [1]
Total	5,267	444	5,267	444	229,000
Federal Government agencies .	2,787	213	973	47	35,300
Industry	2,310	141	[2] 3,747	[2] 163	164,100
Colleges and universities [3]	125	62	[2] 443	[2] 208	25,200
Other nonprofit institutions [4] ..	45	28	[2] 104	[2] 26	4,400

[1] For the most part, consists of full-time personnel plus full-time equivalent of personnel engaged part time in research.
[2] Includes funds from the Federal Government for the conduct of research and development at research centers administered by organizations in this sector under contract with Federal agencies.
[3] Includes all State and local funds, received by public institutions of higher education, which were used for research and development.
[4] Includes State and local funds, received by such nonprofit institutions as museums, zoological gardens, and academies of science, which are used for research and development.
Source: National Science Foundation; records.

Biographical Information

Who's Who

Who's Who in America

International Who's Who

Current Biography

Webster's Biographical Dictionary (Includes pronunciations)

Twentieth Century Authors (See also its *First Supplement*)

Directory of American Scholars

American Men of Science. The 9th and latest edition of this work is in three volumes: *The Physical Sciences; The Biological Sciences; The Social Sciences.*

For the most part, the sources above contain information about *living* persons, although Webster's lists famous persons of all time. The first and last publications below contain only the noteworthy dead. The notices are highly authoritative.

Dictonary of American Biography (Americans only)

National Cyclopedia of American Biography

The Dictionary of National Biography (United Kingdom only)

All three works have supplements which bring them up to date.

Collection of Noteworthy Quotations

Probably the best and the most available is John Bartlett's *Familiar Quotations,* the 13th and centennial edition, completely revised. Here the speechmaker can often find some of his ideas superbly and tellingly expressed. Even the novice speaker should be conversant with it.

TAKING NOTES

If one undertakes his reading with a subject in mind and if he wants to save time and help his memory, inevitably he takes notes. Possibly there are as many techniques of note-taking as there are readers. Each speaker, investigating his subject, will eventually settle upon his own techniques. Yet in selecting his own methods, he should be aware of the standard timesavers and conventions. Our observations on the note cards below will serve to point up the more important standards.

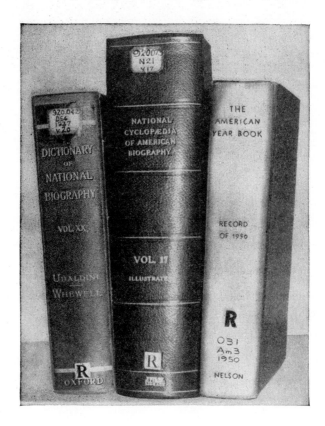

Note Cards

Extent and Effectiveness of Strikes (foreign countries)

On April 1, 1958, a 24-hour strike in France involved 1,000,000 public workers.

"Transportation was brought to a virtual standstill throughout the country. . . ."

The World Almanac (1959) and Book of Facts, p. 99.

CARD 1

Meanings of *cross*

Objects, like words, carry meanings. For example: *cross.*

Says Suzanne Langer, It is "the actual instrument of Christ's death, hence a symbol of suffering; first laid on his shoulders, an actual burden, as well as an actual product of human handicraft, and on both grounds a symbol of his accepted moral burden; also an ancient symbol of the four zodiac points, with a cosmic connotation; a 'natural' symbol of cross roads (we still use it on our highways as a warning before an intersection), and therefore of decision, crisis, choice; also of *being crossed*, i.e., of frustration, adversity, fate; and finally, to the artistic eye a cross is the figure of a man. All these and many other meanings lie dormant in that simple, familiar, significant shape."

Philosophy in a New Key (Baltimore, Pelican Books, 1948), p. 231.

CARD 2

"Reason and Morality," by Kai Nielsen. *Journal of Higher Education,* XXVIII (May, 1957), 265–275.

Theme: Morality is a kind of activity which regulates our desires and interests and guides us to rational choices among them.
 1. It helps one to realize his individual desires when to do so does not hurt others.
 2. It is the exercise of practical wisdom in human conduct; it involves right and wrong choices in particular cases.
 3. It is not scientific knowledge, for this gives us information about what *is* and does not tell us what we *ought* to do.
 4. Science, by supplying knowledge about nature and about ourselves, can help us make choices and justify them.
 5. Choice is not an arbitrary or capricious decision; it is rational and can help reduce or avoid frustrations.

CARD 3

Fermi, Laura C.   (Peaceful Uses of the Atom)

Wife of Dr. Enrico Fermi, winner of Nobel Prize in Physics for 1938 and University of Chicago professor before his death. Mrs. Fermi was familiar with her husband's work on uranium, as shown in her *Atoms in the Family*, 1954.

Appointed by the U.S. Atomic Energy Commission to attend the International Conference on the Peaceful Uses of the Atom, Geneva, 1955. Her book, *Atoms for the World*, records her impressions of the Conference. The New York *Herald Tribune* said of the book: It "combines domestic detail with a careful presentation of the problems . . . we must face as a result of the opening up of a vast new field of energy."

Current Biography (1958).

CARD 4

Cards, 3 x 5 or 4 x 6, or half sheets of paper are better than full pages. They are faster to handle and sort when one gets to the stage of grouping and classifying one's ideas.

In general it is best to restrict each card to a *single* idea or topic, whether the idea be general or highly specific. A card could well contain but a single fact, or a single example, with its appropriate head. Card 2 cites a single object having many meanings. Other cards might have as their headings other objects and list their meanings. The heading of Card 1 points out two ideas, but they are so closely related that the note-taker put them together.

When one starts his reading, often he does not know what *specific* ideas, facts, examples, or quotations he will eventually use in his speech. He gets hold of likely looking books and articles and explores them. He proceeds wisely to summarize, as briefly as he can, each article, book, or important section thereof, on a single card. Card 3 is an example of such a summary. In shaping up the ideas of his speech at a later date, he may suddenly realize that such-and-such a book is relevant. He uses its card to recall its content and whether it contained usable facts and illustrations. A summary card, then, guides one back to a source and to pointed research for special items. Summary cards are valuable in another way. When one reviews a number of them together, they may suggest the central idea of the speech, or some of its leading ideas.

Card 4 is an author, or "authority," note. On such cards one records just the information the speaker needs to identify the person for his audience and to show the author's connection with his subject. The words in parentheses may reflect the speaker's idea of a possible main head or topic within his speech. If so, another card, or cards, would bear the same heading, Peaceful Uses of the Atom, and would record appropriate ideas, materials, examples, or the like.

Always indicate the *source,* the *date,* and the *page* of the material, and in recording them, be accurate. You may need to use any or all of such bits in your speech. Or you may need to go back to the source for checking or further search. If an essential bit is missing, you will have to fumble around. Observe that each card above would take you directly to its source.

A person may not go far in his reading before he discovers ideas and information suitable for his speech. Along with such discoveries, he may sense that his subject is opening up and radiating outwards. If he is fortunate, he will experience this sense of direction before he enters upon systematic reading. He will have found his compass through cogitation and conversation. But if he has not been fortunate, he probably won't find his direction until he has completed two or three summary cards. Once he has his bearings, he will be able to decide readily what materials should go on cards and what their headings should be. In fact, with a sense of direction established, he will discover possible ways of classifying ideas, and the classification may be reflected in the card headings, as it is in the heading of Card 1, "(foreign countries)." The writer had discovered a possible division in the subject, the effects of strikes, between foreign countries and the United States. Another card would have the same heading as Card 1, with the addition (U.S.). Thus the organization of ideas begins during reading and note-taking.

How many note cards? A good rule is: Many more than you think you will need. Later on in building up the speech, it is a lot easier to eliminate superfluous cards than it is to make additional trips to the library for further reading. You are more comfortable and efficient when you have too much material at hand rather than too little. If you think you will save time by taking only a few notes on your initial reading, you will realize in the end that you have wasted time.

HANDLING MATERIALS

Possibly after you have begun thinking over your subject and have begun collecting information, and certainly after you have completed your reading and note-taking, you need time to contemplate and brood over what you have been putting into your mind. This means that an efficient and productive workman begins his speech preparation *early* and spaces it at intervals. At planned intervals he thinks *consciously* about his subject, reading, taking notes, conversing, reviewing his materials, grouping and classifying ideas, adjusting his subject to meet the time limits of his speech, and looking forward to the actual building of the outline. These are the moments and hours of *deliberate* thinking. But much of our most productive, creative thinking goes on *subconsciously,* between the periods of deliberation. Our minds cook, stew, boil, and mix our experience when we are entirely unaware of the process. Psychologists sometimes refer to the process as the *incubation* period of thought, and out of it springs the unexpectedly bright idea whose appearance seems so mysterious and inexplicable. In his preparation, an intelligent speaker gives himself incubation periods between the periods of deliberate thinking and effort. He "rests," and when the bright idea flashes out, he jots it down to consider later. So *schedule* your periods of speech preparation, lay them out methodically. Give your mind a chance.

ORIGINALITY

We have described briefly what is entailed in becoming saturated with a subject—conversing about it, investigating it directly when possible, reading up on it, and assimilating it into the system during intervals of deliberation and incubation. The person who goes through such an experience will come out with an *original* speech, though he may not be the first one in the world ever to have talked or written on his specific subject. He will produce an original speech because, first, his product will differ from any one of his sources. It will be a compound brewed from diverse ideas and materials. It will not be a copy of somebody else's product, nor will it be a weak imitation in the shape of a digest or summary. Second, it will be *his* peculiar reaction to the many sources of stimulation to which he exposed himself. It will reveal his individuality.

Whatever is original has something of the *new experience* about it, and the new experience seems to be any experience that *differs* appreciably from the old experience—from what has been going on in the same old way. Change or movement gives rise to our notions as to what is new or old, for without change every experience would be old and familiar; all would be monotony. Consequently, we can say that the new is that aspect of an experience that is *different.* Suppose you hear a lecture or read an article about the frontier and you plan to make a speech on that subject. Will your speech be *significantly different* from the lecture you heard? Will your speech be new in the sense of *adding* materials and ideas to those of the lecture, or in the sense of presenting the ideas of the lecture *in a way that is appreciably different* from the order and style of the lecture? An original speech, from the speaker's point of view, is a product that differs significantly from the sources that gave rise to it. The report, the summary, the digest, and the précis do not differ appreciably either in substance or in treatment from their originals; they are imperfect copies. Indeed, in making a report—and the report has value as intellectual training—a speaker does not intend to make his product significantly different from the original; in fact, he tries to adhere closely to the thought and structure of the original. The reporter merely wishes to act as transmitter of another's ideas, and he endeavors to transmit as faithfully as his time will allow.

An original speech reveals something of the speaker's individuality; it bears his stamp or trademark. It is the way that only *he* can react to the ideas that gave birth to his speech. Three persons, A, B, and C, might be asked to read a certain article, "In Defense of Politicians," and to make speeches based on it. A, B, and C would react differently to the article; we would hear three different speeches—different in their point of view, their type, and their treatment of ideas. Each person will react as his past experience dictates, and out of his past each will bring something different to bear on the article; or, to put this idea in another way, the article will stir up different associations in A, B, and C. At this point we can put our definition of an original speech in this way: An original speech is a product that differs significantly from the sources that gave rise to it and that bears the imprint of its maker's personality.

Ethics of Acknowledging Sources

Although a person recognizes that his speech is original, he must not side step explicit acknowledgment of his sources. To refer to his sources, of course, gives the speaker personal authority and prestige with his hearers, for they draw the inference indirectly that he has paid them the great compliment of preparing carefully for them and that he is more widely informed than they. But there is also a moral obligation to acknowledge indebtedness. A man who has put out great effort to make information available or one who has expressed an idea with striking effectiveness has some right to be recognized. It is not only right but courteous to recognize a man's labor and inventiveness.

Although it is not easy to know when to acknowledge sources and when not to, these few general suggestions should be followed scrupulously:

Whenever you quote or when you paraphrase closely, be sure to cite the source. To use the ideas and phraseology of another without acknowledgment is plagiarism—literary theft.

An idea or a fact that has added to your knowledge or has set you thinking, or an effective and unusual expression that you *know* you have derived from a definite source, you should acknowledge. Try to cultivate some awareness of the difference between such ideas and those that are the common stock of everyday conversation on a subject or those that you have assimilated so thoroughly as to have forgotten their original source beyond recall. Obviously you cannot pay your respects to a forgotten source; and common ideas and expressions on a situation or a problem need not be acknowledged, for such materials belong to everyone.

Phrasing Acknowledgment

With a little oral practice in referring to sources, you can make your acknowledgments swift and smooth. *Without* special rehearsal you will find your references awkward and stiff.

Some common ways of managing the reference:

Early in the speech, probably in the introduction wherever convenient and relevant, refer to your principal source or sources. If you do this, no other acknowledgment elsewhere in the speech is necessary. For example:

> In discussing the influences that made Robert E. Lee a kind and honorable man, I have been greatly helped by Douglas S. Freeman's four-volume biography of Lee, and by the same author's first volume on *Lee's Lieutenants*. Professor Wilkes suggested in history class last week that Lee's sense of honor was not derived from tradition merely. The remark set me thinking.

Work in acknowledgments wherever they can be put conveniently and logically. Usually the "spot" acknowledgment concerns a fact, a particular idea, a quotation, or a striking phrase or figure of speech. It can precede the reference:

> Goethe expressed his advice on the acknowledgment of source materials in this way: "The most foolish error of all is made by clever young men in thinking that they forfeit their originality if they recognize a truth which has already been recognized by others."
>
> Goethe has said that "the most foolish error. . . ."
>
> According to Goethe, "the most foolish error. . . ."

The reference may be dropped neatly into the middle of the quotation or the idea being expressed:

> "The most foolish error of all," said Goethe, "is made by clever young men. . . ."
>
> "This machine," so the American Match Company states in a recent pamphlet, "turns out 5,000 matches every minute."

Acknowledgment may follow the reference:

> "An idea is his who best expresses it," Bacon said.
>
> "The most foolish error . . . recognized by others." In those words Goethe expressed his conviction.

Where the trustworthiness or the recency of information is important, make your reference *explicit* and as complete as is necessary to be accurate. For example:

> As to the proper method of pronouncing foreign place names, W. Cabell Greet, in his 1944 edition of *World Words,* says that a good rule is "to adopt the foreign pronunciation insofar as it can be rendered by customary English sounds in the phrasing and rhythm of an English sentence."

Rarely in a speech is it necessary to cite volume number and page. Avoid the popular habit of saying "quote" and "unquote." Show by your voice and manner of speaking that you are quoting, or use plain statements: "I shall quote," "That is the end of the quotation."

Form for References

If a reference list is called for, adhere to the following form of arrangement, punctuation, and capitalization. It represents standard practice.

REFERENCES TO YOUR OWN EXPERIENCE, TO CONVERSATION, AND TO LECTURES

Briefly describe your experience: "My experience as a department store salesman."

For reference to conversation, interviews, and lectures, describe briefly: "Conversation with students," "Interview with Professor A. F. Jones," "Lecture notes in American history." Be as *specific* as possible.

REFERENCE TO BOOKS

> Marckwardt, A. H., *Scribner Handbook of English* (New York, 1940).

If a book has two authors, treat them thus:

> Jones, R. F., and J. S. Black, . . .

REFERENCE TO ARTICLES

1. Magazine articles:

> Wilson, J., "Handling the Apostrophe," *The English Journal,* XXI (June 1923), 187–200.

2. Articles appearing in books:

> Hazlitt, William, "On Going on a Journey." In R. S. Loomis and D. L. Clark, eds., *Modern English Readings* (New York, 1942), pp. 117–122.

3. Articles appearing in general reference books:

> "Rhetoric," *Encyclopaedia Britannica,* 14th ed. (London, 1929).

In citing any *Britannica* since 1932, it is preferable to use the date of printing; thus:

"Rhetoric," *Encyclopaedia Britannica* (1952).

4. Citation of newspapers:
   a. For the signed article and editorial:

Steinbeck, John, "The Attack on Salerno," *New York Times* (September 1, 1943), p. 32.

   If the paper has numbered sections, alter the citation thus:

. . . (November 1, 1943), sec. 3, p. 32.

   b. For the news article and unsigned editorial or article:

"Moscow Conference a Great Success," *The Washington Post* (November 5, 1943), p. 1.

REFERENCE TO PAMPHLETS WHERE NO ONE PERSON IS CITED AS AUTHOR OR AS EDITOR

Colonies and Dependent Areas, World Peace Foundation (Boston, 1943).

The reference list should accompany the speech outline and is usually placed at the end.

CHAPTER FIVE

Use of Materials: Amplification

WHEN THE SPEAKER has finished exploring his subject, he must next decide, in broad terms, how he wants his audience to respond. He should think of the specific audience and occasion. Does he want his hearers to *understand* his subject, or some segment of it? Or does he wish his listeners to adopt his *opinion* or *belief* on the subject? In making his choice, he is deciding whether to make an informative speech or a persuasive speech. Recognizing that both kinds utilize many of the same materials and methods but that each kind of speech has its special materials and methods helps him to organize and develop better what he is going to say. In this chapter we deal with the materials common to both informative and persuasive speeches and with the characteristic materials of the informative speech. We will give brief attention to the materials and methods of persuasive speeches in Chapter 11.

PURPOSE AND MATERIALS

The general purpose or effect of an informative speech is *understanding*. The materials and ideas which comprise information spring from three basic questions: what? how? and why? What is it that we are trying to understand? What is its nature? Or if we are interested in the operation or function of something, we ask, How does it behave? Or we may be concerned with why something behaves as it does. This book, for instance, may be regarded as an example of informative discourse, for it presents answers to these questions: What is public speaking? How does one build a speech? Why is it thus built? But whatever the scope of the informative speech, its materials are regarded by both speaker and audience as settled and demonstrable, calling for understanding rather than belief.

MEANS TO UNDERSTANDING

The basic means of securing understanding are two: organization of the speech as a whole and amplification of the "element" of the informative speech, the *statement*. Organization is satisfactory when the listener can follow the structure of the speech, when he can grasp the central idea of the speech and can see how the parts of the speech develop in making clear the central idea. For the speaker, organization is accomplished by making a speech outline. The steps in building the outline we present in Chapter 7. Now we shall concentrate on amplification.

Amplification is the process of enlarging upon a statement, or upon some part of it, in order to bring its meaning within the experience of the hearer. The speaker may understand the statement, but to the hearer it may be strange and unclear. If this be so, the speaker must enlarge upon it by translating it into familiar language. Or the language of the statement may be familiar to the hearer, but he cannot grasp its full meaning on the instant. When this is so, the speaker has to take more time to extend the statement until it registers. A single broad principle underlies amplification: *Understanding is secured by associating the new and the strange with the old and familiar.*

The means of amplification fall into two groups: (1) There are the *techniques* through which the meaning of a statement is reinforced but remains essentially unchanged. They are the techniques of repetition. (2) There are the *methods* by which the meaning of a statement is developed by the addition of relevant ideas and facts. When a speaker uses repetitive techniques, he turns a statement around, dwells upon it, stays with it, until his hearer "gets" it. When he employs additive methods, he extends the idea of the statement, he moves it along, by giving it substance and reality; he enlarges the statement, makes it bigger and hence more capable of commanding the attention of the audience. We shall reverse the order of (1) and (2) and shall treat first the methods of amplification, then the techniques.

METHODS OF AMPLIFICATION

Factual Information

Factual information is data which can be verified and can stand independent of the speaker who is using it. In speaking to University of Maine students on Scholarship Day in 1939, William T. Foster, former President of Reed College, stated as one of his points, "Good students in high school are more likely than others to become good students in college." Foster had had access to a study done at the University of Wisconsin which compared the records of hundreds of Wisconsin students with their records in high school. He amplified his point by saying that 80 per cent of those who were in the top quarter of their high school classes were in the upper half of their college classes during each year they were in the university. On the other hand, over 80 per cent of those in the lowest quarter of their high school classes never averaged more than "C" during their college days. These are facts, assembled by persons at Wisconsin who studied the grades of the students in question. Presumably other persons analyzing the same records would come up with the same results.

Kinds of Factual Information

The kinds of factual information are many. To offer an exhaustive classification here would be confusing and unnecessary. Nevertheless, the speaker on the lookout for factual materials will be aided if he recognizes the principal kinds. We have mentioned some of them in Chapter 2; now let us be more explicit.

First is the single, isolated fact or event, historical or present. The X corporation will spend a quarter of a billion dollars on new machinery this year. James took a "B" in the history course last semester. Franklin was present at the Constitutional Convention in Philadelphia in 1787.

The second kind of fact is statistical data: a number of facts classified and grouped for whatever purpose the investigator has in mind. If a dean wants to know the grade average of the sophomore class in the academic year 1950–1951, he gets out the records of his 400 sophomores, lists each grade (perhaps 2000 in all), and strikes his average. The average, then, is merely one way of describing the academic performance of 400 sophomores. Conceivably the dean might want to know how many of the sophomores took History 220 as compared with Mathematics 170. Again he would come up with a statistic. In newspapers and magazines we are always running across statistics. To get some idea of the many ways statistical data are classified, inspect *The World Almanac, Information Please Almanac,* and *The Statistical Abstract of the United States.*

A third kind of fact is represented by scientific laws and principles. Like statistics, they are ways of describing and classifying a large number of single, related events. From our knowledge of elementary economics, we have all learned that in a free market the greater the supply of a commodity, the lower the price; in other words, the more oranges, the lower the price of oranges. This is the old law of "supply and demand." From our first brush with electrical phenomena, we learned that like charges of electricity repel, unlike attract, and that electricity flows from the positive pole to the negative pole; and from psychology we know that every stimulus has its response, every response its stimulus. Indeed, all our sciences and disciplines have established principles and laws. They may be considered general statements of fact, because they describe the behavior of many individual events under conditions of controlled observation.

Use of Factual Information

The first suggestion cannot be overemphasized: If the speaker does nothing else, he should hunt for factual information on his subject. It is axiomatic that above all a speaker must *know* whereof he speaks. A conscientious speaker, therefore, will build up a storehouse of information which he can draw upon when he is ready to start organizing his speech. Then as he constructs the outline, he can consider each statement and ask himself whether it can be developed by the facts at hand. True, not all statements in an informative speech can be amplified by facts. But wherever they can, one should use facts. The facts not only secure understanding for the listener; they secure respect for the speaker.

SIMPLICITY AND ACCURACY

In presenting statistical data, be as simple as possible without sacrificing essential accuracy. For the popular audience, round numbers are usually sufficient. Unless the difference between 974,232 and 974,251 is vital to the point, better to say "over 974,000." The accountant may demand that the current standing of the national debt be expressed down to the last dollar and cent, but to the layman a statement of the national debt to the nearest million, or probably to the nearest billion, would be adequate. In referring to the tolerance in a bearing in an airplane engine, the engineer will appreciate the difference between .0016 and .0018 of an inch. But for most of us, an approximate figure of one five-hundredth of an inch would be easier to grasp and would be quite as useful as the more exact figure. Hence, unless minute accuracy is called for, use the round figure. Furthermore, simplicity can be gained by a visual presentation of the statistics. In a speech where considerable data of this kind is necessary, use charts or graphs. The ear often needs the help of the eye.

In handling statistics, also, make the fact meaningful and vivid by bringing it within the experience of the audience. A reliable way of doing so is through comparison. To say, for example, that the grade average of your class in public speaking is 80 may be quite true and exact, but the statement gains meaning and force if you add that the average of last semester's class was 83. Most persons find it hard to visualize linear and cubic dimensions without some standard of comparison. To say that a new building will be 330 feet high may be the strict truth, but the dimension will be more instantly meaningful if you add, "If laid on its side, it would be longer than a football field."

Accuracy in using factual materials is important at all times, but especially when the information is common to both speaker and audience. The speaker who is at all sensitive to what his audience may know realizes that people do read newspapers and magazines and are more or less familiar with the current best sellers. Student groups, in particular, have in common many of the same textbooks, courses, and lectures. They know something about the basic information, principles, and laws of the subjects they are currently studying. Such materials, though they occupy but a small portion of a speech, must be presented with strict accuracy.

SOURCE, DATE, RELIABILITY

Finally, whenever factual information is introduced into the speech, sound practice requires the source and date also. If the speaker is dealing with the newest development in textile fibers, he must be up-to-date and will make clear that he is. If he is treating an old and traditional subject, he should take advantage of the latest information on the subject. He may be explaining the ground plan of ancient Athens, yet he will need to know what archeologists have discovered in recent years. On most subjects, with a popular audience, it is sufficient to state the year, or the month and year. The specific day of the month becomes important only when new information on a subject is published frequently. When, for example, we were getting a stream of news reports and articles weekly, almost daily, on the amount and effects of radiation from the hydrogen bomb and other sources, it was important to know that Professor X had reported so-and-so on February 10 and that Dr. Y had found so-and-so on February 23.

Naming the source of information is highly desirable. It heightens the significance of the facts by giving the hearer some sense of their reliability. In a speech on the rising costs of college education, you could simply state this illustrative fact: "At Yale in 1939, tuition was $450; in 1959 it was $1400." Or you could introduce the fact thus: "The Research Bureau of the National Education Association has gathered information from colleges and universities about their tuition costs over a twenty-year period. As reported in *Newsweek* in April 1959, Yale's tuition in the fall of 1959 was to be $1400. In 1939 it had been $450." If you frame the information thus, we learn who is responsible for the fact, when the survey was made, and for what purpose the information was collected. Such items lend weight to the single fact of tuition costs. Do not take easy refuge in the lame words, "Statistics show . . . ," unless you are prepared, upon questioning, to tell when and by whom they were collected, and for what purpose. The informative speaker is like a scientist or a historian; he not only knows his facts but he knows whether to trust them. An audience also shares something of the same attitude. It appreciates facts and likes to know that they are reliable.

Example

An example cannot be understood by itself alone. It must always be an example *of* something. In speechmaking (and in all discourse), the something is the statement to be amplified. The example extends the meaning of the statement by supplying a particular case or circumstance. To illustrate the relationship of the example to the more general statement which it amplifies, take the following:

> One function of advertising is that of reminding persons of the product over and over again.
> In my town the Methodists still ring their church bell every Sunday morning.

A particular instance is thus used to exemplify a more general idea. Accordingly, the example, by definition, is a particular case, incident, or circumstance of the more general idea expressed in the statement which the example amplifies.

Kinds of Example

Examples are grouped into two principal kinds: short or long, real or invented.

The short example has the technical name *instance*. It is present whenever a speaker sets forth a particular case in the briefest possible time and is still clear to the listener. If the instance is well chosen, if the listener can grasp it immediately, it needs only the barest mention. An example of such an instance is the ringing of the church bell every Sunday.

The long example bears the special tag *illustration*. This builds up and fills out the particular case by giving it a setting and supplying narrative and descriptive details. The example thus becomes a sort of compact story or a thumbnail sketch of the circumstances. The illustration is the example *illuminated*.

THE ILLUSTRATION

Speakers have found the illustration especially useful in two types of situation. It is employed in place of the instance when a speaker wants to be vivid and at the same time to give the hearer some sense of action and reality. This is what Bruce Barton did in handling the church bell example (For the complete speech, see the Appendix). Instead of presenting it as an instance, he chose the illustration:

> A member of my profession, an advertising man, . . . was in the employ
> of a circus. It was his function to precede the circus into various communities, distribute tickets to the editor, put up on the barns pictures of the
> bearded lady and the man-eating snakes, and finally to get in touch with
> the proprietor of some store and persuade him to purchase the space on
> either side of the elephant for his advertisement in the parade.
>
> Coming one day to a crossroads town our friend found that there was
> only one store. The proprietor did not receive him enthusiastically. "Why
> should I advertise?" he demanded. "I have been here for twenty years.
> There isn't a man, woman, or child around these parts that doesn't know
> where I am and what I sell." The advertising man answered very promptly
> (because in our business if we hesitate we are lost), and he said to the
> proprietor, pointing across the street, "What is that building over there?"
> The proprietor answered, "That is the Methodist Episcopal Church." The
> advertising man said, "How long has that been there?" The proprietor said,
> "Oh, I don't know; seventy-five years probably." "And yet," exclaimed the
> advertising man, "they ring the church bell every Sunday morning."

The example offered as an instance would have taken about ten seconds;
the illustration probably occupied about a minute and a half. Note the
swift, narrative setting, the dialogue which heightens the impression
of a real event, the careful ordering of details to lead into the point—
and the touch of humor.

In the second type of situation, the illustration is almost indispensable.
When the content of the example is not instantly intelligible to the
listener, when its information is novel and technical, the speaker must
give his listener time to understand.

To an audience not knowing much about filibustering in the U.S.
Senate, a classroom speaker used an illustration with telling effect.
Pretty much in the words of the dictionary, he defined the filibuster as
"delaying tactics employed in parliamentary debate and usually involving long speeches on topics irrelevant to the subject." He amplified
immediately:

> You are all members of some organization—your literary society, your lodge,
> your farm club, your church, your young people's society. Now, as you
> know, such an organization holds a business meeting once in a while—
> called a deliberative meeting. If you were governed by the present Senate
> rules, it would be possible for any member of the organization to stand up
> and talk just as long as he wanted to on any motion that was brought before
> the house. In fact, he would not have to talk straight to the point all the time,
> either. He could start off by making it appear that he was going to talk about
> a certain point involved in the motion, and then he could say or read anything he pleased. He could recite poetry, or read a novel, or give a lot of dry
> statistics from some departmental report a hundred years old. He could do
> anything he pleased to kill time, and the rest of the members would have to
> let him keep right on for at least two days and perhaps much longer unless

they could get two-thirds of the members together to put through a device for stopping him. Of course, you would not all have to listen to him, for you could go out and eat and sleep and do anything you pleased. But, in the meeting, that member would have the floor, and nobody could take it away from him.

It is useful to consider examples not only as short or long, but also as real or invented. The real example is real in the sense that its content is actual. It is an event, a case, a situation that has actually happened. All the examples we have so far included in this section of the chapter are real.

FICTITIOUS EXAMPLE

The invented example, often called the hypothetical or fictitious example, is precisely what its name implies. Drawing upon his imagination and judgment, the speaker makes up an example. He does not produce what has happened; he offers what *might* have taken place. Recently we heard a football coach explaining the theory of the off-tackle play. He explained that more than most plays it depends upon perfect timing. Each man, he said, must do precisely the right thing at the right moment, and if he does, the play always gains yardage. The coach knew his faculty listeners could not be relied upon to remember an off-tackle play they had seen; so he did not use an instance of one. He felt he could not take the time to describe a case of such a play and so did not try a factual, detailed illustration. He had at hand no film of the play. So he amplified by saying, "Now if you were to execute the off-tackle play as it should be done, you would do so-and-so, and so-and-so. . . ." In two minutes he made his audience see a perfect play through his invented illustration. The hypothetical example, then, amplifies an idea by presenting something that might be, or might have been.

Young speakers sometimes hesitate to use fictitious examples. Their reluctance in part is well grounded, for in preparing to speak on most subjects, one can usually find examples of past events, and the historical instance or fact always has the ring of truth. Nevertheless, for purposes of amplification there are times when the invented example is superior to all other kinds. They are the occasions on which one is trying to explain the theoretical and the ideal condition. For the ideal house or electoral system there can be no real example; the communicator must construct one.

Through the invented example the speaker may give rein to his imaginative powers and he may create not only fictions nearer to perfection than imperfect actuality will provide, but fictions more real, more engaging, and perhaps more amusing than literal actuality. Through the invented example the poet and the dramatist in the speaker may come out to good advantage. We do not know whether Christ was reporting an actual case of robbery on the Jericho road when he told the illustrative story of the Good Samaritan. It never occurs to us to care. That tale has engaged more interest and has illustrated a point better and longer than any newspaper story ever written. We do know that the myths with which Plato sought to clarify the more difficult of his philosophical and ethical ideas *are* fictions. They are fictions which draw the reader or the listener pleasantly and surely into a grasp of the ideas. The myth of the chariot, for example, in the *Phaedrus* illuminates Plato's idea of the struggle of spiritual love and sensual love in the soul of man. What Christ or Plato did, and good speakers have always done, the student with a spark of inventiveness can attempt with profit.

Selection of Examples

One must keep in mind certain considerations which govern the selection of examples.

EMPHASIS

In a speech the most important statements and points deserve examples —the points which would be fatal to clarity if the listener did not understand them. The illustration with its specific, vivid details is the longest-lived reminder of an idea. When minor ideas are to be exemplified, one should prefer the short example—the instance—to the illustration.

RELEVANCE TO STATEMENT

Although it is obvious that examples should be directly relevant to the statements they amplify, speakers are constantly tempted to squeeze and torture examples to try to make them fit. Perhaps you have found a fascinating illustration; so you feel you ought to use it somehow. Resist the impulse. Find an example that is relevant, or invent one. Straining an example into a bad fit only puzzles an audience. Like the funny story dragged in by the skin of its teeth, it may be interesting, but it always distracts from the main thing.

RELEVANCE TO LISTENERS' EXPERIENCE

In amplifying an important idea by example, use a variety of examples so selected that they will touch the experience of the chief interest groups in the audience. Examples drawn from country life will strike the imaginations of some members of a general audience; those drawn from city life, others. Examples from mechanics and science will help clarify ideas for some kinds of persons; those from business and the arts will appeal to others. Very few examples will be equally effective with all persons found in general audiences. There was a time, now gone, when examples drawn from the Bible would be familiar to almost all Americans. Today there seems to be no single source of examples effective with all audiences. The wise speaker, therefore, will know as much as he can about the experience of his audience and will choose his examples to fit the main areas of that experience.

The particular, recent experience of his audience, if the speaker is aware of it, is a good source of examples. For instance, is there any connection between his subject and the railroad or airplane accident nearby, a strike in a local industry, Saturday's football game, the latest murder or divorce, or the current lesson in algebra, history or zoology?

Infallible and comprehensive rules for the successful use of recent familiar events cannot be given, for a speaker can be given no substitute for a keen, retentive, active mind. Useful as current and local circumstances may be, however, the speaker must not appear to force them into association with his ideas or to distort them to his uses. They should appear to be related plausibly and naturally, or they should not be used at all.

INTEREST VALUE OF EXAMPLES

Examples, in themselves, tend to be interesting. In selecting the material for his examples, however, the speaker may enhance their capacity to stimulate interest if he will associate them with some of the fundamental, perennial interests common to all normal people. Any of the materials of amplification, of course, may be associated profitably with these interests, but examples, because they are specific and concrete, are especially effective when they touch such springs of interest as sex, health, wealth, sensual pleasure, sentiments, human beings, and activity.

Love, marriage, procreation, the beautiful human form make up the most universally interesting of all stories. Anything, therefore, which is associated with the relations between the sexes is a perennial source of interest. A picture of a beautiful woman is apparently a valuable part (sometimes the only part) of advertisements intended to interest men, and even women. When an advertiser adorns his advertisement for George IV Cigarettes with the brightly colored figure of a beautiful blonde, he is trying to transfer the interest in sex aroused by the picture to the text of his blurb. A resourceful speaker will not neglect the discreet, fitting, and honest use in his examples of this the liveliest of all sources of interest.

Likewise, people are normally interested in what preserves life, health, and well-being, and in what promotes wealth. Let the speaker, therefore, associate his examples with these interests when he can. For example, workers in a factory never listen with so much ready interest to a lecture on safety methods as they do just after one of their fellows has been injured through careless handling of the machinery. "There's a right way and there are many wrong ways to write a check," says a speaker who is cashier in a bank. "Only last week we paid a check for *ninety-three* dollars against the account of one of our depositors because he had been careless in writing a check for *three* dollars." Here the pocket-book interest with the added interest of the concrete example is associated with instructions on how to write a check.

So also the interest of people in things affecting their pride, their sensory pleasure, and their sentiments may be enlisted to give strengthened force to examples. Even when, though seldom, there is no interest operative in a student, other than the competitive interest in grades in school, that interest is often converted into an interest in the subject matter of study. Again, examples touching the glories of the old Alma Mater interest loyal alumni; those which call up memories of the "old gang" interest most people; and except in times of the utmost cynicism, reminders of our affection for our country interest all of us.

The appeal of activity should also influence the speaker's choice of examples. In the explanation of a process or a machine or a maneuver in football, tennis, or war, for example, the interesting speaker will not stop with the essential details of bare exposition. He will show his audience someone performing the process or will show an article of manufacture going through the process; in his explanation he will have the machinery running, and if possible someone running it; he will describe armies or players maneuvering or men fighting battles.

We are all interested in what people are doing and saying. Wherever practicable, therefore, what a speaker would interest an audience in should be associated with people. The university photographer, wishing a picture which will interest the public in the new power press in the mechanical engineering laboratory, poses two or three engineering students with hands on the levers and controls of the machine. He is giving a *human* touch to what otherwise might, perhaps, have been a fuller, clearer picture, but a *dead, unhuman picture.* That is using human interest—the interest of the newspaper-reading public in the breakfast, lunch, dinner, and bedtime snack of the bartender's helper who just won the Irish Sweepstakes.

Interest in personality, like any other valuable avenue of access to people's minds and feelings, can be overworked, cheapened, and discredited by the uses to which it is put—from advertising useless facial preparations and patent medicines to exploiting the ephemeral marital episodes of Hollywood celebrities. The perennial, irrepressible interest of man in his fellow man, however, may be as readily directed to the worthy, the important.

HUMOR AND THE EXAMPLE

There can be no doubt that humor in examples is one of the valuable sources of interest. What we have just said about emphasis and relevance in the choice of examples, and our advice later on appropriateness, apply with special force to the use of the humorous example.

Not everyone who can appreciate a joke has a talent for telling one, and the person who is a poor raconteur generally is not likely to shine in telling a humorous anecdote. We have heard inexperienced debaters trying to enliven their statistics with funny stories (usually at the expense of their opponents). They have been so cumbersome and heavy-footed in their narratives, however, that they have made themselves ridiculous instead of enlivening or illumining the subject. Perhaps the infrequency of the talent for humor among politicians, rather than its impropriety in political discussion, was principally responsible for the uproar from the opposition over the wit in Adlai Stevenson's campaign speeches several years ago. We would encourage the student speaker, nevertheless, to experiment with humor in his examples. Perhaps he will find that he can cultivate a real talent. Let his guides be *relevance, propriety,* and *freshness.*

Stories and anecdotes, of course, may be funny quite independently of any context in which they are told, but unless they are plausibly and securely *relevant* to the speaker's ideas, the audience's interest in the story will stop there and will not be extended to the idea. A speaker should not drag stories into contexts to which they have no appropriate relation unless he is so desperate for the audience's attention that he must have it whether or no; and he shouldn't say, "That reminds me of a story . . ." unless there is something in what he is discussing which really should remind him of the story.

On the matter of *propriety,* let us add only a kind of last word from Cicero. Humor, he said, should not be "too frequent, lest it become buffoonery; nor . . . of a smutty nature, lest it be low farce; nor pert, lest it be impudent; nor aimed at misfortune, lest it be brutal; nor at crime, lest laughter take the place of loathing; nor should . . . [it] be inappropriate to the speaker's own character, to that of the jury, or to the occasion; for all these points come under the head of propriety." [1] In short, when in doubt, don't!

The *freshness* of a humorous story depends, of course, upon who is

[1] *Orator,* trans. by H. M. Hubbell (Cambridge, Mass., Harvard University Press, 1942), p. 371.

telling it to whom, when, and how. The story which went very well in the freshman history lecture (for everyone *has* to hear a story for the first time!) may be pretty stale fare at the senior banquet. Nevertheless, on some after-dinner or sportive occasions a speaker, especially if he has the reputation of being a wit, can get a laugh with almost any threadbare wheeze or feeble pun. People laugh, at such times, simply because they want to laugh and are waiting only for an excuse. Most of the time, however, audiences want fresh humor or fresh application of old humor. An inexperienced speaker, at least, will avoid thumbing through joke books and anthologies of wit and humor, not because the contents of such books are not amusing (or at least were not amusing originally), but because they are everyone's property, the audience's as well as the speaker's. Likewise retelling stories and jokes published in such popular magazines as *Reader's Digest* and in the comic strips is not always as effective as the speaker expects it to be. The humor was very good when published, but most of the audience has already read it and has heard others repeat it again and again since its publication. In spite of the habits of the locker room and the club house, a speaker cannot get away from the consequences of his stale joke by merely changing the characters or by prefacing it with "Stop me if you've heard this one." An old story, in order to be effective, should be given a new twist or a new application or a disguised setting. Then the audience may be interested in recognizing the essentials of the story and be pleased at the surprise elements.

We conclude, then, that in managing his examples the speaker will do well to consider the factors of interest and to associate what he wants to make interesting with what, to audiences in general and to his audience in particular, is already interesting.

APPROPRIATENESS TO SUBJECT AND OCCASION

Tact and taste are not easily subject to rules. Should one use humorous illustrations on a solemn occasion? Does copious use of fictitious examples indirectly tell an audience that the speaker does not know enough to have discovered factual examples? It all depends on whether a speaker enjoys the respect and confidence of his hearers. Within very wide limits examples may properly be drawn from any areas of common knowledge or common experience. A speaker should exercise care, however, that in his choice of examples he does not depart widely from the tone and spirit which the occasion demands and his purpose requires. Extreme cases of faulty taste may easily be cited. In a speech honoring Washington's Birthday, it would seem incongruous for a speaker to couple Washington's conduct at Valley Forge with Benedict Arnold's at Quebec in illustration of the various kinds of courage evinced by a great hero. It is impossible to lay down rules for good sense and tact in choosing examples, but inexperienced speakers should err on the side of caution.

APPROPRIATENESS TO SPEAKER

Examples which seem proper to the subject and the occasion may offend a particular audience or may seem to that audience unbefitting a particular speaker. An audience composed largely of churchgoers may be antagonized by an illustration from a lay speaker suggesting the liability of the clergy to err; yet the same audience would probably take no offense at the same example used by a clergyman. The trouble with the example would not be that it failed to exemplify the speaker's idea, but that it raised distracting and competing ideas in the listeners. College students, speaking before audiences of businessmen, may make the mistake of choosing their examples, however pat, from those areas of business about which they themselves will seem too young and inexperienced to know anything. The natural response of those audiences is not, "I see the point; he hits the nail on the head," but, "What does that youngster know about business?" A speaker cannot expect his listeners to concentrate on his point if he sets them thinking about his *choice* of examples.

Handling Details of Examples

ORDER OF DETAILS

The proper placing of details in an example is a matter of some importance. Examples and illustrations are *picture-forming*, and *the pictures will be formed* once the speaker has set the audience's imagination working, whether he provides the ingredients or not. Hence, if he does not provide details at the proper time, the audience will invent its own details which may not be the ones the speaker wanted. Very seldom can repair work be done afterwards, no matter how often the speaker inserts, "By the way, this house I am speaking of was built on sand." The audience already has it built on granite, and there it will stand. Remember! the speaker has the picture already formed for himself; so any details he mentions, in whatever order, will seem satisfactory to him. But his audience has to form its image as well as it can from what he suggests or fails to suggest, in the *order* in which he suggests it.

NUMBER OF DETAILS

Examples, and particularly illustrations, should include a sufficient number of details to be clear, and details unessential to clearness should be edited out. The speaker has to judge how much knowledge and experience his audience can bring to bear on the example. Much knowledge will suggest few details; little knowledge will demand more detail. If he were talking to a city audience and drew upon an example from farm life, he would have to use a larger number of descriptive details than he would if he were speaking to a rural audience.

Speakers who draw illustrations from their personal experiences are tempted to include too many details and some that are completely unnecessary. How often have we heard the exuberant storyteller interrupt himself with "Oh, that's not important anyway!" Or with some other parenthetical self-correction such as "No, I believe that it wasn't Wednesday, the third; I think it was Thursday, the fourth." Overdrawing and overloading an illustration with detail causes confusion and breaks up any impression of movement and pace.

Comparison

As a means of amplification, comparison extends the idea of a statement by pointing out some likeness with another idea, object, or situation. When a likeness is expressed tersely, it is often a *simile* or a *metaphor*. When the likeness is developed at some length, it is usually called an *analogy*. As an instance of the short comparison, Joseph Wood Krutch compared protoplasm with jelly. He asserted that protoplasm was the simplest form of life, and amplified the idea immediately with the statement, "It is a shapeless blob of rebellious jelly." Much of our conversation is filled with comparisons, and much of our slang consists of metaphors. The special virtue of comparison is its power to make an idea strong, sharp, and intense as well as larger through the addition of information.

The short comparison takes time to mention only a single point of likeness. The analogy, or long comparison, recognizes a number of points of likeness between objects or situations. One of the masters of analogy in the popular lecture was Thomas Henry Huxley. Among other things he often tried to make ordinary English workingmen understand what a liberal education was all about. One of his favorite statements was that education consisted in learning about Nature. Then, knowing that his audience knew something about chess, he would say that learning about Nature is like learning to play chess. The world is the chessboard; the phenomena of nature represent the pieces; and the laws of nature are the rules of the game. Education, then, is mastering the rules of the game of life.

In pondering this example of analogy, observe the precise points of likeness. First is the controlling idea of the comparison: learning is to chess what learning is to Nature. Then this idea is amplified by three points of similarity: world and chessboard, phenomena and pieces, laws and rules. Successful use of analogy depends upon seeing precisely the points of comparison and of stating them clearly.

Literal Analogy

Analogies, like examples, may be either real or fictitious. When the analogy is real, it is called the *literal* analogy. When fictitious, it is named the *figurative* analogy. To distinguish the one from the other, a person needs only to recognize that most objects and actions can be grouped into logical classes, such as animal life and plant life, animate objects and inanimate objects, voluntary acts and involuntary acts. Such classifications and subdivisions of them are almost endless. The literal analogy always draws comparisons within the same class of things; it compares man with man, flower with flower, game with game, machine with machine, and the like. So Jones' behavior can readily be compared with Smith's, city government in St. Louis with that in Detroit, one farm with another, one dress with another, and so on. Within a class of things, there are always many points of correspondence. Hence a speaker has a rich mine of comparisons when he can liken his subject, say the sports program at X university, with a sports program his hearers know all about.

Figurative Analogy

The figurative analogy compares objects and events which fall into unlike classes. Strictly speaking, it states an *identity of relationship* between two unlike contexts. The short figurative comparison is a *simile* or a *metaphor*. William James observed, for example, that a gas jet was like the moon. In days when gas was used for illumination, gas jet and moon could be thought of as identical in *function*, the gas jet lighting up a room and the moon lighting up the earth. Huxley was using a figurative comparison when he likened the game of chess to the game of life. Successful chess playing and successful living are two quite different orders of things, yet with respect to the act of learning he found a number of similarities. In speechmaking, the analogy is especially useful, because no matter what one's subject may be, it is always possible to compare it with something. Any two ideas or objects may at first thought seem entirely unlike, yet upon probing they may reveal a similarity in function, in purpose, in materials and qualities, in the causes which produced them, or in the effects which they produce. At first glance, for example, race horses and athletes may appear to have nothing in common, but if you consider their treatment and training, you can discover some interesting comparisons.

As illustrations of the analogy you are probably familiar with the Parable of the Sowers or the Parable of the Wise and Foolish Virgins. You probably recall Aesop's fable of the boy who cried "Wolf!" As an instance of a figurative analogy, consider Lincoln's comparison between Blondin, the tight-rope walker, and the position of the federal government during the critical days of the Civil War.

> Gentlemen, I want you to suppose a case for a moment. Suppose that all the property you were worth was in gold, and you have put it in the hands of Blondin, the famous rope-walker, to carry across the Niagara Falls on a tight rope. Would you shake the rope while he was passing over it, or keep shouting to him, "Blondin, stoop a little more! Go a little faster!" No, I am sure you would not. You would hold your breath as well as your tongue, and keep your hand off until he was safely over. Now, the government is in the same situation. It is carrying an immense weight across a stormy ocean. Untold treasures are in its hands. It is doing the best it can. Don't badger it! Just keep still, and it will get you safely over.[2]

The figurative (invented) analogy may serve admirably (so of course may the fictitious example) to modify the tone of an exposition which runs the risk of becoming too serious and sober and consequently dull. Thomas Huxley wished to exemplify the notion that the laws of scientific induction and deduction come within the scope of everyday experience. To underscore his point he drew a figurative comparison, not from his own invention but from literature: "There is a well-known incident in one of Molière's plays, where the author makes the hero express unbounded delight on being told that he had been talking prose during the whole of his life. In the same way, I trust that you will take comfort and be delighted with yourselves, on the discovery that you have been acting on the principles of inductive and deductive philosophy during the same period."

Contrast

As a method of amplification, contrast is the opposite of comparison. It carries out the idea of a statement by showing how it is *unlike* another idea. Basically contrast involves two objects, conditions, or ideas which in some way stand opposed to each other. Any contrast therefore always entails *some degree of difference*.

The following example of contrast comes from a speech by the late

[2] Carl Sandburg, *Abraham Lincoln: The War Years* (New York, 1939), II, 125.

Secretary of State, John Foster Dulles. Speaking to the American Federation of Labor in New York City, he used contrast simply and effectively to underline what a production worker's time was worth in New York and in Moscow:

> To buy a pound of butter in New York, it takes 27 minutes of work; in Moscow over 6 hours of work. For a pound of sugar, 3½ minutes in New York, 8 minutes in Moscow; for a quart of milk, 7 minutes in New York, 42 minutes in Moscow; for a dozen eggs, 25 minutes in New York, nearly 3 hours in Moscow; for a cotton shirt, nearly 1 hour in New York, 22 hours in Moscow; for a man's suit, 3 days in New York, 47 days in Moscow; for shoes, 1 day in New York, 13 days in Moscow; and for a woman's wool suit, 22 hours in New York, 22 days in Moscow.

A special use of contrast is called *definition by negation*. Novice speakers find it particularly effective in pinning down the meaning of a fuzzy word or concept and in making clear the purpose of a speech. In partial explanation of the old notion that man is a rational or reasoning animal, one student said:

> When I refer to man as a *rational* being, I do not mean that he is distinguished from other animals because of his ability to reason—at least they *learn,* and learning often calls for reasoning. Nor do I mean to set man off from animals because he can generalize and discover principles, for the dog will show much "generalizing" behavior, based on analogy, when he stops chasing skunks. He may have chased two or three with unfortunate results; so he "reasons" that all skunks will give him pain, and he keeps his distance thereafter. No, man is not rational, in contrast to other animals, if we mean only that he learns, reasons, and generalizes.

One student, who talked on the process of flue-curing tobacco, gave emphasis to his special purpose somewhat as follows:

> Perhaps I should say that I am going to speak only about flue-curing tobacco. Interesting as the process of sun-curing tobacco is, I am not concerned with it now. Furthermore, we shall assume that the tobacco has been harvested and has been brought to the flue shed ready for handling. Also, we shall stop with the process as soon as the curing has been finished and the tobacco is ready to be taken down and carried to market.

Contrast is a means of amplification which builds up the meaning of an idea by increasing its precision and accuracy. It enhances precision because it helps prevent ambiguity and misunderstanding. The comparison promotes understanding in a positive way, for the listener is told that his experience applies to the idea. He is helped to grasp the new or strange information by adding to it the old and familiar. The contrast, on the other hand, enhances understanding in a negative way. The listener is asked to set aside his experience, to rule it out, as not being applicable at the moment. The difference in the psychological effect of comparison and contrast is compressed in this example: "My house is ranch type, but it is not L-shaped." Comparison helps us see a statement in the right light; contrast prevents our seeing it in the wrong light.

Causes of Effects

Another means of amplification is that of explaining an effect by its cause. If the statement calling for amplification asserts some condition or event to be accounted for, a curious person would want to know *why* it came about. So it is natural for a speaker to follow such a statement with a discussion of the cause or causes of the condition. For example:

> States seem reluctant today to make large increases in funds for educational uses. (Why?)
> The burden falls principally upon property taxes in most states.

To explain an effect by its cause or causes is an important and fundamental way of extending information. We are ever curious, always asking why. It rains—why? The temperature soars to 100 degrees—why? One substance we may eat is nourishing, another poisonous—why? Uranium 234 is more readily fissionable than other atoms—why? One person is an "A" student, another a "C" student—why? Almost any state or event or condition we think about or learn about can be regarded as an effect, and when it is so regarded we inquire into how and why it came about. Students of communication, particularly students of speechmaking, should reflect that they are right in the middle of cause-and-effect relationships. We say that a speech is effective. What is its effect, or effects? What were the causes?

The amplification of effects by their causes is useful in informative speeches and for a wide variety of subjects. Hence in preparing for their speeches, students do well to keep a sharp eye out for materials which help to explain the events and conditions they are dealing with. In particular look for relevant principles and laws, especially the general principles of natural phenomena which the natural and social sciences deal with and which the audience may be familiar with or have at least heard about. For example, in explaining the operation of the vacuum tube, you would draw upon the familiar law of electricity: like charges repel, unlike attract. The improvement of one's tennis game involves the application of the familiar laws of learning. Wages and prices depend, in part at least, upon the economic law of supply and demand, and the maintenance of health and avoidance of disease upon principles of exercise and nutrition. A felony or a crime, juvenile delinquency, and divorce reflect habits and principles of human behavior, of motivation and social status. It would be hard to find a subject, even for a short speech, which would not lead the speaker to consider effects and their causes.

A word of caution is in order. Remember, first, that any effect may have not one cause, but several. Hence a statement which asserts an effect may be amplified by a number of statements, each pointing out a cause. This fact poses a problem in selection. How many causes should a speaker present? How complete should he be? There are no pat answers. In the short speech to a popular audience, probably he does best to point out and discuss the single cause that in his judgment seems most important. He would know that superior intellect has something to do with an "A" record, yet talking to an audience of average students he might appropriately emphasize habits of hard, persistent study. The old rule of action applies here: Do one thing well rather than three things superficially.

Logical Definition

As a method of amplification, logical definition illuminates a word or an idea in a statement by first placing it within its class and then by distinguishing it from its class. The method combines camparison and contrast and through them makes clear the *special* meaning the speaker is attaching to the word. In discussing the nature of religious experience, a speaker said that "it always involved faith. And faith," he added promptly, "is belief which cannot be verified scientifically." Thus he swiftly put faith into the classification of beliefs and then pointed out that it differs from some beliefs because it cannot be proved scientifically. Later he tried to distinguish faith from superstition and prejudice. Another speaker, talking about a new kind of synthetic rubber, defined *rubber* as an elastic substance—a kind of substance having the power of resuming its shape after being compressed. Thus he implicitly compared and contrasted rubber with other substances in order to point up its special characteristic, elasticity.

Requirements of Definition

In using definition, speakers should be aware of four requirements.

1. It should cover all cases or instances of the word, idea, or thing being defined. If *elasticity* is said to be a property belonging to all rubber objects, it must be true that every rubber object is elastic. If the use of language is said to distinguish man from other animals, then it must be true that every man uses language.

2. The definition of the word or idea must *exclude* all else not bearing

the same name. If *elasticity* properly distinguishes rubber, it must not be applicable to any other substance. If the use of language really distinguishes man from other animals, then it cannot be characteristic of any other animal. By observing these two requirements, a speaker can do much to make his meanings accurate and precise.

3. The word or idea being defined should be amplified in language that is familiar and clear to the audience. To say that a conservative politician is one who rarely thinks beyond the *status quo* would not be so clear to most persons as to say that he is one who prefers whatever is settled and established and who distrusts what is new and untried.

4. The definition should be as brief as is consistent with accuracy. In a short speech there is rarely time to define exhaustively. Instead the speaker picks out the essential defining idea, which he can do if he observes rules (1) and (2) above. He omits the less significant characteristics. This Jonathan Swift did in defining style as "proper words in proper places." There are other characteristics of style, but in the context in which he was using the word, he was content to name but one of its essential features.

TECHNIQUES OF AMPLIFICATION

Restatement

We have set forth various *methods* of amplification: factual information, example and illustration, comparison, contrast, causes of effects, and logical definition. These are ways of expanding a statement by adding significant substance and information to it. In turning attention now to *techniques* of amplification, we shall deal with three basic ways of enlarging upon a statement, not by adding information, but by repeating the idea of the statement itself. The principle is that of *restatement*: one makes the statement again in different language, either in different words or in different form.

An example of saying the same thing in different words occurred in a student speech explaining how an architect goes about his work: "Before he can start to draw at all, he must have a design in his head. He needs a plan. He must have something to aim at." Obviously the second and third sentences are repeating essentially the same idea announced in the clause, "he must have a design in his head." For an example of restatement involving a shift in the form of expression, observe this simple case: "He must have a design in his head. A design or plan he must have clearly in his mind." Repetition of this sort occurs frequently in extemporaneous speaking and in our conversation. We can scarcely avoid it, for we feel that the hearer must fix his attention on the idea and grasp it firmly before he is ready to hear it discussed and amplified in other ways.

In using restatement, it is well to keep firm guides in mind. First, use it to underscore the most important statements of the speech when you first introduce them. The important statements are probably the statement announcing the purpose of the speech, statement of the central idea or theme of the speech, and statement of a main head which leads off a unit or block of ideas, a unit corresponding roughly to a written paragraph. Then follows the restatement with substantial amplification. Second, finish off a unit of closely related ideas with a repetition of the statement which started off the unit. If the unit were to commence with "An architect has in mind a design from which he works," it might end with "An architect tries to settle upon a clear design for a house before he does anything else." Third, restatement finds a ready place in the conclusion of a speech. One presents a summary by repeating the thought of the central idea and of each main head. Respect repetition of idea, and employ the technique wisely. Don't expect every audience to understand a statement just because you have said it once.

Synonym

A synonym provides a quick way to make a strange word intelligible by associating it with a familiar word whose meaning is the same or nearly the same. The use of the synonym probably springs from the need and desire to be accurate and precise. An informed speaker regards himself as an expert on his subject. He is related to his hearer as an expert is to the novice. And as a result of his study and experience, he has acquired exact and precise ideas. He respects these and takes pride in them. So he desires, quite rightly, to use the precise word in his speech although he knows that it will be strange to the hearer. What must he then do? He has two courses. He employs the exact word and immediately follows it with synonyms. If, for example, he were explaining the chief ways people respond to other people, he might say: "One of the typical ways of responding to another person is with aversion, a feeling of dislike, a sort of running away from the person and avoiding him." Thus *aversion,* the special word of the psychologist, is associated swiftly with the more familiar words, *dislike, running away,* and *avoiding.* If the speaker does not resort to synonyms, his other alternative is that of logical definition. This way to precision we have discussed above.

Quotation

Viewed as a technique of amplification, quotation is simply restatement through the use of a statement by somebody other than the speaker. In discussing some of the problems of intercollegiate athletics, suppose one said:

> Planning a program of intercollegiate athletics and carrying it out is a complex business.

The idea could be restated by quotation, thus:

> In making a general appraisal of organized athletics in the United States, Harold Stoke observes: "Most of the larger colleges and universities, private and public, are organized into athletic conferences managed by highly paid commissioners. Through them, complicated athletic schedules are worked out with all the finesse of the international bargaining table, and considerations of finance, publicity, the prospective careers of coaches and even of presidents, are balanced in equations which would baffle electronic computers."

A speaker uses quotation principally because its language expresses an idea better than he can. The superiority of expression may represent a happy marriage of conciseness and clarity. The quotation, to use a slang expression, may say a mouthful in a hurry. For example, one might restate the idea that modern architecture is functional by drawing on Francis Bacon's terse language: "Houses are built to live in, and not to look on." Or the superiority of another's words may rest in some striking quality which rivets the listener's attention. This quality may be evident in a sharp image, a simile or metaphor, an antithetical contrast, or some neatly balanced language. In other words, the quotation may have some literary excellence the speaker wants to take advantage of. If, for instance, he were to state that authorities on children's literature always remind us that some books are good, some less good, he might follow with another familiar statement from Bacon: "Some books are to be tasted, others to be swallowed, and some few to be chewed and digested."

In handling the quotation, it is well to avoid the barbarous, distracting device of introducing it with the words, "Now I quote," and concluding it with "Unquote." Of course the speaker must make clear that he is using the language of another. But he can manage the acknowledgment more deftly by naming the author. He can preface the quotation with a quick phrase, "As Francis Bacon said. . . ." A short sentence giving the setting will also work well before the quotation, such a sentence as "Francis Bacon expressed the idea in this manner." Note above how the quotation from Harold Stoke has been introduced. Furthermore, naming the author is not only a good way of signaling the quotation; it also gives the effect of authority.

AMPLIFICATION AND INTEREST

The methods and techniques of amplification are more than ways to clearness and understanding. They are also ways of controlling attention and maintaining interest. The informative speaker who observes them need not worry about being uninteresting if he will but keep in mind the basic principle of interest—the association of what is novel with what is familiar—and if he will respect the need for variety.

Novelty and Familiarity

The completely new and unfamiliar has little power to control our attention. It is the familiar in a new setting which compels attention and prompts recognition and understanding.

The novel and the familiar may be combined in two ways. A speaker may first present what he thinks is new to his audience and then immediately relate it to something familiar, or he may offer the old idea and then show its new application. To Americans of recent generations, assembly-line methods of manufacture are familiar, and shipbuilding is an old and well-known process. What made Henry Kaiser's procedures interesting was the application of assembly-line methods to the building of large ships; the familiar principle had been put to new use. Architects' blueprints are completely uninteresting to many persons until the one who is trying to explain them says, for example, "Here is the kitchen, here is the door to the basement, here is the window under which we will put the sink." Then the listener becomes interested because she (or he) begins to find something familiar in the unfamiliar.

Variety

We know that action and movement help to control attention. Nevertheless, movement is ineffective unless it is varied. Monotonous action can be as deadening as inaction. Hence, as his speech unfolds, a speaker will endeavor to give variety to his ideas. Two ways of securing variety are especially to be noted: (1) varying the *kinds* of amplification used and (2) changing the *point of view* from which the audience looks at the materials presented.

1. In discussing examples, we advised that they be chosen from a number of fields, in order to touch the experience of as many members of the audience as possible. This procedure has the additional value of securing variety. The principle should be extended to variety among the kinds of amplification used. A chain of explanatory statements, for instance, should be varied by the introduction of example, or testimony, or comparison. The presentation of information, especially of statistics and figures, should be varied by the offering of examples of the significance of these figures or of the application of these figures. Statistics offered to show that rise in position in the business world is accompanied by increase of vocabulary should be followed (or preceded) by specific cases of measurable vocabularies of men at various levels of salary and authority in business. A presentation of the specific benefits to accrue to the agricultural states from a soil bank program should be varied by the citation of opinions of persons known to be familiar with the needs of the Central states, the Plains states, and the Southern states. Furthermore, examples should be presented of the way the program would help a farmer in Kansas or a cattle raiser in Montana; and comparisons should be made with the benefits obtained from other forms of agricultural assistance.

2. Variety in the point of view as the speaker develops and amplifies his ideas is also highly to be desired. In describing the campus of the university, the interesting speaker might take his listener on a walk along the campus paths. Before the listener is weary of walking, the speaker might put him in a car and whisk him over the campus roads and around the outskirts. The speaker might then take him up in the library tower or up to the top floor of the administration building and let him look out over the campus, or he might give him a bird's-eye view from an airplane. In explaining the new state constitution, the speaker who wished to avoid wearying his audience might turn from description of the executive department to the effects the revision would have on farmers. From farmers he might turn to urban property owners, and from them to labor and to business and to education. In short, a speaker will maintain one view long enough to fix it clearly in his audience's mind, but not so long as to stupefy his audience with monotony. Beware the habit of Washington Irving's Wouter Van Twiller, who always conceived a subject on so vast a scale that he had no room in his mind to turn it over and look at all sides of it. This device of varying the angle of vision has been developed so far in the movies that any one continuous scene photographed from the same spot and at the same angle or distance seldom lasts longer than 50 or 60 seconds. There must always seem to be order in the variety, however. Otherwise interest will give way to jumble and confusion.

CONCLUSION

In conclusion, we remind the informative speaker that his speech consists of a series of statements and that the important ones cannot be understood without amplification. In preparing his speech, the speaker must consider each important statement and ask himself, "What methods and techniques of amplification can I use to make this idea clear to my audience?" From his resources he selects the methods and techniques he thinks will be most effective. Only rarely can a statement be enlarged upon satisfactorily by a single method. Usually the speaker must use several methods, if his readers are to understand, if he is to avoid being misunderstood, and if he is to be interesting.

FURTHER READING

PHILLIPS, A. E., *Effective Speaking* (Chicago, 1908), Ch. 3, "The Principle of Reference to Experience."

WINANS, J. A., *Speech-making* (New York, 1938), Chs. 7–10, "Interest and Speechmaking."

CHAPTER SIX

Visual Aids to Amplification

IN EMPLOYING FACTS to amplify statements, speakers have long recognized the advantages of such visual aids as drawings, diagrams, charts, graphs, pictures, models, and objects. Because most persons are more eye-minded than ear-minded, visual materials serve the speaker in two ways: they promote clearness and they are a powerful source of interest.

Visual materials make for clear impressions because they appear to make the meaning of spoken words tangible and "real," and they promote interest chiefly because they involve a change from one activity to another, from hearing to seeing.

About the invention, selection, and use of visual aids, many experts have written many books. Some of them are mentioned at the end of this chapter. We shall limit ourselves, however, to the information and suggestions which most speakers can put to use without having to call on the technicians who specialize in making motion pictures, film-strips, lantern slides, artistic drawings, and elaborate layouts.

KINDS OF VISUAL MATERIALS

Although visual materials are of many kinds and may be classified in different ways, we shall group them as simply as possible. Each group has its principal advantages, proper use, and common abuses.

Blackboard Diagrams and Sketches

These kinds of illustrations are best used when a speaker needs to build up his sketch, step by step. He draws the first feature and explains it, draws the second, and so on, until the illustration is fully developed. The device is especially adapted to the explanation of processes and procedures (if they can be stripped down to their essentials) and to simple operations and machines.

Preliminary planning and methodical rehearsal make the blackboard sketch effective. First, the prospective speaker should see the diagram as a whole. Then he should determine how many separate parts are needed and in what order to present them. Finally, the diagram must be made part of the language of the speech by incorporating it into the rehearsal period. In rehearsal, indeed, there is no substitute for a blackboard. It allows one to judge how large to make each feature and still complete the picture without crowding. It shows one how best to work and not unduly block the view of his audience. Above all, this kind of practice gives the best chance of learning to look at the audience as much as possible.

The ineptitude of some blackboard speakers needs only the briefest mention. Who has not seen—sometimes in his teachers—a person who addressed his blackboard rather than his audience? Who has not seen a speaker cover up his drawing, forcing the listener to crane his neck, to peer and squirm, finally to resign himself to confusion? Has anyone escaped blackboard work that is too small or too faint to be seen easily or so badly planned that repeated erasures were necessary before some feature was just right? Have we not all experienced those wasted periods of flat silence which we endured with speakers who never learned to talk and draw at the same time? Persons need not be so unskilled if they remember that effective blackboard illustration needs planning and practice, and if then they will actually plan and practice until they can proceed with assurance.

Models and Objects

A model is a materialized example. It is a three-dimensional representation of an object, small enough to be displayed in place of the real object or large enough to be seen when the object itself would be so small as to be invisible. The small-scale airplane and railroad, miniature furniture, the tiny house with its landscaping, and the stage set are familiar illustrations of models reduced in size. Oversized models are often used by the anatomy teacher: models of the heart, the ear, the larynx. Occasionally, also, some models may be taken apart and reassembled in order to show the innermost parts of an object, or the parts may be moved about so as to show how they work or how they appear in different positions. A model of a living room with scale furniture may be used effectively to show the principles of arranging furniture in the house. Sometimes, of course, models may not look much like the real thing, for they may be designed to show the structural relationships between the parts of an object. Chemistry teachers, for example, use models of various kinds of atoms and molecules which resemble tinker-toy constructions more than they do their unseeable counterparts.

Another kind of model is the mock-up, used with great success by teachers in the sciences, in engineering, and in the armed services. It usually consists of real objects, or parts of an object or machine, so mounted on a board as to illustrate how the parts function. For example, light bulbs, wire, a dry cell battery, and switches are often arranged to show the fundamental principles of electric circuits.

Occasionally a speaker finds he can employ objects themselves. In demonstrating the fundamentals of the golf swing or of tennis strokes there is no substitute for the club or the racket. Within recent years student speakers have displayed disassembled ribbon microphones, a baseball cut in half, the chief parts of a small generator, a knocked-down electric drill, a thermostat, a silent mercury light switch, magazine advertisements, musical instruments, and drawing materials. One can readily guess what purposes the speakers had in mind.

The model is especially useful when one wishes to uncover and make clear the inner parts of a mechanism, to show how the parts are arranged, or how they work. The speaker who finds himself with a subject which involves three-dimensional objects should always ask: Can I secure—or make—a simple model?

In learning to use a model skillfully, a speaker should: (1) Rehearse with the model until he can handle it easily and surely, introducing each part precisely when needed. (2) Point out with a pencil or other pointer each feature and part as it is introduced. *Identify it unmistakably.* Naming the part is not enough; the connection between the name and the thing must be made visually. (3) Keep his eyes on the audience as much as possible; don't glue them to the object. (4) Make the model large enough to be seen by *everyone.* An object too small to be easily seen is worse than no object at all; it only irritates the audience.

Charts

A chart is a drawing, a sketch, or any arrangement of lines and colors on paper or cardboard prepared prior to the delivery of a speech and exhibited during the speech as the speaker needs it. Since charts are extraordinarily useful for presenting all kinds of information in many different forms, speakers representing business and industry have long used them widely. Student speakers should employ charts more often than they do. Some of the kinds of charts, easily and inexpensively prepared, are mentioned and illustrated below. All of them show how rather difficult ideas, such as those dealing with the structure and arrangement of clubs, societies, and institutions, or those dealing with data and statistical information, can be made concrete and clear.

STRUCTURE OF A UNIVERSITY

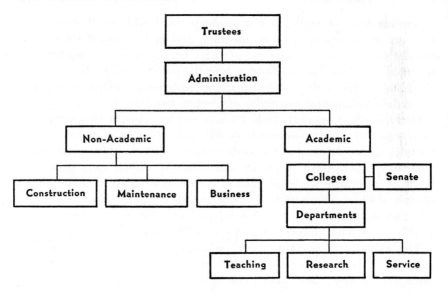

Fig. 4. Organization Chart

WHO FINANCES U. S. NATIONAL DEBT

Approximate Percentages

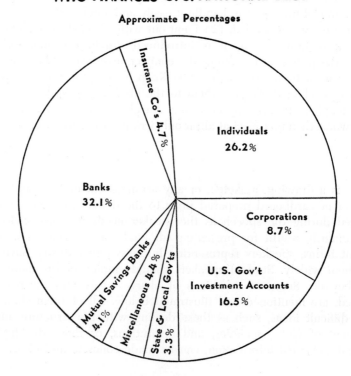

Fig. 5. Piece o' Pie

Organization Chart

Figure 4 shows how a speaker, wishing to explain the basic organization of a university, might visualize its structure. Note that the chart is functional, for each group (name enclosed in a block) has duties and purposes which distinguish it from every other group.

Piece o' Pie

This (Fig. 5) is a common, easy way of presenting simple statistics so that their relative size may be appreciated.

Cut-a-Way

Figure 6 is a neat illustration of the cut-a-way technique which permits one to show essential aspects of the interior of a mechanism or object. Observe that the sketch is designed to make clear two sets of relation-

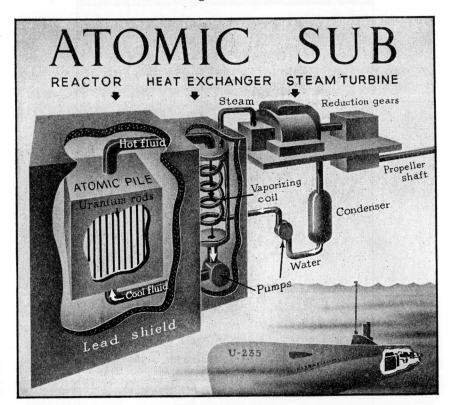

Fig. 6. Cut-a-Way

ships: (1) the *spatial* arrangement and *positions* of one part with respect to another and (2) the operational relationship between parts. In this respect, its underlying principle is like that of Figure 4. It goes one step farther than Figure 4, however, for it uses labels which attempt to suggest directly the function of each part and feature.

Observe, finally, how uncomplicated a complicated mechanism can be made to appear when only the barest essentials required to reveal basic parts and their operations are selected. The result for both speaker and audience is simplicity and clarity. Animated cut-a-ways have come to be used often on TV programs, both for serious exposition and for advertising.

Maps

A map is designed to show certain features of land and sea. The map maker includes only the features which serve his purpose. In producing

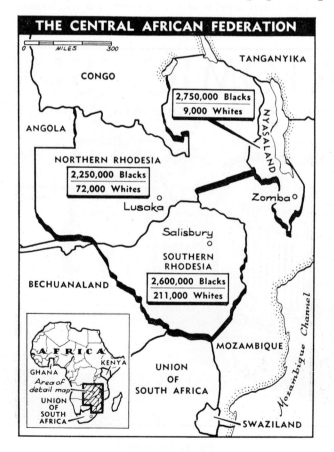

Fig. 7. Map

road maps, for example, he assumes that the prime purpose of a motorist is to get from place to place without getting lost and to drive on the best available roads. A speaker, similarly, makes a map to suit only *his* purpose. He includes only the essentials, uncluttered by useless and irrelevant details. Figure 7 is a map designed to accompany an article dealing with the chief sources of tension in The Central African Federation (Rhodesia and Nyasaland). The countries of the Federation are depicted in large scale and are located in relation to the continent of Africa on a small-scale map. Figure 7 also illustrates how additional information, if simple, can be laid on a map without cluttering it. Here the information included underscores the prime source of tension in the area—the great disparity in population between blacks and whites.

Graphs

The kinds of charts we have mentioned are devices for visualizing factual materials the understanding of which depends on "seeing" their function, operation, structure, and position. Their arrangement would be impossible without our notions of *time* and *space*. The graph, however, is a visual device for presenting facts generally involving *number* or *quantity* in relation to *time*. The graph is the eye of statistics. Only the commonest kinds of graphs will be briefly considered here, those that speakers themselves can readily construct from data they discover in their reading and investigation.

The *line graph* is a swift way of showing how sets of related facts compare with each other. The right-hand graphs in Figure 8 show that the bill for veterans' pensions would have been reduced if the Congress had passed legislation under debate in the spring of 1959. The *profile graph* is twin brother of the line graph. By shading or coloring the area under the curve, the effect is made sharp and dramatic as in the left-hand graph of Figure 8. Either kind of graph can be used to present two sets of comparable facts, as is shown in Figures 8 and 9.

The *bar graph* is a device of emphasis for presenting two facts in comparison with each other, usually without showing how the facts changed from time to time. The line graph is best adapted to show how facts change and develop according to some common measure of reference, usually from period to period, time to time. But the bar graph often simply confronts one fact with another, one set of results with another set. It presents final results, the end product, without trying to show the intermediate data which may have been necessary to obtain the final results. Observe that the bar graph in Figure 10 is concerned only with comparative results; it compares the results of the new plan of flight instruction with the old or traditional method of teaching a person to solo.

When it does not risk confusion and does not have to use too many labels, the bar graph can sometimes show effectively more than one set

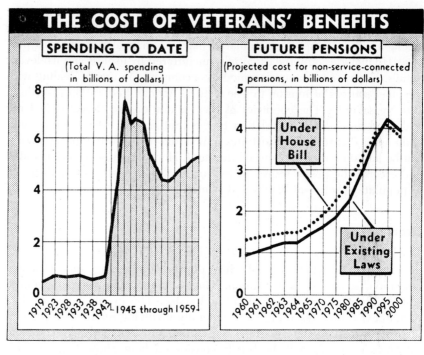

THE COST OF VETERANS' BENEFITS

SPENDING TO DATE

(Total V. A. spending in billions of dollars)

1919 1923 1928 1933 1938 1943 1945 through 1959

FUTURE PENSIONS

(Projected cost for non-service-connected pensions, in billions of dollars)

Under House Bill

Under Existing Laws

1960 1961 1962 1963 1964 1965 1970 1975 1980 1985 1990 1995 2000

Fig. 8. Profile Graph and Line Graph

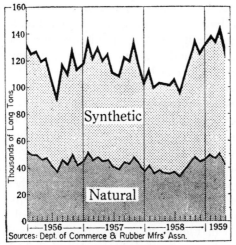

Synthetic

Natural

Thousands of Long Tons

|—1956—|—1957—|—1958—| 1959
Sources: Dept. of Commerce & Rubber Mfrs' Assn.

Rubber Consumption, 1956–1959

Fig. 9.
Profile
Graph

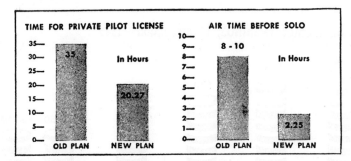

Fig. 10. Bar Graph

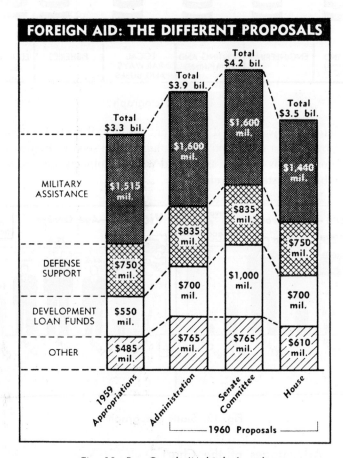

Fig. 11. Bar Graph (Multiple Items)

of facts, as in Figure 11. Sometimes, also, the bar graph can be dressed up to suggest concretely what is being referred to. In this respect, as in Figure 12, it has borrowed the technique of the pictograph.

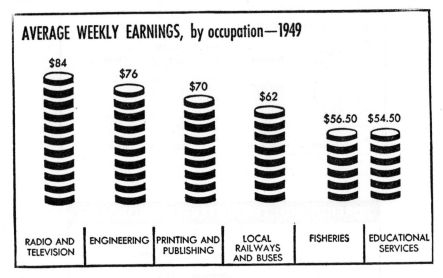

Fig. 12. Bar Pictograph

The pictograph is designed to present numerical facts in a comparative light by using a simplified picture, as may be seen in Figure 13. The picture, moreover, is directly associated with the objects, events, or situations to which the statistics refer.

Fig. 13. Static Pictograph

Advantages of the Chart

The chart, like the model, has four distinct advantages over the blackboard sketch or diagram. It can be used faster in the speech than the blackboard can. Accordingly, it makes possible a swift-running speech. Even when a speaker employs a series of charts, he can learn to display the right one at the right time, say what is needed about each, and move on. The chart also usually makes it relatively easy for a speaker to keep his eyes on his audience; the blackboard, on the other hand, requires him to attend to it as he draws, rather than to the audience. The chart, furthermore, can be more readily used in rehearsal than the blackboard. Few speakers have available a sufficiently large blackboard when they are ready to rehearse, and student speakers cannot always find an empty classroom to rehearse in when they want it. Finally, charts give opportunity to use color and lines of different breadth. Contrasting colors can be employed to secure both emphasis and interest; heavy lines can be used to outline prominent features, light lines for subordinate details; shading and cross-hatching can be put in to suggest thickness. Such refinements add variety and interest as well as promote clearness.

In the classroom student speakers sometimes are troubled about where to place a chart—whether to thumb-tack it to the blackboard frame or desk edge, to prop it up on a desk, or to pin it to some nearby handy surface, such as a curtain. Wherever a special stand for holding charts is not available, the best solution is for the speaker to manage the size and material of the chart so that he can hold it in front of him when he wants it. For this purpose, the largest practicable dimension seems to be about 24 × 30 inches. The material need be only stiff enough to support itself. A chart like this, if its features are bold and uncluttered with detail, can be easily seen by a group of fifty persons. A speaker can readily learn to glance down at it from above and point out its features with a pencil.

Other Aids

The blackboard sketch or diagram, the model, the object, and the chart all hold great possibilities for securing both clearness and interest in a speech. Speechmakers often use other types of visual aids, such as photographs, lantern slides, film strips, and motion pictures. We have restricted our suggestions here to the aids which student speakers themselves can manufacture without technical assistance, and can use without special projectors and darkened rooms. Of course the photograph is often employed effectively, but in our experience the student speaker has found its merits outweighed by its drawbacks. Most photographs are too small to be seen, even by an audience of fifteen persons. They must be enlarged, and enlargement is costly—far more expensive than the materials for a chart. Unless originally taken for the special purpose of the speech, moreover, the photograph usually contains more features and more detail than are needed. Thus the audience, if not confused, is often distracted from the business at hand. In fact, the more unskillful the speaker the more his hearers will welcome any excuse to explore a picture for features which recall familiar, pleasant associations.

Line and Color

In preparing visual materials, the speaker will want to give special attention to the use of line and color. The width of lines can do much to secure
distinctness and contribute to emphasis. A wide or heavy line is reserved
for the chief feature, say for the curve in a graph; a medium-weight line
for a less significant feature, say for the boundaries (or ordinate and
abscissa) of a graph; and a light-weight or narrow line for a background
feature, say for the squares of a graph if they should appear. Sometimes
when there are two features of the same importance a solid line is used
for one, a broken for the other. Similar considerations govern the size and
heft of labels and lettering.

Color contributes markedly to emphasis. A little observation of charts
and drawings encountered every day and inspection of some of the books
listed at the end of this chapter will show a speaker what to do. Unless
he wants to paint realistic pictures he will restrict color to lines or to the
dominant one or two features of his material. Occasionally he may wish
to shade in a background feature; for example, the territory underneath
the curve of a graph. The main rules of thumb appeal to one's common
sense: (1) Use no more than three colors; (2) use colors of contrasting
hues (these are in the regions of the primary hues: red or red-orange,
bright blue, and bright green or yellow-green); and (3) use the same
color for the same feature, whether the feature is repeated in the same
diagram or chart or appears in successive charts which show the same
thing. If one draws up the plumbing diagram of a house, the hot water
lines could well be in red. They should remain red no matter where they
occur in the same diagram or in successive diagrams. Consistency governs
style in line and color as well as style in language.

USING VISUAL MATERIALS

When introducing each kind of visual device and discussing its special
advantages, we have offered some suggestions for its use. For emphasis,
we restate—and add other suggestions which apply to *all* kinds of visual
aids.

Size   Whatever kind of visual material is used, it must be *large*
               enough for everyone to see clearly and easily. Don't guess;
               be sure.

Details   Include only those features and details which are *essential*
               to clearness. Above all, avoid useless labels and names on
               a chart or graph. If labels are to be seen, their lettering

must be large, and many labels will therefore give a cluttered effect.

Artistry   Any chart or sketch, no matter how simple, must be *precise* and *neat*. An impression of carelessness and sloppiness reflects unfavorably on the speaker. Furthermore, a chart which is elaborate with extra decorative touches of line and color is as ineffective and inefficient an aid to verbal communication as is muddy drawing. Even if a speaker happens to be superior at picture-making and draftsmanship, his job is to communicate ideas, not tell his hearers what a fine artist he is.

Eyes   The audience's eyes, not the speaker's, are to be kept on the visual materials. The speaker's eyes should not stray from his hearers longer than is absolutely necessary.

Setting   Any visual device needs a verbal setting when it is first displayed, just as a verbal illustration or story needs a setting if its point is to be understood. Perhaps the best, swift setting is secured when a speaker follows this formula: (1) state first what the device is intended to show; (2) point out next its *main* features, so that the listeners have some grasp of the whole.

Pointing out   Use a pointer, pencil, or finger to *locate* the specific feature or detailed part being talked about at the moment. Even some veteran speakers make the mistake of assuming that a properly labeled, clear chart held prominently before an audience is sufficient and that all eyes will spot each feature as the speaker refers to it. But because any sketch, chart, or graph is found to contain more than a single item, spectators' eyes roam over the "picture"; they are visually curious. To control roaming and to direct focusing, pointing is necessary. But when the spot is located, look at the audience, not at the spot.

To Use or Not to Use Visual Materials

Many earnest persons who take their speechmaking seriously find it easier to organize ideas, to manage details, to present them orally—in other words, to apply the methods and techniques of speaking—than to judge what ideas and materials are the most appropriate and effective for a particular audience and occasion. The problem of selecting the right idea, right phrase, right word for the right time and right persons is not easy. Nor is it easy to decide whether in a particular speech to use visual materials. Two criteria, however, may help a speaker make his own decision in a given case. Helpful, too, may be a list of some of the kinds of subjects for which usually—but not invariably—a speaker should appeal to the eye as well as to the ear.

Visual materials should be used when speech alone is not likely to secure clearness and understanding without them. This is the criterion of effectiveness. Visual devices should be called upon when speech alone takes considerably more time to achieve clearness than would be necessary with visual aids. This is the criterion of efficiency.

Probably the following kinds of subjects cannot readily be made clear through speech alone, and visualization is almost always a requirement for audiences who are hearing about them for the first time:

The how-something-is-done subject. *Examples:* laying out a garden; planning a house; conducting a laboratory experiment.

Explanations of operations, machines, physical and natural events. *Examples:* commercially separating cream from milk; the carburetor; drilling an oil well; the universe of an atom; the vacuum tube; development of the human embryo; transmission of nerve impulses.

Subjects dealing with the structure or organization of something—how one part is related to another. *Examples:* The Chicago Board of Trade; county manager form of government; the Red Cross; the university players club; the X Chemical Company; the Illinois Central Railroad.

Subjects requiring much information in the form of statistics and demanding summaries of factual material. *Examples:* The law of supply and demand; income tax *vs* sales tax; purchasing power of the dollar—1962 *vs* 1938; steel profits and wages; crop rotation and yields; grades as related to intelligence; pure metals *vs* alloys.

Through observation and experience we know that some factual materials, in both the informative and the persuasive speech, may be communicated more swiftly and efficiently by visual devices than by speech. In a few seconds the eyes may see and comprehend what the ears might require two minutes for. Suppose, for example, that a speaker were arguing that the federal budget should be reduced. If one of his supporting points were that "the proportion of national income needed to pay the federal bill has become uncomfortably large," he might wish to amplify as follows:

In 1930, out of each dollar of income, the government took six cents; in 1935, 10 cents; in 1940, 12 cents; in 1945, 30 cents; in 1950, 33 cents.

This would not be unclear, when expressed orally, but the full force of the comparison might not be instantly grasped. So, to secure greater emphasis and make attention easier, the speaker decides he will try to put the ideas this way:

In 1930, out of each dollar of income, the government took 6 cents; twenty years ago each one of us paid to Uncle Sam 6% of every dollar we received. In 1935, five years later, we paid 10 cents, or 10%. In 1940, we were contributing 12 cents, and by 1945, because of World War II, the 12 cents had more than doubled—it had become 30 cents. In 1950 we were supporting our government with 33 cents. In twenty years, our government bill multiplied over five times.

This is less compact, easier to follow, and probably more effective communication than the first statement. The speaker realizes, however, that he is devoting over twice the time to the same material. He has other similar passages in the speech. He must stop speaking on time. He doesn't want to cut out the evidence or an entire section of his talk. Therefore, he decides to appeal to the eye, and with the first passage uses a bar graph:

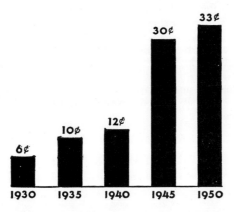

He produces the graph as he starts the passage and by the end of the passage he has used but little more time than he would have used had he spoken it without the graph. He has made his hearers' eyes do what in the second passage he had to do through restatement and some diffusion of language. In brief, through a visual aid he has become more efficient.

Whether to use or not to use visual means of presentation depends on the speaker's judgment. He must decide for the speech at hand whether he can use them and whether by using them he can better secure understanding and can attain higher efficiency than he would without them.

FURTHER READING

ARKIN, Herbert, and R. COLTON, *Graphs: How to Make and Use Them*, rev. ed. (New York, 1940). A full, practical treatment.

BRINTON, Willard C., *Graphic Presentation* (New York, 1939). Containing hundreds of examples of all kinds of charts and including suggestions for constructing them, this book seems designed primarily for persons and business firms with special facilities for preparing graphic aids. Nevertheless, an hour's time with this book will suggest almost infinite possibilities to a speaker who wants to visualize part of his speech and has not discovered how to do it.

CARSKADON, Thomas R., and Rudolph MODLEY, *U.S.A.: A Measure of a Nation: A Graphic Presentation of America's Needs and Resources* (New York, 1949). A fine example of visual materials in use.

DALE, Edgar, *Audio-Visual Methods in Teaching* (New York, 1946). Ch. 4 classifies visual materials according to their "distance" from real objects of experience.

DALE, Edgar, ed., *Display for Learning* (New York, 1952). Part Two, "Materials for Display," contains many suggestions and illustrations useful to the speaker.

KINDER, James S., *Audio-Visual Materials and Techniques* (New York, 1950). Ch. 7, "Graphical Visual Materials," contains many detailed suggestions which apply to the speaker as well as the teacher.

ROSE, L. A., B. B. BENNETT, and E. F. FOSTER, *Engineering Reports* (New York, 1950).

WEAVER, G. G., and E. W. BOLLINGER, *Visual Aids: Their Construction and Use* (New York, 1949), Ch. 4, "How to Make, Display, and Use Charts."

WITTICH, Walter A., and Charles F. SCHULLER, *Audio-Visual Materials: Their Nature and Use,* 2nd ed. (New York, 1957), Ch. 5, "Graphics." An excellent survey.

CHAPTER SEVEN

Organization and Outlines

THE SPEAKER who has collected a good deal of information on his subject, and who has begun to mull over his material—defining, illustrating, comparing and contrasting—with a view to making his information clear to his hearers and making his recommendations forceful with them will discover that many items and separate bits of fact and information are clear and understandable by themselves. But he realizes also that the separate items won't have sufficient meaning or force for either him or his hearers unless he orders and arranges them into a significant pattern, with every item in its right place.

Organizing and patterning ideas in building a speech involve three principal steps: (1) determining the *specific purpose*, (2) deciding what materials and ideas are relevant to the specific purpose and what do not belong, (3) organizing and patterning the relevant ideas so that both speaker and audience can perceive them clearly and remember them easily. This step always means (*a*) formulating a central idea, a dominating theme, or what we call a *governing statement*, that holds together the ideas which will promote the purpose; (*b*) phrasing *main* heads that manifestly relate to each other and directly support and explain the governing statement; (*c*) ordering and planning *subheads and details* that support the main heads and promote interest as well as clarity. The visual product of ordering and patterning is the Speech Outline.

PROCEDURE

Settle on the specific purpose and state it as an infinitive phrase. For example: to explain what a symbol is; to gain contributions to the United Fund.

In determining the specific purpose, keep this in mind: Regard the specific purpose as the *response* wanted from the hearers; or regard it as the final or ultimate *result* of the speech.

Coin the governing statement. For emphasis we call the governing statement of the informative speech the *subject sentence* and of the persuasive speech the *proposition*.

In either case it is a statement that to the speaker as master of his subject "says it all"; if the speaker were his own audience, the governing statement would be the *one* statement that he could accept as being a general and accurate explanation of his subject or fulfillment of his intention. From the uninformed hearer's point of view, it is the one statement that through amplification and discussion becomes so meaningful, so enveloped and enriched with the ideas used to extend and support it, that it works upon the hearer as a single great *stimulus* sufficient to bring about the response desired by the speaker. For example:

Specific Purpose: To explain what a symbol is.
Subject Sentence: A symbol is something which stands for something else.

Specific Purpose: To get my listeners to study more systematically.
Proposition: Systematic study yields more progress in less time than your usual methods.

STATING THE SUBJECT SENTENCE

First we will offer suggestions for formulating *subject sentences* for informative speeches, and then we will add special advice on framing *propositions* for persuasive speeches.

The subject sentence *defines* or *characterizes* the subject being discussed. As a definition or characterization it classifies and differentiates the subject so accurately that the resulting statement cannot be applied to anything else; that is, the resulting statement is *peculiar* and *distinctive*. Suppose, for example, one wished to make a distinguishing statement about the appearance of a zebra. It might be this, "A zebra is a striped horse." The zebra is put into the familiar class of animals, the horse, and is also distinguished from the class by the word *striped*.

At least three specific suggestions can be made for inventing a good subject sentence:

1. *Try to formulate a* LIMITED *definition.* In the subject sentence point out *one important way* in which the subject—whether it deals with an object, a play, a novel, a process, a mechanism, a word, a person, or an institution—is also distinguished from other, closely related subjects.

Boys' Town is an institution for training in citizenship.

The Constitution of the United States was the result of an economic movement.

Elihu Root's career was governed, not by political expediency, but by principle.

Silas Marner is the story of a man redeemed from greed by the love of a child.

Behrman's play, *End of Summer,* is the portrait of a woman without a mind.

A distinguishing feature of the University of Virginia is its Honor System.

2. *Formulate a* FULL *definition.* In the subject sentence state *all* the peculiarities that set your subject off from closely related subjects.

> Burglary is breaking and entering the dwelling-house of another in the night time, with intent to commit felony in the same.

> Polo is a game played on horseback, usually with a light wooden ball and with mallets having long flexible handles, with four players on a side, whose effort is to drive the ball between their opponents' goal posts at the opposite end of the field.

> A co-operative store is a store or shop belonging to and supported by a co-operative society, with the purpose of supplying its members with goods at moderate price, and of distributing the profits, if any, among the members and regular customers.

Important: A great help in coining a full definition, especially when you are dealing with a process, a mechanism, or an operation, is this procedure. Divide a sheet of paper into three columns: Purpose of the Process, Materials Used, Manner of Handling Materials. With the process in mind, jot down ideas appropriate to each column. Then study them carefully and write a single concise sentence that incorporates the ideas.

Suppose one wished to explain the manufacture of plain linoleum; here are the columnar data:

Purpose of Process	*Materials Used*	*Manner of Handling Materials*
Floor covering	Linseed Oil	Mixing machines
Will be waterproof	Rosin (ground)	Pressing cork into burlap
Won't dent easily	Cork	Oxidizing
Will outlast wood	Burlap	

The resulting sentence might be this: "The manufacture of plain linoleum is accomplished by mixing linseed oil, ground rosin, and cork, pressing the mixture into a burlap foundation, and allowing it to oxidize, thereby making a floor covering that is resilient, durable, and waterproof."

3. *Name the principle (or principles) on which the explanation of the subject depends.*

> A modern reformatory operates on the assumption that vocational training, good food, and proper environment can make a bad boy into a good citizen.

> The jet engine applies in a new way the laws governing the behavior of gases under pressure.

In determining and phrasing the subject sentence, take special pains to avoid loose, ill-considered statements like these: "Polo is a unique

game"; "A holding company is not as complicated as it seems." Such statements do not point out the distinctive features of their subjects. Almost
always, they are signs that the speaker has not taken the trouble to decide
what he really is talking about.

STATING THE PROPOSITION

Almost always a proposition will be one of two kinds of statement:

1. *It may be an evaluative or critical statement,* which will reflect the
speaker's belief or judgment about a problem taken as a whole, or about
some aspect of a problem. In his concern over the prevention of war, a
speaker might want to tackle broad problems of U.S. foreign policy; so
his proposition might be:

> The U.S. does not spend enough money on its own preparedness, the pre-
> paredness of friendly nations, and the economic growth of underdeveloped
> countries.

Or he might wish to limit himself to a single condition:

> The U.S. isn't giving enough money to India for her economic development.

2. *The proposition may be a statement of policy,* which will reflect the
speaker's views about the way, or ways, a problem should be solved.

There are two main kinds of policy statement, one specific, the other
general. The former passes judgment on a *particular* proposal which is
being discussed as a solution to the problem at hand. For example:

> Students should support the proposal to build a new field house to be
> financed by an increase in student fees.

> The Secretary of Agriculture should be appointed by the Governor.

> Students should attend the rally for the Michigan game.

Instead of advocating a specific solution, the general statement of policy
simply calls for a change—any change. It says, in effect, that the audience
ought to get ready to consider or to do something. For example:

> Colleges and universities ought to construct some needed buildings by in-
> creasing student fees.

> Departmental heads should be appointed by the Governor.

> Athletic rallies ought to be better supported.

The evaluative proposition registers dissatisfaction with the present
state of affairs. It tells the audience that there *is* a problem which it has
not recognized or felt keenly enough about. It defines the problem. Or it
locates the causes and conditions which gave rise to it. The proposition
of policy, on the other hand, tells the audience that it ought to consider

solving a problem it may already be aware of, that it ought to change its thinking either in some general direction or in a specific direction. The accent is on the future—what ought to be believed or done.

PATTERNING MAIN HEADS

The selection and phraseology of the main heads of a speech involve two problems: choosing heads that are directly *relevant* to the subject sentence; patterning the heads so clearly that one head suggests other, related heads.

The problem of relevance is easily solved. A main head directly amplifies a subject sentence if main head and subject sentence make sense when *for, because,* or *in that* is used as a connective between them. For example:

> *Subject Sentence:* The gaseous content of a city's smoke blanket impairs health.
> (*for*)
>   I. It irritates sensitive membranes.

The second problem, that of organizing main heads into a pattern, is more difficult. Yet to both speaker and audience its solution is absolutely essential if clarity of idea and ease of utterance are to be attained. A *pattern* is an arrangement of ideas or things into a system such that any *one* item in the system suggests and implies *other* items and such that all essential items have been included and all unessential and irrelevant items have been excluded. Note in the example which follows that because the materials have been organized so that (1) any one head implies another, and (2) the parts of the whole take in all the classes of people affected by the explanation, the parts make a whole that is inclusive.

> *Subject Sentence:* Group hospitalization insurance is designed to spread the costs of hospital care so as to benefit everyone.
>   I. It benefits the patient.
>   II. It benefits the physician.
> III. It aids the hospital.
>   IV. It benefits the community.

The better the pattern of main heads in the speech, the easier it is for the speaker to recall and react swiftly to ideas as he talks.

As a speaker sets to work at organizing the material of a speech, probably a pattern will not leap instantly into his mind. His mind will be engaged in shuttling—in going back and forth from possible main heads to subject sentence to specific purpose. He may hit upon a neat pattern for the main heads only to see a moment later that one or two of the heads aren't directly relevant to the subject sentence. So he adjusts the phraseology of the subject sentence—and perhaps will also rephrase the stubborn main heads. All seems in order until his eye catches the subject sentence and the specific purpose. Now as he again inspects these in relation to each other, he discovers that the subject sentence as newly phrased doesn't quite jibe with the purpose. Accordingly he adjusts his statement of purpose, and so the process of critical synthesis goes on, with frequent shifts and adjustments until a whole is planned and knit firmly together.

Only after organizing a number of speeches will one discover patterns with some ease. Practice at making ideas systematic gradually builds up a habit of logical arrangement; and when the habit has once been formed, organizing materials is easy and rapid. In *forming* and *fixing* the habit, however, one must go through the whole process, no matter how obvious some of it may seem at first.

Though some subjects almost automatically fall into obvious patterns, there are times when the obvious divisions do not serve the speaker's purpose so well as other divisions would. A speech on healthful menus would divide itself almost without help into breakfast menus, luncheon menus, and dinner menus. If the speaker, however, were mainly concerned with balanced meals (whether breakfasts, luncheons, or dinners), he might wish to emphasize his purpose by making his basis for main divisions the different essentials of diet, such as starches, proteins, vitamins. He might then *subdivide* his main divisions according to breakfast, luncheon, and dinner menus.

Standard Patterns

Through long experience, speakers and writers have found that a comparatively few plans or patterns serve satisfactorily for breaking down the majority of subjects. Learn to use these patterns and to recognize the kinds of subjects to which each is well adapted. Some of the patterns are more likely to fit informative speeches; others, such as the last four or five described below, persuasive speeches.

The Time Pattern

Narrative speeches and such speeches as involve the explanation of a process, for example, or instructions on "how-to-do-it," are more or less naturally chronological. One item comes before another in the speech because it comes before it in the process. For such a speech, the speaker should try to find a limited number (two or three in a short speech) of time-divisions into which to group the many chronological items of his material. He should avoid having many main divisions. Grouping helps him remember and helps the audience to grasp the entire speech. For example:

Subject Sentence: Planting a garden involves careful preparation of the ground and seed planting at the right time in spaces appropriate to the crop desired.
    I. The ground must be carefully prepared.
    II. Use of the space must be well planned.
    III. Sowing the seed must be done at the right time.

Subject Sentence: Fabricating a steel helmet consists of pressing steel into a cap form which is finished and supplied with accessories.
    I. The steel cap itself must be pressed into its form.
    II. The cap is then given its proper finish.
    III. The accessories must be arranged in the order of their assembly.
    IV. The accessories are attached.

(Notice that these main supporting statements are *characterizing* or *generalizing* statements, capable of detailed expansion and development. For main supporting statements avoid such pure statements of *fact* as "The sheet of steel is placed in the press." This would be merely one of the supporting facts under I.)

Subject Sentence: The Russian Victory offensive in World War II developed in three great movements.
    I. First, all the Soviet Union was cleared of Germans.
    II. Next, the border countries were liberated.
    III. Finally Germany was invaded.

Subject Sentence: George Gershwin rose from the slums to Carnegie Hall.
    I. He spent his childhood in the slums of New York.
    II. As a young man he struggled in Tin Pan Alley.
    III. By the time of his death he had become a major figure in American Music.

(The date of Gershwin's birth, the title of his first song, and the date of his first concert in Carnegie Hall—all are too limited to serve as main heads. They are amplifying facts.)

In using the *time* pattern, it is not necessary, of course, to maintain the chronological sequence. The reverse of the chronological would equally represent a time *relation,* or a speaker might start with one period of time and move on to what came before that time and then to what came after.

The Space Pattern

The division on the basis of *spatial* relations is natural and obvious for some kinds of subject matter. For instance, most news casts are so divided: international news, Washington news, other national news, local news. Besides geographical subjects, others may profitably be organized to proceed from front to back or back to front, top to bottom or bottom to top, inside to outside or outside to inside, near to far or far to near. For example:

Subject Sentence: The books and material on the open shelf sections of our library are distributed in three rooms according to a definite scheme of classification.
  I. The center reading room contains general literature.
  II. The small room on the left is for periodicals and newspapers.
  III. The larger room on the right holds the technical and reference books.

Subject Sentence: In fractional distillation of petroleum the several products boil off in different parts of the tower.
  I. The high volatile fuels rise to the top.
  II. In the middle are the low volatile fuels and the oils.
  III. At the bottom the tars and paraffins settle out.

Subject Sentence: The control panel of the powerhouse is arranged for greatest convenience of the operator.
  I. Close in front of him are the instruments which he uses most often.
  II. Farther away to the sides are the less-used dials and levers.

Because many persons are strongly visual-minded and are likely to connect things they wish to remember with places, the *space* pattern of analysis has another distinct advantage. In listening to the explanation of a process, for example, if the listener can visualize part of the process going on in one place and part in another, he often finds it easier to keep track of details and to remember them.

Topical Pattern

Any speech in which the heads spring from the natural or conventional divisions of the subject itself is topically organized. The broad divisions in medicine, for instance, are based on *structure* and *function;* in matter and in science, on *animate* and *inanimate;* in law, on *civil* and *criminal.* Narrow, specific subjects break into logically appropriate divisions also. Accordingly, the forms of the topical pattern are greater in variety than those of other patterns. The following samples further illustrate the qualities of the topical pattern:

Subject Sentence: A car requires a good motor and good gasoline for economy of operation.
  I. A good motor will last a long time.
  II. Good gasoline will further reduce costs.

Subject Sentence: My job with the Otisko Mills is a good job.
    I. The work is interesting.
    II. The physical and human surroundings are good.
    III. The pay is satisfactory.
    IV. The future is bright.

Subject Sentence: The Junior Women's Chamber of Commerce provides a variety of worthy activities for its members.
    I. It has a varied social work program.
    II. It offers educational opportunities.
    III. It provides excellent recreational activities.

Subject Sentence: A metropolitan newspaper is like a university.
    I. Each has its social studies departments.
    II. Each has departments devoted to the humanities.
    III. Other departments in each are comparable.
    IV. Recreation and sports have places in each.

One kind of *topical* pattern, so often useful that special attention should be given to it, analyzes the material on the basis of *the persons, groups, or categories of people affected.* For example:

Subject Sentence: The daily newspaper provides something for each of many kinds of readers.
    I. It serves those persons who want information and opinion on public affairs.
    II. It provides for those who wish to be entertained.
    III. It guides the shopper.
    IV. It serves the business man.

Proposition: Skill in public speaking is a valuable vocational asset.
    I. It is essential to many professional men.
    II. Business men need it more and more.
    III. Working men find more and more use for it.
    IV. Persons of influence in civic affairs need it.

The speaker is most likely to discover various "natural" divisions of his subject through reading. Accordingly, even if he is working on an expository subject which he knows intimately through personal experience, he would do well to dig up a book or article related specifically or generally to the topic, and to read enough to become aware of the author's divisions and classifications.

Causal Pattern

In dealing with events and their forces, one can often use a pattern like the following:

Subject Sentence: A labor "riot" is the product of _____

    I. Its ultimate cause is _____
    II. Its contributory causes are _____
    III. The immediate cause may be _____

Purpose-Means Pattern

This is especially useful in arranging the ideas of a process or a mechanism.

> *Subject Sentence:* The manufacture of plain linoleum is accomplished by mixing linseed oil, ground rosin, and cork and pressing the mixture into a burlap foundation, thereby making a floor covering that is resilient, durable, and waterproof.
> I. The purpose in making linoleum is to secure waterproof floor covering that is durable and resilient.
> II. The principal materials are cork, linseed oil, jute, and rosin.
> III. The methods of using these materials to make a desirable floor covering are principally grinding, pressing, baking, and oxidation.

Question Pattern

Here the system of main heads *answers* the four questions: what is it? what is it not? in what manner? why? For example:

> *Subject Sentence:* In ancient Rome, rhetoric was the art of speaking well.
> (What it is) I. Rhetoric included all those operations which were thought necessary for speaking well.
> A. It included the invention of ideas.
> B. Etc.
> (What it is not) II. Although associated with poetics, rhetoric was not identified with it.
> (In what manner or what way) III. Much emphasis was given to the manner of presentation, particularly the style and delivery.
> (Reason why or cause) IV. Audiences were expert in judging the quality of oratory.
> A. Roman education always included much training in speaking. An educated man was an orator, and vice versa.
> B. They listened to many fine speakers.

Such patterns of main heads as are peculiar to the persuasive speech grow out of the problem-solution situation.

Problem-Solution

> *Proposition:* Tipping ought to be made illegal.
> I. It creates numerous problems.
> II. Abolishing tipping would remove the problems.

Theory-Practice

Proposition: Union books should be independently audited.
    I. Independent audits are good in theory.
    II. They would work out well for unions.

Practicable-Desirable

Proposition: Diet X should be followed by persons who are overweight.
    I. It will work.
    II. Losing weight has beneficial results.

Disease-Remedy

Proposition: Uniform methods and rules for traffic regulation are needed in the United States.
    I. The present traffic confusion badly needs remedy.
    II. Uniform methods and rules would remedy the confusion.
    III. Such rules and methods would not inconvenience drivers.
    IV. Nothing else will do any good.

MAKING THE SPEECH OUTLINE

With the broad pattern of the speech decided upon, the speaker is ready to construct his speech outline. It is the visual product of organization and patterning. It contains all the ideas he plans to use and in the order in which he wishes to say them. The speech outline should be his guide in rehearsal and in presentation.

Rules of Form and Arrangement

1. The speech outline should show five distinct parts: Title, Introduction, Subject Sentence or Proposition, Development, Conclusion. (See Outline Form.)

2. The relation between heads, subheads, and so on, must be indicated by a consistent set of symbols and by indentations: I, A, 1, *a*, (1), (*a*).

3. Each item down to the level of illustrations or specific detail must be a complete sentence.

    I. A chemical solution is not a mixture.
      A. Turbid water is not a solution.
        1. It is pieces of matter in suspension.
          a. Dirt thrown into beaker and stirred.
            (1) Note particles.

OUTLINE FORM

TITLE

INTRODUCTION

(Attention Material) _____

(Orienting Material _____
including Specific _____
Purpose) _____

Subject Sentence ⎫
    or   ⎬ _____
Proposition   ⎭

DEVELOPMENT

I. (Main head) _____
   A. (Sub-head) _____
      1. _____
         a. _____
            (1) _____
            (2) _____
         b. _____
      2. _____
   B. _____
II. _____
      Etc. . . . .
III. _____
      Etc. . . . .

CONCLUSION

(Summary and other _____
rounding off _____
material) _____

Rules of Logical Structure

4. Each head should be a simple sentence which expresses a single idea only; avoid compound and complex sentences.

   Wrong: I. Since they feel they are being charged extra, patrons do not like
            tipping.
   Right: I. Patrons do not like tipping.
           A. They feel that they are being charged extra.

5. The governing statement should state clearly and completely the theme or governing idea of the speech; in other words, it should characterize or epitomize the ideas that are selected to achieve the purpose of the speech. It will *normally* appear in the outline between the introduction and the development, will be labeled *Subject Sentence,* or *Proposition,* and will not be numbered. When the speaker wishes to indicate that he will postpone his governing statement until he has presented some or all of his development, he may place the subject sentence, or proposition, in the outline at the point where he wishes to introduce it. It will still be *labeled,* carried out to the *left margin,* and *not* numbered.

6. A main head should be a statement that directly supports the governing statement. Words that will test for the proper subordination of main heads to the subject sentence are *for, because, in that,* and *to be specific.*

Subject Sentence: Napoleon was a greater general than Caesar. (for)

Development

I. He was the greater tactician.

7. The main heads when viewed together should show a logical pattern, division, or classification of the ideas that are used to develop the governing statement. Avoid overlapping main heads.

8. Subheads and all subordinate details should develop the main heads directly and unmistakably. Tests for proper subordination are as follows:

a. When a subordinate head follows a main head, the two should be related by such connectives as *in that, for, because, to enumerate.*

I. Social settlements are down-to-earth, practical agencies for relieving poverty in slum areas. (for)
   A. Their staff of professional men and women live in tenement neighborhoods. (because)
      1. In these neighborhoods the needs of working people can best be seen.

b. When a subordinate head precedes its main head, the two should be related by using such connectives as *therefore, thus, hence, as a result, consequently.*

      1. In tenement neighborhoods the needs of working people can best be seen. (hence)
   A. A social settlement's staff of professional men and women will live in the tenement neighborhood. (thus)
I. Social settlements are down-to-earth agencies for relieving poverty in slum areas.

Rules of Rhetorical Effectiveness

9. The order and progression of ideas should be appropriate to the speaker's purpose, his material, and his audience; therefore, the subject sentence or proposition, *labeled as such,* may be placed wherever it seems most appropriate.

INTRODUCTION

A. _____

B. _____

Subject Sentence: _____

DEVELOPMENT

I. _____
  A. _____
II. etc. _____

CONCLUSION

_____
_____

INTRODUCTION

A. _____

B. _____

DEVELOPMENT

I. _____
  A. _____
II. etc. _____

Proposition: _____

CONCLUSION

A. _____
B. _____

10. Transition and signpost statements and phrases should be written in full and should be included in parentheses; do not give them symbols for they are not part of the logical structure.

   I. Antioch College correlates the study of technical and cultural subjects.
     A. _____
     B. etc., etc. _____
       (But it is not only co-ordination in the study of subject matters that makes Antioch unusual; co-ordination is gained in another way.)
  II. Antioch co-ordinates the study of theory and its application by requiring every student to work half his time in a job related to his studies.
     A. _____
     B. etc., etc. _____
       (Well, it's proper here to ask, how has this system of unifying and correlating life and study worked out?)
 III. Antioch's plan has worked well.

Rules for the Introduction

11. The introduction will ordinarily have two parts: Attention Material and Orienting Material, so labeled.

INTRODUCTION

A. *Attention Material*
    1. _____
       a. _____
       b. _____
    2. _____
B. *Orienting Material*
    1. _____
    2. _____

12. The Attention Material must be designed to secure the interest of the hearer and must be appropriate to the content of the speech. Do not use ideas, no matter how interesting, that are irrelevant.

INTRODUCTION

A. *Attention Material*
    1. What does a college aim to do?
       a. Our college newspaper recently carried an article by Professor Dabney, saying that colleges should aim to produce "intellectual aristocrats."
       b. Last Monday in this class Mr. Kushner defended the not-too-serious purpose of the average student.
    2. Many are the attacks on college education; and some colleges have met the criticism by various reforms and new schemes. Examples are,
       a. University of Chicago plan.
       b. St. John's College plan.
       c. Antioch College plan.

13. The Orienting Material may include any of the following types of idea, alone or in combination, that will lead the hearer to understand the development of the speaker's ideas:
Background and historical material,
Special point of view and purpose, including mention of what is *not* the purpose and other matters not to be discussed,
Preliminary definitions,
Explanation of how the speech is to be developed.

B. *Orienting Material*
    1. It is the Antioch plan that I think will interest you.
    2. Founded by Horace Mann, in 1853, who left upon the college this motto: "Be ashamed to die unless you have won some victory for humanity."
    3. Dr. Arthur E. Morgan, known as "Roosevelt-baiter" or "ex-TVA" Morgan, was president of Antioch from 1920 to 1936.
       a. As an engineer he had seen the failure of technical education to produce educated men.
         (1) Culture and skill didn't seem to go together.
       b. Dr. Morgan decided they could be brought together.

Subject Sentence: Antioch College seeks to co-ordinate technical and liberal subjects and to make both apply to life.

Rule for the Development

14. The development must contain the methods and means of amplification which develop the subject sentence or the materials of proof which support the proposition; moreover, it should outline such materials in detail. (Details usually consist of descriptive settings, images and figures of speech, examples and illustrations, comparisons and contrasts, and references to charts, diagrams, models, quotations, etc.)

Subject Sentence: A solution is a body of homogeneous character, whose composition may be varied continuously within certain limits.

DEVELOPMENT

I. Homogeneity is an essential of all true solutions.
   A. Homogeneity means "identity or similarity of kind or nature."
   B. Salt in a glass of water is a good example.
      1. Take glass, water, salt, and demonstrate.
      2. Stir for a few seconds; observe.
         a. Crystals cannot be seen
            (1) By eye.
            (2) By microscope.
      3. Different physical states cannot be detected.

Rule for the Conclusion

15. The conclusion may consist of the following types of material, alone or in combination: a concise but deft summary, the governing statement, an illustration that vividly expresses the sense of the subject sentence, or proposition; a striking and appropriate quotation, a final appeal or suggestion to the audience.

CONCLUSION

We see, then, that Antioch College, which Dr. Eliot of Harvard once referred to as one of the most significant experiments in American education, succeeds by correlating technical and cultural studies on the one hand, and study and life on the other.

Antioch will produce no Ph.D's whose sole ambition is "to know more and more about less and less, until they know everything about nothing." Its students do not leave college expecting that the world owes them a living; rather, Antioch students serve an "apprenticeship to life." Guided through their critical days by careful, experienced hands, they become a part of the society that counts, the society that is spelled with a small *s*. They have the virtue, courage, sensitiveness, and intelligence that college education should develop.

USE OF THE SPEECH OUTLINE

The speech outline is designed to give a complete sequence of ideas, arranged in the order in which they are to be presented in the speech; it is the path or trail the speaker pursues from beginning to end. Accordingly, *he should use it in rehearsal.*

In your first speeches try to make your presentation follow the path of the speech outline as closely as you can. Do not try to memorize its items; through practice and repetition become so thoroughly familiar with its *ideas* that the material spontaneously finds its own language. Try to avoid consciously and deliberately burdening your mind with arbitrary associations; for example, avoid associating a main head with its symbol or with its special place or spot in the speech and avoid memorizing sequences of *words* as such. In other words, try to make the association of ideas natural and logical rather than arbitrary. You should dominate the outline; don't let the outline dominate you.

Carefully follow the method of rehearsal that has been outlined for you in Chapter 8; it is designed to help your mind associate ideas logically and naturally, rather than arbitrarily.

SPECIMEN OUTLINES

The Jet Stream

This specimen is the outline of a speech presented in a public speaking class consisting of men and women students whose major interests represented six different departments and colleges in the university.

INTRODUCTION

A. Attention Material
    1. One day in the fall of 1918, Major Rudolf Schroeder, chief test pilot for the Technical Section of the air service, encountered an aerial mystery.
        a. When he reported his mystery to meteorologists, they did not believe him.
        b. Later when he set an altitude record of 38,180 he told the same story.
    2. During World War II our pilots found that Major Schroeder was correct. They encountered mighty air streams at high altitudes.

B. Orienting Material
Specific Purpose: I would like to tell you about the Jet Stream and its principal effects.

Subject Sentence: The Jet Stream is a mighty river of fast moving air in the upper atmosphere, which affects weather and aviation.

DEVELOPMENT

[First we want to look at the Jet Stream itself.]

I. The Jet Stream is not an occasional atmospheric freak, but an ever-present, though varying, component of the general circulation of the atmosphere.
  A. The great wind systems are caused by the fact that the earth receives more heat in the equatorial regions than at the poles.
    1. The warm air rises because it is moist and light.
    2. The cold air falls because it is dry and cold.
    3. Vast warm fronts meet vast cold fronts and push one another around.
  B. Though they show variation, the great winds move in general patterns.
    1. Like our prevailing ground winds, the Jet Stream moves from west to east.
      a. On the sunlit side of the earth air is warmed; on the dark side it is cooled.
      b. Cool air, being heavier, rushes into and under warm air.
    2. In our north temperate zone, the Jet Stream moves from a northerly direction to a southerly direction.
      a. Movement tends to be from cold zones toward the torrid zones.
        (1) An airman rode the stream from high over the state of Washington into Texas.
    3. The stream varies somewhat in altitude.
      a. Over Washington the pilot found it at about 34,000 feet.
      b. Over Texas the pilot was at 26,000 feet.
      c. A very large warm air mass may push down on an incoming, relatively small stream of cold air.
        (1) This is what occurred during the Washington-Texas flight.
    4. The great winds are usually found between 30,000–40,000 feet.
  C. Although the Jet Stream reveals general patterns of movement, it is often difficult to locate.
    1. It is very high and moves around from region to region.
    2. The peculiar twinkle of a prominent star may tell a weatherman where it is.
    3. Certain cloud formations may indicate it.
    4. There is a variety of other telltale signs.
      a. Unusual gustiness of wind at ground level.
      b. Persistent cool, crisp air.
      c. Generally blue skies with visibility unlimited.
      d. Precipitation which is limited to sporadic sprinkles of rain or snow.

[Now that we know something about the circulation of the Jet Stream, we can consider briefly some of its effects on weather and aviation.]

II. The action of the Jet Stream may help explain major weather disturbances.

A. It is thought to influence the movement of the lower air.
   1. Tornadoes, for example.
B. Weathermen study the big wind, hoping to predict ground weather.
   1. They use jet airplanes, rawindsonde balloons, and radiosonde balloons.

III. This mysterious weather phenomenon directly affects aviation.
   A. It will affect military planes in wartime.
      1. Russia thinks that the Jet Stream is more to her advantage than to ours.
   B. It is already considered an aid to commercial planes.
      1. Pilots flying the continent, the Atlantic, and the Pacific search out the stream to get a lift from it.
   C. New facts about the great winds appear promptly in such aviation magazines as *Flying*.
      1. New information is available almost as soon in the *Science News Letter* and *Scientific American*.

CONCLUSION

We are gradually accumulating more and more information about the river of the great wind and how it moves about over the world. We shall be able to predict ground weather more accurately than at present. We shall be helped and so will our high-flying pilots.

The Making of Plain Linoleum

This outline was the basis of a speech in a public speaking class. It is a fine example of how to handle a process or operation.

INTRODUCTION

A. Attention Material
   1. Probably you have all heard of "battleship" linoleum.
      a. It is superior to wood.
      b. Why is it that many public buildings, such as our classroom buildings, use linoleum rather than wood as floor covering?
   2. Man has made a floor covering that has all the advantages of wood and none of its disadvantages.
      a. The linoleum on the floor of our library lobby has been in use for 20 years and probably will last for another 20 years.
      b. How does man make such superior material?

B. Orienting Material
Specific Purpose: To explain the manufacture of plain linoleum.
Subject Sentence: The manufacture of plain linoleum is accomplished by mixing linseed oil, ground rosin, and cork and pressing it into a burlap foundation, thereby making a floor covering that is resilient, durable, and waterproof.

[We can best look at this process if we take it apart and consider it step by step.]

DEVELOPMENT

I. The first step consists in converting linseed oil into a viscous, rubbery substance.
   A. The oil is heated to boiling.
      1. The impurities must be made to rise to the top where they may be easily skimmed off.
      2. Boiling causes the oil to oxidize more rapidly.
   B. The boiled oil is made to drip slowly over scrims until they are thinly coated.
      1. Scrims provide much surface to facilitate the oxidation of the oil.
         a. Usually the scrims are large sheets of muslin, 3 x 25 feet, hung 2 to 4 inches apart.
      2. Troughs at the top of the scrims hold the boiled oil.
      3. Coats are applied at half-day intervals until sheets about one-half inch thick are produced.
      4. Upon oxidation linseed oil breaks down into fatty acids which are gummy and tough.
         a. Frederick Walton, an Englishman, first discovered this phenomenon on his paint pot.

II. The second step in manufacture consists in combining the oxidized linseed oil sheets with rosin and gum so as to produce a cement.
   A. The linseed oil sheets are ground finely.
      1. Only in fine particles can they be combined successfully with the rosin.
   B. Rosin is the residue left after turpentine is distilled from pine sap.
   C. The ingredients are heated for several hours in large kettles at high temperatures.
      1. This produces a viscous mixture called cement.
         a. The lower boiling liquids boil off.
   D. The ingredients, in cement form, are allowed to age.
      1. The relative firmness of the cement determines the type of linoleum to be made.
      2. Aging gradually hardens the cement.

III. The third step is the preparation of the cork.
   A. Cork gives elasticity to the linoleum.
   B. Two-ton millstones grind the cork very fine.
      1. A powder must be made that is fine enough to pass through a screen having 2500 openings to the square inch.
         a. A fine texture is absolutely necessary to the finished product.
            (1) Fine texture leaves no rough spots.
            (2) Fine texture does not destroy the elasticity of the cork.

IV. At stage four a mixture of aged cement and ground cork is pressed into a burlap foundation.
   A. Experience has demonstrated that burlap affords a hard, even foundation.
   B. Heavy rollers press the mixture into the burlap until it is one piece.
      1. The burlap serves as a mat.

V. The final step is baking.
  A. The linoleum as it leaves the pressing rolls is easily marked and dented.
    1. It is soft and doughy.
  B. Baking produces a hard sheet of flooring.
  C. In the baking room, the soft sheets are hung in festoons from batons placed at the top of the room.
    1. This arrangement allows the free even distribution of heat.
  D. Baking is carried on until a firm but elastic sheet results.
    1. A plunger forced against the linoleum for 60 seconds must not break the surface, nor leave a mark that does not disappear in 5 minutes.
    2. A revolving, vertical shaft pressed into the linoleum must not break or dent the product.

CONCLUSION

With simple, everyday materials—linseed oil, rosin, cork, and burlap—man has developed means of treating them—principally through mixing, pressing, and oxidation—so as to turn them into a durable, resilient, and waterproof floor covering that improves on Nature's own.

If You Must Tan, Tan Sanely!

This speech outline served as the guide of a twelve-minute talk to a public speaking class at Iowa State University. Although girls made up the bulk of the audience, the men found the speech interesting and received it with applause. The speaker, a young lady, supplied the marginal notes; they indicate that she knew what persuasive methods she was using.

INTRODUCTION

(*Use of imagery, contrast, and humor*)

A. Attention Material
  1. On the first warm Sunday in June, hundreds of thousands of people are on the beach at Coney Island.
    a. There are many nationalities.
    b. There is a riot of color.
    c. There is a great variety of activity and amusement.
  2. At Carr's Pool on the first Sunday in June, many of us gather, amid much splashing and fun.
  3. Many of us go swimming primarily to get a good coat of tan, to get that "outdoor look."
B. Orienting Material
  Proposition: We should get our sun tan sanely.

(*Tact*)
  (Now I don't mean to imply that we don't have sense enough to tan gradually; we simply don't realize the difficulties involved.)

DEVELOPMENT

I. Sunburn is harmful, for

(*Vanity and personal reputation*)
    A. It destroys beauty, for
        1. Imagine a blistering sunburn with a formal dress!
           a. I saw a girl at the Memorial Union last night in such an attire.

(*Ridicule*)
(*Imagery*)
              (1) What a contrast between the spanked-baby red and the black lace!

(*Desire for social approval*)
              (2) Many of the dancers noticed her.
        2. Sunburn gives the face a weatherbeaten look.

(*Imagery and simile*)
           a. The skin sometimes gets hard, crusty, and looks like old leather.
           b. Would the sweet young thing want the face of a sailor?
    B. A sunburned skin menaces the whole body, for

(*Health motive*)
        1. Poisons spread to all parts of the body.
           a. The blood carries them.
           b. A poison is a poison anywhere.

(*Facts*)
        2. In 35% of the cases of severe sunburn, poison spreads to other parts of the body.

(*Authority*)
           a. Dr. James F. Cox reported this in a study he made at Atlantic City.

(*Self-preservation and fear of consequences*)
    C. Blistering of one-third of the body may cause death, for
        1. John Cacorma's death, reported by the Associated Press, was due to severe sunburn.

(*Metaphor*)
        2. The body can't "breathe," in that
           a. It can't discharge waste materials fast enough.

(*Figurative analogy*)
           b. It is as if an auto were discharging only one-half as much exhaust gas as it should.

(*Transition to point II*)
    (Sunburn, however, does far more than injure our beauty and imperil our health.)

II. It is responsible for great economic loss, for
    A. New York City's laborers annually lose 200,000 working days.
        1. Dr. Charles F. Pabst, dermatologist at Greenpoint Hospital, arrived at this figure after a careful survey.
        2. With these lost days 1000 carpenters could build the dwellings of Ames in a year.

(*Opinion evidence*)
    B. Dr. Pabst thinks that illness from sunburn costs workers $1,400,000 a year.

(*Transition to point III*)
    (If careless exposure to the sun costs us so much money and is injurious to health, what can be done about it?)

    III. Each of us can work out a sane plan of getting our sun tan, for

      A. We can expose our skin gradually, for

(Suggestion)   1. It is easy to regulate first doses according to the type of skin.

             a. Brunettes should take 10–12 min.

             b. Blondes can take 5–7 min.

             c. Red-heads must absorb only 3–5 min.

(Humor?)   (Has any one ever said that brunettes couldn't take it?)

         2. What I can do you can do.

(Emulation)   3. This is the program followed by many of the movie actresses.

      B. Even if your skin won't stand sun, you can get tanned successfully,

(Suggestion)   1. Use Glucoside stain.

(Pocket-book motive)   *a.* Sixty-cents worth will do the trick.

Conclusion

(Summary and appeal)   If we value what good looks we have, if we are sensible enough to think twice about our health, if we want to avoid discomfort and loss of income, then we should submit to the sun's rays judiciously. Remember that the sun shows no mercy.

     Don't be careless and foolish. Some people, after all, can't get a tan.

(Fear of consequences)   A. You must have a certain amount of skin pigmentation for a tan, and

      A′. You may not have enough, for

         1. This is the case with one of my friends.

CHAPTER EIGHT

Delivery

DELIVERY is a comprehensive term for all aspects of a speaker's mental, audible, and visible behavior while addressing an audience. The study and practice of it are grounded on a single basic principle: *Ideas dominate utterance and bodily behavior.* Ideas dominate the listener. They dominate the speaker. In delivery which is judged good, listener and speaker fully realize or grasp the idea at the moment of utterance. In delivery that is less than good, some competing stimulus—an irrelevant idea, for example—prevents the speaker or the audience from concentrating on the relevant idea. One cannot fully concentrate on any statement on this page if he is at the same time thinking of going to the movies.

The principle is derived from observations of the mind at work in lively, direct conversation. Of course we cannot see the mind at work; we can only make our best guesses. A speaker can come close to achieving that quality of delivery, realization of idea at the moment of utterance, by minimizing the kinds of distractions which claim his attention and compete for the dominance of idea.

From our experience in conversation, almost any of us can point to things which divert us as listeners from the message being spoken. They may be some unusual features of dress or of the face which momentarily command attention. Or some mannerism of posture, movement, or gesture. Or some bothersome trait of speech, such as long pauses, frequent pauses, rapidity of utterance, indistinctness of speech, novel pronunciation, "uhs" and "ers." Or some sign of indirect communication, such as dullness of tone, immobility of face or body, averted eyes. Or some quality of voice or gesture which we interpret as insincerity, affectedness, or lack of interest in us. Or perhaps an unrecognizable word or phrase. These are a few of the distractions. If you can catch yourself in conversation when you are attending *only* to what is said, you are being dominated by ideas and nothing else.

In the formal, public speaking situation, the listener may be subject to the same distractions that he encounters in conversation. But they may strike him more forcefully and be more bothersome, because the speaker plays a more prominent role than he does in conversation.

Furthermore, we do not *expect* such irrelevancies from a good speaker. We expect his speech and gesture to claim our attention utterly and hold it; we expect to "think" along with him.

Like the listener, the speaker is dominated by ideas during utterance when other factors do not compete for his attention and divert him from concentrating on meaning. Some of the competing elements are primarily emotional, such as nervousness, anxiety, and (in extremely rare instances) stage fright. More often the distraction is a *feeling* of inadequacy, springing from inexperience in public speaking, from a sense of having nothing worth saying, or from insufficient preparation (such as poor organization of ideas and inadequate rehearsal). Hence the struggle to concentrate gets in the way of thinking itself. When the speaker is talking in the absence of distracting experiences, he is living ideas and meaning.

THE STANDARDS

In keeping with the basic principle, the psychology of delivery centers on four standards. (1) The audience should be unaware of the physical aspects of delivery. (2) The speaker should be concentrating on his ideas during his moments of utterance. (3) The speaker should experience a sense of communication with his audience. (4) The speaker's bodily action should reflect his ideas and serve the needs of communication. James A. Winans was the first writer to call the last three of the standards, taken together, "the conversational quality" in delivery.

Inattention to Physical Events

The speaker's object is to stir his audience to thought, not to invite his listeners to speculate about his pitch, loudness, timbre, rate, and gesture. A speech is not a performance, and the speaker cannot afford to let his audience regard him as a performer. If at the conclusion of a speech, a listener responds with such comments as "What a wonderful speech," "His voice is squeaky," "What silly mispronunciation," "His gestures were lovely, but such an awkward stance," the speaker knows that his hearers have been distracted by the manner of his presentation. If, on the other hand, the audience is talking about what was said, if the hearers respond with discussion and questions, with objections and arguments, the speaker knows that he has stimulated thought. A good practical test of delivery under any circumstances, even in the classroom, is this: "Did the audience forget that I was making a speech?" The beginning speaker will be wise to ponder this apparent paradox:

If nobody notices delivery, it is good; if delivery is talked about, whether in praise or in censure, it is to some extent deficient.

The Goal: Spontaneity

When delivery is good, when vocal behavior and gesture are utterly in the service of ideas, listeners will often describe the dominant quality of delivery as *spontaneity*. They may know or suspect that the speaker has prepared, but he doesn't sound as if he had. Voice and gesture do not show signs of artificial manipulation. Consequently, young speakers are well advised to ponder the four standards set out above and while gaining experience in public speaking return to them again and again. The standards direct attention, so far as language can, to the *mental activity* of a person *who speaks to others*. They can be thought of as the psychological requirements of delivery, not the physical requirements.

This point is a good one to remember when the speaker is in the rehearsal stage of his preparation. In rehearsal he will find himself taking his mind off his ideas and giving conscious attention to the management of language. If he has voice problems, or if he must work on details of gesture and posture, these things he will have to do deliberately. He thus works consciously (even self-consciously) in order to build physical behavior into mental behavior, to bring body into mind and mind into body until he can acheive a body-mind package which is his speech. Handling himself in practice as if he were his own experimental animal, he should learn to recognize those moments when he is dominated by idea and thought, when he feels "real," when he feels as if he were talking animatedly with a friend. These moments represent the same kind of mental experience he should have on the platform. He engages in self-directed techniques of practice until his mind is in complete command. Not until mind dominates all is the speech ready for the platform. There is no place or time on the platform for artful rehearsal. The speaker must trust that prior practice will pay off. His only concern is to reconstruct and relive his speech so that his listeners may think that he is delivering it for the first time.

I. REALIZATION OF IDEAS DURING UTTERANCE

The speaker during delivery should be as fully responsive to ideas and their meaning as he is in good, everyday conversation. Now what happens when you speak in everyday situations? You get an idea, you say, and you just utter it. Precisely. You don't get the idea, frame a careful sentence that is grammatically correct and beautifully balanced, and then utter it. You don't decide that a particular sentence requires a downward inflection of the voice, that you must say it one way rather than another, or that you must pause at one place for one-tenth of a second, at another place for two seconds. Not at all. You get an idea, or the germ of an idea, and start speaking. You think-as-you-speak; and the vocal inflections and gymnastics, often incredibly intricate as sound patterns, are at one with your thought. Utterance, accordingly, is genuine and spontaneous, and if your acquired *habits* are good, so is your utterance. Your listener is not even aware of it as utterance unless it is in some way peculiar and therefore distracting. We call that mental activity which results in genuineness and spontaneity of delivery, *vivid-realization-of-idea-at-the-moment-of-utterance*. It is perhaps the most desirable aspect of delivery.

When you speak before a group for the first time, does your mind behave as it would in private conversation? Perhaps it does; if so, you are fortunate. Most of us, however, realize that we are no longer engaged in private, informal colloquy; the platform is a new situation and our minds have not been at work there. Consequently, in the face of some self-consciousness and perhaps a touch of fright, we go ahead, and by gaining experience in the speaking situation, we become accustomed to it. That is, we *learn* to think-and-talk on the platform as the occasion and circumstances demand. Actually our mind does not behave in a new and strange manner; it is only learning to adapt, to function freely in a new and different situation.

PROCEDURES FOR PRACTICE

Securing Vivid-Realization-of-Idea-at-the-Moment-of-Utterance

Rehearse Aloud

The emphasis is on practice *aloud*. Reading over your outline of your manuscript a dozen times is not so beneficial as speaking two or three times. At this point in your preparation, you need practice not in reading silently, but in speaking. The stimuli that prompt your mind during utterance are not on a page; they are in your mind, and you need to gain facility in controlling them.

If you have never tried oral rehearsal before, you may find that the first time is not very satisfactory. There's no audience, no real stimulus. Never mind; go on even if the result is strange. The next trial will be easier, and so on. Frequently you can overcome the absence of an audience by imagining one. Many students pair off and practice on each other. Use a classroom for rehearsal when possible.

How Often to Rehearse

No one can say accurately. This is an individual problem, and you will have to decide it for yourself. Some few students may need to rehearse very little, if at all. But do not let your ego rush forward here and put you into this rare group. Over thirty years of teaching public speaking to hundreds of college students (a teacher hears no less than 700 student speeches a year) have shown us that 19 out of 20 students prosper by rehearsal. Some rehearse three times; some practice as many as twelve times. On this point especially, as we have said, there is sound advice in the three old rules for public speaking: *practice, practice, practice.*

When to Rehearse

Do not rehearse until you have finished your speech outline on paper, for not until then is your sequence of ideas clear and complete. For speeches three to seven minutes long, do your best to rehearse the first two or three times no later than 24 hours before you expect to speak. This gives you a chance to do some last-minute tinkering if first rehearsals suggest *minor* improvements in your outline. (*Caution:* Don't make *major* changes in your outline the day before, particularly such a drastic change as abandoning your outline and making an entirely new one.) Later rehearsals may well come the night before your speech. Some students prefer to practice early in the evening before they undertake some other studying; others prefer to practice after all other study is done and the speech will remain the last thing in mind.

Where to Rehearse

For the first few speeches you would be wise to pick a place where you won't be interrupted. Your own room will do nicely when your roommate isn't there, or when he will consent to be audience. Or use a vacant classroom. If possible rehearse once in the place where final delivery will take place so you can get adjusted to the sound of your speech there. Some learners find a favorite outdoor spot and do most of their practice there. The important thing in first practice is to avoid having your attention diverted by distracting stimuli.

How to Rehearse

Although there is no single procedure that will fit all individual needs, try the procedure below, following it meticulously for your first speeches and later changing it if necessary to fit your own requirements. The scheme is based on this psychological fact: the mind gives preference to a whole over its parts, to the stream of ideas in a sequence rather than the eddies. To use this procedure is to provide good insurance against omitting the main logical items and forgetting at joints and transitions. The procedure is designed, also, to keep your attention on *ideas,* not on language and phraseology.

Get acquainted with the general pattern of ideas.

Read through your speech outline silently, slowly, thoughtfully, from beginning to end. *Repeat.* (*Caution:* Don't backtrack for any reason; and don't go back for details.) Read the outline aloud, thoughtfully and deliberately; don't hurry.

Abandoning your outline, again go through your speech aloud *from beginning to end.* Don't back up for any reason, even if you know that you have forgotten a major item, and even if what is to be a 5-minute speech takes only a minute.

Silently reread your speech outline once again.

Practice aloud, again going through from start to finish without backing up.

If by this time the speech isn't running pretty well for you, continue to alternate silent study with oral practice.

Present an oral abstract of your speech. Include items in this order: the purpose of your speech, the governing statement, and the main heads. Your ability to whip through an abstract should mean to you that your mind has clearly grasped the chief parts of a patterned sequence.

Polish the details.

Once you have control over your speech as a whole, you can afford to pay attention to details that you have been omitting or to parts that you have been stumbling over. If details are already in hand, you need not be concerned with the steps below.

Practice *transitions.* These are the hardest details for most speakers— even experienced ones—to manage well. Practice on them helps in keeping your attention on the relationship of one part of the speech to the next part and hence strengthens your grasp on the path and structure of your ideas. In a conventionally arranged speech the chief transitions are signpost sentences or phrases at these points.

From statement of purpose to governing statement.

From governing statement and its preliminary explanation to main head I.

From main head I and its treatment to main head II, and so on.

From the final head and its treatment to the conclusion and summary.

Practice *other parts that have given you difficulty,* the conclusion, the introduction, examples and their details, comparisons, contrasts, quotations.

Assimilate, Do Not Memorize

Should you memorize your speech? If the word *memorize* means to you verbatim recall, the answer is *no.* Through rehearsal you should aim to stamp in, to assimilate, a sequence of *ideas.* What you memorize and learn to handle through controlled association of ideas is a *pattern of thought.*

Phraseology will vary from one rehearsal to the next and from your last rehearsal to delivery on the platform. Remember that the most important task in acquiring good delivery is learning to think and talk as you do in good conversation. Of course, if you rehearse to the point where you have gained control over a pattern of ideas, you may be repeating some phrases, sentences, and perhaps even chains of sentences, in the same words. This is well and good, and it means only that ideas and their word-symbols have become so completely associated in your mind that they are inseparable. You react to an idea, and its verbal counterpart springs into being automatically. What you should avoid during practice is any attempt to memorize words, *deliberately* and *consciously*. If you try to memorize by rote your attention is on remembering language, not the ideas carried by language.

A very few individuals may find some verbatim memorization helpful at first. Those whose opening sentences are excessively slow, halting, and uncertain may find it advantageous to memorize the initial sentence or two. By having language definite and fixed, they are certain that they can get off to a good start. But if the device works, there is a temptation to repeat it and even to memorize verbatim more and more of the speech until one finds oneself wedded to memorization. Intending originally to develop a habit of extempore phraseology, the speaker falls into the opposite habit, a habit that is next to useless in discussion and conference and in the political and legal debates outside the classroom. It may be wiser to bear with the awkwardness and hazards of phraseology than to adopt hastily what looks like a speedy shortcut. In the long run, it will be best to plan and practice and let your ideas find their own words.

Remember that there is no essential difference between the way your mind should work on the platform and the way it operates in conversation. Public utterance is an *enlarged* conversation.

Know Your Speech Plan Thoroughly

Know the plan or outline of your speech so thoroughly that it has become *a part of you*.

The following suggestions may guide you in determining at what point in rehearsal you have satisfactorily *assimilated* ideas:

Do you have *to struggle to remember* the principal ideas? Are you afraid you will forget? Although no human being can be utterly sure that he will say everything he wants to and at the proper place, he can work over his ideas orally—in rehearsal and in conversation—to the point where he feels *reasonably certain* that he can make clear his essential ideas.

After you have planned your speech thoroughly and perhaps have rehearsed two or three times, try this test of understanding and assimilation: Draw some acquaintance into conversation on your subject or a closely related subject. As the conversation develops, work into the dialogue at various times the ideas of your speech. Probably the best person for this purpose is someone else who is studying public speaking. Students are always inquiring of each other what they are going to speak on. Seize the opportunity. It will not only give you a chance to talk and think freely; you may pick up an idea or an illustration you can use, or you may be asked a question that suggests what your audience would like to hear and what you hadn't provided for.

Can you change the order of your speech and still present the chief ideas so that they remain a unit? Try starting out with your best illustration; go from this to the head it illustrates, and thence to the next broader head until you have completed one logical unit. Then proceed to the next head that pops into mind, and so on. Summarize fully at the end.

Although it is probably sound practice in the first speeches *not* to change the sequence of ideas once it is fixed satisfactorily, shifting ideas about during rehearsal *makes* you think, and thus utterance regains the spontaneity that you may have lost through frequent practice. Furthermore, if the change in sequence works out all right, you gain some confidence, for you know that if you should not get started on the platform precisely as you expected to, you could still go on, make a reasonably clear presentation, and the audience would be none the wiser.

II. SENSE OF COMMUNICATION

The speaker on the platform should have a keen sense of communication with his hearers. By a *sense of communication* we mean a *feeling* or *awareness* that two or more minds are engaged in mutual action and reaction. The feeling is evident in almost every conversation. Both parties to a live conversation are well aware that two people are engaged; neither is talking at a stone wall. Furthermore, in addition to some mental interaction, the feeling of communication, of being with another, is helped by the conversationalists' confronting and looking at each other. This identical relationship between speakers in normal conversation must also be evident in the "public" situation between speaker and audience. Recognition of this relationship led Emerson to say that public speaking is only enlarged conversation and that the speaker is a gentleman conversing.

Although you may have to make a number of speeches before you feel in close touch with your audience from the beginning of your speech to the end, you may have moments of direct contact even in your first speech. If you are looking at your audience (and *seeing* them), you may be aware that your hearers are looking at you rather than shifting their eyes restlessly about, or fixing them on the pages of a covertly placed textbook or newspaper. You may discover that their faces are alive with interest, and no longer bear that stony mask of polite attention. Or a frown, a grin, a nod or shake of the head, may be the sign telling you that some idea has struck its mark. The speaker talks to *others;* or, to express the communicative quality of delivery in its strictest sense, the speaker talks *to* and *with* others, not *at* them. Speaker and hearer feel that they are in touch with one another.

===== **PROCEDURES FOR PRACTICE** =====

Securing a Lively Sense of Communication

Enhancing the Desire to Speak

The influence of emotion and feeling on a speaker's delivery can hardly be overvalued. Wanting to speak will give to presentation, first, an earnestness (earnestness is sincerity *plus* ardor) that any good speech should have. Second, it is a powerful source of vocal variety and of genuine gesture. Third, it helps you to overcome self-consciousness, because the desire to talk to *others* tends to take your attention off yourself and to direct it to your task. Finally, it helps in remembering the pattern of your ideas. Emotion holds together the data of experience as effectively as—perhaps more effectively than—formal logic. Hence, if the plan of your ideas is dominated by and is shot through with the desire to speak, the desire will do much of your remembering for you.

To promote a genuine desire to talk to others, observe the following suggestions:

Settle upon a *specific purpose* for your speech that really *fits* your audience.

Remember that *all* speech is provoked by and is directed to others. A speech isn't a performance. How you regard yourself is not nearly so important as how your ideas affect your hearers.

State *clearly* and *precisely* why your audience should be interested in what you are going to say. This may give you some sense that your speech is going to be worth the time and attention of your hearers, and if worthwhile to them, it should be worthwhile to you. (Incidentally, this may suggest a possible introduction to your speech, perhaps built on an *implied* theme, "This subject is significant and worthy of your attention.")

Be bodily alert, both during rehearsal and on the platform. In rehearsal, stir yourself up. Perhaps pace about some, throw in some gratuitous gestures, engage in a minute of calisthenics. In private one can overstep the modesty of conventional conduct in ways which in public would detract from the purpose of the speech. What would offend judicious persons if it were seen need not bother the speaker in rehearsal.

Keeping Eyes on the Audience

You can't expect to feel attached to your listeners, nor they to you, if you ignore them. Spraying your gaze over them is not enough. Look at individuals and see them.

Using the Style of Direct Address

Use the pronouns *we* and *you* in talking. They help give you and the listeners a sense of being one group.

Use an occasional question, especially in introducing a new point. Questions, obviously enough, are directed to others, and you cannot use them without becoming somewhat aware that you have business, not with yourself, but with the listener. Particularly helpful are those questions that you think your audience would like to ask if it saw fit to interrupt as you go along. Anticipate them, state them, and answer them.

At the start of any speech employ a salutation as "Mr. Chairman, Ladies and Gentlemen," "Gentlemen," "Friends," "Classmates," or any mode of address that is appropriate and easy for you. A salutation is not only good manners, it makes you become definitely aware of your hearers, and they of you.

Recognizing Persons by Name

If after one or two speeches you are still having difficulty in establishing direct contact, try an expedient that is permissible in the classroom, though inadvisable elsewhere. Recognize three or four individuals by name in as many different places in your speech. Perhaps something like this: "Now, Mr. Richards, as a student of biology, you may be interested in learning that this improvement to the microscope will. . . ." Or, "Mr. Wilson, if this plan for a simplified rushing procedure is workable, would you be willing to support it?"

Getting "Set" Before Speaking

The following suggestions may not only aid in heightening your sense of the audience, but will also help in minimizing self-consciousness and nervousness:

Just before you are called on to speak, try to recover that desire or impulse to communicate. In effect, say to yourself, "Here's my chance to do a real job for these people. I believe I can make them understand; I think I can claim their attention and interest. Let's see how they react." In other words, try to make the audience the essential stimulus that prompts you to action and speech. Don't review mentally what you want to say; appreciate and heighten the stimulus that should make you say it.

Adopt a *positive* physical approach to the platform; proceed *directly* to meet your task, rather than evade it.

After facing your hearers, *look at them* for perhaps five seconds until they are for the most part paying attention to you. Continue to breathe regularly, and at this time, if you wish, review your opening ideas. Address the chairman and the audience, and start in!

III. BODILY ACTION—GESTURE

Body and mind are so closely linked that an idea vividly experienced not only prompts speech but gesture also. But gesture does not break through into meaning, it cannot aid communication, unless the body is *free* to respond to idea. Hence, poise is necessary if the speaker is to gesture spontaneously.

Basically, poise simply describes bodily behavior that is efficient; it is movement that fits a particular situation with economy and without obtrusiveness; it is, in brief, activity that is *fully adaptive.* Like good speech, poise in behavior is never noticed. Like poor speech, behavior without poise is conspicuous because of its inadequacies; it may be random, needlessly repetitious, gratuitous, or awkward. Good platform behavior, accordingly, is bodily activity that fits the communicative situation.

Freedom to Gesture

Learning to become bodily expressive on the platform does not mean that the speaker is becoming a pantomimist or an actor. Action must not usurp the role of speech. Nor does it mean that the speaker deliberately invents gestures and plants them wherever he may think them appropriate. The hallmark of good gesture, like good speech, is its apparent genuineness and spontaneity.

Learning to become physically responsive involves, in the first place, getting the body *free to respond* to the meanings of the mind. Accordingly, the beginning speaker seeks to maintain his normal freedom of action on the platform. In learning to gesture, then, the process is one of adaptation to the new situation through guided experience and practice. The beginner learns, accordingly, to handle himself so as not to *inhibit* bodily responses that ordinarily accompany vivid and vigorous thought.

Discipline of Gesture

Learning to become bodily expressive on the platform, in the second place, implies discipline of gesture. After the speaker has become bodily alert and responsive, he is not utterly free to behave as his old, everyday impulses dictate. He must recognize that because he is standing before others, or otherwise assuming a more prominent place than is customary in conversation, his position has become emphatic. Consequently, some behavior that is inconspicuous and proper in daily intercourse may become glaringly evident on the platform. Such, for example, are *mannerisms*. They are repetitious behavior that is peculiar to the individual. In fact, they are so distinctive of the individual that his friends and associates have come to accept them as being part of his personality. Hence, by a man's friends his mannerisms escape notice or are charitably tolerated. On the platform and in the presence of strangers, they yell for attention. What is natural and acceptable in one environment is no longer natural and acceptable in another. Accordingly, under the guidance of his instructor and his classroom listeners, the student may need to eliminate certain mannerisms. They may be such habitual quirks of behavior as stroking the hair, pulling the collar or the nose, adjusting the tie, wagging a hand, rubbing the knuckles, smoothing the dress, or fussing with the necklace or earring. Whatever they are, they compete with ideas for the hearer's attention.

Beyond the discipline required to eliminate mannerisms, most beginning speakers must undertake some training to smooth out gesture, to iron out such roughness and awkwardness as may distract attention. The training is begun *after* the speaker finds that his body is responding with considerable ease and freedom. Only after action on the platform begins to be spontaneous and habitual can the novice afford to be self-conscious about his gesture. In the early speeches the important first steps are (1) handling one's body so as not to inhibit action, (2) responding freely to all impulses to activity, and (3) breaking up distracting mannerisms of behavior. The refinement of gesture comes later in the speaker's development.

PROCEDURES FOR PRACTICE

Securing Poise and Freedom of Action

The directions here may seem extremely elementary. They are. Nevertheless, they are basic to gesture and to efficient, unobtrusive platform behavior.

Posture and Carriage

The first step is learning to *stand* quietly and at ease.

Feet

Stand with the feet not more than six inches apart, with one foot somewhat behind the other. Observe that in this position the weight is not evenly distributed on both feet. (Avoid standing with toes in line and with feet tight together, for this tends toward stiffness.) Try to get the sensation of the floor being *solidly* yet *comfortably* beneath you; if necessary bend your knees and come back into position sharply, thus driving your toes into the floor. Finding and learning a basic stance is necessary for freedom of movement about the platform.

Body

The chest should be up, without being thrust out. The shoulders should be erect, without being pushed back. Avoid a military, at-attention posture, for this feels stiff and looks stiff to an audience. To help loosen the shoulders so that they will rest easily, rotate each shoulder, then raise the arms and let them fall like dead weights. When your torso is well poised, you feel as if your shoulders and upper body were *suspended*, rather than borne up laboriously from below. You are then free to respond readily with gesture.

Legs

The chief directions here are negative. Don't stand with the legs far apart, thus giving yourself a planted or propped-up appearance. Don't let one leg bend or sag so much that your body is thrown out of line. Don't stick one leg out in front of you, for this also twists the body and breaks its general smoothness of line. All such positions attract attention to your stance; no matter how natural and comfortable they may seem to you or how acceptable they are in everyday life, they don't look natural on the platform. If, in avoiding such positions, you find that you feel strange and stiff, *practice* in private until you can be easy and comfortable.

Head

Keep the head erect without throwing it back. Don't let it sag forward or fall to one side.

Arms and Hands

The arms and hands must be ready to act, so that impulses to gesture are instantly translated into spontaneous, real movement. Accordingly, find a position that you can become *comfortable* in, and make it the basic or *rest* position from which you will gesture.

One good position is with arms hanging freely—not stiffly or rigidly—at your sides. To find the position, raise the arms to shoulder height, relax and *let them fall*. Another easy position, especially when a lectern is available, is to rest one forearm and hand on the lectern, with the other arm hanging free, or brought up to waist level. If you like this position, guard against leaning or otherwise propping yourself on the stand.

Still another position is with both forearms up to waist level, the palms of the hands up and the fingers partially extended (avoid clenched fists or fingers rigidly extended). In this position the hands will just about meet at mid-body. Practice this position until you *feel* as if your forearms were *resting* on chair arms. This position is probably the easiest of all from which to gesture. (*Caution:* Don't clasp your hands in front or behind you, keep them out of your pockets, and in general avoid any position that inhibits spontaneous movement.)

Stand Still, at Ease

After you have checked these positions carefully, *stand still until the new position no longer seems new and strange.* Stiffness won't depart instantly and magically; only practice and experience will bring results. Many students have used a watch to advantage. Using the position you like best, stand for one minute, relax, and check up. Stand for two minutes and so on until you reach five minutes. If you can stand still and *like* it for even three minutes, you have a base of operations from which you can move when the spirit impels you.

Movement on the Platform

The next step is learning to move about the platform with ease and without attracting the listeners' attention to movement as such. One cannot say flatly how often a speaker should move, or how much. All one can say with assurance is that any speaker who is keenly alive to his task doesn't remain stock-still in one position. Nor can one state at precisely what places in a speech a speaker should move. When his own body and his ideas demand action, he will be impelled to shift position—often without realizing it. What the beginner should do is to learn to handle his legs with ease and grace so that he moves when the impulse hits him. After you have learned to stand easily, practice the following:

From your standing position, move first to one side and then the other two or three paces.

Move on an angle, rather than directly sideways, thus:

(audience)

Lead with the right foot when you go right; lead with the left foot in going left. In this way you don't have to cross your legs; hence you will feel easy, and you won't trip over your own feet.

Initiate the movement lazily (sudden movement attracts attention) and cease it lazily.

Keep the shoulders on a level, and avoid the sailor's roll.

Keep your eyes on the audience.

After you have learned to move unobtrusively, learn to move about a speaker's stand or lectern. (At home substitute a straight-backed chair or a small table for the lectern.)

Stand behind the lectern; move far enough to the side to clear the stand, and then ease forward as far as you wish.

Keep your eyes on your hearers.

Keep one hand on the stand as you move; the hand will guide you, and you'll appear to the observer like a normal human being, because human beings normally use furniture in this way rather than avoid it.

Stand beside the lectern. If you wish to move to a spot behind it, first back up a half-step or two until you have cleared the back corner; then turn and continue to your destination. (*Caution:* Avoid dragging or scuffing the feet as you move backward.)

Keep a hand on the lectern, even though in this maneuver you will be shifting hands at the back corner of the stand as you turn. Keep your eyes on the listeners.

If you are willing to work conscientiously for twenty to thirty minutes on these initial positions and movements as part of your preparation for one of your early speeches, you will see considerable improvement in platform behavior at once. But unless you are unusually skillful, you will not acquire acceptable platform behavior in a single, thirty-minute practice period. Remember that no habit is acquired magically; it is built in through directed practice and the desire to establish the habit firmly. If, then, after you have delivered a speech, your audience or your instructor points out inadequacies of behavior, jot them down and as a preliminary to your *next* speech, practice the positions and movements again, giving special attention to your inadequacies. Repeat this procedure on subsequent speeches. Not until your audience ceases to be aware of your behavior can it be called adequate.

If you can learn to handle yourself well on the platform, you will have taken three fundamental steps toward acquiring a good delivery:

You will help your listeners to keep their attention on what you say, rather than on your behavior.

You will be ready to gesture; perhaps you will discover that you are already gesturing.

You will have the confidence that comes from knowing that you can handle yourself without appearing wooden and awkward.

Improving Gesture

Once a speaker discovers that he is moving freely on the platform and is gesturing spontaneously and unself-consciously, he should consider two questions: (1) Are hand and arm gestures sufficient in number and in variety? (2) Are gestures graceful, free of ungainly, awkward, and jerky movements? On these questions the speechmaker will do well to consult his teacher or some candid critic who will tell him the plain truth. If the time has come to develop gesture in variety, number, and smoothness, the suggestions below will serve as guides. They should receive attention relatively late in the private rehearsal period, at about the time when the speaker can move the main ideas of his speech along without breaks. Recognizing the main kinds of gesture helps one see greater possibilities for gesture. One reviews his speech and sees an opportunity to use a gesture where he hasn't done so before.

Gestures Suggesting the Relationships between Ideas

CONTRASTING IDEAS

One hand marks one idea, the other hand the other, the hands moving away from each other and implying the notion of difference. In expressing a contrast, one often says, "On the one hand. . . . On the other hand. . . ."

COMPARING IDEAS

Each hand marks one half of the comparison; then the hands approach each other to suggest that similar ideas belong together.

ONE IDEA SUBORDINATE TO ANOTHER

An example, an illustration, or a statistic which follows and amplifies a general statement is often ushered in with a hand gesture which says, "Let me show you." A similar gesture is natural to use when offering a hypothetical illustration or a conditional statement such as "Suppose it were. . . ." or "Now if it is true that. . . ."

Gestures That Describe

These suggest the size, shape, position, and movement of objects. They are perhaps the easiest for a speaker to learn to manage. They are natural, indeed virtually inevitable, in the informative speech. To illustrate their possibilities, gesture your way through this passage:

Out in front of me was a large table. On one side of it was a round ball about two feet in diameter. On the other side was a rectangular column, about a foot across and three feet high. From it to the ball was stretched a wire. Just under the wire and at the half-way point was a small monkey who was rhythmically plucking it. Two feet in front of the monkey was a steel ball, about the size of a baseball. The ball would move back and forth in time with the monkey's plucking of the wire. With one pluck, the ball would roll to the right six inches; with the next pluck, it would roll back to the left, and so on.

Gestures That Suggest Emotion and Feeling

To illustrate these gestures get into the mood of the following ideas and speak them:

I shall have absolutely nothing to do with the proposal.

I am quite willing to admit that I was wrong.

I'm sorry, but it can't be helped.

What's the difference; we may as well give up.

No, no, it won't work. I'm warning you.

Put the idea out of your mind.

Gestures That Give Force and Emphasis

These gestures can be illustrated by the following ideas:

We shall fight and struggle and toil on to the bitter end.

Perjury and infamy on one hand; truth and honor on the other.

Some may choose subjection and slavery, but as for me, give me liberty or give me death!

Can you say that we should avoid the issue? I believe we should face it, now, once and for all.

There's not a word of truth in it.

Smoothing Out Gesture

In working additional gestures into the speech during rehearsal, the speaker should practice them enough so that they spontaneously accompany ideas. If they don't become second nature to him, they may strike his audience as being planted and artificial. But the risk of looking a bit artful at times should not deter a speaker from gesturing more, if he needs to. Indeed, his public speaking class may well be the only place he will ever be able to improve his action.

We shall hazard the opinion that the modern speaker does not gesture enough. He seems to be made of clay or to be tied into a bag. The body-mind complex is a functional *whole*. To a remarkable degree in delivery, action sharpens thinking and gives force and variety to the voice. Gesture amplifies meanings and their expression. The student speaker scorns it to his disadvantage.

In working for smooth and graceful action, one tries to attain, first of all, a feeling of easy limberness in the shoulders and arms. Then one proceeds to iron out any awkwardness of arm movement. The exercises and directions below should prove helpful.

Shoulders and Arms

Roll the shoulders, first one shoulder and then the other. Roll both simultaneously. Practice at intervals during rehearsal, and continue practice until you feel like a coiled spring gently compressed, ready for release. Once you have experienced this sensation, you can produce it readily with three or four "rolls." Loose and ready shoulders encourage arm movement.

Practice to secure a relaxed feeling in the arms. Lift the arms, extended in front (but not stretched), to shoulder height and *let them drop of their own weight*—simply *relax*. Then lift the extended arms to shoulder height at the sides; let them drop. Continue practice until you feel your arms *hang*. They should be loose as a rag doll's.

With the arms and shoulders loose and easy, practice the time-honored double-loop exercise. It is perhaps the best single exercise to secure graceful arm movements. First, go through the movement with one arm almost completely, though not entirely, extended in front of you. The points of the loop, *a* and *b*, should be well beyond the sides of the body; the points marked *x* should be somewhat above shoulder height; and the points marked *y* should be at about waist level. This gives a large figure 8, and the arm moves through most of the planes on which gesture takes place. Second, repeat the figure with the left arm. Finally, perform the figure with both arms simultaneously. (*Caution:* At no time must the arms be fully extended nor must they become rigid. It is the easy swing you are after.)

Practice this exercise before you start a rehearsal of your speech.

Arm Movement

First, make sure that both arms are in the arm-rest position, that the forearms are *horizontal*. See that the hands, almost touching each other in front of you, are palm uppermost and that the fingers are in the position they would take if you were holding a fairly large apple or orange. Rigid, extended fingers look unnatural and awkward. See, also, that the elbows lightly touch the sides of the body; to let them stick out looks ungainly. With the arms in this position and *resting* easily, you are ready for the three stages of arm movement.

PREPARATION

A gesture has a beginning, middle, and end. Neither the beginning movement nor the end carries meaning. The beginning movement is called the preparation stage, because it takes the arm and hand to the point where the meaningful action, called the stroke or climax, takes place. The concluding movement, the return, simply brings the arm back to a position of rest, ready to respond again to an idea.

With the arms in position, start a movement with the right arm to the right, observing these directions:

Keep the elbow at the side of the body until the movement is well started. Leading with the elbow is awkward.

Start the movement by letting the *wrist* lead; the hand *follows* at first and gradually catches up by the time the stroke is reached.

Start the movement rather slowly, for sudden movement attracts attention to itself. Vigorous, swift activity—if any—takes place on the stroke.

Practice the preparation first with one arm, then with the other arm, and finally with both.

STROKE

The preparation stage of a gesture culminates in a rather sudden movement that communicates meaning. Speak the following sentence, starting the preparation movement as you start speaking, or just *before* utterance:

The plan is extremely *dangerous.*

Remember the actor's old rule: action *always* precedes speech unless you desire a comic effect. As you make the point, *dangerous,* hand and arm will execute a short, swift movement that marks and gives emphasis to the idea. With good preparation, the climax of a gesture will almost invariably take care of itself. What happens at the climax will depend entirely on the idea expressed. Use each arm alone and then both arms in saying the sentence above.

RETURN

After the stroke, the arm should come to rest. Sometimes it will come back to the starting point of the cycle; sometimes it will return only slightly, especially if another gesture is to follow immediately. For example, experiment with the following sentence:

The plan is extremely *dangerous, vicious,* and altogether *reprehensible.*

After the stroke on *dangerous,* the arm will remain where it is and from that point will execute the next two strokes, on *vicious* and on *reprehensible.* When the series is complete, the arm may return to mid-body, or drop lightly to the side.

Be sure to let the arm return rather slowly; if the action is swift the observer's attention will be attracted.

Do not watch your gestures—unless you want to appear ridiculous.

In encouraging student speakers to improve the quantity and quality of their gestures, we are not implying that the speaker should be as active as the actor. Obviously, the speaker is not an actor, and accordingly his gestures, as a rule, are neither so numerous nor so extensive as the actor's. Nevertheless, the function of gesture is to the speaker what the function of gesture is to the actor: it helps to describe ideas, suggest emotion and attitudes, and provide emphasis.

DELIVERY AS A HABIT

The delivery of a speech is complex behavior. Nevertheless, it does not differ essentially from the act of speaking in any situation. In every speaking situation, there is a stimulus that calls forth the act; it is essentially a person-to-be-spoken-to. What he says or does provokes utterance. In every speech situation there is a response; it consists of vocal sounds and gestures of face and body. Furthermore, the response is immediate and habitual. Similarly, speech on the platform is vocal and bodily response to an audience. You step to the platform. There is an audience-to-be-spoken-to, and in response to it, you speak. "Ah!" but you say, "I am not in the *habit* of speaking to an *audience*." That is precisely the point. You recognize that platform speaking presents a new situation to which you have not learned to respond habitually. Your efforts, consequently, will be devoted to the acquisition of a new habit.

Method and Practice

If the speaker is to work intelligently in his efforts to acquire the habit of public speaking, he will profit from knowing something about what happens when one sets out to build a habit efficiently. In the first place, the process is methodical, rather than hit-and-miss. It involves knowing the goal; one must understand what he is after. A swimmer cannot learn the Australian crawl unless he knows what it is. Similarly, one cannot acquire a good delivery unless he understands its principles, which have been presented in this chapter. Nor, for that matter, can one learn to construct a good speech unless he knows the principles of speechmaking. Habit formation is methodical, also, in that it involves practice and repetition. The importance of practice in acquiring a good delivery can hardly be overestimated. It is, in fact, so fundamental that if one were forced to resort to only three rules of speechmaking, they might well be these: practice, practice, practice. Although the student may have frequent opportunities to speak to a classroom audience, he will discover that preliminary rehearsals in his own room or in a vacant classroom are extremely helpful. After each section of this chapter we have recommended procedures to be followed in rehearsal.

As important as practice is, however, it will not by itself build a good habit. First, there is some danger of practicing the wrong thing. The adage that "practice makes perfect" is a great truth, but it is two-edged. Practice alone will perfect undesirable behavior just as readily as it will perfect desirable behavior. Hence, anyone who sets out to acquire a new habit must see clearly what the new habit is to be. Certainly if this is essential in forming relatively simple habits like running the 100-yard dash, it is doubly essential in forming a complex habit like public speaking. Just standing-up-and-saying-something, then, is not enough; one needs and should encourage the criticisms and comments from both instructor and listeners who should help to keep one on the right path. The learning speaker, therefore, performs routines exactly, such as full outlining according to form, which may seem needless to the experienced speaker, who already *has* the *habits* which the learner should be acquiring.

Motivating and Sharpening Experience

In the second place, the process of acquiring a habit is always facilitated by one's mental "set" and experience during learning. If practice is made a fetish, there is danger of overlooking two conditions of learning that are just as important as practice. One is *motivation;* the other is *intensity* of perception and understanding. The results of experimental studies on learning agree that the *desire* to do a thing helps in the doing. To one who expects to acquire a good delivery this leads to a great axiom: the *desire* to speak to *this* audience on *this* subject is a powerful stimulus to facility, fluency, and variety of utterance. Experimental studies suggest, also, that the more intense an experience is, the readier and longer the retention of the experience.

This knowledge applied to delivery means that the clearer and sharper one's ideas are as he works them over in preparing, framing, and rehearsing his speech, the easier they come back to him on the platform. Indeed, if the student can learn to work methodically in preparing a speech, if his ideas can be marshalled into an unmistakably clear pattern and sequence, and if he can make them *vivid* and intensely meaningful to himself, he will discover that for the most part they will spring from him spontaneously and easily; he will not have to "remember" them, consciously, deliberately, and painfully. This is the difference between remembering ideas by rote and assimilating them until they are part of experience. Acquiring a good delivery, then, is far more than putting in time in rehearsal; it involves learning to handle, to govern, and to *control* one's own thinking by getting oneself emotionally "set" for speaking and by sharply appreciating ideas in a sequence. A speaker's mind on the platform is a free-running machine, not a machine that needs laborious and frequent priming and restarting.

Public Speaking Not Instinctive

In the third place, as the student goes about building a habit of good delivery, he should not confuse habit with instinct. A habit is learned behavior that meets the needs of a situation; an instinct is unlearned behavior in response to a situation. Experimental psychologists now seem to agree that there are at most only three situations that call forth instinctive behavior: fear is the unlearned response to falling; fear is the instinctive reaction to loud noise; and cooing, smiling, and similar manifestations of "love" behavior always attend the caress. These responses are evident at birth, or shortly thereafter. If the psychologists are right, then, all other behavior is learned. There is, consequently, no instinct to speak; we must all learn to speak, as indeed we do, slowly and haltingly, over some three or four years in early childhood. Speaking, then, becomes one kind of response to communicative situations. As communicative situations multiply in number and diversity, speech responses become more complex and diversified. There is, further, no instinct to speak on the platform or in the "public" situation, and assuredly no instinct or unlearned capacity to speak there with fluency and ease and appropriateness. A man must learn to adapt to the stimulus of the "public" situation, and in order to make the adaptation efficient, he seeks to make it habitual, rather than random, uncertain, and self-conscious.

Miracles Don't Happen

Accordingly, if effective utterance on the platform is not instinctive, there is at least one important corollary for him who would learn: Don't expect miracles. One can learn only through doing, by handling himself mentally and bodily as the situation demands. One may adapt rapidly; one may adapt slowly and through error. But whatever happens, after delivery is over one should check up and seek to know why he succeeded, why he failed, and handle himself accordingly in the next speech. Don't expect that an instructor can find some special formula or touch some hidden spring that will render one instantly and invariably at ease and will release a flow of brilliant, clear, and fitting language. An instructor can only act as friendly guide and sympathetic critic. Imagine what he would have to do, or better yet, what *you* as a speaker would have to do, if adaptation were to be instantly perfect and invariably successful. You would have to construct a situation that fitted you to *perfection*. The audience would have to be selected so as to fit your special information, desires, and idiosyncrasies of emotional and mental make-up. It might have to be specially coached, so that it would respond each moment in a way that would encourage you. It would have to assemble at a place where you felt perfectly at home. Finally, it would either have to be primed and prepared to overlook your peculiarities of delivery, or else the individuals themselves would have to possess or to approve of those peculiarities. In other words, if without training you were to speak well you would have to tailor your audience to fit you, rather than to tailor yourself to fit your audience. In a democratic society such tailoring is, of course, absurd, because the individual counts only so long as he recognizes that other individuals may count as much as he. It is in a tyrannical society that the speaker, like Hitler and Mussolini, can hand-pick his listeners, govern their applause, and stage-manage the setting. Moral: If a person wants to speak without the pangs of learning, he should be a dictator!

As the student endeavors to build up a habit of speaking in the audience situation, he should recognize, in the last place, that the acquisition of a habit always involves some initial self-consciousness. Trying anything for the first time makes a man aware that *he* is doing something new, and trying to do something according to principles and directions makes him aware that he is trying to *control* his conduct. Accordingly, as you seek to adapt to the audience situation in your first speeches and as you endeavor to conform to the first principles of delivery, you may not escape some feeling of self-consciousness. But as you continue to make speeches, you will discover a comforting fact: As a result of practice and experience, self-consciousness disappears when the mind is fully occupied with ideas.

Full mental responsiveness to ideas at the moment of utterance and a keen sense of communication and appropriate gesture are probably most evident and are most readily achieved in what we call the *extemporaneous* and the *impromptu* modes of delivery. The training and experience of the young speaker will be primarily in these modes.

FURTHER READING

PARRISH, W. M., "The Concept of 'Naturalness,'" *Quarterly Journal of Speech*, 40 (December 1951), 448–454.

WINANS, J. A., *Public Speaking* (New York, 1917), Ch. 2, "Conversing With an Audience."

CHAPTER NINE

Speaking Impromptu and Reading Aloud

IN OUR PREVIOUS TREATMENT, we have given principal attention to delivery in extemporaneous speaking, that is, in speaking which is carefully prepared, is preferably rehearsed, but is not committed to final language until the time when the speech is made. This mode of delivery has usually been highly prized, and it is the norm by which other modes are measured. There are occasions, however, when persons must speak impromptu, that is, without advance notice, and there are other times when they are expected to read from manuscript or the printed page. In this chapter, accordingly, we present suggestions for impromptu speaking and for reading aloud.

IMPROMPTU SPEAKING

Perhaps nothing so satisfies our egos as success in speaking impromptu, in speaking unexpectedly without having had a chance to prepare for the occasion.

Unfortunately, however, most impromptu speaking is bad, because the speaker, surprised in deep water, loses his head and thrashes and flounders about. His delivery is halting and hard, and his remarks are usually inane and irrelevant, repetitious and disconnected. In alarm and desperation, he clutches at any idea that pops into mind and without examining it hopes that somehow it will save him. When impromptu utterance is good, it is very, very good. Delivery, in particular, may be excellent; it may exhibit the verve, sparkle, and spontaneity that one struggles to attain in the extemporaneous speech. Most public speakers have observed that their impromptu delivery is at times superior to their prepared efforts. A speaker may recognize that he talks well when the circumstances of communication are just right. When the preceding speaker stirs him strongly or when discussion starts him thinking, when he springs to correct another speaker's information, to criticize an argument, to express a different point of view, he has simultaneously an idea to communicate and the impulse to say it—and presto! the job is done with vigor and dispatch. He should recognize, however, that the fortuitous combination of circumstances, just the right situation, brings about his success. Indeed, when the circumstances are made to order, who can fail?

We are concerned here with the situation in which the circumstances are not perfect, in which a speaker, called on unexpectedly, must, like an aggressive athlete, make his own breaks and take advantage of the opportunity to speak instead of letting it slip by.

In coping with the impromptu situation, a speaker should recognize above all, paradoxical as the observation may seem, that he is not wholly without preparation. He has a background of experience and information upon which he may be able to draw. *The problem is how to make his past work for him.*

In such a situation you may be able to enjoy considerable success by attacking the problem in the following ways:

Listen Carefully

This should not be difficult if discussion from the platform or from the floor succeeds in claiming your interest. But if the speechmaking and the discussion do not readily interest you and if there is the slightest possibility that you may be called upon to speak, follow the talk as closely as you can, even if you have to force yourself to attend. The ideas you hear expressed may touch off your information and experience, and thus prompt some kind of reaction. The reaction may be any of these, or others: "The speaker has overlooked an important point"; "I could add an illustration to that point"; "he is being inconsistent"; "that argument is weak"; "he believes so-and-so, but I think the opposite (or, but I believe he is only partly right)." When such ideas strike you, make a note of them wherever they occur. Make the note brief— only a phrase or two—so that you don't lose the trend of the speech or the discussion. Thus, you will soon have a record of your reactions.

Control Alarm and Panic

If you are called on to speak, you may experience a wild moment. "What shall I say; oh, what shall I do! I can't say anything! I'm caught; I wish I were out of here!" Such a reaction is emotional, and emotion, as we know, feeds on itself and makes the experience more intense. Now recognize such an emotional response at once, and cope with it. Ease yourself physically by relaxing and thus reducing muscular tension. Breathe regularly. With a little practice, you can learn to ease off thus in four or five seconds. Then turn your attention to the situation and meet it squarely. Has a specific question been asked that demands a definite answer? If you can answer it, start walking to the platform and decide what your answer will be. (If necessary to gain time, ask for the repetition of the question. This gives the mind something to do!) Your decision will probably suggest a reason or two or at least an illustration to back it up. At this moment you have, whether you recognize it or not, what amounts to a central idea with which you can lead off, and one or two ideas to follow and support it. You can conclude by restating your opening idea. If you cannot reply to the direct question, two roads are open to you. Either decline to speak, excusing yourself as gracefully as you can, or say in substance, "I don't have anything to say to that question, but if I may, I should like to comment on such-and-such a point." Here is where your notes come in handy, for your decision to comment on another point may be prompted by a glance at them. You use them to recall swiftly your earlier reactions.

If, on the other hand, a general question is asked you—such as "Would you care to comment on so-and-so's remarks?"—you fly at once to your notes for suggestions. To one inexperienced in impromptu discussion, notes are here invaluable because a general question or invitation suggests no possibilities. It isn't specific enough to give one a mental start, and the review of notes may prompt an idea.

Become Thoroughly Habituated to Useful Patterns of Thought

So far we have been concerned principally with suggestions that aid the impromptu speaker in selecting something to say. Now we shall present some aids to the rapid organization of his ideas. The impromptu speech, like the extemporaneous speech, requires a speaker not only to have something to say but to say it as clearly as he can. The least to be expected of him is that he will contrive a simple, sensible governing statement and support it with an example or two. Anything more which he may be able to accomplish is clear profit.

The patterns below, intended primarily to promote clarity of expression, may also serve to suggest ideas. The student would do well to practice them so thoroughly that they become part of him; he should, in other words, assimilate them completely. They then stand a good chance of coming to his aid, unrecognized and unheralded, in those few moments of preparation in the impromptu situation, to provide form for his thoughts. In classroom practice if the teacher can manage to give the student an extra moment or two before speaking, he can review them deliberately and select the pattern most appropriate to his reply.

1. Lead off with what has been said. Express your reaction. Support it. (*A variant of this:* Start with the question asked you. Answer it in one sentence. Explain or give your reasons for the answer.)
2. Lead off with an illustration. Conclude by stating the point it suggests.
3. Say that an important point has been omitted. State it. Support it.
4. Express disagreement with a certain argument. Give reasons for disagreeing.
5. Express disagreement in terms of the problem discussed.
   a. The evils have been exaggerated. State why.
   b. The solution is bad, for
      (1) There is a better one. State it. Give reasons.
      (2) It is impractical. Give reasons.
6. The reasoning in such-and-such an argument is in error, because of
   a. Insufficient or untrustworthy facts. Explain.
   b. Inadequate or untrustworthy testimony. Explain.
   c. Faulty analogy. Explain.
   d. Faulty cause-and-effect reasoning. Explain.
7. The argument shows an inconsistency. Explain.

Impromptu Speeches about Speaking

The formula above will aid greatly in discussing impromptu the content and reasoning of any speech, in or out of the classroom. In the classroom, also, considerable discussion may be directed to speaking as such. Impromptu speaking about speeches has special values for the student. It lays the foundation of good criticism, not only of class speeches, but of all speeches, anywhere. It affords, moreover, additional training in speech for both parties to the criticism, for the student speaker secures further practice in impromptu utterance and the student criticized learns about his successes and failures from one of his peers. Finally, the speaker, familiar with the standards, methods, and techniques of speechmaking, has knowledge which he can use on the spur of the moment.

The patterns already set out above will be useful in criticizing a speaker's argument; those below will aid in organizing impromptu criticism of other phases of speechmaking.

SPEAKER'S SUBJECT

The subject of Mr. *X*'s speech was appropriate (was inappropriate), for
   I. A good speech subject, as we all know, should. . . .
      (Here you remind your audience of the *standards* by which a subject should be judged. Reference to standards in this pattern and in those following gives you ready material for your opening remarks.)
   I'. And his subject meets (does not meet; in part meets) the requirements

of a good subject, for. . . . (Here you go on to support your judgment.)

SPEAKER'S INFORMATION AND CHOICE OF IDEAS

X's speech was worth (was not worth) listening to, for
    I. A good speech should enlarge our information (or influence our thinking and action).
    I'. And I learned something (little) from X's speech (or X's argument on . . . appealed [did not appeal] to me), for. . . .

DELIVERY

X's speech was well (poorly) delivered, for
    I. A speaker's delivery should show qualities of. . . .
    I'. X's delivery showed (did not show) such qualities, for
        A. He was (was not) mentally alert to ideas, for. . . .
        B. As for sense of communication, he. . . .
        C. As for vocal qualities, he. . . .
        D. As for pronunciation, he. . . .
        E. As for bodily responsiveness
            1. To ideas, he. . . .
            2. To the platform situation, he. . . .

Observe that an impromptu criticism might well be limited to *one* of the aspects of delivery alluded to in *A–E* above. For example:

The vocal qualities of X's delivery were acceptable (inacceptable), for
    I. Desirable qualities are. . . .
    I'. X possessed (did not possess) these qualities, for. . . .

SPEECH ORGANIZATION

X's speech was clear (clear in part; not clear), for
    I. Its purpose was (was not) evident, for. . . .
    II. Its subject sentence was (was not) evident, for. . . .
    (If the subject sentence was evident, cite it and thus support your judgment; if it was not clear, try to suggest why it wasn't.)
    III. Its main heads were (were not) recognizable, for. . . .
    IV. It effectively used (did not use) some of the methods of securing clearness, for. . . .

Rarely will an alert individual find himself completely unprepared for the impromptu situation. Although he cannot prepare specifically for the unexpected occasion, he can equip himself and condition himself for meeting such occasions. (1) He can confirm the habit, which ought to be a normal consequence of his education, of reading, inquiring, conversing, observing, and thinking widely on those general and particular subjects which men in society at all times and at a given time concern themselves with. He will find, what frequent speakers have always found, that within wide limits the same lines of thought, developed in much the same way, will be adaptable to many speaking situations. He will accumulate, therefore, a store of such lines of thought, which he will be able to call to mind and to adapt properly to a variety of circumstances. (2) Like the contestant in an honest quiz show or like a student preparing for an examination in special circumstances, he can pay special attention to the basic ideas and information which are likely to be needed in the situation he is going to face. (3) He can train himself to listen closely, take note of his reactions, and develop the knack of swiftly arranging his remarks. The more speaking experience he gains, the more resources of idea, information, and illustration he accumulates, the more readily will possible supporting and amplifying material cluster about an idea. A good impromptu speech, with an idea worth remembering, cannot be made from an empty or lethargic mind.

READING ALOUD

One's Own Material

Reading a speech from a manuscript (or from some equivalent such as a teleprompter) is perhaps more common today than ever before in the history of public speaking. In part this is due to the influence of radio and TV. In part it is caused by the pressure of business and public life, for many men in industry and government are too busy to take time to prepare well enough for extemporaneous utterance. In part, too, reading a speech assists one to speak with accuracy and to avoid the hazards of misquotation. But in large part, the greater use of reading is probably due to this circumstance: Fewer men in responsible positions today have had the training in public speaking that their counterparts enjoyed almost as a matter of course three or four generations ago.

Hence although extemporaneous delivery is still the most common method used by speakers, the modern student of public speaking should have some experience in reading a speech from manuscript and in speaking impromptu. In these times when much communication is by radio and television, most leaders in political, business, and civic life will appear at one time or another before the microphone. For most of these appearances, they will be required to prepare written versions of their speeches and to read them. Furthermore, with the multiplication of organizations, committees, conferences, and conventions in all phases of our business, industrial, social, civic, and educational lives, comes more and more demand for the reading aloud of minutes, reports, documents, and communications of all sorts. That this reading should be competent rather than incompetent is greatly to be desired.

Reading

To read aloud well is difficult. It requires intelligence, training, and practice. For this reason colleges often devote entire courses to reading aloud, and those persons who expect to read in public, especially those preparing for political and administrative positions, for the law, for the ministry, for acting, for performing on radio and television, and for teaching, should take intensive instruction in reading. We do not propose to offer such intensive instruction here, and we will have nothing to say about what is known as the oral interpretation of literature. We wish merely to present a few, basic suggestions that should set the reader on the proper road to competent, work-a-day, prose reading.

The goal of all oral reading is utterance which sounds like direct communication. A reader tries to express *ideas*. He tries to *react to the meanings* of the written words and hold the meaning in mind, concentrating utterly upon it, while he says the prepared language. In brief, his reading should reveal two qualities of good delivery: full realization of meaning at the moment of utterance and a keen sense of direct communication.

Preparation of the Written Speech

Prepare a Speech, Not an Essay

In planning for the written speech, one should, of course, prepare as thoroughly as for the extemporaneous speech. This observation needs emphasis, for many speakers mistakenly feel that because they can lean on written language they need not give so much care to preparation as they would to the construction of an extemporaneous speech. Often they regard the written speech as an essay. Consequently, they select a subject which is too broad to be treated adequately without using more abstract and general language than an audience can understand. As a result, vivid, specific illustrations and details, and the many other ways of adapting and fitting ideas to an audience, tend to be left out. Frequently a written speech is fuzzy and unclear because the speaker thought he could write before he made a complete speech outline, that is, before he clarified and ordered his mind on the subject. Our advice, accordingly, is this: Plan the speech, outline it, and write it out *in every detail* just as if you expected later to discard the manuscript and talk extemporaneously. If you have the opportunity and facilities, try dictating the speech from the outline. The written speech should in every respect reveal a real person talking to a specific audience on a specific occasion. As the speech is being written, the speaker should visualize himself *talking* to his hearers.

Before preparing the final draft of the speech, the speaker should check the text methodically with these questions in mind:

Does the introduction really claim the interest of the hearers and establish direct contact with the audience? Is each illustration detailed enough to be clear and vivid?

Are there enough transitions and signpost phrases to keep the audience from getting lost?

Is the style of direct address used when referring to people? In general, prefer *we, our, us, I, you,* to *they, people, a person, the reader, the author.*

Are there many abstract words and phrases? Can you substitute *concrete* and *specific* words and phrases? (Time spent in inspection and substitution will repay a speaker a hundredfold.)

Eliminate from the Manuscript All Sources of Distraction

Give yourself maximum opportunity to concentrate on ideas by eliminating what may distract your attention. Accordingly:

Type the manuscript on one side of the paper only; this facilitates handling. Triple space the lines, for this reduces the danger of re-reading a line or of skipping a line. If you cannot type the manuscript or have it typed for you, write in a large, bold hand.

Have the copy absolutely clean; do not clutter up the page with last-minute additions between the lines and in the margins. Don't cross out material and transpose word order. Visual clutter distracts attention.

Practice Aloud

Handling the Manuscript

A reader may handle his manuscript in one of two ways: (1) He may hold it in his hands somewhat above waist level, high enough so that he can see it easily without bending his head and not so high as to hide his face. One hand should hold the manuscript, and the other hand should be free to shift pages and to gesture. (2) He may place it on a speaker's stand, or on a table, but only if either one is high enough to permit him to consult the paper readily without bending over. If it is on a stand, both hands are free to gesture.

The speaker should check both positions carefully with this fact in mind: The head should be erect, because in this position the eyes can be readily kept on the audience. Bending-over tends to keep the eyes riveted to the manuscript, and the reader needs to do everything he can to keep in physical touch with his hearers. *Let the eyes, not the head, drop to the paper.*

Two cautions should be observed: Do not try to conceal a manuscript (or notes, for that matter) from an audience; do not apologize for reading.

Look at Your Hearers

Inexpert reading tends to make delivery indirect; both speaker and audience are usually robbed of any feeling of direct communication, principally because the speaker glues his eyes to his manuscript. Consequently, in practice reading a speaker must spend much of his effort in learning to keep his eyes on the audience. *He should practice until he can look at his hearers 90 per cent of the time.* For at least nine minutes of a ten-minute speech he should have his eyes on his audience.

Achieving such directness involves great familiarity with one's manuscript and ability to find one's place unerringly. Both can be accomplished through persistent practice.

Practice in keeping one's place should proceed in this manner:

Take a long look at the words ahead and do your best to concentrate on their meaning; then look up and speak them. When you can go no farther, drop the eyes to the proper place, take another look ahead, look up, and speak again. Repeat again and again.

Practice in this way should continue until you determine your maximum memory span, until you discover the longest language groups you can hold in mind before you need to consult the text for another glance ahead. Let us illustrate briefly. Suppose the opening paragraph is represented by this passage from Huxley:

Suppose it were perfectly certain that the life and fortune of every one of us/ would, one day or other,/ depend upon his winning or losing a game at chess./ Don't you think we should all consider it a primary duty/ to learn at least the names and the moves of the pieces;/ to have a notion of a gambit,/ and a keen eye for all the means of giving and getting out of a check?/ Do you not think we should look with a disapprobation amounting to scorn,/ upon a father who allowed his son,/ or the state which allowed its members,/ to grow up without knowing a pawn from a knight?

Upon first reading this aloud, you might discover that you would have to pause and look down frequently, perhaps at the end of each thought-unit, as indicated by the slant lines (/). With further practice, you could easily speak each sentence, and therefore would need to consult the text only three times; and with still more work, you could probably speak the entire paragraph. As you work through your manuscript in this manner, you will discover that your memory span will depend on whether the ideas are abstract and general, or concrete and specific; accordingly, the frequency with which you glance down will vary considerably, for sometimes you will be able to hold only one sentence-idea in mind, sometimes a number of sentence-ideas. The object is to practice until you have to consult the text as little as possible. When you have located the spots where you *must* glance down, you may *mark* them with some convenient symbol. (Many students like to use a small circle in red ink.) The marks will guide your eyes and prevent confusion.

Concentrate on Meaning and Idea Rather Than on Words

Cultivate and build up the feeling that you must speak to this audience at this time, that you are in touch with your hearers and they with you. Since you have constructed the speech, you are intimate with its ideas and with the way they are related to each other. You built the speech; therefore you should understand it fully. Consequently, the most practical aid to the re-creation of its ideas is to feel the force of the object that prompts the speech. That object is your audience and the feeling that you have business with it. To experience this feeling and to keep in touch visually with your hearers will do much to prompt you to react to ideas rather than to words merely, and will do much to secure the proper emphasis, loudness, and inflection.

Acquire the habit of speaking no passage until its meaning has a chance to hit your mind. This means, essentially, that you must learn to pause, for it is during the pause that the mind is most active in concentrating and preparing for what is to come. Unskillful readers almost invariably read too fast—so fast that they have little chance to react to ideas; both body and mind are wrapped up in mere utterance—in articulating sounds.

Silence in reading is golden. First, train your ear to recognize how much of the total speaking time is taken up by silence. A practical way of doing this is to try reading the first 125 words of your speech in no less than one minute. Although rate of utterance and pausing depend upon the speaker's personality, his material, and the size of his audience, 125 words for the opening minute will not be far wrong. In experimenting with the opening minute, be careful not to drag out individual sounds and words. Utter them with normal distinctness, as you would if you were talking. You will then notice that the total time needed for a given passage is influenced by the *number* of pauses and by the *length* of pauses.

Second, having made this observation, let the number of pauses be dictated by the ideas. Pause wherever the sense dictates a pause, wherever you would pause in speaking the same ideas in the same language in conversation. When you try this, you will realize that you pause oftener than punctuation dictates.

Third, not only pause often enough to appreciate ideas, but also pause long enough to give your mind a chance to get set for the next idea. Construct an idea before uttering it. Don't hurry ahead for the language; wait for its meaning to strike you and then utterance will reflect idea. Where ideas are closely related to each other and follow each other swiftly, pauses may be quite short—a second or less in duration; where a major thought sequence ends and another begins, as at the major divisions of a speech, pauses may be several seconds long. But whether the pause is short or long, the mind is getting set for the next idea.

As you work on the pause and try to subordinate language to sense, don't worry if at first you find yourself substituting new words and phrases for what you've written. Such substitution is in fact a reliable sign that you are reacting to ideas; you are thinking so well that other words naturally come to express the same idea. Brush up on precise phraseology late in rehearsal.

Make Prominent the Structure of the Speech

After your reading begins to sound and feel like live conversation, give special attention in a final rehearsal to the major ideas that reflect the pattern of the speech as a whole. Such ideas will be at least those passages that state or allude to the purpose of the speech, the central idea, and the main heads. These must be given emphasis. Do not, however, give them prominence by merely reading them louder, for this is likely to be mechanical and artificial. Rather, during the pauses preceding them, *realize that they are the most important* of all your ideas. Such realization should produce the proper emphasis as you speak them.

In brief, if one has a speech to read, not a general essay, and if one practices assiduously with ideas uppermost in mind, one can usually read very acceptably and often can appear to talk spontaneously. In any event, a speaker should *prepare* to read when he has to stick to a text. There is no excuse for stumbling awkwardly about, for reading like a race horse, or for dull, lifeless communication.

Material Not One's Own

Reading aloud from the printed page or from written, typewritten, or duplicated material not of one's own composing is essentially the same process, presents most of the same problems, and calls for much the same advice as reading from one's own manuscript. The standard of excellence and effectiveness is the same: speaking which approximates lively, direct, spontaneous communication. It reveals in the reader the two essential qualities of all good delivery: full realization of meaning at the moment of utterance and a keen sense of direct business with a listener. Furthermore it is achieved by adaptations of the same procedures which we have just discussed. We shall now discuss certain other considerations which may assist a reader.

Oral Effectiveness Depends in Part Upon the Kind of Material

We have remarked that a speech which is to be read aloud should not be an essay but should exhibit the important qualities of concreteness, specificness, vividness of illustration, and lucidity of structure which characterize good extemporaneous speaking.

Obviously whatever materials are to be read aloud will be capable of being read most effectively if they resemble good speeches. When the reader has a choice, therefore, he should select passages of that kind and should test them with the questions and considerations which we present on pages 159–160. Usually, however, the reader's choice, if not dictated by circumstances, is at least limited. He should try, therefore, to treat the passage for reading as if it were his own finished manuscript.

Master the Meaning and Structure

He should become as thoroughly master of its meanings, its structure, its purpose and implications, its mood, its vocabulary and sentence structure as if it were his own. This means preparation and rehearsal whenever remotely possible. No one reads well at sight material of any complexity of thought, vocabulary, or structure.

What we have said in the sections Concentrate on Meaning and Idea

Rather Than on Words and Make Prominent the Structure of the Speech applies as well to reading another's prose as your own. If you are going to concentrate on meaning you must know thoroughly what the meaning is, over all and sentence by sentence, and you must re-think that meaning as you speak. If you are going to emphasize the structure of a passage, obviously you must yourself, in advance, have a lively sense of what that structure is—in the passage as a whole, and sentence by sentence. Such knowledge of a passage of any length or complexity cannot be had in a quick glance-through or by letting one's eye wander ahead while one is reading aloud. It must come through advance preparation. One must answer for oneself clearly the following questions:

What did the author intend to convey to his reader? What do I intend to convey to my listener by reading this passage?

How are the ideas and information in the passage developed? How can I make that development available to my audience?

How would I speak these words and sentences to this audience if I had composed this passage in these words?

Gain Command of the Vocabulary

Since the vocabulary, the language, of a passage may very well not be the language you would normally use, you must give special care to mastering that language, both in meaning and in pronunciation, so that it becomes as easy for you as your own. All of us respond vaguely to many words which we do not understand well, and we all under-stand, and even write, words of whose pronunciation we are ignorant, uncertain, or misinformed. An essential phase of preparation for read-ing, therefore, is getting oral command of the vocabulary of the ma-terial one is to read. Do not minimize your own limitations. Look the word up and try it aloud until you pronounce it easily. The person who staggers drunkenly through proper names which he has had a chance to learn, or who turns *statistician* into a cough and sputter, cannot excuse his blunder with a vapid giggle and the remark "Oh, I never could p'nounce that word anyhow!"

Certain special complications in reading another's prose aloud arise also from the difference of convention between oral and written lan-guage—the one meant to be comprehensible to the ear, the other to the eye.

Punctuation and Reading Aloud

Punctuation is a guide for the eye, but at best it is an inadequate and unreliable set of signals for the voice. The principal function of punctuation is to assist a reader in a quite conventional fashion to grasp the structure of the written sentences. It serves the kind of function for the eye which stress, pause, inflection, and other manipulations of the voice serve for the ear. When a reader, therefore, has grasped the meaning and structure of a sentence, he no longer has need of the punctuation. He speaks the sentence to mean what he intends, quite independently of punctuation.

If one is ever placed in the situation where he must read absolutely at sight, where when he launches into a sentence he has no clear idea where he is coming out, he may have no choice but to govern his pauses and inflections by the punctuation. He may resort, perhaps, to the old convention of pausing momentarily at each comma, a little longer at a semicolon, and longest of all between a period and the next capital letter. He may try to exclaim at an exclamation point and inflect his voice upward at a question mark. These, however, will be uncertain expedients and no substitutes for full-realization-of-idea-at moment-of-utterance.

In the first place, current conventions do not demand punctuation at all pausing places. Often the relations among the words themselves are enough to make obvious the proper pausing places, and at other times commas are used to show structure where no pauses are either necessary or desirable. In the sentence, "The longer you live the wiser you grow," the structure is plain without a comma, though the writer may use one for good measure. On the other hand, pausing at the comma in the following sentence produces a very curious effect: "Ah, but eyes can only look; that is not observing." The journalistic convention of omitting the comma before the conjunction in a series illustrates especially well the unreliability of punctuation marks as signals for oral reading. "Tonight the policemen, firemen and other city employees hold a meeting." In the normal speaking of that sentence there is no more pause after *policemen* than after *firemen*. To put more pause there couples firemen and others as one unit set off against policemen. Unskilled and unwary readers sometime cause much confusion in radio news-reporting, for example, by reading series as we have indicated.

At best the person who reads-in the punctuation sounds dull and mechanical; at worst he is confusing and deceptive. The person who takes the trouble to use punctuation to help understand his text in advance and then goes ahead to think the text while speaking it will seldom go very far wrong, punctuation or no punctuation.

In actual practice, the central problem of reading aloud well, whether one's own or another's text, after one has mastered the meaning of the passage, may be suggested thus: To get back into the *reading* voice and speech those live variations in stress, pace, inflection which characterize *spontaneous* or *extemporaneous* speech. Our earlier suggestions for reading your own speech will help you get lifelikeness into the reading of passages not your own. Some additional suggestions and warnings may be helpful:

Recognize that the normal tendency is to read *too fast.* The words are there before you with nothing to hinder you from buzzing ahead as fast as you can. Besides, *you* know the meaning already; so almost any sound you make will seem clear to you. The listener is not so fortunate. You must take time to articulate clearly—especially the key words, the proper names, and the numerals. The context of a sentence will seldom reveal what an unclear name or number should be—in speaking or writing.

Recognize that written language is relatively uniform in appearance, aside from certain conventions such as capitalization, paragraphing, quotation marks, and occasional italics: in size of letters, spacing, style of letters, darkness or lightness of print. Good spoken language, however, is most various and un-uniform—in speed, in length or shortness of pause, in force on words and syllables, in movements of pitch. Don't let the uniformity of the written or printed language infect the spoken. For example, though almost all words *look* equally prominent, except for their length, only a very few words in any passage become prominent in a spoken passage. The tendency of readers to even out the stress among the words in a sentence is one of the most frequent sources of dullness, of deadness in oral reading.

"When we get to the river, we'll decide." In one meaning of that sentence, *two* words at most will be prominent: *river* and *decide*. Lifelike reading will emphasize those words and depress the others, not to a blur but to barely articulated speech. In general the words which will be prominent are those which carry new ideas and those which carry the elements of a contrast. Most other words will be dropped into the background through absence of emphasis. These words are of three general sorts: (1) *echoes*, words repeating, or echoing, ideas recently spoken; (2) *implications*, words whose meaning is taken as obvious and implicit in the language; and (3) *form* or *filler* words, those words demanded by the structure of the language but carrying little significance in themselves. Emphasizing either of the first two kinds gives a false or confusing meaning to a sentence; emphasizing the form or filler words distorts or clutters meaning. All through the previous sentences, for example, we have been speaking of words. In presenting these sentences orally, giving prominence to the word *words*, therefore, after we have well begun the discussion, would constantly make a listener think that we meant something different or had lost our minds. "A man's mind is his most precious possession." The meaning of *man's* is implicit. If the word is given prominence, there seems to be a suggested contrast with some other mind, a woman's, for example; and a false meaning is injected into the sentence. Emphasis on the form words may be illustrated from the habits of the *and—*, *of—*, *in—*punchers. These readers have a sense that emphasis is needed—but they somehow use emphasis to obscure meaning rather than to reinforce it. "This proposal is *both* economical *and* practical." No doubt the reader's meaning can be gathered. How much better, however, to give prominence to the main ideas, "This proposal is both *economical* and *practical*."

These suggestions for reading aloud do by no means exhaust the useful instruction which may be offered for developing that valuable skill. Most colleges offer a course intended to develop students' ability in oral reading and in the oral interpretation of literature; and there are various good textbooks on the subject, including those listed at the end of this chapter. We recommend both the courses and the textbooks.

In summary, the following suggestions and warnings will guide the speaker who would achieve good public reading aloud of practical prose:

1. He will prepare or will choose selections adapted to ear-comprehension —speeches, not essays.
2. He will eliminate from his manuscript or his text all sources of distraction.
3. He will become thoroughly familiar with the thought and language of his text.
4. He will practice aloud, learning to manage his manuscript or book gracefully, and to look at his hearers while he is speaking.
5. He will concentrate on meaning and idea rather than on words.
6. He will make prominent the structure of the passage.
7. He will learn to use punctuation as keys to structure rather than as signals for manipulation of voice.
8. He will curb a tendency to read too fast and will avoid the flat, uniform dullness, by stimulating in himself (1) a reconstruction of

the active thought of the passage while he is reading it, and (2) a lively sense of communication with his listeners.

Use of the Microphone

So widespread in these times is the use of public address systems—of electronic amplification in any and all sorts of places where speaking is done, from large convention halls to street corners and conference rooms—that a microphone now seems to be a normal accessory to any public rostrum. Because the microphone is perhaps most often associated with speaking from manuscript, some brief advice on using it seems appropriate here.

Under present-day circumstances, obviously a young speaker ought to learn to use the microphone and to accept it as a normal part of his equipment. For the most part, whether he be speaking on radio or television or be merely using the microphone on the platform or on the table in front of him, the speaker will succeed best if he accepts the instrument as a normal aid to his ordinary speaking, requiring little special attention from him.

A speaker on radio or television will be wise to seek and to accept the directions of the experienced studio people. Hence we shall not attempt to advise him in particular. To the novice, the many distractions of clock, control signals, camera, lights, operators, microphones, and manuscripts will be least bothersome, even at first, if he devotes himself wholeheartedly to his message, if he maintains a full realization of idea at moment of utterance and a lively sense of communication with an audience. He should speak in a moderate, room-sized voice and generally should avoid sudden and great changes in loudness, for which the control men will find it difficult to compensate.

The speaker using the microphone of a public address system also, of course, should occupy himself first and foremost with his audience and his message. He should accept the microphone as a normal piece of furniture and should not let his attention become focussed upon it. He should speak always to his audience, not to the microphone; but he should stay near enough to the microphone (a foot or two) so that it can overhear him easily and the amplifier can assist him as it should.

The function of a public address system is to make an ordinary voice easily audible over distances and under circumstances of competition with other sounds where it would not ordinarily be so. Hence the sensible speaker will give the equipment a chance to do the work, and will then let it do the work. He will speak firmly, without straining or shouting on the one hand or crooning softly on the other, and he will let the instrument make him loud enough for the room.

Some kinds of persons who fancy themselves as men of action and power on the platform make a point of avoiding the assistance of amplification. Either they demand that "that thing" be turned off, or they step out of range of the microphone with the remark, "I'm sure I can make you hear me without that." As if there were some special virtue in the mere expenditure of energy! Of course, an audience does not like to see a speaker hug a microphone as if it were a broom handle; but he had better do even that—and be heard easily—than tantalize and frustrate his audience.

Let the speaker, then, be prepared to use the microphone and loud speaker without apology and without special behavior. In summary our advice is this:

1. Stand or move about normally within close range of the microphone.
2. Keep attention (and eyes) on the audience, not on the microphone.
3. Speak clearly in a firm, normal voice; don't shout or murmur—*let the equipment do the work.*

SELECTIONS FOR PRACTICE IN READING ALOUD

With the following passages the student may practice the basic skills of reading aloud material not of his own composition. He should practice, of course, upon written versions of his own speeches also. His object will be to become proficient (1) in the unobtrusive handling of manuscript or book, (2) in keeping good eye-contact with his audience and a lively sense of communication, (3) in maintaining a full realization of meaning at the moment of utterance, and (4) in responding to meaning with appropriate bodily movement—all while referring to the printed or written page for his language.

The verses from the comic operas of Gilbert and Sullivan provide amusing material with which to develop accuracy, distinctness, and agility of articulation. The student should practice them with increasing speed as he learns to articulate more easily and sharply. At all times, however, he should strive for liveliness and for *intelligible* fullness of meaning. He should not be content to drop into a rapid, singsong monotone. Meaning must dominate even when, as in selection No. 3, the meaning is entertaining nonsense.

The prose selections represent various kinds of discourse appropriate for oral presentation. Similar materials may be found in the Speeches for Study and Practice in the Appendix.

1. From *H.M.S. Pinafore*

When I was a lad I served a term
As office boy to an Attorney's firm.
I cleaned the windows and I swept the floor,
And I polished up the handle of the big front door.
    I polished up that handle so carefullee
    That now I am the Ruler of the Queen's Navee!

As office boy I made such a mark
That they gave me the post of a junior clerk.
I served the writs with a smile so bland,
And I copied all the letters in a big round hand—
    I copied all the letters in a hand so free,
    That now I am the Ruler of the Queen's Navee!

I grew so rich that I was sent
By a pocket borough into Parliament.
I always voted at my party's call,
And I never thought of thinking for myself at all.
    I thought so little, they rewarded me
    By making me the Ruler of the Queen's Navee!

Now landsmen all, whoever you may be,
If you want to rise to the top of the tree,
If your soul isn't fettered to an office stool,
Be careful to be guided by this golden rule—
    Stick close to your desks and never go to sea,
    And you all may be Rulers of the Queen's Navee!

W. S. GILBERT

2. From *Pirates of Penzance*

I am the very model of a modern major general,
I've information vegetable, animal, and mineral,
I know the kings of England, and I quote the fights historical,
From Marathon to Waterloo, in order categorical;
I'm very well acquainted too with matters mathematical,
I understand equations, both the simple and quadratical,
About binomial theorem I'm teeming with a lot o' news,
With many cheerful facts about the square of the hypotenuse.
I'm very good at integral and differential calculus,
I know the scientific names of beings animalculous;
In short, in matters vegetable, animal, and mineral
I am the very model of a modern major-general.

W. S. GILBERT

3. From *The Sorcerer*

Oh! my name is John Wellington Wells,
I'm a dealer in magic and spells,
　　In blessings and curses
　　And ever-filled purses,
In prophecies, witches, and knells.

If you want a proud foe to "make tracks"—
If you'd melt a rich uncle in wax—
　　You've but to look in
　　On our resident Djinn,
Number seventy, Simmery Axe!

We've a first-class assortment of magic;
　　And for raising a posthumous shade
With effects that are comic or tragic,
　　There's no cheaper house in the trade.
Love-philtre—we've quantities of it;
　　And for knowledge if any one burns,
We keep an extremely small prophet, a prophet
　　Who brings us unbounded returns.

For he can prophesy
With a wink *of* his eye,
Peep with security
Into futurity,
Sum up your history,
Clear up a mystery,
Humour proclivity
For a nativity—for a nativity;
With mirrors so magical,
Tetrapods tragical,
Bogies spectacular,
Answers oracular,
Facts astronomical,
Solemn or comical,
And, if you want it, he
Makes a reduction on taking a quantity!
　　　　　Oh!

If any one anything lacks,
He'll find it all ready in stacks,
　　If he'll only look in
　　On the resident Djinn,
Number seventy, Simmery Axe!

He can raise you hosts of ghosts,
　　And that without reflectors;
And creepy things with wings,
　　And gaunt and grisly spectres.

He can fill you crowds of shrouds,
   And horrify you vastly;
He can rack your brains with chains,
   And gibberings grim and ghastly!

(Repeat first two stanzas.)

W. S. GILBERT

4. From *The Gondoliers*

There lived a King, as I've been told,
In the wonder-working days of old,
When hearts were twice as good as gold,
   And twenty times as mellow.
Good-temper triumphed in his face,
And in his heart he found a place
For all the erring human race
   And every wretched fellow.

When he had Rhenish wine to drink
It made him very sad to think
That some, at junket or at jink,
   Must be content with toddy.

He wished all men as rich as he
(And he was rich as rich could be),
So to the top of every tree
   Promoted everybody.

Lord Chancellors were cheap as sprats,
And Bishops in their shovel hats
Were plentiful as tabby cats—
   In point of fact, too many.
Ambassadors cropped up like hay,
Prime Ministers and such as they
Grew like asparagus in May,
   And Dukes were three a penny.
On every side Field-Marshals gleamed,
Small beer were Lords-Lieutenant deemed,
With Admirals the ocean teemed
   All round his wide dominions.

And Party Leaders you might meet
In twos and threes in every street
Maintaining, with no little heat,
   Their various opinions.
That King although no one denies
His heart was of abnormal size,
Yet he'd have acted otherwise
   If he had been acuter.
The end is easily foretold,

When every blessed thing you hold
Is made of silver, or of gold,
   You long for simple pewter.
When you have nothing else to wear
But cloth of gold and satins rare,
For cloth of gold you cease to care—
   Up goes the price of shoddy.

In short, whoever you may be,
To this conclusion you'll agree,
When every one is somebodee,
   Then no one's anybody!

W. S. GILBERT

5. How to Read [1]

The process of making monotonous black characters on the page vividly stir the latent sense-perceptions is . . . relatively slow and irksome. Few people have ever learned to do it consistently; and hence it is fair to say, few have ever truly learned to read. The moral is, read slowly. Take ample time. Pause where the punctuation bids one pause; note each and every comma; wait a moment between a period and the next capital letter. And pause when common sense bids you pause, that is, when you have not understood. As the line of sentences comes filing before the window of your soul, examine each individual expression with the animus, and more than the animus, you would maintain were you paying-teller in a bank; saying to yourself continually, "Do I know this word?" and, "What is this phrase worth?" . . .

Read aloud; read slowly; read suspiciously. Re-read. What a busy man has time to read at all, he has time to read more than once. . . . The most industrious student forgets a large part of what he tries to retain. The best-read man is the one who has oftenest read the best things.

LANE COOPER

6. A Liberal Education

Suppose it were perfectly certain that the life and fortune of every one of us would, one day or other, depend upon his winning or losing a game of chess. Don't you think we should all consider it a primary duty to learn at least the names and the moves of the pieces; to have a notion of a gambit, and a keen eye for all the means of giving and getting out of a check? Do you not think we should look with a disapprobation amounting to scorn, upon a father who allowed his son, or the state which allowed its members, to grow up without knowing a pawn from a knight?

Yet it is a very plain and elementary truth, that the life, that the fortune, and the happiness of every one of us, and more or less, of those who are connected with us, do depend upon our knowing something of the rules of a game infinitely more difficult and complicated than chess. It is a game

[1] From Lane Cooper's *Two Views of Education* (New Haven, 1922), pp. 117–118.

which had been played for untold ages, every man and woman of us being one of the two players in a game of his or her own. The chess-board is the world, the pieces are the phenomena of the universe, the rules of the game are what we call the laws of Nature. The player on the other side is hidden from us. We know that his play is always fair, just, and patient. But also we know, to our cost, that he never overlooks a mistake, or makes the smallest allowance for ignorance. To the man who plays well, the highest stakes are paid, with that sort of overflowing generosity with which the strong shows delight in strength. And one who plays ill is checkmated—without haste, but without remorse.

Well, what I mean by a liberal Education is learning the rules of this mighty game. In other words, education is the instruction of the intellect in the laws of Nature, under which name I include not merely things and their forces, but men and their ways; and the fashioning of the affections and of the will into an earnest and loving desire to move in harmony with those laws.. A man so educated, and no other, I conceive, has had a liberal Education, for he is, as completely as a man can be, in harmony with Nature.

Adapted from THOMAS HUXLEY

7. The Four Freedoms [2]

In the future days, which we seek to make secure, we look forward to a world founded upon four essential human freedoms.

The first is freedom of speech and expression everywhere in the world.

The second is freedom of every person to worship God in his own way everywhere in the world.

The third is freedom from want, which, translated into world terms, means economic understandings which will secure to every nation a healthy peacetime life for its inhabitants everywhere in the world.

The fourth is freedom from fear—which, translated into world terms, means a world-wide reduction of armaments to such a point and in such a thorough fashion that no nation will be in a position to commit an act of physical aggression against any neighbor—anywhere in the world.

That is no vision of a distant millennium. It is a definite basis for a kind of world attainable in our own time and generation. That kind of world is the very antithesis of the so-called new order of tyranny which the dictators seek to create with the crash of a bomb.

To that new order we oppose the greater conception—the moral order. A good society is able to face schemes of world domination and foreign revolutions alike without fear.

Since the beginning of our American history we have been engaged in change—in a perpetual peaceful revolution—a revolution which goes on steadily, quietly adjusting itself to changing conditions—without the concentration camp or the quicklime in the ditch. The world order which we seek is the cooperation of free countries, working together in a friendly, civilized society.

This Nation has placed its destiny in the hands and heads and hearts of its millions of free men and women; and its faith in freedom under the guidance of God. Freedom means the supremacy of human rights every-

[2] Excerpt from an address before a Joint Session of the Houses of Congress, January 6, 1941.

where. Our support goes to those who struggle to gain those rights or keep them. Our strength is in our unity of purpose.

To that high concept there can be no end save victory.

FRANKLIN D. ROOSEVELT

8. The Prodigal Son

And he said, A certain man had two sons: And the younger of them said to his father, Father, give me the portion of goods that falleth to me. And he divided unto them his living. And not many days after the younger son gathered all together, and took his journey into a far country, and there wasted his substance with riotous living.

And when he had spent all, there arose a mighty famine in that land; and he began to be in want. And he went and joined himself to a citizen of that country; and he sent him into his fields to feed swine. And he would fain have filled his belly with the husks that the swine did eat: and no man gave unto him. And when he came to himself, he said, How many hired servants of my father's have bread enough and to spare, and I perish with hunger! I will arise and go to my father, and will say unto him, Father, I have sinned against heaven, and before thee. And am no more worthy to be called thy son: make me as one of thy hired servants. And he arose, and came to his father.

But when he was yet a great way off, his father saw him, and had compassion, and ran, and fell on his neck, and kissed him. And the son said unto him, Father, I have sinned against heaven, and in thy sight, and am no more worthy to be called thy son. But the father said to his servants, Bring forth the best robe, and put it on him; and put a ring on his hand, and shoes on his feet: And bring hither the fatted calf, and kill it; and let us eat, and be merry: For this my son was dead, and is alive again; he was lost, and is found. And they began to be merry.

Now his elder son was in the field: and as he came and drew nigh to the house, he heard music and dancing. And he called one of the servants, and asked what these things meant. And he said unto him, Thy brother is come; and thy father hath killed the fatted calf, because he hath received him safe and sound. And he was angry, and would not go in: therefore came his father out, and intreated him. And he answering said to his father, Lo, these many years do I serve thee, neither transgressed I at any time thy commandment: and yet thou never gavest me a kid, that I might make merry with my friends: But as soon as this thy son was come, which hath devoured thy living with harlots, thou hast killed for him the fatted calf. And he said unto him, Son, thou art ever with me, and all that I have is thine. It was meet that we should make merry, and be glad: for this thy brother was dead, and is alive again; and was lost, and is found.

THE BIBLE, Luke 15: 11–32.

9. From Lincoln's Second Inaugural Address

Neither party expected for the war, the magnitude, or the duration, which it has already attained. Neither anticipated that the *cause* of the conflict might cease with, or even before, the conflict itself should cease. Each looked for an easier triumph, and a result less fundamental and astounding. Both read the same Bible, and pray to the same God; and each invokes His aid against the other. It may seem strange that any men should dare to ask a just God's assistance in wringing their bread from the sweat of other men's faces; but let us judge not that we be not judged. The prayers of both could not be answered; that of neither has been answered fully. The Almighty has His own purposes. "Woe unto the world because of offences! for it must needs be that offences come; but woe to that man by whom the offence cometh!" If we shall suppose that American slavery is one of those offences which, in the providence of God, must needs come, but which, having continued through His appointed time, He now wills to remove, and that He gives to both North and South, this terrible war, as the woe due to those by whom the offence came, shall we discern therein any departure from those divine attributes which the believers in a living God always ascribe to Him? Fondly do we hope—fervently do we pray—that this mighty scourge of war may speedily pass away. Yet, if God wills that it continue, until all the wealth piled by the bondman's two hundred and fifty years of unrequited toil shall be sunk, and until every drop of blood drawn with the lash, shall be paid by another drawn with the sword, as was said three thousand years ago, so still it must be said "the judgments of the Lord, are true and righteous altogether."

With malice toward none; with charity for all; with firmness in the right, as God gives us to see the right, let us strive on to finish the work we are in; to bind up the nation's wounds; to care for him who shall have borne the battle, and for his widow, and his orphan—to do all which may achieve and cherish a just and lasting peace, among ourselves, and with all nations.

10. The Educated Citizen [3]

You who have spent four years on this campus know better than most people that your greatest satisfactions, your greatest rewards, resulted from the free interplay of ideas. You know that your most penetrating insights resulted from the exchange and the interchange and clash of ideas. And I would remind you that just as a great university cannot operate in any but an atmosphere of intellectual freedom, neither can a great government. It is the function of the democratic form of government to nurture freedom. No less does the democratic form of government require freedom as the condition in which it can function at all.

I would suggest, then, that it is the duty of an educated man in America today to work actively to put good men into public office—and to defend them there against abuse and the ugly inclination we as human beings have to believe the worst. I would suggest that it is not enough merely to vote but that we, all of us, have the further obligation to think, and to maintain steadfastly the rights of all men to think freely. It is always true that when the citizens of a democracy become apathetic, a power vacuum is created, and corrupt men, or incompetents or worse, rush in to fill it. But today our situation is even more dangerous than that. In ordinary times the corrupt or the incompetent can be suffered for a while and then ejected. But these are no ordinary times. The world's fate now hangs upon how well or how ill we in America conduct our affairs. And if a bad man is elected trustee of a sanitary

[3] From *What I Think* (New York, 1956), pp. 176–177. Reprinted by permission of Harper & Brothers. Copyright © by R. Keith Kane.

district, or if an able man in Washington is left to shift for himself in the face of unjustified attack, then our government is diminished by that much —and even more because others will lose heart from his example. So you as educated, privileged people have a broad responsibility to protect and improve what you have inherited and what you would die to preserve—the concept of government by consent of the governed as the only tolerable way of life.

We in our country have, indeed, placed all of our faith, we have placed all of our hopes, upon the education, the intelligence, and the understanding of our people. We have said that ours is a government conducted by its citizens, and from this it follows that the government will be better conducted if its citizens are educated. It's as simple as that. We believe that the people will find their way to the right solutions, given sufficient information. We believe with Lincoln, "Why should there not be a patient confidence in the ultimate justice of the people?" (although I must confess to having entertained certain private, fleeting doubts upon occasion). We have bet all our chips, if you please, on the intellectual improvement of our people. This is a magnificent gamble—but it is a gamble, for it raises the question whether we have reached the awesome pinnacle of world power we now occupy too soon, before we have sufficiently elevated our national mind to lead the world wisely. Only the educated man entertains doubts, and doubt is the beginning of wisdom; but doubt is not wisdom's fulfillment, and in a time of crisis the man who doubts may fall prey to the strong dumb brute— to the man on horseback.

Adlai Stevenson

FURTHER READING

Grimes, Wilma, and Alethea Smith Mattingly, *Interpretation: Writer, Reader, Audience* (San Francisco, 1961).

Lee, Charlotte, *Oral Interpretation* (New York, 1952).

Parrish, W. M., *Reading Aloud*, 3rd ed. (New York, 1953).

Woolbert, Charles H., and Severina E. Nelson, *The Art of Interpretative Speech* (New York, 1956).

CHAPTER TEN

Voice and Pronunciation

THE DEMANDS OF ORAL COMMUNICATION

By far the larger part of verbal communication is for the purpose of reporting events, explaining and teaching, transmitting information and instructions, and persuading. Hence the first necessities of such communication are clarity and exactness. When the communication is oral, as it is in public speaking, it should be accomplished with quick and easy intelligibility of utterance. Clear, informative, instantly understandable utterance, therefore, is highly desirable for anyone who would address others, formally or informally.

The reasons for the high degree of clarity and lucidity necessary in speaking, even above that needed in writing, are not far to seek. If the listener does not understand at once the sense of something he hears, he cannot take time to go back over it, mull it over in his mind, and puzzle it out. If he doesn't know at once the meaning of a word he hears spoken, he cannot stop the speaker in order to go off somewhere to look up the word or to confer with a friend about it. He either lets it go, and its meaning along with it, or he takes time out to puzzle over it. In the latter situation, even if he finally decides what the word means, by the time he turns his attention back to the speaker, he has missed some of what followed the puzzling word. Likewise, if a word or passage is inaudible or indistinctly spoken, the listener is likely to miss it or what follows it. Furthermore, he does not have time to go back over sentences which have bothered or distracted him, except at the cost of losing track of what follows. Neither can the listener slow down a speaker (usually) to the speed of the listener's comprehension. It is sometimes possible in oral communication of the conversational sort, whether face to face or over the telephone or the two-way radio, to get a speaker to repeat something or to say it another way. Still, there is a loss of valuable time, often at those moments when time is precious. Hence we can lay it down as a rule that, under most conditions, *unless a listener understands a speaker at once, he will never understand at all.* Furthermore, it must follow that *when the listener doesn't understand the words and sentences uttered, or gets a wrong impres-*

sion from tone or quality of voice, it is probably the speaker's fault.

Nevertheless, voice and pronunciation as the carriers of spoken language can receive but scanty treatment in a course or book devoted to public speaking. The improvement of voice and diction must rest upon extensive special knowledge of the speech and hearing mechanism, of the anatomy and physiology of breathing, of voice production, and of hearing. Such knowledge can barely be presented in a special course, to say nothing of one dealing with the processes of speechmaking. Voice training, when undertaken to improve the vocal qualities of speech, requires much time and concentrated practice. The labor is long even for the person with a normal voice. It is even longer for a person whose voice shows certain abnormalities which require the skill of corrective specialists. The improvement of articulation and pronunciation, when desirable and necessary, also is time consuming. A knowledge of phonetics and the behavior of speech sounds underlies intelligent and permanent improvement, not to mention the hours of persistent practice. The student in his first course in speechmaking finds little protracted time for such knowledge and practice. Nevertheless, if his speech shows serious defects, he must find the time to correct them, either in a special course or under the guidance of special teachers. This he should do, not merely to become a better speechmaker, but to improve his everyday speech.

Although his speech habits may be acceptable for everyday conversation, the student speechmaker can almost always teach himself to use his equipment better than he does. He can speak loud enough to be heard easily, and he can speak distinctly. He can often improve vocal quality, and sometimes he can secure greater flexibility and variety of vocal sound. In working for such gains, he must realize that the guides for improvement must be in harmony with the natural behavior of the vocal mechanism. To work with Nature is better sense than to work against her; to work against her sometimes does damage to the voice. In this chapter we shall describe briefly the mechanism of voice and offer some suggestions for improving voice and articulation.

THE SOURCE OF VOICE

Sound is produced by a vibrating body which sets into motion air waves which strike the ear and are "interpreted" by the brain. The vibrating material may be air itself, as in the organ pipe; or it may be strings, as in the piano and the violin; or it may be a reed, as in the clarinet; or it may be flesh, such as the lips of the mouth (as in cornet playing) and the vocal lips or bands of the larynx. Obviously, a vibrating body cannot set itself into motion; it must be struck, plucked, or agitated by some means. So it is with the vocal bands. They are set into vibration by breath under pressure. The amount of pressure varies from soft tones to loud tones, and from low-pitched sounds to high-pitched sounds. For most speakers, improved control over the breath is needed in order to secure adequate loudness.

ANATOMY OF BREATHING

The vocal bands are set in a group of cartilages, of which the most evident is the wedge-shaped thyroid cartilage at the front of the neck, which is popularly called the Adam's apple. This group of cartilages, known as the larynx, stands on top of the windpipe which connects the larynx with the lungs. Located in the upper region of the chest, the lungs, so far as voice production is concerned, are an intricate system of interconnecting air sacs. Although they are elastic and will spring back into shape after being compressed, much as a squeezed sponge does, they cannot compress themselves. There are no muscles in them, and no muscles are attached to them. Hence control over breathing has nothing to do with control over the lungs. Control, as we shall see, is secured elsewhere.

Just below the lungs is the diaphragm, partly muscular, partly cartilaginous, a dome-shaped partition which separates the lungs and heart above from the abdominal organs below. Surrounding the lungs in the walls of the chest are the ribs, which are equipped with muscles which raise and lower them. Surrounding the viscera are the muscles of the abdominal walls. These three sets of muscles—the *diaphragm,* the *rib muscles,* and the *abdominal muscles*—work in conjunction to press upon the lungs and to provide air pressure against the vocal bands. To see in brief how these provide pressure is to understand the few principles that underlie the control of the breath stream.

THE BREATHING CYCLE

When one inhales and then expels breath, these events occur: (1) The diaphragm muscles contract and thus flatten out the diaphragm's dome. This creates a partial vacuum in the region above the diaphragm. The rib-raising muscles may also contract—especially in deep breathing, such as is needed in violent exercise—and the consequent rise of the ribs also helps to create a vacuum. In response to lowered air pressure in the lung region, air rushes in from the outside through the nose, mouth, and windpipe, and inflates the lungs. This entire process constitutes *inhalation.* (2) The pulling-down of the diaphragm causes a squeezing of the organs below and this in turn causes the abdominal muscles to distend. Most of the distention takes place in the region at the front of the body, between the belt line and the inverted V formed by the ribs. (Place your hand or a book on this region and observe the *outward* movement during inhalation.) (3) The diaphragm muscles relax; the ribs lower, permitting the chest walls to press against the lungs; and the abdominal muscles push the viscera up against the diaphragm and thus bring pressure from below against the lungs. With the squeezing of the lungs, air is expelled. In this manner, *exhalation* is accomplished.

VOCAL SOUND

When the vocal bands come together and the air stream from below is forced between them, the bands vibrate and sound waves are produced. The waves move up the throat passage, most of them emerging from the mouth but some going out through the nasal passages. These sound waves, set up by the vocal bands, are reinforced by a combination of resonators, some of which—notably the bony structure of the upper chest and of the head—act as sounding boards, and others—principally the throat passage, the mouth cavity, and the nasal passages—act as air-column resonators.

The sound made thus has all the characteristics of any sound: *pitch, loudness,* and *timbre* (or quality). Some notion of what these characteristics involve may be gained from the table below. Observe especially that sound may be understood in two aspects: its *physical* properties (behavior of the vibrating body and waves), and its *psychological* properties (interpretation of the sound waves by ear and brain).

	As Physical Phenomena	As Psychological Phenomena
Pitch	Frequency or rate of vibration of vocal bands.	Interpreted on a scale from *low* to *high*.
Loudness	Intensity. Relation between amount or distance traveled by vibrating bands and frequency of vibration. *Amplitude* is the distance that a wave impulse oscillates.	Interpreted on a scale from *soft* to *loud*.
Timbre	Relation between the native character of the vocal bands, the degree of complexity of vibration, and action of the resonators. The complexity of a wave's form.	Interpreted as what makes a voice recognizable and distinctive, and pleasant or unpleasant.

The public speaker is interested in his voice for two fundamental reasons: (1) He wishes to avoid those voice qualities that distract his hearers' attention from what he is saying—such qualities as harshness, shrillness, nasality, hoarseness, sameness of pitch, and sameness of loudness. All these invite attention to themselves. Many of these distracting qualities constitute special, individual problems, and in most cases where they are present, a speaker would do well to secure special counsel from his instructor or from an expert on voice. (2) The speaker desires to make his vocal instrument as flexible and as responsive to meanings as is possible. He should realize that the *sound* he makes, quite apart from what he says verbally, carries meanings and may command or discourage attention. The more change and variety and color the sound has, therefore, the easier it holds attention and compels interest. In securing *maximum* flexibility of his voice, the speaker should undertake *intensive* training and exercise, a program too specialized to present in this book. Nevertheless, he can appreciably and rapidly help himself by applying the following suggestions.

Breath Control and Loudness

To increase loudness, when needed, one applies extra pressure against the lungs. He does a little more of what comes naturally. First he makes certain that he knows what his abdominal muscles and chest are doing during exhalation. Some persons will discover that the main movement is in the chest region, others in the abdominal region. Still others will find that chest and abdomen move simultaneously. But whatever one's habit, one should follow it. Second, during exhalation one applies a little additional muscular pressure in the same direction. The result is to increase air pressure against the vocal bands. They travel a greater distance, thus sending "stronger" sound waves to the listener's ear. The sound heard is louder than it would be if no additional pressure had been applied. The process is easy, yet the speaker who needs to talk louder must establish conscious control over the process until it becomes habitual.

Increased loudness for the speaker also entails more air and somewhat deeper breathing than he uses in ordinary conversation. So in *inhalation* he takes in somewhat more air than he needs otherwise. Yet at the same time he must not take in too much air, nor gulp it in suddenly with an obvious heave. Deep inhalation often causes a quick release of excessive air, producing a burst of loudness inappropriate to meaning. The effect is like a quick sigh. When repeated over and over, this process produces a downhill loudness pattern, ranging from too loud to not loud enough. When one gulps a large amount of air, he feels compelled to get rid of most of it instantly. Gulping, too, often gives a breathy quality to the voice.

When one increases loudness, he breathes oftener than ordinary conversation requires. The rule is to breathe as frequently as one needs to, using enough breath to increase loudness, but no more. To get the knack of speaking louder, some students will need a brief coaching session with a teacher.

Improvement of Voice Quality

The speaker who sets out to improve voice quality must *give the throat and mouth maximum opportunity to function as resonators.* This is by far the most important single endeavor.

The procedure is to *relax* the muscles of the jaw, neck, and upper torso until one feels lazy and easy. Stiffness, tautness, and tension must be removed, because tension in the muscles of the neck often gives a pinched, shrill, or harsh quality to tone. Some muscles are attached to the larynx; others rest against it. When these muscles are taut, they pinch the voice box unduly, and through a kind of sympathetic action the vocal muscles of the larynx; and the deep, constrictor muscles that constitute the inner walls of the lower "throat" also become tense and rigid. Furthermore, taut jaw muscles frequently cause a muffled or a harsh quality in the voice, because they won't let the jaw drop enough to allow tone to come out of the mouth freely. The "open" throat is absolutely essential to good voice production.

Even if a speaker's voice has no distracting qualities, it can become better if the throat and mouth resonators are open and free. This will be at once evident when one realizes that the action of these resonators to a considerable degree influences three components of vocal sound: the pitch we hear, the loudness, and the quality or timbre. First, although the changes of pitch in the voice are in part due to the adjustments of the muscles of the larynx—adjustments which determine the tension, thickness, and length of the vibrating bands—the pitch we hear is also due to the voice resonators, for these resonators strengthen some vibrations and damp out others. If the throat, mouth, and nasal passages are free to respond instantly and fully to a wide range of pitches, the key, the inflection, and the melody of the voice will be made the most of. Second, although loudness is partly the result of breath pressure exerted against the vocal bands, it is also influenced by the resonators which increase the intensity of vocal sound as does a box resonator upon which a vibrating tuning fork is placed. Finally, although the quality of voice depends in part upon the texture and the complexity of vibration of the vocal bands, voice quality also depends upon the action of the resonators. Their action reinforces some parts of the complex pattern of vibrations and damps out others. It should be clear, therefore, that the human resonators play an essential role in determining the kind of vocal sound we hear. To improve voice in any of its aspects—pitch, loudness, or quality—give the resonators a chance to function freely and efficiently. Avoid undue throat and jaw tensions; *relax.*

Improvement of Vocal Variety

In their delivery, most speakers are capable of greater vocal variety than they exhibit; that is, they are capable of greater inflection (changes in pitch) and greater changes in loudness and rate of utterance. In their private conversations, especially in moments of excitement and keen interest, their voices show all the range that is natural to them. The endeavor, then, is to secure the same range in formal delivery. The fundamental condition, of course, is to be as concerned and interested in talking to an audience as one is in his best conversation. Some persons, however, do not experience their full vocal range on the platform because they do not *associate* it with speechmaking. What is needed is to establish the association, to hear and feel what their voices can do in a speech.

One method of working is through deliberate exaggeration of vocal quality during the rehearsal period. After you have your speech running along fairly smoothly, try shouting what you regard as the most important ideas. You will then feel and hear what great changes of loudness you yourself can command. Try saying the principal ideas with deliberate slowness and racing through a detailed illustration. Again, you will be aware of what great change of pace you are capable of. Finally, try saying your principal ideas first on a fairly high pitch-level, then on a very low one. Thus you can experience what your voice *can* do in a speech.

In employing exaggeration, remember that its chief purpose is to give you the *sensations* of vocal change and to associate the sensations with the presentation of the speech. But although exaggeration may be useful during practice, mechanical manipulation of the voice has no place on the platform. Monotony may be better than artificiality. When you face your hearers, speak as directly and as genuinely as you can. Your primary business is to relive ideas; you haven't time to coach yourself with reminders: "I must speak louder here"; "This must go slower"; "This requires a high pitch, this a low pitch." If you have practiced intelligently and diligently, the results of your practice will be revealed automatically. Trust your mind and voice to respond correctly.

Mental Activity and Vocal Variety

The public speaker who is in search of variety of voice and who does
not need special voice training to overcome monotony must never
overlook the intimate relationship between mind and voice. The more
sharp, vivid, and intense mental action is, the greater and surer is the
vocal response and the greater are changes of pitch, of loudness, and
of rate of utterance. In short, a speaker can train himself to react sharply
and fully to the communicative situation and to what he is saying as he
says it; he can strive to achieve a *full* realization of meaning at the
moment of utterance and a *keen sense* of communication with his
hearers. His voice will respond accordingly.

Natural Key

Both in delivery and in working on voice, one must keep to his own
natural pitch-level, or key. This is the pitch that is heard most often—
the dominant pitch—which is appropriate and peculiar to one's vocal
mechanism. Determined by heredity and the laws of physical growth,
the vocal bands and resonators produce sounds which are *naturally*
appropriate to them. A bass voice, for example, is by nature bass and
not tenor. For most persons, their habitual pitch-level is their natural
pitch-level, but a few persons may through habit speak in a key that
is higher or lower than their natural key, a practice which should be
avoided.

In any speaking situation, one's natural key should prevail. An unnaturally high pitch may cause shrillness. Moreover, a high pitch
seriously limits the speaker's pitch range and thus restricts his opportunity of securing variety of inflection. A high pitch gives him little
range above it. On the other hand, a person's natural key provides for
considerable range above and below it. An unnaturally low pitch often
causes hoarseness, gutturalness, and harshness. It, too, limits a speaker's
vocal range, for there is little opportunity to go below it. Consequently,
tune your ear to your own conversation; note the dominant pitch-level
and use it on the platform. If you are relaxed just before you start
speaking and then begin with quiet directness, you'll probably hit
your natural key. Tenseness will usually shoot the pitch up.

One special caution is in order here. If the key is naturally high, do
not try to lower it; if it is naturally very low, do not try to raise it.
Few people can change their natural pitch-level without risking damage
to their voices. The system of muscles regulating pitch has been built
into us; it is determined by the laws of heredity and of physical growth.
Its physical character cannot be altered. All a speaker can do is to

strengthen and render more flexible his natural mechanism, to make the most of his potentialities.

PRONUNCIATION

The word *pronunciation* has two meanings for the student of speaking. Taken broadly, it refers to the whole action of producing speech sounds. In this broad sense, pronunciation includes *articulation*, a term referring to the *positions* of the tongue, teeth, lips, and soft palate in forming speech, especially consonant sounds, and to the distinctness and precision of utterance. In its narrower sense, pronunciation refers to the *correctness* of speech, whether the stress and accent of words are acceptable (*re' search* or *research'*), whether sounds have been improperly omitted (*jellm'n* for *gentlemen*), or substituted (*substantuate* for *substantiate*), or improperly added (*athaletic* for *athletic*).

Distinctness of Utterance

Public speech should be distinct enough to avoid confusing and distracting the hearers; utterance must facilitate, not obstruct, the ready perception of meanings. In judging whether he speaks with adequate precision, the speaker should be guided by three considerations.

In formal communication, first of all, the articulation of consonant sounds needs to be more careful and precise than in informal conversation. Although most people are intelligible enough in the normal leisurely conversation of their ordinary lives, they are not so adequately equipped for special circumstances: when they speak to an audience, when time is precious, and when confusion and misunderstanding cannot be tolerated. Hence, one who speaks in public should not assume that his everyday utterance is sufficiently clear and precise to meet the demands of the more exacting situation until he has proved that it is. He can learn whether articulation is adequate by enlisting the aid of a competent observer, such as his instructor, and by recording his speech and listening to it. Remember that your best friends won't tell you or are so accustomed to your speech that they don't notice imperfections.

Second, *sloppiness* or *slovenliness* is perhaps the chief fault of articulation. By this is meant what is often called lazy, blurred, or mushy speech. It is like bad, undecipherable handwriting or a private system of shorthand that can be understood only by the user. One common sign of sloppiness is a slighting and obscuring of consonant sounds in many-syllabled words and at the ends of words, especially the consonants *t* and *d*, *f* and *v*, *k* and *g*, *p* and *b*, particularly when these

consonants are followed by vowels. Examples are *bake* for *baked,*
wunnerful for *wonderful, definly* for *definitely, inresting* for *interesting,*
unnerstan for *understand, pain it* for *paint it, summarine* for *submarine,*
couldn' for *couldn't, wouldn'* for *wouldn't.* Even when slovenly speech
is sufficiently intelligible, it lowers the speaker's standing in the opinions
of many listeners, though they themselves may be guilty of the same
fault.

Another sign of slovenliness is the telescoping and cluttering of words
and sentences. Utterance is so rapid or incomplete that the speaker
seems to have a hot potato in his mouth. He says *gumn't* for *government,*
binnis for *business.* Both the telescoping of sounds and the obscuring
of consonants are almost invariably accompanied by the omission and
substitution of sounds. An example is *jiss gonna git* for *just going to get.*

On the other hand, utterance that is overdistinct is also unacceptable.
It is usually as distracting to the hearer as is sloppy speech, for it is
likely to strike him as pretty, fancy, elegant, and highbrow. Furthermore, many contractions, omissions, and elisions of the sounds of everyday speech have come to be accepted. A listener is tuned to them, and
when a speaker tries to get in every sound, spelling-book fashion, the
result is confusion. For example, *boy 'n girl* is more acceptable than
a carefully pronounced *boy and girl.*

In general, the speaker is a little more careful with his public utterance than with his informal conversation.

Correctness of Pronunciation

What constitutes correct pronunciation is often a difficult and much-
disputed matter—difficult, first, because every person has his pet opinions on the subject. Moreover, as a good democrat a person often holds
that his pronunciation is as good as anybody's. Possibly he is right,
for it may serve his purposes in the circle of his own friends and associates. Furthermore, those who study the behavior of speech sounds
—the phoneticians—do not always agree on whether a particular pronunciation of a word is correct. Some, for example, interested primarily
in the history of spoken language, will tolerate variant pronunciations
because they know that if a new pronunciation catches on and becomes
accepted through usage, it will be regarded as correct. And how is
one to judge whether a new pronunciation will catch on?

Since it is true that pronunciation has changed, is changing, and
will continue to change, how is one to judge whether his pronunciation
is correct? Most authorities face the fact of change and say that current,
cultivated or educated usage is the measuring stick for pronunciation.
A speaker would be wise to accept this standard, for if his pronunciation

reflects current usage, his manner of speech will not distract the attention of his listeners.

To help in deciding what current usage is, the public speaker may profit from a few suggestions. They are offered here solely with his needs in mind, and his needs are governed by at least two conditions. (1) Public speaking is as a rule more formal and more careful than informal and familiar conversation. (2) The public speaker is often addressing hearers, especially if he is on the air, who represent considerable variety of pronunciation, and his own pronunciation can scarcely reveal such variety.

Study the usage of the dialect region to which you belong through long association, and conform to its usage. Although there are hundreds of local dialects in the United States, there are three dialect regions: the territory east of the Hudson River, including some parts of New York City and Long Island (Eastern speech); the region south of the Ohio River and Mason-Dixon Line east of the Mississippi, and including Louisiana, the eastern portions of Arkansas, Oklahoma, and Texas (Southern speech); the rest of the United States (General American speech, spoken by three-fourths of all Americans). If you were born and brought up in one of these linguistic areas or lived in one of them during your formative years, you will reflect the pronunciation of your regional family.

If some of your pronunciations are peculiar to the narrow locality you have been reared in, listen to the speech of those in your community who are well educated and who have traveled about. Such people tend to reflect in their pronunciation the wider usage of the region, and they can be accepted as fair models. Listen also to the network radio and TV announcers and to the speech of movie actors who play straight rather than character parts. Such people use a slightly modified General American speech that is intelligible everywhere. But if you use Southern or Eastern speech, do not try to make it over to conform to General American, for only the expert who knows language behavior and who practices methodically over a long period of time can do a good job, free of inconsistencies which any person with a normally sharp ear will laugh at as affectation. Unless for some special purpose, such as making your career that of the actor or the announcer or commentator, it is unwise and unnecessary to copy a pronunciation foreign to the accepted usage of a large dialect region. (Even the large broadcasting systems today permit wider usage in pronunciation than they did a generation ago.) Broad, rather than provincial, differences in pronunciation are tolerated, and a listener easily adjusts to them.

Where two pronunciations of the same word occur with about the same frequency, either one is acceptable.

For words used infrequently, consult the pronunciation recommended by a good dictionary. For words in constant use, the dictionary is not always a reliable guide. First, as the dictionary makers themselves acknowledge, it takes from ten to fifteen years to get out a new edition, and although the makers do their best to record current usage, the accepted pronunciation of a word may have changed by the date of publication. Constant use modifies pronunciation fairly rapidly, as in the accent on *quintuplet,* which has shifted from the first to the second syllable in the last thirty years. On the other hand, a word used infrequently is subject to little change, and your dictionary usually can be relied on.

The pronunciations in some dictionaries must be followed cautiously, in the second place, because their makers have not always found it possible to indicate differences between the pronunciations of the same word in the major dialect regions. Most dictionaries reflect, for the most part, the usage of the General American area. A notable exception to this practice is John S. Kenyon and Thomas R. Knott, *A Pronouncing Dictionary of American English* (Springfield, Mass., G.&C. Merriam Co., 1944). This work records the pronunciations of words as they are used in ordinary conversation in each of the three dialect regions.

As for place names, note where your dictionary lists them—whether in the general text along with other words, or in a special section. Their pronunciations may be shown. Observe, too, whether the names of famous people are listed and whether the pronunciations are indicated. For the pronunciations of some 12,000 foreign names and words, consult W. Cabell Greet, *World Words: Recommended Pronunciations* (New York, Columbia University Press, 1944). Note in particular Greet's discussion of pronunciation on pages 1–4 and his excellent advice for the anglicizing of foreign words: ". . . adopt the foreign pronunciation insofar as it can be rendered by customary English sounds in the phrasing and rhythm of an English sentence."

Above all, in consulting a dictionary for pronunciation, become thoroughly familiar with the key sounds and symbols it uses to show pronunciation. The symbols are usually discussed at length in a separate section at the front. If you use a dictionary infrequently, *always* consult the key words listed at the bottom of every page. It is easy to forget what the pronunciation symbols mean, and the key words keep you straight.

The pronunciation of the public speaker, then, should be clear and intelligible. It should reflect the best, widespread usage of the dialect region to which he is native. In a word, it should be free of localisms and idiosyncrasies of pronunciation that would distract the listener's attention.

===== EXERCISES FOR PRACTICE =====

Persistent and careful practice of the exercises which follow will help promote good voice and diction. Continued correct practice, however, is necessary. Consult with your instructor as to whether you are doing the exercises frequently enough and properly. Frequent short periods of practice (5–15 minutes) are preferable to less frequent longer periods.

I. *To promote relaxation of the "vocal" muscles*

   A. Establishing the sensation of relaxation

      In good voice production the breath seems to flow through the throat and mouth as if there were nothing to interrupt it. The exercises below are designed to relax the muscles of the throat and jaws.

      1. Let the head fall forward; roll it gently to one shoulder, to the back, to the other shoulder, and to the starting position again. Keep muscles of neck and jaw *relaxed*.

      2. With head erect *yawn*. At the height of the yawn, massage with both hands the muscles of the jaws and neck. Do this until your jaw *hangs* open and you can insert three fingers vertically between your teeth. Jaw and neck should feel *completely* relaxed.

      3. Let the lower jaw drop and the head fall forward. Shake the head vigorously until you can feel the jaw wag back and forth. If necessary, push the jaw first to one side and then to the other as far as it will go.

      4. Relax the jaw. Utter in groups of three: *yah-yah-yah; yo-yo-yo; yee-yee-yee; yoo-yoo-yoo.* Be sure that the jaw drops *open* after each triplet. Repeat, using numerals in groups of three.

      5. Practice the exercises described in Chapter 8 (pp. 146–147) for securing the relaxation and poised ease of the arms, shoulders, and upper chest. The sensation of being relaxed in these parts of the body helps to secure, and to maintain, the relaxation of throat muscles.

   B. Keeping relaxed while speaking

      You can hardly expect to maintain the "open throat" during a speech unless you make the *definite and persistent* attempt to associate relaxation with the act of speaking.

      1. As you undertake each rehearsal of your speech, practice the exercises above. *Feel* relaxed about the throat and upper body region before you begin to speak.

      2. Just before you start speaking to your audience, check to see whether you feel easy about jaws and neck. (*a*) Manage a covert yawn, wag your lower jaw a bit, as you leave your seat. (*b*) As you take your position at the stand or lectern, *settle* your body into position, letting your shoulders and chest sag imperceptibly. *Take your time;* you don't have to rush into your talk; get set before sounding off. (Remember: getting bodily set contributes to your peace of mind as well as to proper use of your voice.)

II. *To promote adequate breathing for speech*

To experience the sensation of breathing and to establish some control over the breathing mechanism are important for a speaker (*a*) who gasps and gulps to the extent that his listeners are aware of his "breathiness," and (*b*) who must speak more loudly and forcefully than he has been in the habit of doing.

A. To get the "feel" of breathing
1. Lie flat on your back. Relax, and as you breathe quietly observe the rise and fall of your body just below the ribs and breast bone. Place your hand or a book there; watch the motion, and observe that (*a*) as you *inhale*, the motion is *upward*, (*b*) as you *exhale* the motion is *downward*.
2. Stand in an easy, well-poised position. Place both hands just below ribs and breast bone, and *exhale*. Note the *inward* motion of the hands. Then *inhale*, observing the *outward* movement of the hands. Now with your hands *press* the breath out of you, at first slowly, then suddenly.
3. Inhale easily and fairly deeply. Hold for 1 second and then relax. Note that when you relax, you *exhale*. Repeat, holding the breath for 2 seconds, and relaxing; for 4 seconds, for 6 seconds, for 8 seconds. (In inhalation, don't let the upper chest and the neck become strained and tense; and don't let the shoulders rise.)
4. Inhale easily, and on exhalation count from 1 to 5, and then release the remaining air. Repeat, counting from 1 to 10. Don't take in so much air that your shoulders heave. Make sure that at the end of each series you have breath left to exhale. Count slowly; don't hurry and don't force exhalation.
5. Intone a series of five short "ah's," taking a short breath before each. Keep your hand on the upper abdomen to make sure that you are pushing in during phonation. Keep the throat relaxed and use the abdominal muscles to start and to stop tone.
6. Intone in triplets, *ha, ha, ha,—ha, ha, ha,—ha, ha, ha*, etc., taking a short breath before each *ha*. You should be able to feel a short abdominal stroke on each syllable. The nearer you come to a laugh, the better.

B. To associate proper breathing with speaking
1. Read aloud the following passage from p. 307. First, pause at the places indicated by the slant lines (/) and take a breath at each pause. Second, breathe at the pauses indicated by the asterisks (*). Reread several times, taking care not to gulp for breath at the pauses, or to run out of breath.

Imagine that we stand/ on any ordinary seaside pier,/ and watch the waves rolling in/ and striking against the iron columns of the pier.*/ Large waves pay little attention to the columns/ they divide right and left/ and re-unite after passing each column,*/ much as a regiment of soldiers would/ if a tree stood in their road;*/ it is almost as though the columns had not been there.*/ But the short waves and ripples/ find the columns of the pier/ a much more formidable obstacle.*/ When the short waves impinge on the columns,/ they are reflected

back/ and spread as new ripples in all directions.°/ To use the
technical term,/ they are "scattered." °/ The obstacle provided
by the iron columns/ hardly affects the long waves at all,/ but
scatters the short ripples.°/

2. Pick up the outline or manuscript of your speech and read it at a
   rather deliberate, easy rate, pausing wherever the sense bids you
   pause and noting at what pauses you take a breath. At the breath
   pauses, be sure that you are breathing easily; take your time.

   As a result of this procedure you should at least experience
   what happens when you breathe during speech. If the experience
   has made a sharp, deep *impression* on you, there is some chance
   of its guiding you in actual delivery.

   *If you have real trouble with breathing during utterance, prac-
   tice these exercises when you rehearse for each speech.*

C. To improve clarity, strength, and firmness of tone
   Note: In these exercises see that the mouth is wide open for the *ah*
   sound. Practice also with *ee* and *oo* in Nos. 1–5.
   1. Inhale; hold upper chest expanded; whisper *ah* by contracting
      at the diaphragm; relax upper chest.
   2. Inhale; hold upper chest expanded; voice *ah,* contracting at the
      diaphragm; relax upper chest.
   3. Repeat No. 2 sustaining voiced *ah* as long as possible without
      relaxing upper chest.
   4. Repeat No. 3 humming an *m* firmly instead of voicing *ah.*
   5. Inhale; sustain voiced *ah* firmly on even volume and even pitch
      as long as possible without straining, first contracting above the
      waist and finally lowering upper chest.
   6. Repeat No. 5, humming an *m* instead of voicing *ah.*
   7. Repeat No. 5 alternating *ah* and *oo.*
   8. Repeat No. 7, increasing the series to include *ee: ah—oo—ee—
      oo—ah.*
   9. Inhale; voice *ah* softly; increase the loudness slowly and evenly
      to the maximum that can be attained without straining. The
      length of the increase and the maximum volume attainable
      should become greater with practice.
   10. Stand, breathe deeply, and hum a loud *m* or voice a loud *ah,* or
       ee, sustaining the tone as long as possible without straining.
       Alternate intoned and spoken vowel sounds.

III. *To improve vocal variety*

If you speak too fast or too slow, too loud or too soft, if your voice does
not reveal sufficient variety of pitch, of loudness, or of rate, if your speaking voice is monotonous in any respect, you may find that the procedures
and exercises below will help you. They are not intended to supplant a
rigorous, sustained program of voice training under the guidance of an
instructor; they are not intended to "build" a voice to the point where
you realize your own vocal potentialities. Rather, they are aimed to show
the public speaker what he *can* do with his voice, to give him the *experience* of vocal variety, and to associate the experience with his speaking.

Recognizing your natural pitch level. Before experimenting with your
voice you should tune your ear to your *natural pitch level.*

Sit down at a piano and intone *ah*. Find the note on the piano corresponding to it; then gradually lower the intoned *ah*, moving down the scale until you find the lowest tone you can make without strain. (Keep relaxed about the throat and jaws!) Observe the corresponding note on the piano. Next, move the *ah* up the scale until you find the highest tone you can produce without strain, and match this on the piano. You will want to repeat the entire procedure several times until you are sure you have found the lowest and highest note you can intone comfortably. Then with your lowest *ah* located on the piano, count the black and white keys up to and including your highest *ah*. Thus you have your vocal range—say 21 piano notes. Divide this range by 4; e.g., $21 \div 4 = 5\frac{1}{4}$. Then starting with the lowest note of your range, count up 5 notes. The pitch of this note, or of the note just above it, is very close to your natural pitch level. Finally, with this pitch level fixed in your auditory memory, observe your conversation and see whether the pitch level of your speech corresponds to the natural pitch level you have discovered. Furthermore, if you record one of your speeches, observe whether its dominant pitch corresponds to your natural pitch level.

In the practice suggested below, if you work at your natural pitch level and in the range of tones immediately above it, you will run small danger of hurting your voice.

A. To experience variety of loudness

    1. In a rather large room, count from 1 to 10 just loud enough, first, to reach your nearest "listener," and second, to fill the room with sound. (Be sure to maintain an open, easy throat. Hold to your natural pitch level, and push the sound out with the abdominal muscles.) Gradually increase loudness until you are shouting. Be especially careful not to let your pitch level shoot up; get lots of sound without much, if any, change of pitch. This procedure should help you to distinguish loudness from pitch and to show you how much loudness you are capable of.

    2. Speak each of the following, first, just loud enough to be heard by your friend if you were conversing with him; and second, loud enough to be heard by a listener in the back row of an auditorium. This exercise should help you to feel and hear great contrasts of loudness.

That can't be so.	Dinner is at eight.
You're quite right.	I'll say so.
I don't know.	That's too bad, old man.
Let me alone.	We can't do that.
Jones is mistaken.	There's no doubt about it.
You don't say so!	We must be prompt.
The train leaves at four.	To see is to believe.

      a. To become aware of smaller differences in loudness, stand in a large room, preferably an auditorium, and speak each of the sentences above (1) to a person standing beside you; (2) to a listener 15 feet away; (3) to a listener seated in the middle of the room; (4) to a listener at the back of the room. (Note: If a recording apparatus is available, record four degrees of loudness, using the statements above; then listen to observe whether you have actually achieved distinct differences of loudness.

b. Speak this passage from Shakespeare, the first half of each line loudly, the second half softly.

Youth is full of pleasure, age is full of care;
Youth like summer morn, age like winter weather;
Youth like summer brave, age like winter bare.
Youth is full of sport, age's breath is short;
Youth is nimble, age is lame;
Youth is hot and bold; age is weak and cold;
Youth is wild, and age is tame.

(Note: If possible, record this exercise also.)

3. When you are practicing your speech, try at least one rehearsal according to this procedure: (a) in the margins of your outline, indicate variations in loudness thus: attention ideas—*fairly loud;* subject sentence—*loud;* main heads—*fairly loud;* principal sub-heads—*not so loud;* supporting details—*soft;* conclusion—*loud;* (b) rehearse at least once observing these loudness directions.

(*Caution:* Remember that such practice is mechanical and is designed merely to give yourself the experience of variations in loudness. On the platform, avoid the mechanics—forget them for the moment and speak directly; have faith that repeated experience during practice will gradually show up automatically in your delivery.)

B. To experience variations of tempo

1. Become thoroughly familiar with the selection on page 174, and then proceed as follows:

   a. Read to a friend or acquaintance in your own room, very much as if you were conversing with him. Time yourself.

   b. In a large room or auditorium, read so as to make the most remote listener understand. Time yourself. Compare the times needed for the two readings. What do you observe as to (1) duration of pauses? (2) duration of individual sounds and words? (3) articulation?

2. Read, and if possible record, the following sentence, first speaking it at a rather brisk, colloquial pace, then pausing for a count of 3 at each of the slant lines:

   History makes men wise;/ poetry, witty;/ mathematics, subtle;/ science, deep;/ philosophy, grave;/ logic and rhetoric, able to contend.

3. Record two or three short prose selections, speaking each as if you were directly addressing a real audience. Compare the pace of illustrative material with that of general, abstract statements.

4. In rehearsing for your speech, practice once by speaking rather slowly your opening two or three sentences, your subject sentence, main heads, and conclusion; and move along your supporting ideas, especially specific illustrations, rather rapidly.

IV. *To improve articulation and distinctness of enunciation*

A. Practice speaking the words and sentences below, slowly at first with exaggerated distinctness and completeness; then increase the speed to that of normal utterance, retaining the sharpness of enunciation. Avoid such pronunciations as "enner" for *enter*, "lasswinner" for *last winter*, "painning" for *painting*, "represennative" for *representative*, "weller" for *welder*, "hunnert" for *hundred*, "grannit" for *granted*, and carefully avoid such telescoping as "gennally" for *generally*, "opportunny" for *opportunity*, "prolly" for *probably*, "materal" for *material*.

accidentally	naturally	inequalities
adjustment	instances	slovenliness
constitutional	shortages	incidentally
representative	individually	acknowledgment
inter-American	appointed	in the morning
quantities	acquainted	one hundred twenty-five
sentences	plenty	articulatory prestidigitation
mountain	advantages	United States Government
hypotenuse	merchandise	antisubmarine gun
adjective	exorbitantly	sent out questionnaires
variety	opportunity	unexceptionable
obstacle	appropriated	coast guard cutter
certainty	seldom	international legion
ninety-six	laborer	library assignment
intramural	numerous	European nationalities
interrogatory	inadequately	officer of the day
noncombatant	experiences	the sacrifices that are necessary
frantically	definitely	let's go
it's wonderful	appointing	language
credit department	understand	take it for granted
customer	interrupt	particularly
heating	contact him	collect
St. Louis	wanting	collection
rental	planting	regularly
solicitor	last winter	generally
intermediate	swindler	materially
recognize	county	cardinal
under	approximately	meter reader
encountered	picture	accurately
encountering	interfere	similarly
directly	printing	deteriorate
welder	handling	invariably
welding	granted	company
gentleman	I can't decide	density
enterprise	I don't know	unscrupulous
twenty	didn't	coerce
penalty	wouldn't	political police
hundred	shouldn't	subsidy
statistics	couldn't	subsidiary
enter	subject	subsidization
interdepartmental	interesting	experimentally
emergency	supply service	created
circulation	environment	temperatures

co-operation	Washington	unhurriedly
accounting	equipment	potentialities
just going to get	regulations	managerial
believe	probably	employee

1. Distinctness of utterance in the relation of facts and in the re-counting of acts presents difficulties which a competent speaker should be asked to overcome.
2. Some gentlemen now ask us to commit ourselves definitely to a kind of international understanding which probably will have to be tested before it is ultimately adopted.
3. Peter Piper picked a peck of pickled peppers, but actually he wasn't too particular or too industrious at tasks of this kind.
4. The microphone, like a good natured gentlewoman, will respond readily to reasonable demands, if it is spoken to in moderate and clear tones.
5. The candidates who are elected to serve as delegates to the Constitutional Convention will be expected to make suggestions and recommendations for the improvement of state, county, and municipal government.
6. A certain soap is said to be ninety-nine and forty-four one hundredths per cent pure.
7. Where was it that we saw those technicolor pictures that presented the customs and tribal habits of the native inhabitants of Tahiti?
8. Last winter, in the course of a particularly and accurately representative business interview, we saw the interesting statistics from a survey separately conducted and similarly reported by the Accounting Department.
9. He didn't say he wouldn't, and he didn't say he couldn't or shouldn't, but he didn't.
10. He plans to go into business in the near future.

B. Write out sensible sentences using as many as possible of the words in the list above, and practice reading the sentences for completeness and accuracy of pronunciation.

C. Practice the exercises and words below until you can do them quickly, easily, and distinctly. Repeat each exercise over in rapid succession. In the first exercises, pronounce the *sound* commonly associated with the letter, not the name of the letter.

$$t - p - d - b$$
$$t - s - th \text{ (as in thin)} - s - t$$
$$d - z - th \text{ (as in then)} - z - d$$
$$ch - sh - zh - dzh \text{ (j)}$$

facts, acts, discs, asked, ghosts, hosts, integral, statistics, statistician, ballistics, fists, twists, resists, mists, lists.

D. Read the verses on pages 171–174, or similar patter verses, with distinctness, accuracy, and speed.

FURTHER READING

ANDERSON, Virgil, *Training the Speaking Voice*, 2nd ed. (New York, 1961).

FAIRBANKS, Grant, *Voice and Articulation Drillbook* (New York, 1960).

GRAY, G. W., and C. M. WISE, *The Bases of Speech* (New York, 1959), Chs. 2–3, "On Voice and Pronunciation."

O'NEILL, J. M., ed., *The Foundations of Speech* (New York, 1941), Ch. 3, "On American Pronunciation"; Chs. 6–8, "Concerning the Voice and Speech Mechanism."

POTTER, Simeon, *Our Language* (Baltimore, Md., 1950), Ch. 13, "British and American English."

CHAPTER ELEVEN

Materials and Methods
of Persuasion

GOALS OF THE PERSUASIVE SPEECH

While he is studying the elements of persuasion as they apply to speechmaking, the student speaker does well to remind himself that the goal of all persuasion is to influence the opinions and beliefs, the behavior and conduct, of persons. In preparing to address a particular audience at a particular time and place, however, a speaker does not simply say to himself, "I want to change the belief of this audience"; rather, he will say, for example, "I want my hearers to believe that the railroads ought to improve passenger service"; or "I want this audience to vote the straight Republican ticket." The goal of a particular persuasive speech, whether expressed or implied, always reveals (1) the speaker's belief about a state of affairs and (2) his intention that his hearers should think likewise.

PRINCIPLES OF PERSUASION

The persuasive speaker endeavors to reach his goal through the application of a single controlling principle. Writers on persuasion have expressed the principle in different ways. The three following are representative. A. E. Phillips called the principle "Reference to Experience":

> Reference to Experience . . . means reference to the known. The known is that which the listener has seen, heard, read, felt, believed or done, and which still exists in his consciousness—his stock of knowledge. It embraces all those thoughts, feelings, and happenings which to him are real. Reference to Experience, then, means *coming into the listener's life*.

J. A. Winans spoke of "common ground." A speaker is on the road to persuasion when he and his audience stand on a common ground of belief, of goals and values, and of emotion and feeling. The speaker recommends his own belief to others in terms of relevant beliefs which he and they share, of relevant values and ideals which they both approve of, and of relevant emotions and feelings which they experience alike. Kenneth Burke has asserted: "You can persuade a man only insofar as you can talk his language by speech, gesture, tonality, order, image, attitude, idea, identifying your ways with his."

In brief, the persuasive speech is likely to achieve its goal when speaker and audience can be shown to share beliefs and attitudes, motives and interests, emotions and feelings which are relevant to the business at hand. The persuasive speaker is always saying, in effect, "Accept what I say because it harmonizes with what you already accept and regard with favor." Borrowing from Burke, we shall refer to the principle as that of *identification* and shall think of persuasion as a process of identification.

MATERIALS OF PERSUASION

Knowledge of Subject

The most substantial way of identification is through ideas and information relevant to a particular problem, audience, and occasion. The speaker must be master of these ideas and information. A persuasive speech, however, is not occasioned primarily, like the informative speech, by a speaker's superior knowledge of a subject which he wants his hearers to appreciate and understand. Rather, he has, or thinks he has, a solution to a problem which matters or ought to matter to them. Hearers are in doubt and are called on to make decisions and choices; they have not made up their minds or acted decisively. So the materials which unite speaker and audience, if speaker and audience are to find common bonds at all, must come from the ideas, facts, opinions, and arguments which are relevant to the problem and appropriate to the audience at a particular time and place.

Any problem, its "solutions," and the decisions and actions taken about it go through well-defined stages of discussion. The speaker can get on common ground with his audience by focusing his speech on the questions and issues which concern them at the time.

Two methods of analyzing a problem are widely used. They tell the speaker what he must know and where he can concentrate his fire. The first was formulated by the distinguished American philosopher John Dewey. The second is an inheritance of the ages.

Dewey's Steps in Analysis

1. Becoming aware of the problem.
2. Defining the precise nature of the problem.
3. Discovering possible solutions to the problem.
4. Deciding upon the best solution.
5. Testing the decision by putting it into practice.

Thinking on any problem always goes through these five stages, although the testing process, except in the laboratory under experimental conditions, cannot be carried out until the solution has been put into practice to see whether it will work. Our legislators discuss and debate and pass a law, but the law is not tested until it has gone into effect.

How does a problem arise in everyday affairs? First, some observer gets the notion that he doesn't like what is going on at present; he may not, for example, like the subsidizing of intercollegiate athletics at X college. So he complains about it; or in more formal terms, he becomes a critic of the present. He may run across others who have been vaguely disturbed over the matter, and discussion goes on. Second, discussion arrives at the point where criticism makes the problem definite. It becomes clear that trouble with the subsidizing of athletics lies not in the awarding of athletic scholarships, but in the awarding of scholarships for athletic ability only. Accordingly the problem is made clear: "Can athletic scholarships be granted at X College on more grounds than athletic prowess?" Third, with the problem clearly recognized, remedies are suggested; and fourth, out of suggested remedies one proposal is adopted by the college. Finally, discussion on this matter subsides and the proposal goes into effect to meet its practical test.

Now suppose you as a beginning speaker were at X College when the discussion of athletic scholarships was going on. Suppose your knowledge and grasp of the situation had led you to see the problem in its five aspects. What would you elect to speak on to a college class? *You would do well to select that aspect of the subject that reflected the current stage of discussion.* If your audience vaguely felt that the problem existed, then you might decide to define the problem and bring criticism to a head, perhaps judging correctly that your hearers were not yet ready to hear of a solution. Or if current discussion were beyond the stage of definition and students were discussing alternative proposals, you might wisely advocate a specific solution. In short, analysis not only helps to understand the problem as a whole, but analysis is of practical value in determining what special view of it is best suited to the particular audience. This is true not only of campus problems but of all controversial problems—regional, national, and international. Indeed, the campus or local problem differs from the international problem only in being closer to home, more concrete, and less broad in extent.

The Traditional Scheme of Analysis

This method of seeing the essentials of a controversy is not unlike the steps of analysis above. It is, however, somewhat more detailed, and some speakers in their preparation find it more practical because it directs attention to the cause and effect mode of thinking and suggests statements (or their equivalents) that may often be used as the proposition or as the main heads of a speech.

I. What criticisms are made of the present situation? Are there evils—effects or conditions we do not like?

I'. What are the causes (both immediate and remote) that have brought about the criticisms and bad effects?

II. What policy, program, or action would if accepted and put into action remove the criticisms and abolish the evils?

A. Does the proposal for remedying the evils make a definite and clearly recognized change from the present state of affairs?
A'. Does the proposed solution specifically recognize new causes and conditions that will remove the old causes that brought about the bad effects?

III. Is the proposal for change the best possible remedy?

A. Is it definitely distinct and separate from other solutions offered?
A'. Is it superior to any other remedy?

IV. If adopted, would the proposal set causes to work whose effects would be as bad as those it would remedy?

A. What drawbacks has the proposal?
A'. Would they really be serious and significant evils?
B. Would the proposal be workable? Could it be put into operation?

Again this method of analysis is useful to the persuasive speaker in the same way as are the Dewey steps. The questions help him survey the possibilities of his subject and help him to decide upon that aspect of it which would be appropriate to the special audience and occasion. On one occasion he would find it appropriate to concentrate on one phase of the subject, at another on some other phase.

Selecting the Specific Goal

Once the speaker has found an area of interest in which both he and his hearers can meet appropriately, he begins to consider his specific goal or aim. He decides what effect, what response, he wants from his audience. He states the effect as his *opinion,* his *judgment,* his *evaluation,* and builds his speech in support of it. He wants his audience to accept it, to have the same attitude toward it that he has. Technically, his opinion functions as the proposition of his speech.

Knowledge of Audience

Some of the basic materials of persuasion are derived from what the speaker can learn about his hearers. He is especially interested in them as *social* creatures, in the kinds of persons they are because they have been brought up among people, not on a desert island alone.

The study of social character is complex. It is best carried on formally in the fields of psychology, social psychology, and sociology. Those who have had an introduction to these fields are in a better position to understand the character of audiences than those who have not. For the young person who has not had the chance to analyze human nature rigorously we offer a few fundamental suggestions which will put him on the road to discovery.

Norms and Standards of Group Behavior

A person in an audience is not a member of that group only, but more importantly he is a member of other groups from which he has derived most, if not all, of his ideals and beliefs. Some significant groupings:

Family
Political groups:
   Democratic and Republican parties
   Liberal, conservative, middle-of-the-road
Religious groups
Racial groups
National and regional groups—U.S.A., the Middle West
Societies and clubs:
   Service clubs—Rotary, P.T.A.
Professional groups—teachers, lawyers, physicians
Economic groups:
   Owners and managers—Chamber of Commerce, trade associations
Farm—Farm Bureau
Big Business, Little Business
Consumers—high income, average income, low income
Labor—A.F. of L., electricians, teamsters

In preparing to meet his audience, a speaker asks himself two kinds of questions: (1) What groups are represented in the audience? (2) What ideals of belief and conduct are the groups committed to? What do they say about their goals and values? What values may be inferred from their actions? Most speakers will find that they know a good deal about groups they themselves belong to; for example, family and religious groups. Upon thought, they can list the ideals, customs, and codes of behavior by which these groups judge the behavior of their members. For knowledge of other groups, they may have to consult books and articles which deal with their aims and principles. Societies of any size and scope issue literature about themselves.

Group norms are the uniformities of ideals, rules, customs, and behavior by which the thought and conduct of group members are regularized. Norms are *"standardized generalizations."* Group pressure is behind them and individuals are expected to conform. As examples of norms expressed as ideals, take our American values as asserted in the Constitution and to which we give allegiance. We respect "justice," and we stand for "liberty to ourselves and our posterity," and for the protection of property and freedom of religion, speech, and press. No man may be "deprived of life, liberty or property, without due process of law," and "all men are created equal," having certain "inalienable rights," such as "life, liberty, and the pursuit of happiness." These are some of the ideals and concepts which bind Americans into a national group.

The force and appeal of group standards are manifold. Norms not only bring social pressure to bear on an individual, but they are bundles of many-sided experience. They announce or imply deep-seated goals and desires. They are associated with motives and emotions. They are responsible for our strongest attitudes—those mechanisms we recognize when we say we are for or against something or regard an object, person, or idea with favor or disfavor, liking or disliking, desire or aversion. And because they channel so much experience into broad streams, they are the chief means by which members of a group can successfully communicate with each other in ways that ensure the preservation, solidity, and unity of the group. One of the widely respected social psychologists, Theodore Newcomb, points up the impact of group standards in this way:

> Group norms . . . determine individual behavior in two ways. They provide both meanings and goals. They provide meanings because . . . the individual is dependent on group norms for his meanings; without them he cannot communicate. They provide goals because the individual cannot be indifferent to the approvals and disapprovals which are associated with the norms. Inevitably, he becomes motivated toward or away from objects, people, institutions, and ideologies whose meaning is provided by the norms.[1]

How are group norms employed in persuasion? They supply the fundamental ways to identification. The speaker draws upon norms

[1] Theodore Newcomb, *Social Psychology* (New York, 1950), p. 275.

which are relevant to the ideas he presents. The identification works in two ways. Knowing that individuals identify themselves with the ideals of a group, he connects his proposals and arguments with their ideals wherever he can logically do so. Thus he establishes identity through common ideas. He also suggests a personal identification, on grounds that persons who approve of the same ideas are to that extent alike.

A striking example of identification is in George William Curtis's speech, "The Puritan Principle," delivered when feeling ran high over the Hayes–Tilden election controversy in 1876. Responsible, thoughtful people were so aroused that they spoke openly of resorting to arms to determine who should be President. Before about 400 influential citizens gathered in New York, Curtis advocated that Congress should set up machinery whereby "a President, be he Democrat or be he Republican, shall pass unchallenged to his chair." He singled out the chief national groupings in the audience—the Irish, French, English, and German— and reminded them of their old-world allegiances by mention of their national flowers. He shifted to their new-world values, to their traditions as New Englanders and as Americans, and to their respect for liberty and for liberty under law. Then he asserted that the traditions of law were directly applicable to his proposal, and Congress should find a legal remedy. The address is supposed to have stopped all talk of a civil war. Serious students of persuasion ponder it as an example of appeals to ideals, values, and emotions which held speaker and hearers in common bond. Somewhat less emotional and less direct is President John F. Kennedy's use of identification in his Inaugural Address, January 20, 1961 (below, pp. 333–336).

Lines of Thought, Motives, and Emotions

When the persuasive speaker has analyzed his subject and has some appreciation of the group norms represented in his immediate audience, he becomes interested in finding the possible lines of thought by which he hopes to achieve his purpose. At this point in his preparation he looks again to the *precise circumstances* which gave rise to the problem under discussion. If he will regard them closely, he will find what people think are the conditions (sometimes referred to as "causes") which are blocking the achievement of their goals. In other words, people and groups are experiencing frustrations in greater or less degree. When goals are not attained and frustrations appear, emotion is almost always the result. The speaker who can thus size up the problem-situation has discovered the logical basis of emotional appeal—blocked motivations and thwarted goals. Helpful in locating such lines of thought are the following guide-questions:

What conditions interfere with the *health* of the audience or of the groups it is interested in? Are there signs of anxiety, worry, fear, discomfort? Are people anxious, worried, fearful, uncomfortable, or disturbed in other ways?

Are there conditions which threaten *economic welfare?* What is hurting wages, salaries, savings, production costs, and prices?

What conditions are harmful to the security and stability *of family life?* What is injurious to the opportunity, education, and comfort of children?

Who or what is working against the *basic freedoms?* Is the situation placing unwarranted checks on freedom of speech, action, or worship? Who is being tyrannical and arbitrary?

What opportunities are being denied to the audience or to groups and persons it is interested in? Who is discriminating against whom? Are conditions in some way unjust? Illegal?

What is damaging to the status and prestige of the audience, the community, the nation? What is insulting to whom?

Is any aspect of the situation damaging to some cherished tradition or custom?

Has any person, business group, labor group, or political group been shirking its social responsibilities, or been reneging on its public promises and commitments?

Have persons or groups involved in the situation been deceitful or untruthful? Has some group or party forsaken accepted ideals of truth, virtue, democracy, religion, or codes of conduct?

The genuine concern of any audience in a problem and its solution is grounded in such motives and in conditions which interfere with the normal realization of goals.

The speaker who thus probes a problem will be more than realistic and interesting. He will also be on the way to acquiring the language of power and emotion. If the circumstances actually *threaten* our values and modes of conduct, there is danger, and we cannot avoid feeling anxious and fearful. In the face of injustice and unfairness, we become indignant. We take pride in our accomplishments, and pride also is the feeling which permeates prestige and coveted status. We feel pride in actions that are honorable and dutiful, and we experience shame in dishonor and unfaithfulness. When we think we can successfully cope with a situation, when we believe that we are ready to solve a problem and when it seems probable that we will, we experience confidence and feelings of security. (What emotions do students experience when they take an examination?) When persons unite, determined to face a problem and sincerely desiring to solve it for the benefit of all involved, they experience feelings of mutual understanding and good will. So the speaker who honestly faces a real problem, who understands it, and who believes that he can help an audience solve it, finds his thought and argument impregnated with emotion, and his language will bear the signs of it.

The young speaker often errs in thinking that he must avoid emotion and feeling and the mention of attitudes that stir men emotionally. He may even feel that it is wrong to reason other than "logically." But there is no valid basis for deprecating emotion generally, and there will be no ethical problem if the speaker's view represents his *considered* opinion.[2] The sincere speaker cannot avoid emotion unless he schools himself against it. He will reveal it in his face, his voice, and his movement. And as he responds to his hearers and they to him, he will often unconsciously refer to "our duty and responsibility," to "our sense of fair play," to what is "right" or "good" to do. If he quotes a well-known passage from the Bible, most listeners will experience a slight feeling of reverence—and so may the speaker, as he quotes it. The sincere speaker cannot be a machine.

Furthermore, the divorce between "logic" and "emotion" is more supposed than real. When one sets out to reason most logically, one may discover that *what* he says speaks as loudly as its logical form and framework. Suppose you were speaking in support of the annual Red Cross drive and you decided that the effective line of attack was to emphasize the little-known service that the local chapter rendered in putting a service man in touch with his family when the normal means of communication had broken down. So you took this as your subject sentence: "The local Red Cross chapter kept service men in touch with their families when other means failed." You knew of a number of instances and arranged your material thus:

    I. The chapter did this in the city.
       A. A well-to-do family was put in touch with their son.
       B. A poor family was put in touch with their son.

    II. The chapter performed such a service in the rural area.
       A. A well-to-do family, etc.
       B. A poor family, etc.

You concluded after four minutes, most of which was devoted to factual description of the four instances. In such a speech the proposition is a limited generalization that is supported beyond reasonable doubt by

[2] See D. C. Bryant, "Aspects of the Rhetorical Tradition: Emotion, Style, and Literary Association," *Quarterly Journal of Speech*, XXXVI (1950), 326 ff.

four instances, and the instances are meant to be typical because you selected cases from both the rich and the poor. Now could you tell whether you controlled the perceptions of your audience *primarily* because of your reasoning? Or was the main effect secured through what you said—the ideas used and the associations they stirred up directly or indirectly? Did there come into play your listeners' sense of duty and obligation to service men, their desire for the soldier's happiness and well-being, their affection for home and family relationships, and their sense of justice (no discrimination because of differences in money and position)? Even when we aim at the logical connections among ideas, the ideas themselves control attention by calling up our accumulated experience of motives, emotions, and attitudes.

The Speaker's Character and Personality

When Emerson said of a speaker, "What you are thunders so loudly I cannot hear what you say," he was only expressing anew what speakers and audiences have always known—that personality and character exert as strong an influence (perhaps an even stronger influence) upon the reception of ideas as do other means of persuasion. Quintilian so keenly appreciated the force of the speaker's character in persuasion that he believed no bad man could secure any honor whatsoever with an audience. Bad character and persuasion excluded each other; consequently, he defined the orator as a good man skilled in speaking.

The impact of character is derived partly from the speaker's prestige and partly from his manner of presentation, his bodily activity, facial expression, and vocal qualities that mean sincerity, earnestness, modesty, courtesy, and geniality. These desirable qualities of personality, not revealed on the surface of language and behavior, shine through presentation and help paint the speaker's portrait.

How can the speaker paint a desirable self-portrait? There are no formulas, no rules-of-thumb. Socially acceptable qualities of personality and character are built up through long training in the home, the school, the church, and association with others. All we can do is to offer some advice which may make these qualities more evident to a person who has them and may show the person who lacks them what is needed.

Prestige and Esteem for the Speaker

One of the significant characteristics of any group of persons is its social structure or system. The structure is evident as soon as well-defined positions have developed, positions whose status or importance can be located on a social scale from low to high. Persons who hold positions having high prestige or status enjoy the esteem of other members of the group. Hence esteem becomes a factor in persuasion.

The speaker-audience situation is a real, though relatively simple, group structure. The social position of the speaker is a dominant one and carries prestige largely because he is expected to possess some, if not all, of the qualities of a leader. One of the chief qualities is that of knowledge, because the speaker, relative to the audience, is supposed to have had the opportunity to know and think. Enough has been said in this chapter and elsewhere in this book about information and knowledge as essential ingredients of speechmaking.

Knowledge is of course made evident by what the speaker says, through the information he reveals on the subject of the moment, and through the general background of knowledge an educated person is supposed to have. To the extent that a speaker possesses the *special* knowledge of the expert, his esteem is heightened and he wields the influence of *authority*.

Other factors that significantly influence the prestige and esteem of the speaker fall into two general categories: (1) traits of good taste, and (2) moral traits that are expected of speakers in a free society. In the former category we shall emphasize courtesy and modesty.

COURTESY

There are two principal *cautions*. Avoid offending the sensibilities of a group by being risqué, by being irreverent toward people they respect or toward religion and God, by using humor when the occasion is solemn, or by attacking cherished ideals and deep-seated opinions by recourse to ridicule and to sustained satire and sarcasm.

The following approaches to the revered authority, the cherished belief or tradition, recognize the hearer's attitude without condoning it:

> We all respect Thomas Jefferson's views on education and find them especially sound for his day and time. But we should not extend less respect to John Dewey whose mature judgment on modern education leads him to say. . . .

> We may all believe that the American Army is the greatest in the world. The opinion is a credit to our patriotism and loyalty. Nevertheless, if we examine the opinion carefully, we may see it in a new light.

The second caution is this: Avoid convicting an audience of ignorance. Present the information they don't have, of course, but don't make such mistakes as saying, "You didn't know this, did you?" Don't dismiss an objection with a shrug, or with a smart-alecky "So, what!" Rather, some formula like this is to be preferred, "I am sure your opinion is well-founded, but my information leads me to another conclusion."

MODESTY

A speaker with a know-it-all attitude is a trial to everybody, anywhere. He is even more obnoxious on the platform. Signs of his immodesty are especially evident in his flat, dogmatic assertions, in his sweeping generalizations, and in his voice and manner which plainly imply "I can't be wrong." The cause of such immodesty lies principally in his failure to recognize that he may possibly—just possibly—be wrong once in a while. He fails to appreciate what most educated persons learn: that in pro-and-con matters, neither pro nor con has a monopoly on truth. Our opinions can be called "possibly true," "probably true," "in all probability, true," but never "certainly" or "universally" true. Scientific conclusions and laws probably carry the greatest certainty. The physicist may have proved that all bodies will fall in a vacuum at a uniform speed. But even for this observation he will not claim too much, for he will preface most of his laws with the phrase that admits the possibility of doubt: "*So far as we know,* all bodies will fall in a vacuum at a uniform rate." Why should the persuasive speaker, without the laboratory experiment to test his conclusions, be more certain than the scientist? Remember that the speaker is often recommending a policy— a belief or action which is to be applied in the future. How can he, without being immodest, say dogmatically that he will prove, or has proved, what will hold true in the future "beyond all shadow of doubt"? Even in the law, where most questions are decided by reference to past happenings and can be testified to by witnesses, documents, and so forth, juries are specifically charged to reach a verdict that is "beyond *reasonable* doubt." Doubt, accordingly, can seldom be banished. A sensible speaker knows this—and so does his audience.

The young speaker should avoid phrases like "I shall prove conclusively," "No one can take exception to this conclusion," "This is proved beyond question." Let him be more accurate and more modest, with such phrases as "It seems to me," "Probably," "Perhaps we can accept this," My opinion is. . . ."

The modest speaker who does not claim too much for his conclusions will avoid another sign of immodesty: exaggeration. He will not say carelessly that "all men are honest" when he really means that "most men are honest"; in other words, he will avoid the sweeping generalization. He will, furthermore, appreciate the value of *understatement* as opposed to *overstatement*. A sailor who described his rescue from a torpedoed merchantman concluded by saying that the experience was "pretty rough." He let his hearers supply the high-flown adjectives, "harrowing," "terrible," "miraculous," "amazing." Indeed, it should be observed that one value of understatement is that the hearer is often ready to concede more than he would permit the speaker to claim.

MORAL VALUES

The persuasive speaker should reveal in himself those moral qualities and social values which we normally expect of ourselves and our friends. Persuasion always involves ethical problems, because an audience must necessarily *trust* a speaker to seek only worthy ends and to use only honest, socially desirable means of persuasion.[3] The audience must be convinced that the speaker is a man of *integrity, good will, sincerity,* and *good sense.* The audience will be likely to see these qualities in him if, in addition to being modest and courteous, he also strives for the general welfare and not simply for his own, respects the opinions of others but respects his own judgment as well, and plays fair with his audience, his opponents, and the issues at stake.

HANDLING THE MATERIALS OF PERSUASION

The speaker who can assure himself that he has found and considered the essential materials for a persuasive speech is ready to think about ways of treating and presenting his ideas.

First, the *methods and techniques of amplification* are as useful in the persuasive speech as they are in the informative speech. As a general rule, it is not easy to persuade an audience to belief or action without making clear what belief is to be accepted or what is to be done. Indeed, if a group is convinced that the time for action has come, sometimes all that is needed is a description of the desired action, presented pointedly, unambiguously, and vividly. Furthermore, the best argument is ineffective if it cannot be understood, and all the skills of identification go to naught if hearers do not see what is being identified with what.

Second, all the *resources of language and style* help in producing persuasion. Particularly important are those ways which impart *impressiveness* to style—the sharp, intense, vivid phrase, image, and illustration.

Third, the attitude of the audience toward the speaker's goal and the position he recommends will greatly influence strategy and tactics. Before he decides finally on what ideas to use and how to handle them, a speaker should ask: How does my audience regard me and my basic

---

[3] For a more complete discussion of the speaker's ethical problem students may wish to consult our *Fundamentals of Public Speaking* (1960), Ch. 17.

position? Are they neutral, partisan, opposed? Are some groups for me, others against me? So at some stage of his preparation, the persuasive speaker should consider his goal, his basic position (to be expressed as a proposition), and his chief lines of thought with relation to the partisanship of his audience. "Now," he tells himself, "I know what I want my hearers to accept and here are the arguments I have about decided to use. How many of my listeners will probably find them congenial? How many will reject them? How many are neutral, ready to be informed and willing to judge on the basis of what I can say?"

To answer such questions accurately would require the speaker to make some kind of attitude poll of his audience, or to discover the results of such a poll. Except under the most favorable and unusual conditions —in the public speaking class, for example—it is impracticable to conduct one's own poll. Consequently, the alert speaker is alive to any polls reported in the newspapers which in any way relate to the subject and materials of a speech he may be planning to make. These will tell him something about the population of which his audience, or some of it, may be a part. Better yet he will discover that by reading widely and by talking with as many persons as possible, he will learn what persons *say* they believe. With such information he can turn his attention to his prospective hearers and group them into at least three main classes: *partisans, neutrals,* and *opponents.*

Rarely will hearers be all partisan, all neutral, or all in opposition. They will usually exhibit shades, tints, and colors of all three opinions. Although no one has discovered sure-fire, scientific formulas for selecting and handling materials for *any* audience, we shall try to present some guiding considerations which have met the test of experience.

Influencing Neutrals

The neutrals, whether well-informed and judicious or ill-informed, haven't made up their minds, and a speaker has a real chance to guide them. In general, these people are the so-called independent voters whose decision to vote one way or another—or not at all—decides elections. If they have had too little information to enable them to commit themselves, they will welcome information. It is therefore easier to cope with neutrals than with opponents, a fact that political campaigns invariably recognize. The election campaign aims at two things: to hold the interest and support of partisans and to swing into camp those who are vacillating.

Select the primary objection (or objections) that has prevented decision, and answer it with the best evidence and argument at your command. Often we vacillate because there is one aspect of a situation or problem that bothers us most. We say, "Yes, so-and-so and so-and-so is true, but there's one matter I'm still doubtful of." Some judicial doubters want to be sure on all important aspects of a problem, and if one aspect bothers them, they will reserve decision and refrain from action.

One of the commonest objections raised by conservatively minded people is this: "In theory," they say, "your idea is all right and we're for it, but you simply can't put it into practice—it won't work." Consequently, if the speaker can show how his proposal has actually worked elsewhere, or if he can draw a vivid sketch of about how it might work, with enough detail to make the plan seem alive, he can often win favorable response. The greatest virtue of the public speaker has often been considered his power not only to make people *understand* but to make them *see*.

Give special emphasis to one aspect of the problem or to one solution, and subordinate or omit other sides of the question and other solutions. Judicious neutrals frequently find no great objections one way or another, but all sides and alternatives look equally attractive; at one moment they lean one way, at the next moment, another. Consequently, the speaker makes his solution look as attractive as possible by (*a*) great concentration upon it and by (*b*) largely excluding rival ideas. Of special importance here will be motives and attitudes that will give force and strength to argument and evidence. Keep attention undivided, and exclude competing, unfavorable ideas. This is not deception unless the speaker is dishonest; it is merely sensible economy.

In addressing the judicious element, use as many facts and as much evidence as is consistent with a and b above. Thus a speaker will tend to satisfy those neutrals who are undecided because of insufficient information. [*Note:* In discussion with potential members of an audience, watch for such responses as "I don't know" (a sign of inadequate information?), "I just can't make up my mind" (a sign of vacillation?), and "I agree, *but* there's one thing that . . ." (a sign that a special objection is hindering decision?).]

Neutrals and Partisans

In addressing the neutrals, one cannot afford to ignore partisans.

Make the entire speech as interesting as possible. Some of the ideas used to address the neutrals—perhaps all of the ideas—will be old and familiar to the judicial and informed partisan. Accordingly, avoid alienating supporters by boring them.

In being interesting one is employing good tactics on the indifferent partisan whose indifference and lethargy keep him from active partisanship. Furthermore, by including information for the ill-informed neutral in the group, one also appeals to the tepid partisan, for his lukewarm attitude may be the result in part of his not having had any real knowledge and argument on the problem.

Avoid ideas that will alienate the partisans. Suppose a speaker were arguing that longer vacations with pay would be a boon to labor and to the country, and some of the hearers were generally sympathetic to labor but didn't like James Hoffa. To mention his name or to cite him as an authority would hurt both the speaker and his argument. Let sleeping inhibitions lie unless there is a real reason for awaking them. This is especially true in addressing prejudiced partisans.

The speaker need not appeal to or condone the prejudice of the irrational partisan. The attitudes that feed his prejudice—such as loyalty to his class and social group—are likely to be so broad that he will apply them automatically to almost anything said or implied.

Influencing Partisans

Often a group is already persuaded of the soundness of an idea or of the desirability of an action. The audience is overwhelmingly partisan. A speaker accordingly will concern himself with one of two goals: (1) to impress upon his hearers the old truth and thus encourage them to act upon it whenever the opportunity comes; (2) to urge them to a definite and specific action to be undertaken immediately or in the very near future. In either case the speaker seeks *to intensify* attitude. Most preachers seek to accomplish the first purpose; they try to keep the virtues of right conduct and of religion bright and appealing to a congregation whose presence indicates sympathy and respect for religion. The advertiser and the salesman ordinarily have in mind the second purpose.

For Sharpening the Impression

The general method is to give the old theme new interest. Accordingly those ideas and methods that elicit imagery and enliven the old idea with new information and interpretations are especially valuable.

Associate the old with the new. (1) Seek a new angle or point of view; (2) use novel illustrations; (3) build up vivid and sharp images. A good illustration of a speech to impress is Bruce Barton's "Which Knew Not Joseph," printed in the Appendix. Mr. Barton spoke of the value to business of persistent advertising, of the wisdom of being always sincere, and of the need for being warm and friendly—all "old stuff" to his audience. Especially effective were his illustrations—the humorous story which has real point, the familiar story of Joseph given a new interpretation, and examples drawn from personal experience.

Apply the old truth to the present situation. For example, what does the old Christian maxim, "Do unto others as you would that they should do unto you," mean to modern business (if one were addressing a business men's club)? To student relationships (if one thought it appropriate to talk on this to his class)?

For Securing Action

Again the speaker's primary job is to keep his listeners' undivided attention on the conduct desired, and avoid ideas that suggest alternative action. An idea of an action, keenly perceived and understood, tends to result in the action.

Of particular value in moving listeners to action are the following methods:

Making the hearer imagine himself doing what is desired. If one would get a friend to shove aside his books or beer stein and go to the movies, one might say, "Just think of that cool, comfortable theatre. Remember the last Disney we saw? There's another one on. And you know how gorgeous Marilyn Monroe is—not to mention Louis Armstrong taking off on the 'Basin Street Blues.' Just think, man!—comfort, Monroe, and music out of this world!" Of course, pleasure and sex are effective motives here, but imagery so chosen as to put the hearer imaginatively into the action desired does the real work.

Awakening the confidence of hearers by showing them that the action is practicable. Perhaps nothing so promotes confidence as to show that other groups, similar to your audience, have acted as you propose and have enjoyed *success.* On an occasion when an all-fraternity council was considering whether to recommend requiring a "C" average for initiation into a fraternity, the strongest appeal was made by a student who took five minutes to explain that the adoption of the measure at X University had been a signal success. Concern and worry were replaced by confidence and considerable enthusiasm.

Enlisting the pride of hearers. Pride is an emotion centering on the self and is stimulated chiefly by the high regard in which others hold the self. Consequently, we cherish our reputation, are cordial to admiration, and expand under anything that enhances our prestige and self-importance. One can enlist pride by showing that the desired action will enhance or protect the reputation and prestige of hearers.

Here the speaker reminds his audience that others—individuals or groups—have regarded them as progressive, as men of good will or men of honor, and suggests that in the face of such regard they will not want to refrain from acting as suggested. A speaker who engineers an appeal to his hearers' reputation must always take two steps: (1) logically associate the action desired with one or more basic motives and values, and (2) definitely indicate that other persons respect the audience for holding the attitudes.

Prior to a local election, a housewife illustrated both steps well. A citizen of Brown Township, stumping for the bond issue that would finance a new school building, she reminded her hearers that they had always supported measures which preserved and enhanced the educational opportunities of their children. "In fact," she said in substance, "you have a reputation for guarding the opportunities of our youth. The *Record* [the newspaper of the neighboring county seat] last month said this about us: 'Some persons are asking whether Brown Township will pass the school bond proposal. We think its people will. They not only can afford it, but more than the people in most districts we know of, the citizenry of Brown Township are mindful of the educational welfare of their children.' "

Making the audience face squarely the arguments—and especially conditions and facts—that call for the desired action. Here the speaker briefly reviews the reasons that have led his hearers to accept the idea of the action that they have not yet taken. In particular he gives great emphasis to the facts—unpleasant though they may be—and to the excuses and evasions that have led his audience to side-step action. One of the weaknesses of human nature is to forget, to put out of mind, unpleasant evils that cry for remedy. We don't like to think of the deplorable conditions in the slums or the poverty and malnutrition in underprivileged countries. We sometimes excuse our failure to hold an opinion on grounds of "having an open mind," our shady financial deals as being "good business," our laziness and procrastination on grounds of being too tired or too ill, our own destructiveness as being students' fun, our dissipation as evidence of being good fellows, and our cheating on examination as a sign of cleverness rather than of immorality and ignorance! There are times when a speaker can and should speak bluntly and plainly; such a time comes when people fail to act as they should because they shut their eyes to facts that demand action and indulge in conscience-saving evasions.

One of the most direct and telling examples of making an audience face the facts of a situation occurred in the course of Clarence Darrow's argument to the judge who was to determine the sentence of two college students, both confessed murderers. Darrow sought life imprisonment for the defendants, rather than execution. He said:

> Your Honor, it may be hardly fair to the court, I am aware, that I have helped to place a serious burden upon your shoulders. And at that I have always meant to be your friend. But this was not an act of friendship.
>
> I know perfectly well that where responsibility is divided by twelve, it is easy to say:
>
> "Away with him."
>
> But, your Honor, if these boys hang, you must do it. There can be no division of responsibility here. You can never explain that the rest overpowered

you. It must be by your deliberate, cool, premeditated act, without a chance to shift responsibility.[4]

The direct suggestion or command is especially effective when an audience is ready to act. A speaker can quite frankly say, "Go and do so-and-so." A student once interested a class in reading *The Grapes of Wrath* and at the end of his speech offered an explicit direction:

All you need to do now, if you are interested in Mr. Steinbeck's book, is to go to the library during the next vacant hour you have and fill out the call card. The call number of the book is PN6167 S112. There are six copies available, and in three minutes you have the book. If you have no class next hour, go at once and be sure of a good book you can start reading this afternoon or tonight.

The oblique form of the same suggestion would have been: "I think you will want to read the book at the first chance you get." Or, "Isn't this book sufficiently interesting to be read at the first opportunity?"

The beginning speaker should always remember this: When an audience is ready to act and wants to act, supply explicit directions. If he can rouse real interest and enthusiasm for the proposal—as he very often can with the partisan audience—he can give the hearers something definite to do. If he wants them to sign a petition or endorse a resolution, he should give them a chance to sign as soon as possible. If he wants them to write their Senator or Congressman, he should give them definite directions and information so that they can. Supply his name and address, and perhaps suggest what they should say. When a speaker fails to capitalize on the readiness of his hearers to act, he blocks and frustrates them. There are few disappointments so great as to want to do *something* and not to know just what to do or not to be able to do it.

Influencing Opponents

Conditions

Ordinarily it is futile to try to make converts out of opponents in a single speech. People usually change their beliefs on a subject, if at all, only over a considerable period of time. The process of radical change-of-front is almost always slow and requires substantial education, exposition and persuasion, many speeches and books and articles, and much discussion.

Nevertheless, the zealous speaker need not feel discouraged about his chances with the opponents in his audience. First, even in the single

[4] Defense of Richard Loeb and Nathan Leopold, Jr. In W. N. Brigance, ed., *Classified Speech Models of Eighteen Forms of Public Address* (New York, 1928), p. 141.

speech it is always possible to get persons to believe less surely. Merely to *soften opposition* in a single effort is a positive accomplishment, and the veteran speaker, as well as the beginner, should regard it as such. Second, converts can sometimes be made on a subject toward which opponents do not respond emotionally and which does not deal with fundamental economic, social, or political questions having wide implications. One would be foolish to try to convert conservative business men and industrialists to state socialism, or even to persuade them to take a *limited* step toward socialism, such as to accept government ownership of railroads. But on less touchy and fundamental questions, there is fair chance of success. The auditing of the finances of extracurricular societies, changing the grading system, shortening the Christmas holidays, altering rushing rules and the regulations governing parties—to mention only a few campus perennials—do not involve social upheavals. These are limited in their social implications, and opponents who are not strongly prejudiced can sometimes be brought around to the advocate's view in a single speech.

There is another time when shift of attitude is quite possible: it is at that stage in a controversy in which discussion concerns *means and methods* of change, rather than the desirability of change. When almost everyone agrees that there are deplorable evils, that the disease has reached a point at which something must be done, discussion turns to the means of cure. Since most people have recognized the need for change, there is a big area of agreement. Hence, there is a favorable attitude toward solution of some kind, and this promotes rational consideration and choice of the best cure. Such an atmosphere even permits acceptance of a cure that is not perfect. For example, the United States Senate accepted the United Nations Charter, an imperfect instrument of world peace.

In framing the statement of the proposition do not ask hearers among whom are influential opponents to make a radical change from their habitual conduct and attitude; choose a statement that requires but little reorientation of habits of action and belief. Be moderate rather than extreme.

Methods

THE JUDICIOUS OPPONENT

Meet the chief objections of the judicious opponent, so far as you can discover them through discussion and reading. The judicious opponent has weighed and considered the question under discussion and, in all probability, has looked at it from all sides—at least he believes so. Since he has reasoned to a conclusion and respects reason, the speaker can meet him directly on rational grounds, can recognize his objections and reason with him directly about them.

New facts and new conditions may lead an opponent to reconsider his opinions. The judicious opponent is usually willing to consider any and all material that is relevant to the problem. He has tried to over-look nothing important in making up his mind. Yet often on problems that keep recurring in different form, such as the best kind of taxation, he has been unable to keep up-to-date and hasn't fully realized that fact.

Mention ideas and opinions that both speaker and opponent have in common. Those experienced in conciliation and arbitration techniques say that conflict is intensified when contending parties emphasize their disagreements and that opposition is minimized when agreements are clearly discerned. Consequently, you would be wise to determine what you and your opponents have in common, and briefly but clearly review the common ground early in your speech, probably in the introduction.

MEETING THE CASUAL OPPONENT AND THE PREJUDICED OPPONENT

If a study of an audience reveals that such opponents are in the minority, the speaker does not have an insuperable problem. First, the casual opponent—he who has happened to hear more against the speaker's opinion than for it—probably lacks information. Consequently, the reasoning and information designed for the neutrals will be fairly effective for him. Secondly, since one is not likely to make a convert out of a prejudiced opponent, one's job is simply to avoid rousing his prejudices and increasing his opposition. A speaker cannot disregard and neglect the prejudiced listener; he simply takes care not to offend him by a careless remark or phrase.

In the lone persuasive speech, a speaker should remember that his major task is to keep his partisans interested and if possible swing the neutrals into line. As for opponents, a speaker does not ignore them; he deals frankly and tactfully with his judicious critics and avoids harden-ing the hostility of his prejudiced opponents.

Much of what we have been advising may seem like no more than common sense. It is buttressed, nevertheless, by the findings of some experimental studies which were designed to determine the effective-ness of recognizing and arguing "both sides" in a controversial situation. It is better to present both sides rather than one side only when listeners possess intellectual and critical ability and when they will continue to be exposed to many-sided arguments.[5]

[5] For example, see Carl Hovland, Irving Janis, and Harold H. Kelley, *Communication and Persuasion* (New Haven, 1953), p. 294.

Logical Modes of Persuasion

We have identified thus far three methods of handling persuasive materials: the ways of amplification, the style of language, the adjustment of ideas to the attitudes of the audience. We consider now one other way of handling materials and ideas. It is the logical mode.

The mode takes advantage of man's tendency to believe when statements (and the ideas they carry) are so arranged as to call attention to their consistency, relevancy to each other, and reliability. The form and support of the combination of statements appeal to *reasonable* men. The force of the appeal is evident in the remark, "That sounds reasonable," or "That makes sense."

The basis of logical support is fact and opinion. If the basis is shaky, doubtful, and untrustworthy, any reasoning that is built upon it seems weak and unconvincing. Hence when the speaker considers facts and opinions as support for his statements, he has a special concern for their accuracy and reliability. Indeed, in a close argument he may be forced to indicate why they can be depended upon. He should therefore be aware of the rules of evidence.

Evidence

Evidence consists of those matters of fact and of opinion which form part of an argument.

Although the law employs an elaborate classification of evidence, we shall treat of two basic kinds, factual evidence and opinion evidence.

FACTUAL EVIDENCE

Factual evidence consists of *data* which have been perceived or observed by somebody. The data are what have been directly registered on the senses—the senses of vision, hearing, taste, smell, and touch. Such data become evidence when they are *interpreted* in more than one way.

Suppose we were playing bridge in our living room. We hear a piercing scream outside in the street. Everyone rushes to the window and beholds this scene: A woman yelling in the road, a car passing by, a man running in one direction, and a dog running in another direction. One observer says, "The man hit her"; another, "The car hit her"; another, "The dog bit her." The facts are the data: a scream, a woman in the street, a moving car, a running man, a running dog. The facts become evidence in each person's interpretation of them.

Factual evidence can be classified according to its *source* and *scope*.

The source of the facts may be *direct,* as it was for each person in the scene above. Each observed the events he himself interpreted. Similarly, the speaker is the source of his evidence when he draws on his direct experience. The source, moreover, may be *more or less remote.* Historical events, for example, reveal different degrees of remoteness. The past event may have occurred quite recently, as when one reads in today's newspaper that Queen Elizabeth landed in Montreal yesterday. The facts of the history books, of course, are more remote; for example, "Lincoln was shot in Ford's Theatre." Nevertheless, the remote fact, like the direct fact, was observed by somebody. It has simply been preserved for later use—for use by a speaker or by anybody else. When a speaker makes use of a past fact, obviously he is not his own witness to the fact. Somebody else must be *testifying* to the fact.

The scope of facts refers to their number—whether there is a single fact or many. In our street scene, there might have been but one fact, a scream; for by the time we looked out the window there might have been no moving objects to be seen. As it was, we were presented with five events. In other cases, the scope of the facts may be very wide indeed. A statistic, for example, may represent a collection of facts. If one reads that there were 11,230 students enrolled at Siwash University in 1961–1962, the figure reflects a large number of observations from a registrar's records. If one reads that steel workers receive $3.37 an hour, the statement conceals a very large number of observations, made by many persons whose data have been interpreted as an average figure. Where facts are extensive and have been gathered systematically through wide investigation and experiment, they are usually called statistics. (See pages 66–69 above.)

OPINION EVIDENCE

Opinion evidence consists of the interpretations and judgments of others on which we rely when the facts themselves cannot be obtained. Suppose a person believes that "fraternity hazing often results in physical injury," because "the Dean of Students at X University says that 'hazing at our college has often broken bones.'" The dean has not gone on to cite cases; he has merely expressed his opinion or judgment. Belief has come about on the Dean's say-so.

The distinctive aspect of opinion evidence lies in its *authority.* It is the interpretation or judgment of an *expert,* a person in a position to know, a person whose competence as an interpreter is accepted. Obviously, when a speaker cannot be his own expert on his subject, he must rely on the expertness of others.

RELIABILITY AND TRUSTWORTHINESS OF EVIDENCE

Since in persuasion many arguments rest on fact and opinion, a speaker levels a critical eye on his facts and his authorities. Partly he does so to satisfy himself of the grounds of his own belief. Partly he does so because he gauges what his audience will accept as fact and authority. We recall the student, given a ticket for illegal parking, who explained to the judge that his car had been pushed close to the fire hydrant.

> "I can't accept that," said the Judge.
> "But," said the student, "I properly parked it, and when I came back the car had been moved."
> Said the Judge, "That's not evidence for me."

There are a few fundamental tests which the critically minded speaker will apply to his evidence.

1. *Are the sources of evidence reliable?* Who observed the fact or who compiled the statistics? Is there any reason to suspect that the observer was influenced by more than ordinary bias? At the present time, the facts about lung cancer and cigarette smoking are many and various. One puts more trust in those coming from an independent laboratory than in those originating in the laboratory of a tobacco company.

The reliability of authoritative opinion must be weighed with special care. Is the person expressing the opinion in a special position to know the facts from which his opinion is derived? Presumably the Dean of Students at X University, because the Dean's office has been in touch with fraternity life over many years, is in a position to know about hazing practices and their results—at least at X University. But would the Dean be as acceptable an authority on hazing in other universities as would some national agency that compiled information on the hazing practices of all fraternities?

Furthermore, does the person expressing the opinion have a reputation for good judgment, that is, for making conservative and valid inferences from the facts that are behind his opinions? Is he free of undue bias and prejudice? A practical way of deciding these questions is to discover whether the authority enjoys the respect and confidence of others who know of him and his work. Has the book from which the speaker has drawn the opinion been favorably received by those who can pass upon its worth? (A convenient source of evaluation is the *Book Review Digest*, where many reviews of recent books are brought together.)

Finally, does the opinion run counter to the author's natural interest and bias? If so, it can be given great weight. When Wendell Willkie, a Republican campaigning for the presidency against Franklin Roosevelt, a Democrat, publicly endorsed Roosevelt's foreign policy and his treatment of the war, the endorsement was especially significant because it was contrary to Mr. Willkie's interests to express an opinion that would help the Democrats and which they would use as a campaign argument.

2. *Is communication of the evidence accurate?* Can the speaker *report* his own observations accurately? Would visual materials help secure exactness? Is there need to write and then memorize or quote?

In reporting the observations of others, the quotation, if read *well,* is very useful. The quotation, in fact, is doubly useful to the speaker: he is satisfied himself that he is reporting exactly and in effect assures his hearers that he is being accurate. If one doubts the value of accuracy in communication, remember that the law prefers the original of a document, and if a copy is presented, it must be sworn to as a true copy.

3. *Is the evidence sufficiently inclusive in scope?* Are there other witnesses to the same fact and do they make the same report? Agreement among a number of witnesses is an excellent check on accuracy. The single evidential fact seldom carries much weight. The law usually insists on more than one witness to a fact.

When a speaker relies on the opinions and judgments of others, he must be sure that a number of authorities hold similar opinions on the same matter. This gives a check on the *consistency* of opinion, as well as its scope.

In securing and using data from others, a speaker is likely to run into statistics. If the evidence is statistical, what do the statistics really mean? Does the observer or reporter indicate for what *purpose* they were gathered? Does he state the *method of investigation* used? Do the statistics cover a large number of cases? If statistics are sufficiently valuable in influencing a speaker's decision and that of others, he should be able to give clear explanations in the speech.

4. *Is the evidence recent?* If the speaker draws on his own experience, is it recent? Remember that memory is imperfect and that the remote event is warped in memory; remember, too, that our recent experiences tend either to correct and supersede remote observations or to substantiate them. In selecting data from his own experience, then, the speaker prefers the recent observation, rather than the remote.

In using the opinions of authorities, the speaker does well to become date conscious. He should prefer the reliable opinion that is most up-to-date. Authorities, like any of us, do change their minds. He should check on the witness, too, who is reporting an event. Does he cite a *specific* date?

Forms of Argument

When reasoning is conducted logically, the speaker works his ideas and evidence into the patterns described below.

DEDUCTION

The deductive pattern applies the meaning of a general statement to a more specific, relevant statement, and thus permits a conclusion to be drawn. The process is one by which the particular is brought within the significance of the general so as to suggest a consequence. For example:

> Contracts should be honored. (*General Premise*)
> Room leases are contracts. (*Specific Premise*)
> Room leases should be honored. (*Conclusion*)

(In deduction, the general statement may be conveniently named the *general premise,* the more particular statement the *specific premise.*) In the example above, room leases as an idea is brought within the meaning of contracts. This done, whatever may be asserted of contracts may also be said of room leases—not all things, of course, but those things thought to be relevant and fitting as measured by the experience of the speaker and listener. The notion of "should be honored" can be applied to contracts, at least as a general rule. Ergo, room leases should be honored.

In use, the deductive pattern may be presented as it is above, with the general premise starting the pattern and the conclusion ending it. More often, however, the order is this:

> Room leases should be honored. (*Conclusion*)
> They are contracts. (*Specific Premise*)
> Contracts should be honored. (*General Premise*)

This is the order and indentation of the speech outline. It is also the order observed in conversation more often than not. Because the sequence seems "natural," we shall observe it in the illustrations below.

To every instance of deductive reasoning, the speaker applies three test questions:

1. *Are the meanings of the premises unequivocally clear?*

2. *Is the predicate-idea of the specific premise properly included within the subject-idea of the general premise?* In the example above, "contracts" in the general premise is taken to mean *all* contracts; so the same word in the specific premise is necessarily included within the meaning.

The necessary connection is ideal and a speaker rejoices when he can show one. If there be any condition which he can claim is "conclusive," "beyond all shadow of doubt," this is it. But in much argument about human problems and behavior, as distinct from matters of science, the perfect general premises—the generalizations without exception—are few and far between. General premises are likely to be true almost always, or in most cases. In other words, they are *probably* true, not invariably true. Hence, the wise, perceptive speaker must often be cautious about claiming too much for his general premises. He does well to keep in mind an ever possible qualification, as for example, "All contracts should be honored except in unusual circumstances." Then he can show, if necessary and if conditions suggest it for the case at hand, that the conditions are *not* unusual or peculiar. We all subscribe to the belief that *no person should lie;* yet there are instances when some high humanitarian motive justifies an exception.

3. *Which premise needs supporting?* In many contexts the general premise is so obviously acceptable to the audience that it barely needs mention, if at all. It is the specific premise which, as a rule, demands support and needs to be established as true.

EXAMPLE

A general statement may be supported by examples. The process is often called generalization from example, or argument from example. In the process, an idea that is wider in scope than the example carries the notion of the *many.* The example bears the notion of the *one.* In addition, the connection between the one and the many derives its force from this implication: what is true of the one is also true of the many. For instance:

> Wars are triggered by provocative incidents. (*Generalization*)
> Firing on Fort Sumter started the American Civil War. (*Example*)

> Students gain confidence in public speaking through experience in public speaking classes. (*Generalization*)
> Jones did. (*Example*)

> Tests of vocational aptitude are useful in choosing one's life work. (*Generalization*)
> They were for Jones. (*Example*)

If the argument from example is to be convincing, at least three key questions must be answered affirmatively:

1. *Is a single example sufficient?* Because of their cumulative force, a number of examples usually carries more weight than a single one. As in statistical inference, the larger the population under observation, the more probable is the truth of the generalization about the population. In numbers there is strength. In a speech, of course, there is not time for anything like an exhaustive enumeration of cases. Yet the lone instance is seldom convincing. The listener is too likely to respond, "But that's only one case; what about others?" The persuader should keep in mind the distinction between the role of the example in exposition and in persuasion. In explaining a general idea, the example *illustrates,* and

a single one may be enough to secure clearness. In argument, the example is intended to prove.

The argument from example is most effective when the instances can be followed by statistical evidence. To illustrate:

> Most students buy their textbooks at X Bookstore. (*Generalization*)
> Peterson does. (*Example*)
> Rhodes does. (*Example*)
> In our largest dormitory, 11 out of 12 students do. (*Statistics*)
> A survey of buyers at X Bookstore last semester showed that 9 out of 10 of them were students. (*Statistics*)

2. *Are the examples truly comparable and relevant?* A generalization arises out of a number of similar instances and asserts what the instances have in common. Sometimes it is relatively easy to see in what respects examples are similar to each other and to the principal idea expressed in the general statement. One can readily recognize, for example, a single point of comparison. In the illustration above, there is but a single point of likeness, the buying of textbooks. On the other hand it is more difficult to perceive clearly and to state exactly *several* points of similarity, particularly when they are buried in an abstract word. For example:

> Students in Y fraternity are responsible persons. (*Generalization*)
> Barnes of Y fraternity is a responsible individual. (*Example*)

What is entailed in responsibility? Various traits of behavior are associated with it, and one would have to make sure which traits before he could know they were common to both the general statement and the example. Upon the presence of the same traits would depend the soundness of any comparison between Barnes and his brothers in the fraternity.

3. *Do the exceptional cases, if any, weaken the generalization?* We recall the old proverb, "The exception proves the rule." It does, in the sense that it *tests* the rule. So any exception must be regarded critically. Is it unusual—so far out of line with other instances that it weakens the force of the generalization? If it cannot be accounted for satisfactorily, a general statement less wide in scope had better be used, or the generalization abandoned entirely.

ARGUMENT FROM ANALOGY

A comparison brings together two ideas, objects, or events and makes the most of their similarities rather than their differences. The argument from analogy is built on a number of similarities between two sets of conditions or circumstances. It specifies that one set of conditions has characteristics *A, B, C, D,* and *E,* and that the second set of conditions also reveals *A*, *B*, *C*, and *D*. Then it concludes that *E* either is true or will be true in the second set. For example:

Jones will do good work at *X* University. (*Conclusion*)
 He did good work at *Y* University. (*Specific Premise*)
 X and *Y* Universities are comparable in ways that affect grades. (*Comparative Premise*)
  Both have similar scholastic standards. (*Condition 1*)
  Both have similar faculties. (*Condition 2*)
  Both place studies ahead of social affairs and campus activities. (*Condition 3*)

Note that the argument from analogy is well named, for it derives its strength and cogency *from* a comparison which is expressed as a premise. Note, also, that the comparative premise is a conclusion with respect to the items of similarity which support it.

Analogical argument is a powerful tool of persuasion if two requirements are met:

1. *The greater the number of similarities between two particulars, the more convincing is the conclusion.* In reasoning that true-false tests will prove successful in elementary economics because they have been successful in elementary physics, the more points of likeness between the two courses, the sounder the conclusion. Both courses are designed for freshmen and sophomores; both courses assume that students are of about the same age and have the same academic preparation; both deal with principles and laws that are matters of fact; both aim to impart knowledge rather than skill.

2. *The dissimilarities between the particulars must not be more significant than the likenesses.* Do the laws of economics—the law of supply and demand, for example—admit of so many qualifications and special conditions that they cannot be tested by a simple true or false answer? And are there fewer exceptions and special qualifications in the laws of physics? If the answers are yes, then the single dissimilarity is far more significant than all the similarities noted above.

EFFECT TO CAUSE

A causal relationship is held to exist whenever one event or condition controls and accounts for the occurrence or behavior of another. In the effect-to-cause pattern, some present or past condition is accounted for by an event or condition which preceded it. The statement to be supported is treated as an effect. The supporting statement, or statements, is regarded as the cause or condition. For example:

Khrushchev's speeches to the West have been provocative. (*Effect*)
 He wants to gain the initiative. (*Cause*)

Persons who desire the initiative almost always speak provocatively. (*General Rule*)

Often, as in this example, the credibility of a cause depends upon the credibility of the generalization which is relevant to it. The general rule expresses the audience's knowledge of similar causal conditions and makes the application to the case at hand. In such situations, the cause to be established is an educated guess. It cannot be taken as a fact. Hence, the speaker must be confident that the generalization is acceptable.

In other situations, the speaker is better off. When he can draw on more exact knowledge than that of opinion and belief, when he can pull in the findings of science and experiment, he can establish the fact of the cause. This, combined with the law or general principle, is highly convincing. For example:

Williams is a dependable student. (*Effect*)
   He always completes his assignments on time. (*Cause*)
   Prompt discharge of commitments always attends dependability. (*Principle*)

Here the statement of cause could be substantiated by enumerating instances and by statistical evidence.

Probably the most convincing situation of all arises when it can be shown that in the absence of the cause there was a contrary effect. For example:

Farmer X produced more wheat per acre than his neighbor. (*Effect*)
   He used chemical fertilizer. (*Cause*)
   His neighbor did not. (*Absence of Cause*)
   Chemical fertilizer always increases the yield of a crop unless some circumstance interferes. (*Principle*)

In selecting a causal argument and in presenting it, a speaker will be guided by a number of questions:

1. *Does the argument deal with events or conditions?* Whenever a speaker can deal with real causes, the argument is more convincing than when he has to depend upon favoring conditions only.

2. *Is the effect accounted for by a single cause or condition?* In locating *the* cause—if there be an only cause—the speaker weighs the possibility of other causes. Human problems are seldom simple. Obviously forest fires, high grades, world peace, radiation effects, and high prices cannot be explained in terms of single causes.

3. *How direct is the connection between cause and effect?* To consider this question is to see the difference between an immediate or trigger cause and a more remote but compelling condition. The immediate cause of a forest fire may be a lighted cigarette thrown from a

car, or an unextinguished campfire. The more remote condition is a habit—carelessness.

4. *In the absence of the cause, would the effect be as probable?* Too often we confuse coincidence and chance with cause and effect. Few people today believe that carrying a rabbit's foot, crossing the fingers, or knocking on wood will keep away bad luck. But some athletes still wear lucky socks and lucky numbers. And some persons say that the atom bomb tests are responsible for the outbreak of unusually violent storms and floods in many parts of the country for the past few years. As yet we do not know of a connection between storms and A-bomb explosions, but there were similar periods of abnormally bad weather long before the A-bomb was invented. Our friend the basketball coach actually does win some games without wearing his lucky socks.

CAUSE TO EFFECT

This logical pattern involves a prediction about the future. The effect-to-cause pattern, on the other hand, is oriented on the present and past. By the nature of his task, the persuader must employ both patterns. To see why this is so helps in understanding and in using the patterns.

The logic of the problem-solution state of affairs can be put simply: a speaker must address himself to either the problem or a particular solution or both. If he talks on the problem, he has these alternatives: He says, "I think present conditions are bad and I want you to think so too." Or he says, "I see what the problem is, and it is of this nature because of certain causes and conditions." If he talks to the solution, he says, "I have a solution, and it will remove the causes and conditions which created the problem." Or—if the audience has reached this stage of discussion—he says, "My solution is better than a rival solution, for the rival solution won't take care of the causes which produced the conditions you complain about." One can see at a glance that causal relationships are inherent in recognizing, establishing, and solving a problem. One can see, also, that the problem-solution circumstances entail two dimensions of time. If the speaker deals with the problem only, he is concerned with present conditions and what has caused them. He looks to the present in the light of the past. If the speaker deals with a solution, he says in effect, "If you accept my proposition and act in keeping with it, the consequences *will be* desirable." He looks to the future. Like a physician, the persuasive speaker is a diagnostician; he recognizes the symptoms of the disease—the accompanying conditions and their signs—and determines their cause. He prescribes a remedy. Consequently, when a speaker talks about a problem and its sources, he is reasoning about effects or conditions and their causes. When he is reasoning about solutions, he thinks of his proposition as a cause or condition which will bring desirable consequences. He is then within the framework of the cause-to-effect pattern.

In the cause-to-effect pattern, statements direct attention to a cause or condition and the predicted effect. In the advocacy of a solution, there are two typical kinds of structure:

1. A single statement may join both cause and effect.

Independent audits of labor union funds would eliminate dishonest union officials.

Note that the subject-idea designates the cause; the predicate-idea names the effect.

2. One statement asserts a condition which entails more than one effect; succeeding statements specify the effects.

It would be desirable to have union officials elected by secret ballot.
The requirement would prevent intimidation of members at election time. It would restore democratic procedures to labor unions which have lost them.

In using a cause-to-effect argument, the speaker encounters two questions: Has the causal relationship held true in the past? If it has been true in the past, is there any reason why it should *not* operate as expected in the future? The relevancy of these questions can be perceived from the following example:

Independent audits of labor union funds would eliminate dishonest union officials. (*Conclusion*)
Independent audits of the funds of any organization discourage dishonesty among officials. (*General Premise*)
Unions do not differ from other organizations in ways which would make an audit ineffective. (*Comparative Premise*)

The general premise is combining two ideas: (1) it implies that a union is an example of an organization in which (2) the cause has produced the effect. Then the comparative premise says that a union, taken as an example of an organization, reveals no condition which would make the cause ineffective. Thus it is apparent that the cause-to-effect pattern involves a prediction whose force depends upon comparable conditions in the present and the past.

The speaker who is familiar with the five logical patterns and who gains experience in applying them in his speeches will gradually realize the sources of their effectiveness. He will see that they cannot make sense to a reasonable person unless the meanings they carry are clear, stable, and unequivocal.

FURTHER READING

BREMBECK, W. L., and W. S. HOWELL, *Persuasion: A Means of Social Control* (New York, 1952), Ch. 24, "Ethics."

COHEN, Morris, and Ernest NAGEL, *An Introduction to Logic and Scientific Method* (New York, 1936).

DEWEY, John, "Authority and Social Change," in *Authority and the Individual* (Cambridge, Mass., 1937).

EISENSON, Jon, *The Psychology of Speech* (New York, 1938), Ch. 17, "Motivation."

FRYE, A. M., and A. W. LEVI, *Rational Belief* (New York, 1941).

GRAY, G. W., and C. M. WISE, *The Bases of Speech*, 3rd ed. (New York, 1959), Ch. 9., "The Semantic Basis."

GRAY, G. W., and Waldo BRADEN, *Public Speaking: Principles and Practices* (New York, 1951), Chs. 3–4, "Motivation and Interest"; Ch. 5, "Occasion and Audience."

HAIMAN, Franklyn S., "An Experimental Study of the Effect of Ethos in Public Speaking," *Speech Monographs*, 16, No. 2 (1949), 190–202.

HOLLINGWSORTH, H. L., *The Psychology of the Audience* (New York, 1935), Ch. 3, "Types of Audiences."

HOVLAND, Carl J., Irving L. JANIS, and Harold H. KELLEY, *Communication and Persuasion* (New Haven, Conn., 1953).

MINNICK, Wayne, *The Art of Persuasion* (Boston, 1957), Ch. 5, "Suggestion"; Ch. 6, "Argument"; Ch. 12, "Ethics."

OLIVER, Robert, *The Psychology of Persuasive Speech* (New York, 1957), Ch. 2, "Ethics"; Ch. 8, "Identification"; Chs. 9–12, on modes of appeal.

PACKARD, Vance, *The Hidden Persuaders* (New York, 1958).

RUBY, Lionel, *Logic, An Introduction* (New York, 1950).

WHYTE, William H., *Is Anybody Listening?* (New York, 1952).

WINANS, J. A., *Public Speaking* (New York, 1917), Ch. 8, "Influencing Conduct."

CHAPTER TWELVE

Style

THROUGHOUT the long history of systematic writing on the principles of public speaking—that is, on rhetoric—the part of the subject which most writers have treated at greatest length and in most detail has been the language of the speech. This emphasis is understandable. Speeches, first and foremost, are tissues of words, words supported by bodily expression and vocal quality, of course, but principally words. Words are the common counters, the standard coinage, through which we conduct our transactions in communication, whether in speech or in writing and whatever the particular purpose. Language, then, and principally the language of words rather than of other symbols and signals, finally makes a speech the thing that it is. Language gives it an existence and makes it live, brings it from something conceived and potential in the mind, feelings, and imagination to something actual and dynamic in human relations.

Another reason why much attention tends to center in the language of a speech is that the language, interpreted by the delivery, creates in the listener the first and quickest impression of the message of the speech, the sort of person the speaker is, and the tone and mood of the occasion. Furthermore, in the long run the way an idea or an opinion is cast into words determines *precisely* what that idea or opinion is. Finally, memorable language in a speech often sticks in listeners' minds and represents for them what the whole speech means. Whatever Lincoln intended in his *Gettysburg Address,* for nearly a hundred years it has *meant* to Americans "of the people, by the people, and for the people." Probably the grandeur of Sir Winston Churchill's language and the stately strength of his sentences had as much to do with sustaining the English in World War II as had any particular messages he gave them from time to time.

DEFINITION AND QUALITIES OF STYLE

There can be no doubt, therefore, of the importance of the speaker's skillful use of language, and hence of what is called *good style.* Broadly conceived, style probably cannot be separated from other factors in a speech, and it involves, as the Frenchman Buffon said, "The order and movement which we give to our ideas." In that sense style comprehends much that we have already discussed. In this chapter, however, we shall attend more particularly to style as *that quality in speaking which results from the selection and management of language.*

The foregoing definition has certain important implications. It implies, in the first place, that style is always present in discourse. Though in common parlance we sometimes say that a speech or a man had style or had no style, the definition implies that style is not limited to good speaking or to certain persons. Style will be good, bad, or indifferent depending on what language a speaker selects and how he manages that language. A second important implication of the definition is that style depends upon the *qualities of the words* and upon the *manner in which the words are worked together* and are made to function in connected speech.

Obviously, whether as words or as connected passages, the speaker's language should serve efficiently the purposes of speaking. That is, good style will assist the speaker in getting the audience (1) to understand his meaning, (2) to believe in him, (3) to remember his message, and (4) to wish to accept his ideas. To promote these ends good style will be (1) clear, (2) appropriate, (3) interesting and attractive, and (4) impressive. These four qualities of style do not correspond exactly, of course, to the four functions which the speaking may serve. Roughly, however, we may observe that to be understood a speaker must be clear; that if his language fits the subject, audience, occasion, and himself, his audience is most likely to respect and believe him; that interesting and attractive language tends to make listening easy; and that impressiveness tends to secure memory and motivate action. The *minimal* qualities required of any satisfactory speaking style will be *clearness*, so that the message may be understood, and *appropriateness*, so that the language will in no way discredit the speaker.

In accordance with the definition of style and the desirable qualities of style, we will discuss (1) the speaker's selection of language, that is, his vocabulary; (2) his management of language in connected speech. Then (3) we will suggest desirable methods for developing a good style.

SELECTION OF LANGUAGE—WORDS

"Proper words in proper places make the true definition of a style," wrote Jonathan Swift to a young clergyman just beginning his career of preaching. We shall begin with the choice of proper words.

Clearness

Clear language is language which is easily intelligible to those to whom it is directed. It registers accurately with the audience *as it is spoken.* Through experience in speaking and through knowledge of his hearers a speaker develops a feeling for clear and easy expression. Nevertheless, even though there is no substitute for experience, a speaker can do much deliberately to improve his clearness by trying to infuse into the language of his speech the qualities of familiarity, concreteness, specificity, and action.

Familiar Words

Words that are in current, general, oral use and have live meanings to most people in the society in which the speaker is talking are to be preferred to the more strange or more "elegant" words. Many people may well have some sense of what is signified by *fallacious reasoning* though normally they do not use the words. Nevertheless the speaker before a general audience who would be sure that he is clear will probably say *false thinking* instead. *Pernicious precedent* may be the most exact expression and in some ways the most preferable terminology, but a speaker had better say *bad example* unless he is absolutely sure that his audience knows the meaning of the previous expression. The skillful speaker might say, "This legislation will constitute a pernicious precedent; such laws will leave a bad example for future congresses to follow."

Strange Words

Strange words, of course, may stir up the curiosity of hearers; nevertheless, they almost always hinder understanding, and speakers must learn not to depend upon them. Even such relatively innocent usages as *cinema* for *movie,* and such slightly foreign expressions as *holiday* for *vacation* and *motorcar* for *auto* may delay comprehension. They may suggest a certain elegance in the speaker's intention, but by attracting attention to themselves, they may divert attention from the simple meaning and thereby cloud it.

One may find statistical accounts of the relative familiarity, based on frequency of occurrence, of various classes of English words. The speaker may find such accounts suggestive, but he cannot be governed by them. He must speak in the language which he can command, but he should say to himself again and again, "Am I sure that my audience will know this word or will understand it as I understand it?" "Is there some more familiar word which would convey my meaning and would not arouse irrelevant feelings or ideas in my listeners?" In using familiar language, however, a speaker should beware of seeming to talk down to the audience. Whatever language a speaker uses, he should use as if it were the natural and obvious thing to do.

Technical Words

The use of specialized and technical terminology, or of a restricted vocational jargon, likewise presents problems of familiarity. As we suggested in discussing definition, a speaker must not expect an audience to understand technical language just because he does, or because, as offenders sometimes say, "Any fool who keeps his eyes and ears open ought to know what that means." The fact is that most people receive only the vaguest and most remote impressions from the special language of an occupation or profession or social climate other than their own. On many college campuses, for example, the term *grade-point average* has a definite meaning and is immediately clear. To unacademic persons, however, it has only the most nebulous meaning, if any at all; and from one college campus to another it may be unclear whether a three-point or four-point system is being referred to. We cannot even safely expect a general audience to have an exact idea of what is meant by such common commercial expressions as *inventory, trial balance, requisitions, flow sheet, form letter,* or such frequently used political expressions as *autonomy, self-determination, log rolling, unicameral.* Terminology of this sort should be used wherever necessary, although many times when it is used a more common expression would serve the purpose just as well. When it is used, however, it should be accompanied unobtrusively by explanation, or it should be used in such a context that its meaning cannot be mistaken. The problem of technical or pseudo-technical vocabulary in the common phases of experience is increasing as the terms of the social and psychological sciences creep into popular parlance. Such words as *fixation, psychosis, complex, freudian slip, culture, statistical significance* have a spurious currency which the speaker who would be clear must beware of. Such terms are likely to mean no more to the general audience than that the speaker wishes to be thought a well-informed fellow, not necessarily that he *is* one.

Perhaps a good aid in checking one's vocabulary for familiarity is developing a healthy respect for the capacity of people to *misunderstand* and to be puzzled by the out-of-the-ordinary. Hence one should cultivate the habit of asking oneself often, "Do these words seem familiar to me because I am the person I am, with certain special knowledge and special experience, or because they are current in the general usage of people such as those I am addressing?" Some conscious attention to this question will soon result in the habit of distinguishing between language that is clear to oneself and language that is clear to one's listeners.

Concrete and Specific Words

The concrete, specific word carries a clear and definite meaning to listeners because it points to real objects and real events and is associated with them in objective experience. Consequently, for most purposes concrete terms are better than abstract, and specific terms are better than general terms. When abstract language is necessary, it should be defined or otherwise explained swiftly. If the abstract or technical term is the most accurate for the purpose and is, therefore, necessary, it cannot be left undefined without producing fuzziness in the minds of the audience.

Democracy is abstract, *the government of the United States* is concrete. *Creature* is abstract, *horse* or *man* or *pussycat* is concrete. *Honesty* is abstract; *refusing a perfectly safe opportunity for cheating on an examination* is concrete. *"Depart from evil and do good"* is abstract; *"Thou shalt not covet thy neighbor's wife"* is concrete. Abstract language like abstract thought has great values. Some of the best philosophical and scientific writing in the world would be impossible without it. With the subjects, however, on which most of us talk most of the time, the more abstract the language we use the less memorable will be our speech. Undoubtedly there are important meanings in such common abstractions as *virtue, goodness, sin, liberty, social equality, profit, justice,* but in themselves they hardly produce *clearness* of idea or intention.

A certain Middle Western city is vague; *St. Louis* or *Chicago* or *Toledo* or *Topeka* is specific and should be used instead (unless there is some special reason for not mentioning the name). *Extracurricular activities* is general; the *campus newspaper,* the *year book,* the *French club,* the *debate team,* the *student senate* are specific. At times, of course, speakers *wish* to be general or vague, expecting their audiences to supply, as suits them, the concrete, specific ideas which the speakers avoid. At such times the speaker, obviously, is not being clear and definite, and his style shows that he is not. Under most circumstances of public speaking, however, although we may express our ideas at first in abstract and general terms in order possibly to get preliminary and vague general acceptance of them, not until we become concrete and specific do we really come to grips with the minds of our audience and succeed in convincing or informing them. The clearness of meaning which comes with concrete, specific language stands out notably in the following sentence from Booker T. Washington's *Atlanta Address* (see Appendix). He wished to say that the progress which the Southern Negroes had made in the thirty years since freedom had not come without struggle and difficulty. Observe the familiar, concrete, specific words he chose.

> Starting thirty years ago with ownership here and there in a few quilts and pumpkins and chickens (gathered from miscellaneous sources), remember

the path that has led from these to the inventions and production of agricultural implements, buggies, steam-engines, newspapers, books, statuary,
carving, paintings, the management of drugstores and banks, has not been
trodden without contact with thorns and thistles.

In connection with concrete and specific language, see the discussion
of the language of factual statement on page 68 and of the citation of
statistics on pages 169–170. The speaker who would be clear will ask himself, "How can I bring my ideas down to cases?" "Can I name names and
mention specific items to replace or supplement my abstractions and gen-
eralities?" "What expressions which I am using seem specific and concrete to me but may seem general and abstract to my audience?"

Action Words

People almost always prefer the moving picture to the still picture. Accordingly, whenever a concrete word or phrase also suggests movement
and activity, we greatly enhance clearness.

A speaker can take at least a few practical steps to make his language
act. First, he can watch for opportunities to use action words in place
of words which do not suggest movement. To say that a machine *runs*
is better than to say that a machine *functions;* to say that something
stands up suggests more activity than to say something *resists rough use*
or *assumes a vertical position;* to say that the town council *debated and
passed* an ordinance is probably superior to saying that the council *considered and approved* an ordinance. The general rule, then, is to use
words, particularly verbs, that tend to conjure up momentary action pictures in the minds of listeners.

Second, speakers should prefer what the grammarians call the "active
voice." This means that the language represents the subject of a sentence
as doing the action indicated by the predicate. It is better, for example,
to say, "The gunner drops the shell into the mortar," than to say, "The
shell is held over the muzzle of the mortar," or, "The shell is dropped into
the mortar by the gunner." "We know we should act" is better than "It
is thought that action should be taken." "Congress created a committee to
investigate the problem" is superior to "The problem is to be investigated
by a committee set up by Congress." "Action by the committee is desired
by the chairman" represents a kind of reverse English compared with
"The chairman wants the committee to take action." "We ate our lunch
quickly by the pasture gate" does not leave the meaning in doubt as does
the passive form "Our lunch was eaten by the pasture gate." The active
voice, in brief, almost always creates a sense of movement; the passive
voice, even when clear, stops movement. Still water is less dynamic than
running, rushing, turbulent water.

Appropriateness

A speaker's words may be very clear and yet most unfitting and inappropriate to him, to his audience, to his subject and the occasion.

To the Speaker

When language is inappropriate to the speaker, the reason is usually that he is either straining for elegance or impressiveness and achieving only inflation, or he is mistakenly trying to "speak his audience's language," "to be one of the boys," and managing only to be degraded and substandard. When the agent of the light and power company, whose customer asked to have the electricity turned off, inquired, "Were you contemplating changing your residence?" he was trying for elegance and achieving foolish pomposity. Had he asked, "Are you thinking of moving?" he would have done his business in not only the most unobtrusive but the most efficient language. When the college graduate, who is assumed to be a person of some education, affects the defective grammar and semiliterate vocabulary of the uneducated, he is not (as he may claim) getting on common ground with his audience. He is insulting his audience, as did Patrick Henry when he talked to backwoodsmen in their dialectal and ungrammatical language. Most listeners recognize the inappropriateness of such vocabulary. They understand simple, correct language, even if they do not habitually use it themselves, and they expect a man to speak to them in that language if he is the sort of person to whom it should be normal.

A speaker should also be cautious in using the special terminology or jargon of a particular class of people or occupation not his own. When a college debater, discussing socialized medicine before a group that included physicians, endeavored to meet the physicians on their own verbal ground, he confused *diagnosis* with *prognosis*. He did not find out until later why some of the medical men smiled. If a speaker is to use jargon, he must use it with complete assurance and accuracy. He must realize that any audience had much rather hear him speak fluently and clearly in the language which he can command than to hear him blunder about cheerfully in an idiom in which he is not at home.

LANGUAGE OF THE SPEAKER AS A PERSON AND AS A SPEAKER

The speaker's language, therefore, first of all must seem to belong to him, to be becoming to him, as *a person* and as a speaker. What language belongs to him as a special individual, what his private habits of speech are, bear upon the fitness of his language; but most of the time listeners are not personally and intimately acquainted with the speaker. They know him as a kind of person—an educated business man, a labor leader, a clergyman, a college student—and what seems becoming to him in that role and *in his role as speaker,* taken together, will be fitting and appropriate.

The sense of what qualities of language become a man *as speaker* over and above what fit him as an individual is a delicate sense. That there is a difference has been recognized from Aristotle's time to our own. The subtlety of the difference has led to many mistakes. On the one hand, it has trapped people into adopting a special "speaking style" (and tone of voice) which can readily degenerate into the ridiculous. On the other, and by revulsion from what is called "oratorical" language, it has led to an exaggerated ordinariness, a deliberate debasing of language below what a self-respecting person would wish to use in careful conversation.

LANGUAGE SUPERIOR TO CASUAL TALK

The most desirable language for public speaking will maintain a nice balance a little on the careful side of good conversation. The language which is normal in offhand, informal conversation does not seem natural in public speaking. Therefore the advice of Professor Winans is excellent, "Public speech does not require a low tone, or a careless manner, or undignified English. . . . Give your thoughts fitting garb; to plain thoughts plain expression, to heightened thoughts heightened expression." In a word, the language of a good public speaker is the language of a "gentleman conversing."

It is impossible to provide samples of the language which all speakers should use in all situations so that their language will seem to listeners to be so normal that it will not be conspicuous. That language, however, will fall somewhere within the scope of the following rough-and-ready prescription: Language which is barely usable in the offhand talk of ordinary conversation, because of its informality and casualness will appear debased when it is elevated to the speaker's platform. Language which seems a little too formal in conversation will seem on the platform just enough elevated or enlarged to be in the proper perspective. The learning speaker who keeps a gentle pressure (but only *gentle,* without forcing) on himself to tone up his language will usually improve satisfactorily.

LANGUAGE OF THE EDUCATED PERSON

Most of the users of this book are educated people, or are on the way to becoming educated people. They are among those people, therefore, who will be expected to use language which does not attract attention to itself as defective in grammar and usage. They will wish to speak so as not to raise the eyebrows or divert the attention of the "judicious," as Hamlet said to the players. Bad grammar and faulty pronunciation, of course, are not moral offenses. Nevertheless, because on most occasions they conflict with what listeners expect of educated speakers, they invite attention away from intended meaning by adding meaning which is not intended—that the speaker is somehow deficient in his education. It may be true no longer that, as Ruskin wrote a century ago, "a false accent or a mistaken syllable is enough, in the parliament of any civilized nation, to assign to a man a certain degree of inferior standing forever." Nonetheless, such grammatical errors as "like I said," "if I would have known," "everybody has their own opinion," widespread as they may be, do a speaker no good. Nor does he gain by such false elegancies as the "usage" of a new gadget rather than the "use" of it, "in lieu of" for "in view of," and "media," criteria," and "curricula" as singulars.

The educated speaker, however, is no prude, and he provides no justification for the ostentatious display of vulgarity with which some popular demagogues try to distinguish themselves from their educated, civilized opponents. As Nicholas Murray Butler told a graduating class at Columbia University half a century ago (see p. 319 below), the educated man "knows the wide distinction between correct English on the one hand, and pedantic, or as it is sometimes called 'elegant' English on the other. He is more likely to 'go to bed' than to 'retire,' to 'get up' than to 'arise,' . . . to 'dress' rather than to 'clothe himself,' and to 'make a speech' rather than to 'deliver an oration.'" Nowadays, perhaps, he would "give a talk" rather than "make a speech"!

In general, then, it is important to remember that an audience *expects* a public speaker to use language which is superior to what he would employ in his casual, off-the-cuff conversation. The speaker who aims "to speak better than he thinks he can" will probably satisfy this expectation in his hearers. His language will help to hold attention; at least his language will not distract attention.

To Audience, Subject, and Occasion

Much of what can be said profitably about appropriateness to audience, subject, and occasion is implicit in our discussion of clearness and of appropriateness to the speaker. Two or three points may be specially fitting here, however.

SLANG AND JARGON

In considering the appropriateness of language to audiences, the speaker should be cautious about using *slang*. The temptation to use it is strong.

Slang is often vivid, sharp, and telling. It seems like a common bond between audience and speaker, and because it is familiar and readily recognized, it seems to be a natural, easy means for promoting clearness. Nevertheless, speakers should be aware of the pitfalls as well as the virtues of
slang. First, slang is a slippery and ever-changing language. Its vocabulary gets out of date faster than popular songs and headlines. Consequently, the slang expressions which seem familiar and clear to the
speaker may be Greek to an audience. The speaker, therefore, must be
sure that *his* slang is also his hearers'. Second, the flavor of informality
and casualness in slang is jarring on many occasions and from many
speakers. Rarely is slang suitable on formal occasions or in a speaker who
is not well known and well liked by his audience. Third, the use of slang
even when accurate often suggests to some audiences that the speaker is
just trying to be a good fellow or is merely talking down to them. In brief,
slang, like humor, can sweeten a speech; like humor, it can sour a speech.

The same observations as those about the use of slang apply directly to
the use of the special terminology and jargon of, let us say, sports writers
and commentators, of the entertainment world as represented in the publication *Variety*, and of such cults as the "Beat Generation" and the "hi-fi"
enthusiasts. A speaker, of course, may show off in any of these idioms,
but by the criteria of clearness and appropriateness it would take very
special audiences and very special speakers to make the language desirable.

EXTRAVAGANCE

The language of exaggeration, of "super," so dear to the tongues and
pens of our advertisers, involves basically the problem of propriety. Perhaps we should not be concerned with this fantastic vocabulary, which
we as listeners *may* tend to discount automatically. We hear so much of
it, however, that we can hardly help allowing it to creep into our speaking on serious and significant occasions, unless we are consciously careful. The common trouble with TV and radio commercials is not that
they are uningenious and ill-executed. Far from it. The trouble is that
they are usually couched in such exaggerated language and are delivered
in such hyperthyroid excitement that they are all out of proportion to
subject, speaker, audience, and occasion. We cannot dress up commonplace matters, such as breakfast cereals and laundry soap, with false
enthusiasm and inflated diction, without seeming absurd and ridiculous
and without losing the respect and confidence of our listeners. After all,
in a vocabulary where "Super-Colossal" describes the normal, usual condition, what does one say to express unusual approval?

KIND OF SPEECH

Finally, two broad considerations may help the speaker judge the appropriateness of language. First, have the occasion and subject given rise to an informative speech? A persuasive speech? A scientific person seeking to impart information at a meeting of scientists will inevitably emphasize the language of fact. Figurative vocabulary will be at a minimum; so also will be the emotionally loaded and the picturesque word. A scientific or technical subject planned for a popular audience—the lecture occasion—will demand the language of explanation, the diction of definition, example, comparison, and contrast. It will keep a nice balance between technical, strange words on the one hand and familiar, concrete, and vivid language on the other. But if the subject be controversial, touching necessarily upon the opinions, attitudes, and prejudices roused by the occasion, the diction of emotion will come into play. For the political speaker urging his hearers to throw the rascals out of Washington, the language of fact gains strength from the language of appeal, exhortation, and power. MacArthur defending his Korean record before Congress, Lincoln debating Douglas or honoring the Union dead at Gettysburg, Henry Grady appealing to the Yankees to understand the New South, Nixon and Kennedy accepting nomination for the Presidency, the student earnestly dealing with race prejudice—none can escape language which moves men's emotions as well as their minds.

SIGNIFICANCE OF SUBJECT AND OCCASION

Second, how important and significant are the subject and occasion? Language, to be appropriate, must correspond to the value with which speaker and audience regard the subject. This means, so Aristotle tells us, "that we must neither speak casually about weighty matters, nor solemnly about trivial ones," unless we are trying to be funny. Which is more important, urging your student audience to attend the football rally or defending your best friend on a charge of disloyalty? The answer depends upon how you size up the occasion which you as a speaker are preparing to meet. Under the circumstances, which subject is the more *pressing?* The decision depends also upon your perspective. If the occasion is not urgent, which subject *should* matter most to you and your hearers? The decision taken will color the language of the speech from beginning to end. The language will either ring true or sound hollow; it will be either in tune or off key.

Interest, Attractiveness, Impressiveness

There can be little doubt that individual words, quite independently of their use in connected passages, may be interesting, attractive, or impressive. The concrete, specific word is not only more clear but more interesting than the abstract, general word. No doubt it is more clear *because* it is more interesting. The active voice of verbs is more interesting than the passive. Some words have special or peculiar attractiveness, are particularly pleasing, either from association, sound, or some more mysterious cause. One is reminded of the elderly lady who told a speaker that she had enjoyed his speech because he had used that blessed word which she loved, *Mesopotamia*. Most of us would agree, furthermore, that there is more dignity and impressiveness inherent in the words *constitutional convention* than in the headline writer's equivalent *code parley*. The one word *peace* has served to focus the whole message of Christian preachers on many notable occasions, and more recently it has become one of the favorite catchwords of the propagandists of the Communist world. Furthermore, perhaps some words are beautiful and others ugly simply because of the sounds in them. It is hard, however, to isolate the beauty or ugliness of words as sounds from the beauty or ugliness they have acquired through association and meaning.

These qualities, however, are most significantly associated with words in connected discourse. We shall proceed, therefore, to the discussion of that aspect of style involving connected language. Again, we shall treat language as clear, appropriate, interesting and attractive, and impressive.

MANAGEMENT OF LANGUAGE—WORDS IN COMBINATION

Clearness

Let us call up again Swift's definition of style, "Proper words in proper places." We have been discussing the proper words; now we will look at the proper places—and first at the management of words for clarity. Usually, clearness is the result of casting familiar, concrete, specific, active words into familiar, direct, uncomplicated sentences and larger thought-units in which the structural and logical relations are easily visible and are marked with connecting and relating words. Declarative sentences in the active voice which are not too long to be spoken easily in one breath will usually be clearer than the longer, more oblique sentences.

Observe the relative clarity of the following two versions of the same passage:

> If waves are watched rolling in and striking the iron columns of an ordinary pier, it is seen that although the larger waves are not much obstructed by the column, but are merely divided briefly and joined again, as a regiment of soldiers is divided by a tree, the short waves are blocked and scattered by the columns.

> Imagine that we stand on any ordinary seaside pier and watch the waves rolling in and striking the iron columns of the pier. Large waves pay little attention to the columns. They divide right and left and reunite after passing each column, much as a regiment of soldiers would if a tree stood in their road. It is almost as though the columns had not been there. But the short waves and ripples find the columns of the pier a much more formidable obstacle. When the short waves impinge on the columns, they are reflected back and spread as new ripples in all directions.

Neither passage is *notably* unclear, at least to a reader. To a listener the first passage would undoubtedly be harder to grasp and to recall. There is little in the words or the structure to focus attention and thus facilitate understanding.

The use of familiar rather than strange sentence structure promotes clearness, as does the sharply constructed paragraph or basic unit in which the *statement* is easy to recognize and the *development* is marked by guidepost words and phrases: "let us take an example," "for instance," "another bit of information," "consequently," "on the other hand."

Clearness, as we have observed, is partly, perhaps largely, dependent upon attention, and attention is much the same as interest. Those qualities which make style interesting, therefore, will be of much help in making it clear.

Appropriateness

As we shall have occasion to observe again when we discuss the means of cultivating style, style in speaking and style in writing are closely akin. Excellence in written style, style which is to register chiefly through the eye rather than the ear, comes most surely from the qualities we have been discussing: clearness, appropriateness, interest, and impressiveness. Thus the basis of good style in writing is the same as the basis of good style in speaking. Yet the difference between the customary circumstances involved in listening and in reading account for certain important differences between oral and written style. Certain elements and qualities are appropriate to the direct, face-to-face, personal encounter between speaker and a particular audience which do not fit so well the more remote relationship between writer and general reader, or even particular reader. Furthermore, the great versatility of voice and facial and bodily gesture in grouping, emphasizing, contrasting, and structuring language as it is spoken perhaps makes appropriate to speaking a less stringent discipline in the selection and management of language than is needed in writing. In brief, we may say that though the essay and the speech are blood relatives, the essay is not simply a written speech or the speech an essay standing on its hind legs.

Oral Style

Let the speaker never forget, therefore, that he is directing his language to a *specific audience* and not at the general reader. This means that the working language of a speech will usually differ in some respects from that of an essay or theme.

DIRECTNESS

First, some elements of language will reveal direct, speaker-to-hearer communication. The language of direct, oral discourse is marked by *I* and *you*, by *we*, *our*, and *us*. It is marked, also, by the more copious use of the question than most readers would tolerate. Indeed, the use of interrogation and the first and second person pronouns show *unmistakably* that audience and speaker are face to face.

The interrogation is easy to use, once a speaker really thinks of himself as a *speaker*, once he finds that talking to an audience is no different from elevated conversation. He should realize, above all, that the question is one of the best ways he has of making hearers respond. The two main kinds of question, the *open* and *closed*, both do this. The first simply invites hearers to consider what is coming next and usually introduces a point or main idea. Thus it "sets" hearers and rouses a kind of expectancy. The closed, or *rhetorical question*, contains an invitation to say yes or no and is often used to tie up an argument.

Both kinds are illustrated in Beveridge's speech which opened the Republican campaign for Charles Evans Hughes in the fall of 1916. Beveridge was attacking Wilson's and the Democrats' handling of the Mexican "incident." A hearer might be responding much as we indicate in brackets.

> Have we been kept out of war with Mexico? [I can't say right off. It depends on what war is.] What is war? [I'll listen—what is it?] Merely a declaration? [Possibly not this, but—.] Our naval war with France was waged for two years without a declaration. Japan struck Russia without a declaration. War means offensive and deadly acts. We invaded Mexico and withdrew; but fighting took place and American marines were killed. Our territory was invaded by Mexicans who were driven out; but again Americans were killed. We invaded that country once more and to-day our military forces, with siege guns, are intrenched in the heart of Northern Mexico. They have fought with uniformed Mexicans and soldiers of both sides have fallen. Almost the whole of our effective military forces are kept on the border and lines of communication established with Pershing's men. Our War Depart-

ment has held officially that a deserter from our army must be punished as
in time of war. The government's censorship of all news from Mexico is
more rigid than that of the European belligerents. If all this is not war, what
is it? [I wouldn't know right now.] If such a state of things existed between
ourselves and any other nation, what would we call it? [Well, war I guess.]
What would the world call it? [War.]

PROFUSENESS

Second, oral language is more profuse, more repetitious than written
language is. It is more inclined to pile up words rather than trust to the
discovery of the single exact word. A student speaker, roused by a local
crime wave, was not satisfied to express a chief point only once. Early in
his speech he said,

> The gangsters warred against each other.

Then, following a few statistics and an example, he put the same idea this
way:

> The racketeers killed racketeers. The mobsters of the Capone days rarely
> molested ordinary people. Murder was just an "occupational hazard."

The same student speech affords an illustration of the piling up of words,
words that are near-synonyms, overlapping in meaning:

> The hoodlums today are the mugger, the knifer, the rapist, the strangler,
> the brute attacker.

In the pressure of extemporaneous utterance, eager to insure clearness,
emphasis, and force, the speaker did not revise his list of hoodlums, as
might the writer, to secure a neat, logical classification of gangsters.
Written language at its best is more compact than this, is more often
content with few synonymous terms and few amplifying phrases.

INFORMAL CONSTRUCTIONS

The language of extemporaneous speech, in the third place, often reveals sentences whose construction is less traditional and formal than
would be proper for the eye alone. The eye must depend upon the
signs of punctuation and capitalization and upon the careful placing of
sentence elements, such as qualifying phrases and clauses, if the reader
is to avoid confusion and distraction. The ear, however, can depend upon
the tremendous resources of voice and gesture to set sentences straight.
Inflection, pause, pace, and emphasis are the oral signs of punctuation;
they tell the listener how sentence elements are related to each other. A
dangling participle to the eye may not dangle to the ear! Furthermore,
in speaking one uses sentences which are more varied in length. A suc-

cession of short, terse sentences which would bother the eye might not hinder the ear.

The following brief passage from a speech of President James H. Halsey to the students of the University of Bridgeport exhibits many of the qualities characteristic of the oral style of direct address. It is dignified but sufficiently intimate and is readable as well as listenable.

> We in college, both faculty and students, must keep this goal of freedom clearly in view, because it is principally from the students in college that our leaders come. You who represent the student body of the University of Bridgeport, and your fellow students in other colleges throughout the land, are a highly selected group—you are one in five of all people your age. Therefore, upon you rests a greater responsibility in this matter of freedom because you are being given greater opportunities. As the potential leaders of people in a free country, you must help us to help you toward an education for freedom.
>
> And so, I would say to you today as we open this twenty-first year of our college, that each and every one of us must keep this goal forever before him. And to the members of the faculty I say specifically that regardless of what we teach, how we teach, or whom we teach, education for freedom must be the ultimate objective.[1]

Oral style, in sum, is the manifestation of the fitness of the language of discourse to the speaking situation: to speaker, to audience, to subject, and to occasion as interrelated elements in a face-to-face oral event.

Impressiveness

Speakers and listeners alike know that the commanding sentence, the lively word, the apt phrase, the vivid metaphor, the amusing epithet, of all the elements of a speech, often make the most immediate and most enduring impression on listeners. Franklin D. Roosevelt's label "horse-and-buggy," which he attached to the economic ideas which he wished to reform, served efficiently for many people to summarize the gist of a series of his speeches. A generation earlier Woodrow Wilson had coined a slogan which summarized the purposes which he had proclaimed for our participation in World War I and our part in the peace settlement. Most Americans knew the slogan "Make the World Safe for Democracy." A happy figure of speech also may serve to focus the whole force of an argument. Thomas Paine, the American patriot and friend of the French Revolution, summed up with such a figure his contempt for Edmund Burke's argument against the French Revolutionists: "He pities the plumage and forgets the dying bird."

Further examples of impressiveness come to mind in abundance: Winston Churchill's tribute to the Royal Air Force, "Never in the field of human conflict was so much owed by so many to so few," and his splendid

---

[1] At the opening Student Convocation in the fall of 1947.

affirmation of the stamina and will of the English people, "We shall fight on the beaches, we shall fight on the landing grounds, we shall fight in the fields and in the streets, we shall fight in the hills, we shall never surrender"; Lincoln's "government of the people, by the people, and for the people"; Franklin D. Roosevelt's coinage, born of the panic days of the Great Depression, "We have nothing to fear but fear itself"; Homer's "wine-dark sea"; Christ's "Render unto Caesar the things that are Caesar's"; William Jennings Bryan's condemnation of the gold standard as "crucifying mankind upon a cross of gold"; the many proverbial sayings, such as "The race is not to the swift"; and sharp word inventions like "The inhibited don't mind being prohibited."

Imagery and the Metaphor

Imagery in the speech involves the selection of words which aim to make the listener use his sensory apparatus as if he were actually in the presence of the things being referred to. Imagery gives the listener a substitute for actuality, or a new and more vivid kind of actuality. One of the characters in a novel by J. B. Priestley attends a concert in which, for the first time, he hears a "modern" symphonic piece. The author describes the effect of certain passages upon the conventional, conservative sensibilities of the listener: "Tall, thin people were sitting around sneering at each other and drinking quinine, while an imbecile child sat on the floor and ran its finger nails up and down a slate." Thus the speaker who wishes to give force and intensity to his ideas tries to turn his abstract and general ideas into concrete and specific imagery.

Antithesis and Contrast

Antithesis is a compressed contrast which brings close together words whose meanings are at opposite extremes. "The educated man has no monopoly on knowledge; the uneducated man has no monopoly on ignorance." Usually, as in this example, the structure of the expression is exactly parallel and is strictly balanced. Thus pattern and thought reinforce each other and carry the punch of a well-aimed blow.

The following sentence, with contrasting balance, effectively communicates the main point of the student speech on pages 309–310. It also distills an image which gives a title to the speech. "Thus we can see that although the conscience is often called 'a little voice inside,' it acts more like 'the old crank next door.'"

Inventing Impressive Expressions

In order to invent impressive language, state the governing idea of the speech in the most concise and accurate way possible. Do the same for the chief supporting ideas and for the conclusion. Summarize the entire thought of the speech in twenty words. More often than not the effort to be both compact and precise results, as in poetry, in vivid, figurative language. And if the main ideas of a speech can be expressed in striking language, the listener will grasp and remember essentials rather than details, as he does with Churchill's statements on pages 247–248. They are brief compressions of entire speeches. We still remember them. Similarly, Lincoln epitomized a speech with "A house divided against itself cannot stand." Expressions like these do for a speech what slogans do for advertisements and campaigns.

Further Considerations

Any writer on public speaking is tempted to enlarge his discussion of language to great proportions, not only because the subject is complex but because it is very important. Under the present limits of space, however, we have thought it best to treat in the preceding pages chiefly the considerations which should govern the speaker's choice of words and some of the elementary methods of bringing clarity and force to connected speech. For economy's sake only, we omit here other important matters which would form part of a fuller treatment, such as activity, curiosity, and humor in language, metaphor and other imagery, rhythm and harmony in the movement of language.

The student who is seriously interested in the best possible achievement, therefore, will wish all the helpful suggestions he can get from the many excellent treatments of style in such works as those listed at the end of this chapter. Perhaps he will wish to begin with Chapter 16 of our *Fundamentals of Public Speaking* (3rd edition, 1960), of which this chapter is an abridgment.

ACTIVITIES FOR IMPROVING STYLE

Speaking Often

Speaking often is one of the obvious ways of learning to use language well. Much speaking, however, may intensify bad habits as well as create good ones. The speaker, therefore, especially while he is a learner, should practice each speech aloud several times before he presents it to his final audience. He should also covet opportunities to give a speech on the same subject before different audiences in order to try changing his language to make it more effective each time. For greatest profit, obviously, the speaker must be keen to the listeners' response to his language, noticing what is puzzling, what is amusing, what is clear, what is dead, and

accordingly altering his technique. Otherwise his practice will be useless
—if not harmful.

Listening and Reading

Perhaps as fundamental as speaking often is reading and listening. One
does not come instinctively by a sense of clearness and fitness in language.
One has to cultivate it. Through extensive and frequent exposure one has
to absorb a sense of what good language is. There are only two sources
of this experience: one is hearing good oral discourse, the other is reading.

There is much good oral discourse to be heard, on the air, from the
pulpit, from the public lecture platform, and even in the college and
university classroom. Furthermore, many good recordings of speaking
may be had. Not always, alas, are these specimens easy to find, and they
are even more difficult to find when one wants them. Therefore reading
good prose and poetry is the speaker's best resource for exposing his mind
to excellent use of language.

As a means of improving the use of language, no one can overestimate
reading *aloud*. We learned to speak in the first instance because we *heard*
and talked long before we learned to read and write. Accordingly, hearing
and speaking remain the most effective avenues leading to improvement
in our command over speaking. To hear and to read orally a vocabulary
wider and more precise than our own is to enhance our own oral vocabulary; to hear and mouth language that is constructed better than ours, is
more rhythmical and impressive, is to improve our own oral patterns.
We urge, therefore, that the earnest public speaker read aloud—and
read aloud as much as he can. He will find courses in oral reading (or oral
interpretation of literature) helpful, not only because there the models
of language will be exemplary, but because a teacher can help him to
listen accurately and critically to himself. But if courses are not available,
he can do much if he selects good materials and will strive to read as if
he were *communicating* with a listener. (See Chapter 9.)

Writing

Writing and speaking need the corrective influence of each other if either
is to attain its maximum excellence. One who is a careful writer often
tests his sentences by reading them aloud, either to himself or to someone
else. Thus he seeks to modify any unnecessarily complicated structure
and to shorten sentences which would otherwise require a reader to carry
too much detail in mind before he gets to the essential action words. One
who is a careful speaker will examine critically his extemporaneous utterance. He can take a recording of his speech, or a stenographic copy of
what he said, and criticize his own language—discovering, moaning over,

and repairing the fragmentation, needless repetition, and inept expression. He can write in, for future reference, those coinages he wished he had used, but didn't!

Writing is at its best only when it permits that lively flow of thought which is characteristic of good speaking, only when it conveys the vitality —the lifelikeness—of spoken language, only when it bears in mind the best lanes of approach to its audience. Conversely, speaking is excellent when it is governed by some of that discipline which controls the best writing: (1) when the speaker has so developed his usable vocabulary that the most accurate and appropriate language which the audience will understand springs readily to his tongue; (2) when something of shapeliness and grace appears in the speaker's normal mode of talk; (3) when sentences take on without rigidity or complexity some semblance of structure, of subordination and co-ordination, clear evidence that some things come before or after others by design rather than by chance.

It follows, we think, that after a speaker has begun to become really naturalized to the speaking situation, to the experience of a lively sense of oral communication with an audience, to a full realization of the force and content of thought at the moment of utterance, he should take to writing as a regular, substantial part of his preparation. After planning and outlining and after some oral rehearsal such as we advised in Chapter 8, the student should write out his speech, or considerable portions of it, just as he would propose to speak it to his audience. He should set the written text aside for a few hours or a few days. Then he should retrieve it, read it aloud critically, and revise the language and the sentences as better or more fitting words come to him and as he discovers sentences which are clumsy or not so clear as they could be. Once more, he should read the new version aloud to a tender and critical ear (his own).

Maintain an Oral Attitude

The main object of our attention in this book is the planned but extemporaneous speech—not the speech which is written out and read aloud or memorized. For this reason there is little in the earlier chapters which gives special consideration to language. Thinking for communication and in communication is the first consideration. If there were to be only one consideration, that would be it. We all come equipped with a usable enough stock of language to get well started. Thinking and using language, however, are so much parts of the same process—thought is so completely dependent upon symbols—that improvement in the one is impossible without improvement in the other. Furthermore, the language of words, rather than thought itself, is amenable of direct study. Consequently in improving his use of language a speaker is improving the materials of what we have called "applied thought."

We come around, then, to the conclusion that the maturing public speaker who would rise above the ordinary, the commonplace, the good-enough-but-undistinguished in his language will speak often, will read silently, will read aloud, and will write. All these activities he will engage in critically, with intent to profit, for the language of clarity vitalized by the language of force, vividness, and memorableness is an indispensable ally of the public speaker.

════ FURTHER READING ════

ARISTOTLE, *Rhetoric*, trans. by John Henry Freese (Cambridge, Mass., Loeb Classical Library, 1939), Bk. III, Chs. 1–12.

BAIRD, A. Craig, and Franklin H. KNOWER, *General Speech* (New York, 1949), Ch. 10, "Language."

BORCHERS, Gladys, "An Approach to the Problem of Oral Style," *Quarterly Journal of Speech*, 22 (1936), 114–117.

COOPER, Lane, ed., *Theories of Style* (New York, 1907), esp. Swift, "A Letter to a Young Clergyman"; Buffon, "Discourse on Style"; Spencer, "The Philosophy of Style." [Republished as *The Art of the Writer* (Ithaca, N.Y., 1952).]

GRIMES, Wilma, "The Mirth Experience in Public Address," *Speech Monographs*, 22 (November 1955), 243–255.

LANGER, Suzanne K., *Philosophy in a New Key* (Baltimore, Md., 1948), Ch. 5, "Language."

LEE, Irving J., *The Language of Wisdom and Folly* (New York, 1949).

———, "Four Ways of Looking at a Speech," *Quarterly Journal of Speech*, 28 (1942), 148–155.

MURPHY, Richard, "The Speech as Literary Genre," *Quarterly Journal of Speech*, 44 (1958), 117–127.

MURRY, J. Middleton, *The Problem of Style* (Oxford, 1925), esp. Chs. I, IV, and VI.

PARRISH, W. M., "The Study of Speeches," in W. M. Parrish and Marie Hochmuth, *American Speeches* (New York, 1954), pp. 1–20.

POTTER, Simeon, *Our Language* (Baltimore, Md., 1950), Ch. 10, "Authority and Usage," and Ch. 11, "Slang and Dialect."

Rhetorica ad Herennium, trans. by Harry Caplan (Cambridge, Mass., Loeb Classical Library, 1954), Bk. IV.

RICHARDS, I. A., *The Philosophy of Rhetoric* (New York, 1936), Lecture V, "Metaphor."

SAPIR, Edward, *Language* (New York, 1949).

THOMAS, Gordon L., "Oral Style and Intelligibility," *Speech Monographs*, 23 (1956), 46–54.

Introductions, Conclusions, and Transitions

INTRODUCTIONS

The introductions to most speeches, as we have suggested in our discussion of outlining, serve either or both of two functions: (1) to get the attention of the audience and (2) to prepare the audience for the speaker's purpose and point of view. The speechmaker, therefore, would do well to plan the introductions to his own speeches with both functions in mind.

Getting Attention

The Familiar Reference

Reference to the occasion or the place. Is there any relationship between the subject and the date of the speech? A scientist lecturing on meteorology at Charlottesville, Virginia, on Jefferson's birthday might well refer to Jefferson's interest in recording data on the weather.

Observe Woodrow Wilson's recognition of the occasion and place in his address on "The Meaning of the Declaration of Independence." [1]

> We are assembled to celebrate the one hundred and thirty-eighth anniversary of the birth of the United States. I suppose that we can more vividly realize the circumstances of that birth standing on this historic spot than it would be possible to realize them anywhere else. The Declaration of Independence was written in Philadelphia; it was adopted in this historic building by which we stand. I have just had the privilege of sitting in the chair of the great man who presided over the deliberations of those who gave the declaration to the world. My hand rests at this moment upon the table upon which the declaration was signed. We can feel that we are almost in the visible and tangible presence of a great historic transaction.

Reference to a recent event or to a familiar quotation. To start with a reference to a local or national event that has made a deep impression on

[1] J. M. O'Neill, *Models of Speech Composition* (New York, 1921), p. 554.

the community and to link it logically with the subject makes a very easy and effective opening. The speaker, however, must guard against the temptation to stretch an event, to squeeze and torture a happening or a quotation, in order to show a connection between it and his subject.

Good use of the local incident was made by a student in an oratorical contest at Evanston, Illinois. Four days before the contest, the assistant state's attorney had been machine-gunned. The student, speaking on the breakdown of the home as a cause of crime, was thus presented with a fitting event that he turned to his benefit. This was his opening sentence:[2]

> The murder of your prosecuting attorney, last Wednesday, has made my subject an unusually timely one for this audience, for beginning with the first recorded human crime—the murder of Abel by Cain—and coming down to this murder in your city day before yesterday, the perplexing question of crime has baffled society.

Reference to what a preceding speaker has said. Where several speakers appear on one occasion, as at banquets, conventions, and in the classroom, an alert speaker can often take his opening remarks from something that has already been said.

At least two possible ways of managing the reference should be considered. After starting with a swift report of what an earlier speaker has said, one can:

1. Explain how his subject fits into the earlier speech, by stating that he will develop a different aspect of the subject. At a meeting of small-home architects, one man spoke of new plumbing layouts, and later in the afternoon another speaker alluded to the earlier topic and added that he was going to report on a new type of valve that regulated water pressure.

2. Show a plausible association between his subject and the previous one. In a round of class speeches lasting a week, one speaker on the first day talked on the proper design of a fireplace. Later in the week an aspiring geologist spoke on how to find water. His approach was somewhat in this vein:

> A few days ago my friend Mack Taylor told you how to build a fireplace that wouldn't smoke. Now I'm going to speak on something that's far more fundamental than designing fireplaces. It's important if you should sometime decide to build a home in the country, and you'd better look to it long before you worry about fireplaces. In fact, you'd better look to it before you even decide just where you're going to put that house.
>
> What I want to do is to tell you where you can find water. The method used is recommended by up-to-date geologists. It is . . . , etc.

[2] M. G. Robinson, "The Eleventh Commandment," *Classified Speech Models*, ed. W. N. Brigance (New York, 1928), p. 19.

Humor

Speakers have always regarded humor as a good method of ice-breaking. The humorous story or anecdote as a means of introduction is effective if three conditions are always respected. (1) The story must be in point and not dragged in. The test for relevance is simple: Could the story be used as a supporting example of a main head or of a subhead? If so, it belongs in the speech and one can lead off with it if he wishes. (2) The mood or temper of the occasion must not be inimical to humor or to this particular humor; the anecdote is out of place when the occasion is solemn or dignified. (3) The story must not take up more time than it is worth. If the speaker has selected his subject well, if it is reasonably appropriate to his hearers, he should get to the heart of his speech as fast as his audience will let him. The extended anecdote often wastes time.

For an example of the humorous story properly used in the introduction see Bruce Barton's speech, "Which Knew Not Joseph," which is printed in the Appendix.

Significance of the Subject

Reference to the significance or importance of the subject is perhaps the most rewarding means of approach for the novice speaker to master. It can be used for most speeches on most occasions and for persuasive as well as for informative speeches. And this kind of approach not only stands a good chance of claiming the hearer's attention; it is also likely to stir the speaker himself to greater energy, alertness, and interest than most types of introduction.

Let the attention section of the introduction be developed around this *implied* theme: my subject is important to *you,* at this *time,* and on this *occasion.* Or in other words, the speaker tells his audience *why* they should listen; he *motivates* them.

In planning to use this scheme, the speaker should note, first, that he does not actually state that his subject is important; to do so would probably result in a colorless, trite statement. Second, he should pick two or three reasons why the subject is significant; he states these and amplifies each, if necessary, to the point where he sees the audience react favorably and attention is won. The speaker can then move on to his purpose and point of view.

The success of this approach depends entirely on whether the speaker really *believes* that there are excellent reasons why his audience should listen to him, on his subject, and at that time. If he has good reasons, then his subject is truly appropriate to both his audience and himself. If he enjoys success with this method, it will be due primarily to two factors: (1) The reasons he picks—if they are significant rather than trivial—will usually reflect those motives, emotions, and attitudes which direct our lives and partially govern what we will attend to and perceive. The responses touched off may well be strong and deep. (2) Since he gives the reasons that led him to settle on this subject rather than some other, he is likely to respond strongly himself; he himself becomes interested, energetic, alert, and direct; he remotivates himself. Any speaker who is slow to warm up to his speech should try this approach.

One of the classic, short approaches of this kind is that employed by Jeremiah S. Black when he argued the right of trial by jury before the Supreme Court, in December 1866. A Federal military court martial had tried and sentenced to death one Mulligan and two associates, all of them civilians. Mulligan appealed; and before the Supreme Court, the military tribunal maintained that it had the power to try civilians during wartime even when the civil courts were open, and, furthermore, that the civil courts were powerless to prevent the military from acting. In the face of such a contention, Black's approach is not overdrawn: [3]

> I am not afraid that you will underrate the importance of this case. It concerns the rights of the whole people. Such questions have generally been settled by arms; but since the beginning of the world no battle has ever been lost or won upon which the liberties of a nation were so distinctly staked as they are on the result of this argument. The pen that writes the judgment of the court will be mightier for good or for evil than any sword that ever was wielded by mortal arm.

(Observe the basic motives and attitudes to which the speaker referred: *rights, liberty,* and the *good.*)

A student interested in insurance once spoke to a class of boys somewhat as follows:

> Perhaps you don't like to be bothered by life insurance salesmen who are always trying to sell you a policy. Forget the men and consider the thing. For the young, unmarried man, insurance can be a means of saving. Upon his marrying, he finds that he has a way of protecting his wife and family from financial worries if he should die. Insurance can also be a means of building up a retirement income that will give a man comfort and security in late life.
>
> I propose this morning to explain the advantages and disadvantages of three kinds of life insurance.

Orienting the Audience

With his attention step planned, the speaker can turn to the second purpose of the introduction, the *orientation* of his hearers.

In the orientation part of the introduction, the speaker should always

[3] O'Neill, *op. cit.,* p. 84.

make a direct reference to his subject. In the informative speech, the reference to subject may consist in stating the specific purpose of the speech, for example, "I shall attempt to explain how dress patterns are made." For some subjects on some occasions no more orientation than this may be needed, and after announcing his purpose the speaker can proceed to his first main idea. But for many subjects on many occasions, fuller orientation is desirable. It may be accomplished by the following materials, alone or in combination:

Present the governing statement. Many speeches present the governing statement fully in the introduction and then restate it at least once. The object is to dwell on it until it registers with the audience. Many a subject sentence, for example, is abstract and general, even a bit complicated and profound, and an audience can't get hold of it without restatement.

State how the subject is to be developed. For example: "In explaining how domestic Roquefort cheese is made, I shall mention first the ingredients, and then take you step by step, from the beginning to the finished product that is ready for boxing and shipment."

Supply background information. A bit of history often helps an audience to see a subject in its perspective. If one were talking on the Frasch process of mining sulphur, he might, for example, supply a brief review of the older mining methods.

The background sketch should be placed in the introduction wherever it will fit in smoothly and logically. It might follow the subject sentence; it could be part of the attention material; or if it contained unusual and interesting facts, it could be the opening sentences.

CONCLUSIONS

The conclusion has at least one main purpose: to summarize and draw together the chief ideas of the speech. The ideas and tone should give a rounding-off and sending-off effect.

The Summary

Some kind of summary is necessary, and we urge that the beginning speaker not leave its formulation to the spur of the moment. Any hearer will welcome a summary, because the summary appeals to his sense of order and proportion; the speech as a whole, the multitude of ideas he has heard, suddenly are revealed again as orderly and systematic, rather than chaotic.

It is of course true that the short speech *which is extremely well organized and is methodically presented* may not require the concluding summary; the speaker may simply stop after he has completed discussion of his last point. But one should not be in a hurry to abandon the summary;

in an overwhelming majority of speeches, it is an effective way of rounding
off ideas, of securing clearness, and of stimulating action.

Summaries may be formal and concise, or informal and somewhat discursive. In either case, the summary should be managed by *restatement*
(recurrence of old idea in different words) rather than by *repetition* (recurrence of old idea in the same phraseology). Accordingly, the shortest
possible recipe for a summary is this: Deftly restate the ideas expressed in
the governing statement and in the main heads.

To illustrate the summary, suppose the governing statement and main
heads were as follows:

> The control panel of a powerhouse is arranged for the greatest convenience
> of the operator.
>   I. Close in front of him are the instruments which he uses most often.
> II. Farther away to the sides are the less used dials and levers.

The formal summary might be this:

> In short, the instruments that control the machinery of a powerhouse are
> arranged on a large panel to suit the convenience of the operator, the in-
> struments most used being in front of the attendant and ready to his hand,
> the instruments least used being at the extreme sides of the panel.

The less formal summary might run something like this:

> To conclude, then: If you were to visit the control room in Urbana's power-
> house, you would see Mike Williams, on the night shift, seated before the
> large control panel—a panel that is arranged like most control panels in
> powerhouses. Immediately in front of him, and easy to reach, are the in-
> struments he may need five or six times during the night. At the far sides of
> the panel are the dials and levers that may be used once a week, or even
> less often.

Governing Statement as the Conclusion

When a speaker discovers that his governing statement is too complicated
and unwieldy to handle easily early in the speech and perhaps too difficult
for his hearers to understand without much restatement and preliminary
explanation, he may save the statement until the end of the speech and
use it as his conclusion. If he does so use his governing statement, he must
be sure to retain in the orientation step the statement of his specific purpose.

The Detailed Illustration as a Summary

Perhaps the most interesting type of conclusion by summary is a detailed
example which illustrates the meaning of the entire speech. The informal
summary cited above is really such an illustration. It would become detailed had the speaker given Williams three or four typical operations to

do, if Williams were to use two or three of the dials and levers near at hand and to use each for a definite purpose, and were he to make use of one of the remote instruments.

TRANSITIONS

Inexperienced persons often find the "joints" of a speech hard to manipulate. Like most elements of a speech, transitional phrases and sentences must be planned; they don't spring, ready-made, into mind. It is good practice to include them in the speech outline and to give special attention to them late in the rehearsal stage of preparation when one is ready to work on details of phraseology.

Introducing Main Heads

Use signpost devices. Number the main heads: *First, Second, Third,* and so on. Variations of this are: *In the first place, The first step, The first matter to be discussed is* . . . , *Let us first discuss.* . . .

Although such labels may seem obvious and somewhat wooden here alone on the page, usually they are not distractingly obvious in a speech.

Use parallel structure in main heads and emphasize by the pause. Here are four heads whose structure is alike:

   I. On the north side of the quadrangle are the dormitories.
  II. On the east side of the quadrangle are the science halls.
 III. On the south side of the quadrangle are the administration and classroom buildings.
 IV. On the west side of the quadrangle is the great auditorium.

Through experience and conditioning we have come to regard things similar in structure and size as equal in value, as having equal claims on attention. Hence, if the speaker phrases head II exactly as he worded head I, a listener senses that both heads are co-ordinate in value. He reacts similarly when he hears heads III and IV. Parallelism of structure, accordingly, holds main heads together.

Parallelism is most effective when combined with the pause. Just before stating a head, pause for five seconds or so. The pause will give emphasis to the idea of the preceding division and will at the same time advertise the beginning of the next division.

Use the flash back and preview device. This consists of alluding at the major points of the speech to what has just been said and to what will follow. Although there are many ways of managing such a transition, perhaps the "not only—but also" formula is the swiftest and easiest to handle. In the example below, the material supporting each main head has been omitted.

I. Antioch combines cultural and practical studies. . . . .
. . . .
(Antioch not only combines cultural and practical studies; it also joins
study with practical experience.)
II. Antioch combines academic study with work in the business world
. . . .
(Antioch has done more than combine culture and practical studies
and join study with experience; it has found that its system works.)
III. Antioch's plan has been successful.

Keeping Subheads Distinct

Adopt a consistent set of conjunctive adverbs, and get into the habit of
using them to start off the discussion of a subhead. A workable group of
such words is this: *moreover, also, furthermore,* and *finally.*

In using these co-ordinating words with the subheads, avoid using the
same words also to designate main heads; and don't use *first, second,* and
so on with the subheads if you are applying them also to main heads.
There's no surer way of confusing listeners than to cross them up by inconsistent labeling.

The rule of thumb, then, is this: Use one set of labels for main heads,
another set for subheads. In all cases avoid, if possible, the useless, un-
discriminating connectives, "and another thing," and "then too."

CHAPTER FOURTEEN

Speeches for Special Occasions

MOST OCCASIONS for public speaking call for speeches whose primary purposes are either to inform or persuade. On many occasions, however, the *main* purpose at least is something else—to extend or receive a courtesy or to provide entertainment for an audience. When these special purposes prevail, the principles and practices of effective speaking which are the subject of this book are just as important and should be just as carefully applied as in expository and persuasive speeches. That is, these special speeches should be carefully prepared, audience and occasion should be carefully analyzed, clear plans and outlines should be developed, ideas should be amplified concretely and vividly, style should be appropriate, delivery should be characterized by conversational quality.

In these speeches, as a matter of fact, certain qualities of content and presentation are even more important than they are in other speeches, because the audience is almost always aware ahead of time what the speaker's purpose is and where his discourse will lead. Neatness and clarity of structure; plentiful and vivid example and concrete detail; ease, audibility, clarity, fluency, and liveliness of utterance; propriety and grace of style—a high premium is to be placed upon each of these in speeches of introduction, of presentation of a gift or an award, of welcome and response to welcome, and in after-dinner speeches and other speeches of entertainment.

In addition to the heightened value to be placed in such speeches upon the qualities which we have just enumerated, the purposes and occasions prescribe for the speaker certain basic and essential requisites of content—certain established formulas, if you will—within which he must function. His success depends upon how well he works out his speech without exceeding his function and without violating the accepted rules of the job he is doing. The rules for each kind of speech are few, but they should be followed, and the opportunities for individual variation are many. In these speeches, however, as in all others, there can be no adequate substitute for good sense, good will, keenness of mind, and a feeling for the fitting and proper.

SPEECHES OF INTRODUCTION

Speeches of introduction are so common and so frequently bad that everyone should prepare himself for the times when he will make them. Many speakers would much rather not be introduced at all than be subjected to, and be present while the audience is subjected to, the "introductions" which they often encounter. Speakers are usually introduced either by friends and colleagues (who may be very poor speakers) who know them well, or by chairmen who know them only slightly by repute but wish to seem well acquainted, or by individuals or functionaries known to the audience but who do not know the speaker at all. This, alas, is a just statement of a dismal situation, and there is not very much we can do to improve it unless those persons who introduce speakers will undertake to improve themselves.

Speeches of introduction are often inexcusably poor in delivery and in substance. The delivery is likely to be either feeble and indistinct or stiff and self-conscious. Introducers often say too much or too little, and too frequently they lack tact and taste. These faults need not prevail, however, if introducers will understand their functions, be content to serve those functions, and take their tasks seriously.

Purposes

A speech of introduction should accomplish, as far as possible, two purposes; and those two purposes accomplished to the best of his ability, the introducer should do no more. (1) It should place audience and speaker on a footing of mutual acquaintance, confidence, and sympathy. (2) It should promote the purpose of the speech. It is no part of the purpose to display the introducer, *his* relation to the speaker, *his* relation to the audience, *his* relation to the subject. Whatever the introducer says should advance one of these two purposes. He must resist temptation to turn aside from them.

Materials

The irreducible minimum of content for a speech of introduction, even when the speaker is thoroughly well known to the audience, is the speaker's *name and identity*. Such brevity, however, is ordinarily undesirable, unless the audience has been brought to attention and quiet beforehand, because the introduction, like the first few speeches of the first act of a play, is likely to be lost in the stir of the audience's settling down. Shailer Mathews' famous introduction of President Wilson, which has become the norm for presenting the President, only *identified* but did not name the speaker. His entire introduction consisted of these words: "Ladies and gentlemen: The President of the United States." In further promoting acquaintance and confidence between speaker and audience, the introducer should mention favorably but *moderately* why the speaker is qualified to talk on his subject: his experience, his position, his special capabilities.

In promoting the purpose of the speech, the introducer will not only try to direct favorable attention to the speaker by referring to his qualifications, but he should lead that attention toward the subject. He should remind the audience why the subject is especially important or significant either in general or in relation to the occasion, to recent events, to coming events such as the anniversary of a person or an institution, or to the particular audience. Again the length or detail of such remarks will be measured by the audience's previous acquaintance with the subject and its significance. The introducer should not labor the obvious; he should remember also that the speaker himself may wish to point out the importance and significance of his subject by way of getting his speech under way.

There may be ideas properly suggested to the introducer by the audience itself: compliments which he, rather than the speaker, might pay in the interest of good will. If the audience is large or especially distinguished, the introducer may compliment it for being so. He should not, however, *call* it large or distinguished if it obviously is not. Such remarks infuse an inappropriate tone of humor, sarcasm, or insincerity into the relation of speaker and audience. If the audience is small, it is well not to mention its size or to apologize for a small audience.

Whenever possible, the introducer should consult the speaker beforehand to confirm the accuracy of his information—especially name and titles—and to find out what the speaker wishes to have said and what he wishes not to have said. Then, unless it is utterly impossible, the introducer should respect the *speaker's wishes*.

Warnings about Content and Language

Be brief and moderate. Use restraint in both length and content. Remember that the introducer is the host or the representative of the host. The audience wants to hear the speaker. It is a safe rule that if the speaker is to talk from *five* to *fifteen* minutes, the introducer should not use more than from *thirty* seconds to *two* minutes, and normally no speech of introduction should last more than *five* minutes.

Use tact and taste. Don't embarrass both speaker and audience by overpraising the speaker. It is very easy, if one is not careful, to let a perfectly genuine wish to do justice to a speaker's excellence get out of control and turn into extravagance. Do not dwell on a speaker's exploits, although you ought to mention those which are relevant. Do not prejudice a speaker's excellence as a speaker by alluding *directly* to his ability. Such remarks as, "You will now hear an interesting and inspiring speech," are usually more harmful than helpful to the speaker-audience relation. It is better that the audience should find the speaker exceeding their expectations than failing to approach the quality predicted. By extravagance the introducer discredits himself as he embarrasses speaker and audience.

Though good humor should always pervade a speech of introduction, the use of humor, especially humor involving the speaker or tending to make light of occasion or subject, is questionable. There are some few occasions, however, where the expert use of good-humored humor is proper, as for instance in Streeter's introduction of Dean Jones of Yale at the inauguration of President Hopkins of Dartmouth.[1] When in doubt, omit humor.

Find fresh, sincere, and plausible substitutes for such trite and hackneyed phrases as "it is an honor and a privilege," "a scholar and a gentleman," "a man who . . . , and a man who . . . , and a man who. . . ."

Arrangement of the Speech

Place the essential information near the conclusion. Essential information includes at least the *subject;* sometimes the speaker's *name.* A sense of anticlimax and impatience to get on with the speech develop in the audience if much is said after the subject is announced. Even when your speech of introduction is very short, do not as a rule put the essential information in the first sentence. The audience may not hear or understand, because of the disturbance of getting settled or because of unfamiliarity with the introducer's voice and manner. Observe a climactic order, but do not strive for something tremendous.

Delivery

It is best not to read a speech of introduction. Even at the expense of some possible fumbling and hesitancy, it is better that the audience and the guest should suppose the introducer to be sincerely uttering his own genuine sentiments than that he should appear to be the impersonal mouthpiece of a piece of paper. Know the ideas thoroughly; plan and practice. The speech must move. But do not read. Maintain a lively sense of communication so as not to sound mechanical and perfunctory.

Pause to get attention before beginning; then speak slowly, distinctly,

[1] J. M. O'Neill, *Models of Speech Composition* (New York, 1921), p. 670.

and loudly enough so as to be easily heard and understood by the guest speaker and by *all* of the audience.

PRESENTING A GIFT, AN AWARD, OR A MEMORIAL

This kind of speech is very often needed because of the many occasions when, in all kinds of societies and business, professional, and civic associations, we wish publicly or semi-publicly to acknowledge the distinction attained by individuals, groups, or institutions or to commemorate a person or event with some tangible token.

Watches, fountain pens, pocketbooks, or wallets are presented by their fellow workers or by management to faithful employees who have served ten, twenty-five, forty years. We gather at the dinner table publicly to bid goodbye to an associate who is moving on to another and better job and to present him with a briefcase or a set of luggage.

Words must go with the medals, ribbons, plaques, cups, trophies, certificates, prizes, and scholarships which we award to individuals or groups who have excelled in athletics, scholarship, business, industry, charity drives, virtue, or good works. On the occasions of most such awards the audience and the individual honored feel let down or cheated unless someone accompanies the presentation with words of praise and appreciation.

Likewise the presentation of a memorial in honor of the dead creates a solemn and dignified occasion which is hollow without proper words of praise and dedication. Whether the university's literary club presents to the library a book fund in memory of a deceased scholar, a gift primarily for *use;* or whether the war veterans present a statue to the city in memory of the honored dead; in all such situations we expect speeches of presentation appropriate to the donor, the donee, the gift, and the person or event being commemorated.

Purposes

The purposes of speeches of presentation are (1) formally and publicly to exhibit the worth of the recipient, (2) to heighten the sense of appreciation or satisfaction felt by the donor, or donors, and (3) usually to represent the gift as a token or symbol rather than remuneration.

Materials

The minimum expectation from a speech of presentation is that the speaker will mention—or at least *name*—the award, the person receiving it, and the donor, and that he will indicate why the presentation is made. In fulfilling these requisites, especially the last, there are several kinds of material which the speaker will be more or less expected to use. These requisites will derive from the fitness of the donee to be honored, of the honor as coming from the donor, and the fitness or significance of the gift itself.

Briefly stated, the speaker will:

Magnify, though not exaggerate, the services, deeds, qualities, accomplishments, and excellences of the recipient.

Say something of the considerations which governed the choice of the gift if these considerations are complimentary to this recipient especially.

Minimize, though not depreciate, the intrinsic worth of the gift.

Go beyond the material characteristics of the gift to discover a deeper meaning, perhaps a symbolic significance (the gift is, after all, a token).

If the donee is a person, name and illustrate with reasonable restraint his deeds and qualities which make him worthy of this distinction. If the recipient has been selected as a symbol of a group or as typical of many other persons, dwell not only on his excellences but on the excellences of others like him. If the recipient is an institution or organization, look especially to the principles and qualities which it stands for.

Especially when the gift is a memorial, the speaker should describe the qualities of the person being commemorated, look to the reasons for his being especially worthy of memory, and mention the qualities and motives of the donor. This last sometimes involves some history of the donor, especially of his relations to the person or event being remembered, and to the donee.

Concerning the gift itself, the speaker should call attention to any special qualities which make it particularly valuable or significant. If, for example, it shows fine workmanship or if it is a rare gift, the speaker should show pride in these qualities. The qualities which it symbolizes or of which it reminds one should be attached complimentarily to the person being honored. If it is intended for use, let the use seem real and seem appropriate to both donor and donee.

Manner of Presentation

Like the speech of introduction, the speech of presentation should seem to express the genuine, sincere sentiments of the speaker and the donor. If possible it should be spoken extemporaneously upon a foundation of preparation and practice. It is better if not read from the page. Its special qualities should be clear, simple organization and felicity or fitness.

If the occasion permits, the speaker should look with satisfaction at the gift when he is speaking about it; and he should address the recipient directly and should look at him, at least when the actual, physical presentation is being made. Though on many occasions the speaker is presumed to be speaking only to the recipient, the audience is in fact a real part of the function and deserves to hear and understand. The speaker should, therefore, avoid the appearance of carrying on a private conversation with the recipient and a few persons close at hand. He should throughout speak *clearly*, *distinctly*, and *audibly*.

ACCEPTING A GIFT, AN AWARD, OR A MEMORIAL

In accepting a complimentary honor, a speaker will seldom offer any ideas or information unknown to the audience. He will, however, be expected not only to *feel* but to *show* appreciation. Sometimes, of course, his "speech" may consist of no more than saying "Thank you." Many situations, however, seem to call for a protraction of the process of acceptance and for gracious amplification of the speaker's appreciation so that a dignity may be infused into or maintained in the occasion and so that the audience may have time to take full satisfaction in the recipient's evident pleasure. Thus the speaker will look for proper and gracious ideas through which to convey his thanks. There are, of course, times when a speaker may genuinely exclaim, "I don't know how to thank you. I didn't deserve it." This formula, however, is shopworn and should be used with great caution. Especially should a speaker avoid introducing an obviously preplanned speech with the statement, "I am speechless; I can't find words with which to thank you."

Materials

On any occasion when more than a mere "Thank you" is in order, the acceptance speaker should include, in felicitous sentences, the following materials:

Admiration, thanks, and appreciation for the gift or the honor.

Expression of appreciation of the kindness of friends.

Minimization, though not depreciation, of his own services or merits.

Sharing of the honor, where it is possible, with others.

In amplifying these ideas the speaker may draw remarks from his own experience, referring perhaps to his trials and difficulties if he can do so without self-glorification—without featuring his personal successes. Whenever he refers to successes, he should let them appear to be attributable to the assistance he has had from other people. It is proper for him to pay tribute to others—his friends and associates. In referring to the gift, the speaker will tell what it means to him beyond its intrinsic worth or its practical use, what it inspires him to accomplish in the future, what it symbolizes with respect to his past associations and his future aspirations and ideals.

On some occasions, when the spirit of the scene is genial rather than sober or formal, the speaker may admit pleasant humor and jest into his speech of thanks. The ultimate effect of his humor must never be to depreciate the gift, himself, or the motives of the donor. Never make a jest for the sake of the jest and then try to set things right by saying, "And now to be serious for a moment. . . ." While receiving the gift, look at the person presenting it; in admiring the gift, look at it; in thanking the donor, don't ignore his presence.

Let there be no relaxing in such essential qualities of all public utterance as *clearness, distinctness,* and *easy audibility.*

WELCOMING AN INDIVIDUAL OR A GROUP

Speeches of welcome put a premium upon tact and taste in the choice of material and upon grace and felicity of style and delivery.

Purpose

The purpose of a speech of welcome is to extend a sincere and grateful greeting to a person or to a group—such a greeting as offers good fellowship and hospitality. It serves the same purpose on a public occasion that a sincere greeting does between individuals, or that the opening of a door does when one is bidding a guest welcome.

Materials

The least a speaker should do in such a speech is:

Indicate for whom he is speaking.

Present complimentary facts about the person or group to which the courtesy is being extended.

Predict pleasant experiences.

In all of this he should take pains to *illustrate,* not to argue.

In elaborating his address of welcome the speaker may have recourse to three general types of materials. First, it is likely that the host thinks favorably of the spirit, purposes, and accomplishments of the guest and the group or organization which the guest represents. The speaker may, therefore, undertake to explain or to point up the purpose or spirit of the occasion—to declare graciously why it is appropriate and significant that the host and guest should come together under the present circumstances. This is the sort of thing which most mayors try to do when welcoming to their cities the conventions or representatives of prominent organizations. Thus was the United Nations Conference welcomed to San Francisco in April 1945, and thus was a new president of a metropolitan university welcomed by a spokesman of the Chamber of Commerce.

Secondly, the host may wish to explain or publicly to rehearse the spirit or purpose of the organization or institution extending the welcome. "This is what we are," says the speaker, "and we trust that you will find us good." Thus might the spokesman of a school or college prepare the way for a visitor from another school or college who has come to observe the operation of a well-established system of independent study for undergraduates. The speaker, however, must take care not to seem boastful or to suggest that the visitor is lucky to be privileged to observe the local wonders. If the visitor comes to impart information or to confer some favor upon the hosts, the welcoming spokesman ought perhaps to refer to the visitor's special qualifications and accomplishments. Welcoming a new director for the Boy Scout organization or the artist who is to paint the murals in the new post office, might well call for material of this kind.

In the third place, and perhaps most frequently, the speaker will think it fitting to pay a tribute to the person or organization being welcomed. Dawes' tribute to the Jewish Welfare Board [2] was an example of this method. The faults of this sort of tribute which thoughtless or ill-prepared speakers will commit are generality and extravagance. The speaker should, if possible, praise the guest for specific distinctions rather than general virtues, and he should keep his praise well within the limits of reasonable plausibility.

General Characteristics of the Speech

The speech of welcome is well organized. The audience is gratified by form and progress as well as by content, is comfortably aware of where the speaker is going and how he is getting there. There is always a central theme which is serious and complimentary. There is usually a definite approach or introduction which leads gracefully to the suggestion of the main theme, and there is a conclusion, brief and dignified.

The mood of a speech of welcome is more serious and exalted (though, we hope, not more stuffy) than the mood of a speech of introduction, for

[2] J. M. O'Neill and F. K. Riley, *Contemporary Speeches* (New York, 1930), pp. 13–14.

on these occasions the guest himself and what he represents, rather than his speech, will be the main attraction. The mood is more dignified and more suggestive of formality. There may even be a touch of ritual in it such as the symbolic offering to the guest of the key to the city. And the mood tends to be strongly emotional. The guest expects the language of emotion; the audience demands it. The speaker must, then, get beyond casual coldness, but he must not exceed good sense by extravagance and spoil everything by gushing.

The speech should exhibit taste and judgment. The manner and the material must fit all elements of the occasion: speaker, audience, guest, time, place, circumstances.

In spite of all the "must's," however—and there are few which good will and good sense will not dictate—there is plenty of room for individuality and originality in the speaker. Newness or freshness (not, however, "smartness") in stating old ideas, or the handling of an old topic in a novel way, provides adequate challenge to the ingenuity of any speaker.

RESPONDING TO A WELCOME

A speech of response is basically only a speech of welcome or presentation in reverse. Hence the speaker will:

Indicate for whom he is speaking.

Express appreciation of the kindness of friends.

Speak complimentary words about the person or group extending the courtesy.

Minimize his own merits, though not depreciate them.

Anticipate pleasant experiences.

In the speech of response, as in the speech accepting a gift or award, the speaker does not, at first, have the initiative. He is following another speaker who has set the pace, so to speak, and has established the tone of the occasion. Whether the previous speaker has done poorly, has shown bad taste and little judgment, or has kept the occasion on a high level of propriety and dignity, the responding speaker dare not abruptly change the pace or tone.

Circumstances, therefore, make the speech of response often the most difficult of all speeches of courtesy because it is the hardest to prepare for and because, when you have prepared, it is impossible to be reasonably sure that what you thought of saying will fit the circumstances. In the first place, the speech of response must often be impromptu, and therefore one is tempted to be content with muttering a few general inanities and letting it go at that—like the average "thank you" letter after Christmas. Furthermore, the response may have to follow different kinds of leads which are frequently unpredictable. One may have to respond to the presentation of a gift or token of esteem or of some mark of honor. Or one may be offered a tribute whose content, and hence the resultant position he may find himself in, cannot be foretold. And then one may be tendered a speech of welcome which cuts the bottom out from under most of what he intended to say. One may, for example, have decided to comment on the spirit, purposes, or virtues of the welcoming group, only to find them already displayed beyond his power to magnify. Or one may have elected to characterize the spirit of the occasion, only to hear the preceding speaker steal every last rumble of his thunder. This kind of speech, therefore, must be composed with the utmost sincerity and as much ingenuity as is available.

Purpose

The speech of response to welcome (with or without presentation of a token) has one purpose only, to express *appreciation*. The speaker will do well to let that purpose thoroughly dominate him and to draw his materials according to an understanding of the full implications of what it is to "appreciate." To appreciate is not merely to thank. It is to *value*, to perceive accurately the *whole worth* of a thing, to *understand*. The speaker will ask himself: Why do I value this address of welcome? this gift? this tribute? the people welcoming me? the group I represent? He will then tell his hosts and his audience.

Materials

He will generally evince his appreciation by elaborating one or more of the following themes. He will express appreciation of the significance of the occasion, what it means and will mean to him and to those whom he represents. He will pay tribute to the organization, institution, community, or persons offering the welcome. He will explain the purpose or spirit of the organization for whom he is speaking. He will, as a matter of fact, adapt to his response the same kinds of material which might have been used in welcoming him.

General Characteristics

In form, the speech of response is much like the speech of welcome. It always has a theme. There are always some ways of finding excellence in an organization or of praising or paying tribute to a person. The speech will always have an approach and a conclusion. The special problem of the approach will be the neat and gracious fitting of the speaker's own theme into the situation left by the preceding speaker. This at times may be no small problem! The speaker must avoid the impression of ignoring, either in his manner or in the ideas he uses, the speech with which he was welcomed. Here again words may "fail," but he should not say so unless they really do. The audience expects him to talk. As a matter of fact, a speech of response is usually much longer than a speech of welcome.

It is, perhaps, useless reiteration to say that the speech must *fit* the occasion. The material must be appropriate. More, possibly, than others, this speech puts emphasis on content. Therefore the speaker must know whereof he speaks. Vagueness or plain ignorance will not serve. Blunders in taste and judgment are less likely if one is well equipped with information.

In summary, the speaker has been the recipient of formal courtesy. He must show his *appreciation* of that courtesy.

SPEECHES FOR ENTERTAINMENT

There is some legitimate question whether a speech which does not, to some extent, entertain an audience can be fully effective in any purpose. Surely, for most purposes it is easier to inform and persuade a pleased and interested listener than a displeased and bored one. Hence we may take it for granted that whatever makes a speech interesting, vivid, alive, and communicative also works to make it entertaining—if we interpret entertainment broadly, as we should, and do not restrict it to mere enjoyment of the funny, the comic, the humorous.

As there are few good speeches, for whatever purpose, which do not also incidentally entertain an audience, so there are few good speeches whose *sole* purpose or effect is to amuse or entertain. This is not to say that entertainment as the primary and avowed purpose for a speech is low, illegitimate, or undesirable. Everyone knows that much speaking which is done in public and in private is prompted by a wish to provide pleasure and diversion for one's friends or one's listeners, whoever they may be. And everyone knows that an entertaining talker, either at the dinner table at home, at the banquet table, or on the platform is a valuable asset to society. It is normally true, however, that except perhaps in vaudeville routine, a speech is more thoroughly and effectively entertaining if the entertainment grows more or less plausibly out of the development of ideas intended to convey information and understanding.

In discussing the entertaining speech, therefore, the most that we need do is to suggest some of the typical occasions for speeches of entertainment and to indicate the kinds of methods and supporting material which will usually predominate in such speeches.

Occasions

Many public (if not academic) lectures, though they often have informative value, are fundamentally for the amusement and diversion of those who attend. World travelers, explorers, adventurers, renowned hunters or fishermen—whether they describe places or people, experiences they have had or thoughts which have come to them amidst their adventures —speak mainly to entertain their audiences, not necessarily to educate them. When the traveler returns from his trip to Mexico, to the Grand Canyon, or to the airplane factory or when he reports his interview with the president of Ecuador, he will want usually to improve the *spirits* of his listeners. If he improves their minds also, he will consider that as so much clear profit beyond what he expected.

Likewise various social and semisocial occasions provide natural circumstances for speeches chiefly to entertain or divert an audience. Club meetings, parties, fraternal gatherings, and especially dinners and luncheons call for conversation and speeches which provide a maximum of entertainment with a minimum of weighty thought or systematic information. Many luncheon and dinner organizations, of course, make it a point to have programs provided with serious and important content. Even so, the speaker who would be heard eagerly and would make his subject acceptable will make his presentation also as entertaining as possible. The luncheon or dinner occasion is, of course, the natural habitat of that most popular of discourses, the after-dinner speech, which is given special treatment below.

Characteristics

In materials the speech for entertainment will favor the novel and vivid over the familiar and the exact, the active and lively over the close and concisely logical. Careful, laborious explanation will yield to lifelike impressions and colorful description. High premiums will be placed on the concrete example, the dramatic anecdote, story, or narrative, the striking comparison and contrast, the apt quotation, the effective introduction of direct discourse and snatches of dialogue. Humorous exaggeration, witty and unexpected phrasing and turns of thought, human interest, human peculiarities and foibles—these factors will stand out in speeches to entertain. In short, we are back to the emphasis of our earlier chapters on clarity and interest; and here, as there, we warn that the means of development, the devices of effectiveness, must serve the function of heightening the meaning of a significant, though not necessarily a complicated, idea.

In his *manner of presentation,* the entertaining speaker will be lively,

vigorous, good natured, optimistic, and kindly. He will keep things moving and will resist the temptation to labor for an effect that seems slow in coming or to milk the last thin drop of humor or wit from a situation or from a gag. He will not expect to rival at their own specialities the high-velocity comedians on the variety programs, and he will shun the easy assumption that his every remark must be a witty gem and that anything he says must necessarily be funny.

He will use *humor* to the best of his ability, but he will not overrate his ability. He will know that humor is only *one* avenue of entertainment, and though a good one, not always the most appropriate. In his use of humor he will be guided by what we said earlier—that jokes, anecdotes, and wise cracks are not the only sources of effective humor. He will understand that comedy is founded in the incongruous—in a painless disharmony between a thought and its expression, between a person and his acts or his language, between an individual and his pretensions or his opinion of himself. Where injury or pain begins, genuine humor leaves off. Though genial parody or take-off and other forms of burlesque are useful, an entertaining speaker will not let himself slip into biting satire or sarcasm. Such behavior, though spectacular and tempting, almost always defeats its own purpose and does more harm than good. The end of entertainment is a glow of friendly satisfaction in the listeners—satisfaction with the speaker and satisfaction with themselves. Only those devices which promote that end are legitimate materials for the entertaining speaker who wishes to entertain again. The audience, as ever, is the measure of the fitting and appropriate.

THE AFTER-DINNER SPEECH

Among speeches whose primary purpose is entertainment, the so-called after-dinner speech is at once probably the most admired, worst abused, and most difficult. To it, all that we have said about the entertaining speech applies with special force. *Hence our particular suggestions to the after-dinner speaker may serve to point up and to summarize the essence of our advice about speaking for entertainment.*

All postprandial speeches are not speeches of entertainment, and many of them are not even intended to be. The essentially serious informative or persuasive addresses delivered above dining tables need not occupy our time now. Most of this book is concerned with those speeches. We will only redirect the student's attention to the principle that such a speech will succeed best if it is adapted to the special conditions of audience and occasion which prevail after a meal in an atmosphere of disarrangement, cigar smoke, and tinkling water glasses and coffee cups.

Purpose

What is normally meant by after-dinner speaking is discourse providing *entertainment primarily,* usually after a meal of the banquet sort. The speaker is expected to present light stuff (though not exclusively frivolous) in an open, discursive, vivid style.

Demands

After-dinner speaking is difficult because it demands humor, because it must be interesting, and because the speaker is usually asked to *speak,* not to speak *about* anything in particular. After eating, people expect to be interested without giving much effort themselves except willingness to be entertained. They resent a speaker's imposing upon their good will by handling a heavy subject in a dry way; and, contrariwise, they are disgusted by a speaker's abusing their good will by pelting them with a string of pointless stories and anecdotes. The form requires wit, grace, charm, good humor, and at least some good sense.

Minimum Essentials

The basic formula for an after-dinner speech is:

Have a single, simple idea which you state vividly and illustrate and develop good-naturedly.

Use humor if it can seem spontaneous and be germane to the subject.

Be brief.

Avoid making other persons ridiculous.

Materials

The after-dinner audience wants to be shown, not to be reasoned with; to watch, not to exert itself. Such concealed argument as there is must not be dry, heavy, or compact. It must be insinuated into the audience's minds, not loaded in or driven in. Hence the materials must be vivid; they must be capable of resting easily on a full stomach. *Illustrations,* humorous if humor is practicable, developed with perhaps more detail than would seem economical on more sober occasions, should occupy the largest portion of the time. *Analogies* which progress in a leisurely fashion rank with illustrations as basic material. Relief and change of pace can be attained by energetic *figures of speech* and *fresh turns of phrase.* A special type of illustration, the *imaginative sketch,* especially when it involves persons and their faults and foibles, is peculiarly appropriate to the after-dinner speech.

At the core of the speech, however, should be an idea or a sentiment which is worth the trouble. Such ideas, for example, as serve to show us the absurdity or the folly of our ways, rather than the viciousness of our sins, or such sentiments as make us aware of the possible charm or pleasure of our relations with our fellows—these may well be amplified in after-dinner speeches. Subject sentences for such speeches (stated or implied) may be exemplified by the following:

> It is far more important for the new Dean of the Law School to charm and please his students than to see that they are prepared for the Law. (Ironic.)

> He who feeds the chickens deserves the egg.

> In many walks of life oversize decisions are frequently made by undersize brains.

> Men harass themselves unduly and plague their wives unnecessarily by wrongly supposing that women's hats are intended to be head coverings instead of ornaments.

> Our school (or our association) provides a basis for good fellowship which is worth all the expense and inconvenience of attending reunions (or conventions).

> The professor is, after all, the collegiate athlete's best friend.

Ideas and sentiments such as these, developed with fundamental insight as well as jocularity and good humor, can make, and have made, entertaining after-dinner speeches. Audiences have come away realizing, agreeably, that they had not only a glow of enjoyment but a feeling that something had been said.

Arrangement

In presentation, the normal forms and divisions of the speech are often done away with in favor of an *apparently* casual and impromptu organization. The introduction and conclusion, however, are very important. The introduction *must* be interesting and in perfect harmony with the mood of the occasion. An anecdote is a good device for effecting an introduction. Sometimes the anecdote, however, is too good; it may set a pace which the speaker will find it hard to keep up, and it may dominate rather than serve the *idea* of the speech. A speaker should beware of permitting himself to drag in a feeble excuse for an idea in order to have a plausible reason for telling a good story. His effort should be to find the story for the idea, not the idea for the story. In any event, his introduction must be graceful, because expression, graceful and charming, may often serve to avert the dismal consequences of weaknesses of idea in a speech, although stylistic excellence can never be an adequate substitute for substance.

The conclusion will be best if it is brief and if it leads to a real climax. At this point also an anecdote may be good if it is short and pointed. Some speakers find an apt and surprising quotation a good means of securing the effect of brevity and climax. The formal, summary conclusion is effective only if it is obviously burlesqued. The conclusion must not, like the "lone and level sands," "stretch far away."

Some smart but unwary toastmaster once introduced a famous after-dinner speaker by likening him to an automatic vending machine. Said he, "Just put a dinner in the slot and up comes a speech." The speaker's retort, deadly but indelicate, paid the toastmaster amply for a personal slur and for misrepresenting the true genesis of a good after-dinner speech. Good after-dinner speeches are not prepared during the consumption of a meal at the speaker's table. They are carefully and thoroughly prepared on a foundation of knowledge of the audience and the occasion. One does not take lightly an invitation to "speak informally." He understands that to mean "Be so well prepared that you will be free to seem informal and casual." One can't debate extemporaneously with other speakers on the program, for argument and debate are not *in* the occasion. One cannot rely on commonplaces, for other speakers may have uttered them already. "If the known practice of many of the best speakers is worth anything," wrote Sears, "it may be inferred that very careful prevision and provision are needful: prevision to see what is likely to be timely and effective; provision to secure it and order it in effective sequence." [3] That is the lesson from successes and failures in after-dinner speaking.

In the long run, we may agree that "good taste, generous sentiment, sober and fond recollection may be more needful than knowledge and zeal." [4] *Fitness* is the one great standard for the after-dinner speech.

SOURCES OF ILLUSTRATIVE SPEECHES ON SPECIAL OCCASIONS

The inclusion of many actual examples of whole speeches and portions of speeches in the preceding pages would, we realize, have some advantages. We believe, however, that they would not be worth the lengthening of the chapter and the interruption of the reading of the text which they would have cost. Though the speeches for special purposes have certain definable requisites, each such speech is so much a function of the occasion which creates it that no one speech is truly illustrative of what another ought to be. For this reason we choose rather to refer the interested student or teacher

[3] "After Dinner Speaking," *Modern Eloquence,* rev. ed. (New York, 1929), III, xxi.
[4] *Ibid.,* xxiii.

to the collections of speeches listed below than to provide him with a selected anthology in these pages.

BAIRD, A. Craig, *American Public Addresses* 1740–1952 (New York, 1954).

BRIGANCE, W. H., *Classified Speech Models* (New York, 1928).

LINDGREN, Homer D., *Modern Speeches* (New York, 1926, 1930).

Modern Eloquence (New York, 1929).

O'NEILL, J. M., *Models of Speech Composition* (New York, 1921).

————, *Modern Short Speeches* (New York, 1924).

O'NEILL, J. M., and F. K. RILEY, *Contemporary Speeches* (New York, 1930).

PARRISH, W. M., and Marie HOCHMUTH, *American Speeches* (New York, 1954).

SARETT, Lew, and W. T. FOSTER, *Modern Speeches on Basic Issues* (New York, 1939).

CHAPTER FIFTEEN

Group Discussion

SEVERAL YEARS AGO a well-known scholar and college president told a gathering of members of Phi Beta Kappa that the two inventions of modern times which have had the most extensive effect on college and university education are the mimeograph and the committee. That idea was not uttered altogether in jest. Nowadays it is hard to imagine a university, or a business house, or a labor union, or a PTA getting along without the service of a mimeograph or some other form of duplicator. It is almost as unrealistic to suppose that the educated, responsible citizen will escape being involved again and again in committee consultation or some of the other forms of discussion. He will be a member of many small groups of roughly three to fifteen people each, who attempt jointly, through talk, to secure information, to form responsible opinion, or to take co-operative decision. Such groups are as likely to appear in a man's or woman's business or employment as in his professional and trade association, his civic activities, and his social organizations. Most of us, as a matter of fact, probably have more opportunities to exercise our abilities in oral communication as members of committees, panels, symposia, conferences, boards, and discussion groups of various sorts than as speakers before audiences in the conventional sense.

To function well under any of these group circumstances, one needs, first of all, skill in public speaking. Although public speaking and discussion are complementary activities, in some respects, their procedures and techniques differ. One needs, therefore, to learn some special skills for discussion.

In consequence, during the past two decades or so, teachers, scholars, and experimenters, both in and out of the colleges and universities, have given much serious attention to the principles and practices of small group activities. They have written textbooks which are worth extensive, systematic study, and we especially recommend the books listed at the end of this chapter as among the most useful for that purpose. In the present chapter we wish only to introduce the student to the most usual and distinctive of the forms of group discourse.

GROUP DISCUSSION

Though the term *group discussion* is often used to signify almost any of the activities we have mentioned, most writers on the subject use it to mean specifically, *a co-operative and systematic attempt by several persons through the joint use of oral discourse to reach a decision on a recognized problem, mutually satisfactory to the participants.* We will think of group discussion in this sense and will regard it as one form of public discussion. Some other forms, which we will discuss also, are the panel, the round table, the symposium, the study group, the colloquium, and the case conference.

Requisites of Good Group Discussion

Good group discussion requires:

A worthy objective acceptable to the group

Recognized, responsible leadership

Responsible, well-informed, thoughtful participants

Participants who have as much skill as possible in speaking

Familiarity with the special principles and techniques of group discussion as distinguished from the other forms of speaking.

Group Discussion and Other Speech Activities Compared

If group discussion is activity in which persons discuss a problem face-to-face in order to find a conclusion satisfactory to all, it is both like and unlike other speaking situations.

First, like public speaking, discussion involves systematic oral communication. One who has learned how to communicate effectively with others, therefore, will find himself well grounded for group discussion. In discussion there is always a speaker—in fact many speakers—even though one speaker may not talk formally and at length. Moreover, the speaker, whoever he is from moment to moment, may be either trying to make himself clear to others or to persuade them. Furthermore, there is obviously an audience—the group.

On the other hand, discussion in certain important respects is unlike public speaking. In the first place, speaker and audience frequently change roles, for a participant in discussion is at one moment the speaker and at the next moment the listener. In listening to a speech, rarely does the hearer participate orally to any great extent, even in the forum, although the good speaker will often think of his listeners as responding with unspoken questions, objections, and arguments, and his speech may thus become a form of colloquy. The discussion, moreover, is usually less formal than the public speech. It is not always so, of course, for some discussions (committee meetings, for example) may be quite formal. Furthermore, the purpose of the public speaker is usually different from the purpose of the participant in discussion. The public speaker or debater, in taking a stand on a controversial problem, aims to influence others to *his* way of thinking; he wants to lead and desires others to follow. The participant in group discussion, on the other hand, does not wish solely to impose his views on others and to make them his adherents; he wishes to think with others, to reach a *common* conclusion. At times, of course, a participant may become an ardent advocate of a position; nevertheless, he realizes that he is making his contribution to a common cause and that his own convictions may well be modified before a final group decision is achieved. In brief, the *purpose* of public speaking and of group discussion may differ significantly: the speaker wants others to agree with him, whereas participants in discussion want to agree with each other.

It should be recognized, furthermore, that group discussion differs from most *conversation* in two respects:

1. Its participants are ordinarily better prepared than most conversationalists. Appreciating the purpose of group discussion, they take special pains to inform themselves on the problem before them, and they endeavor to think as earnestly and as deeply as they can about it.

2. The purpose of group discussion—to make a decision on a problem —is not so keenly felt in conversation, and, consequently, even among well-informed people talking about a definite problem, few conversations are carried through to a decision.

Group discussion, finally, must not be confused with the type of conference or committee meeting in which the chairman or leader uses the outward forms of discussion to facilitate selling his own program and winning acceptance of his views. He may give the appearance of encouraging discussion and at the same time manage to have only his own ideas before the group. Discussion thus becomes an indirect means of leading others to agree with him. Although in many situations such tactics produce effective persuasion, they are incompatible with group discussion. Participants, naturally, may enter into group discussion bringing pet ideas and preconceived positions which they will present with force and enthusiasm. What comes out of a group discussion, however, is a *new* product, a conclusion that is usually different in some ways from the conclusions held by the participants at the start of the discussion. The attitude of a participant is essentially this: "I shall use the methods of persuasion to make the best of my own views, of course, but I shall also use them to secure the best decision to which we can all agree."

Subjects for Group Discussion

It is impossible to draw a sharp distinction between the *subjects* of group discussion and of speechmaking. Almost any subject about which men deliberate and into which men inquire publicly may be considered profitably in a speech or in a group discussion. The question whether speechmaking or discussion is more appropriate at a given time on a given subject can be answered only on the basis of the purpose and the circumstances. If the object is to canvass the possibilities latent in a problem and to arrive jointly at a solution or a decision satisfactory to the limited group—a committee or a board, for example—then the methods of group discussion are likely to be the most satisfactory all around. On the other hand, if a solution or decision has been arrived at, or at least formulated, and the object is to recommend it for the approval of a group—the city council or the electorate, for example— then one will choose public speaking or debate.

Since many learning groups, in the classroom and elsewhere, do not have subjects made to order for their discussions, the selection of a good subject may become a problem. The qualities in a subject or the elements in a situation which suggest group discussion as an effective procedure suggest also that a good subject for discussion will be:

Controversial

Interesting and important to the group

Stated impartially as a question

Capable of being discussed significantly in the time available.

Selecting the Subject

The distinctions between *questions of fact, questions of policy,* and *questions of value* help in recognizing a desirable subject and getting it properly stated. Issues of *fact* are not normally subjects for discussion. "Have prices risen?" "How much have prices gone up?" "What is inflation?" "Are there enough people interested in establishing a community forum series?" Discussion on such subjects is not likely to be sustained, for as soon as the facts are in, discussion ceases. This is especially true of subjects dealing with "How to do it" and "What is it?"—for example, "How is rayon made?" "How is the Red Cross run?" "Upon what principles does democracy rest?" Moreover, the search for facts looks only to information, not to a group opinion, belief, or policy. In other words, a search for information culminates in *understanding*, not in *agreement;* and it is on subjects where people seek to agree that group discussion is most useful and necessary. Group discussion, of course, cannot get far without facts; indeed, any discussion will go through a fact-finding and information-seeking stage, but its real goal is to *use* facts and to *interpret* them in order that its participants may reach a common belief. Accordingly, some of the foregoing questions might well be turned so as to permit discussion on the practical problems which the questions are really aiming at: "What (if anything) should be done to control rising prices?" "Should a community forum series be inaugurated?"

Value judgments sometimes offer opportunities for group deliberation. We consider values in such questions as, "Does participation in intercollegiate football build character?" "Are fraternal organizations assets to the community?" "Are general education courses advisable for all Freshmen and Sophomore students?"

Discussion does not get far, however, with such *value* questions as, "Is pleasure a better guide for conduct than duty?" "Is Protestantism preferable to Catholicism?" "Does the end justify the means?" "Is science in conflict with religion?" All such questions about human, religious, and philosophical values, often exceedingly interesting subjects for informal or speculative discussion, are difficult (frequently impossible) for people to agree upon. Since *group* discussion aims at securing agreement, value judgments are best left to other forms of discussion.

Group discussion is usually best adapted to exploring *questions of policy.* Such questions typically contain the word *should* and require a decision as to what course of action, if any, is to be taken. "Should the finance committee recommend that dues be raised?" "Should Metropolitan University openly subsidize varsity athletes?" "Should the Federal government own and operate the nation's railroads?" "Should the President of the United States be elected by direct vote of the people?" Each of these subjects requires the group to reflect and decide upon a recommended course of action.

Usually discussions will prove most successful if the subject can be phrased as a *question of policy.* Assume, for example, a situation where the participants can profitably and interestingly consider the following question of value: "Are fraternities beneficial to a university community?" Much the same information and experience would be called upon, but a better discussion would probably result from consideration of one of the following subjects:

Should Blank University banish fraternities?

Should this group go on record as believing fraternities are an asset to this campus?

What changes, if any, should be made in the fraternity-sorority system as it now operates on this campus?

A successful type of subject for group discussion is often one which concerns the means of accomplishing a given end. For example, the question, "Should a community forum series be started?" assumes that people have felt the need for some means, other than newspapers, magazines, radio, and TV, of extending community thought and discussion. The real question is about the best means of meeting the need. The great advantage of such a question is that discussion starts in an area of agreement; therefore there is a good chance of securing a final consensus and of avoiding splitting the group with a majority and minority decision. We do not mean to suggest, however, that group discussion should be used only when people are ready to consider rival proposals on a problem. Many subjects proper to group discussion may well require consideration of the problem itself, its nature, and the conditions that create the problem, for not until the subject has been approached thus can possible solutions be fully examined.

Phrasing the Subject

PUT THE SUBJECT IN THE FORM OF A QUESTION

Right: Should American colleges abandon intercollegiate athletics?
Wrong: *Resolved,* that American colleges should abandon intercollegiate athletics.

Discussion that starts off with a resolution or a proposition runs the danger of beginning in an atmosphere of pro and con, of attack and defense. On the other hand, a question points up the problem-solving aspect of discussion somewhat better than does a proposition.

STATE THE QUESTION IMPARTIALLY

A loaded question may give bias and one-sidedness to discussion. It makes fair and complete exploration of all relevant means of coping with the problem highly difficult.

Right: Can the participation of voters in primary elections be increased?
Wrong: Why don't more voters participate in primary elections?

Sometimes, too, question-begging terms and conclusions whose truth is assumed creep into a question and make difficult a fair approach to the problem. The question, "What can be done to rescue our outmoded railroads from oblivion?" makes two unwarranted assumptions: (1) that the railroads are outmoded, (2) that they are passing into oblivion.

STATE THE QUESTION CLEARLY

Although during most discussions it is necessary to define the problem in controversy and to clear away misunderstandings over the meanings of words—especially words with loose, popular significance or specialized, technical meaning—needless definition can be avoided and time saved by using clear, unequivocal language in the question itself. In the question above, for instance, precisely what does *oblivion* mean? A less figurative and confusing word or phrase can be substituted.

SYSTEMATIC STEPS TO DECISION

In Chapter 11 we outlined Dewey's steps in the analysis of a problem. These steps are fruitful in many areas of problem-solving, but perhaps in no activity are their immediate, tangible benefits so obvious as in group discussion. Since they represent the stages which discussion on any controversial problem must go through if a wise decision is to be likely, they suggest an excellent guide for carrying on discussion systematically. These steps are:

1. Becoming aware of the problem.
2. Defining the precise nature of the problem.
3. Discovering possible solutions to the problem.
4. Deciding upon the best solution.
5. Testing the decision by putting it into practice.

Although the solution of any problem demands passing through each of the five steps, the amount of time spent on the several items may vary widely. The group may seem to have ignored, for example, the definition of the problem, but participants can never reach agreement on a solution, if they have not, at least in their minds, defined the important terms in the same way. In many discussions over education, for example, few persons attach precise meanings to terms like *intellectual* and *cultural*. These require special definition.

Quibbling over precise definitions, however, can be deadly boring and time-consuming. Participants, particularly the leader, must decide when the group is confused because of ambiguity in terms or when further refinement of definitions is not of sufficient value to justify taking an additional amount of the total time available.

Although the normal order is from 1 to 5 through Dewey's steps, discussants may feel the need of redefinition at any step. Discussion of possible solutions (step 4) often makes for a new awareness of some phase of the problem (step 2). Sometimes a group can give only a limited time to a particular subject and may agree to omit one or more of the steps.

Group discussions usually end with step 4 (deciding upon the best solution) rather than with step 5 (testing the decision by putting it into practice).

Preparation for Discussion

The Outline

Few people would be so naïve as to expect a systematic development of any program without previous planning. The chairman or certain of the members should prepare in advance an outline which anticipates the sort of questions to be answered during the discussion.

The items should be stated as impartial questions. They should never constitute a rigid guide, but should simply suggest the type of questions to which answers are sought. Members are expected to modify, add, or eliminate items during the actual discussion if the need arises.

Each participant should receive the outline long enough in advance so that he can do whatever investigation and advance thinking may be necessary for him to be a *responsible, well-informed member*. The following outline indicates the sort of advance planning which should be made.

Should the Federal government establish uniform driver's license requirements for all United States citizens?

CHAIRMAN'S INTRODUCTION (2–3 minutes)

DISCUSSION PROPER

I. What conditions involved in the licensing of drivers cause some people to believe there is a problem?
   A. How serious is the problem of highway accidents in the United States today?
      1. How many people are killed and injured each year?
      2. What is the economic cost to the nation of automobile accidents?
      3. Does the situation seem to be improving?
   B. How nearly uniform are requirements for drivers' licenses throughout the nation?
      1. What are the specific requirements in certain of the states?
      2. How widely do the requirements vary?
         a. What is the earliest age at which one may receive a driver's license anywhere in the U.S.?
         b. What is the oldest any state demands that a person be before he can qualify for a driver's license?
         c. What variation is there in such other matters as the nature of

written tests required, requirements to pass vision tests, requirements to pass driving tests, amount of license fee, etc.
C. Are there good reasons to believe that driving license requirements are too lax in some states?
  1. Is the number of accidents related to the laxity of driving examinations?
  2. What justifications (if any) are there for the belief that stricter licensing laws would decrease accidents?
    a. What does one's common sense decree?
    b. What do authorities say?
    c. What do available statistics reveal?
D. Are there valid reasons to believe that *uniformity* in examinations would decrease accidents?
  1. Do accidents occur because of discrepancies or variations between the regulations of various states?
  2. Are drivers confused and less efficient because of the present situation?

II. What solutions might handle present problems?
  A. Would greater efforts to educate drivers be a feasible solution?
    1. Through what agencies should (could) education be given?
    2. What subjects or areas might be stressed in such a program?
  B. Would a Federal law establishing minimum requirements (but not maximum) be of help?
    1. Which items might be covered by such a law?
    2. Would such a law be consistent with present relations between the Federal and State governments?
  C. Could legislation be enacted which would take the power of licensing drivers from the various states and give it to the Federal government?
    1. What possible forms might this action take?
    (Congressional enactment, Constitutional amendment, etc.?)
    2. Would such a law be consistent with present relations between the Federal and State governments?
  D. Can the problem be ignored or left to resolve itself?
  E. What other solutions seem possible?

III. Which solution is most desirable?
  A. Which solution would most effectively erase the problems previously discussed?
  B. Would the solution favored create significant problems which need to be considered before the solution is approved?
  C. Would the favored solution receive the support of the public and of officials?

CHAIRMAN'S (OR RECORDER'S) CONCLUDING SUMMARY.

Note the form of this outline. Items are stated as complete questions. Although the approach obviously rests upon Dewey's five steps, it does not follow them exactly. In this discussion, the answers to Part I would probably lead through both *awareness of the problem* (Dewey's first step) and the precise *nature of the problem* (his second step), but this order need not and should not always be followed meticulously. In the actual discussion consideration of possible solutions may at the same time determine the best solution. Other variations are frequently desirable. *The group should never feel obligated to follow the exact order, to confine itself only to items listed, or to include all matters which were thought important in the advance planning.* To be guided by such an outline would permit orderly procedures. Probably no important information or ideas would be overlooked.

THE CHAIRMAN

Responsibilities of the Chairman

Though some groups seem to accomplish certain kinds of desirable ends without specifically designated chairmen, under most circumstances the chairman is the key to the efficiency of the group. Seldom does a group resolve a problem successfully through discussion except under the guidance of a recognized leader or chairman. The chairman's *responsibilities* include the following:

Obtaining background information on the subject. This will enable him to understand the significance and implications of contributions so that he can steer the discussion within profitable channels.

Planning the discussion outline or the agenda. The chairman may do this entirely unaided; he may share the responsibility with certain group members; or the group may hold a preliminary session simply to develop agenda. In any event, the chairman should see that an outline proposing an order of discussion is prepared and is made available to the group in advance.

Providing for the physical comforts of participants. The chairman should make sure, for example, that a table is actually available if he wants members seated around a table. He should be certain the seating arrangement (with ample elbow room) will be the most desirable possible. He must recognize that procuring and setting-up proper facilities is one of his responsibilities, and he will do the best he can under the circumstances.

Introducing the subject. This responsibility is met through the techniques set forth in Chapter 13. The chairman should get attention and orient participants and audience (if any). The suggestions offered for getting attention in the introduction to a speech apply also to a chairman's opening remarks. The orientation normally takes longer in the introduction to a discussion than it does in a speech.

Inexperienced chairmen frequently fail to realize the importance of the introduction. Certainly one would not give a thirty-minute or an hour talk without a skillful, complete introduction. The introduction to an hour of discussion should, if anything, be planned even more carefully than the opening remarks to an hour lecture. The group must be ready to start thinking.

Guiding the discussion. The chairman strives to keep the group from heading off on tangents. Whenever remarks seem to be irrelevant or off the point, he should encourage the speaker to explain how they relate to the matter of the moment. He can say tactfully, "Mr. X, will you explain how your remark relates to so-and-so?" or "Mr. X, we are considering such-and such a point. What light does your statement throw on it?"

He seeks also to keep his associates moving forward through the agenda. He is alert to opportunities to crystallize and summarize their contributions, agreements, and points of conflict so that their deliberations will be as efficient as possible.

He seeks to consolidate opinion toward a consensus to which the participants will commit themselves. When it appears that the group favors a particular proposal or decision, he may try phrasing it and ask whether there is general agreement. When it appears that agreement is not possible on a single proposal and a majority and minority division seems inevitable, he may ask a representative of each group to phrase its proposal. In terminating discussion, it is essential to crystallize opinion so that all can recognize a concrete result which no one person has provided, but in which each has had a hand.

He must meet all of his responsibilities with tact and good humor. Each participant should feel that he is important to the discussion. The chairman can encourage this feeling; at least he should do nothing to destroy it.

Maintaining his own impartiality. The leader should not take sides when differences develop among the participants. He should not take a definite stand on a controversial issue which may differ from the position taken by some participants in the group. Yet if he becomes aware of a matter which ought not be ignored, he may say, for example, "Do any of you care to express the point of view which I have sometimes heard that . . . ?" or "Jack has expressed himself very strongly. Do any of you care to take a different stand?"

Only if the chairman remains neutral will the group freely express its ideas. He must encourage participation. To do that he should remain the impartial moderator, a person willing and eager to have all views aired. It is possible, of course, that a chairman may find himself in a dilemma: if he remains impartial, the wrong decision may be made by the group; if he takes sides, he cannot remain impartial. The way out of the dilemma can depend only upon the chairman's evaluation of the situation. Perhaps the decision to be made is sufficiently important for him to sacrifice himself as group chairman and exert his influence upon the right side. Only in rare circumstances, however, will he find it necessary or advisable to give up his role as the unbiased group leader.

Summarizing the collective opinion or decisions of the group. In some discussions, the chairman (or the recorder) can make a major contribution with brief summaries which pull together what has been done and said so that the group is ready to move forward in common understanding. This is an extremely important duty of the chairman, for when a group loses its way and begins to wallow, confusion and a sense of futility set in. Undirected and unguided discussions, too often the rule, are to a large extent responsible for the feeling that discussion gets nowhere. Furthermore, random discussion makes a true consensus difficult, if not impossible.

The ability to summarize concisely and accurately is not easily acquired, but it can be learned through practice. Where and when to summarize, it is impossible to say; the leader must listen attentively to the discussion and exercise his best judgment. As a rule, however, summaries should at least be employed at each of the major stages of discussion.

> It seems evident, then, that the conditions giving rise to our problem are so-and-so, so-and-so, etc. Are we ready now to see exactly what our problem is?
>
> Do we agree that our problem can be defined as so-and-so?
>
> For such-and-such a proposal, we have heard the following reasons. . . . Does anyone wish to comment further on them?
>
> Such-and-such proposals have been made. Does one of them seem to be superior? Which one is most desirable? Most practical?
>
> Such-and-such weaknesses have been urged against such-and-such a proposal. Shall we reject it?
>
> Mr. X interprets the evidence of such-and-such an argument in this way; Mr. Y in this way. Which interpretation shall we accept?
>
> We agree on these points . . . ; we seem to differ on these. . . . Can we resolve the disagreement?

The chairman (or the recorder, if one has been designated) should also summarize at the conclusion of the conference. The temptation to omit such a summary is often great. The chairman may think that anything he says will be so obvious to all as to be a waste of time; he may feel incapable of stating the exact results of the meeting; since the group has disagreed upon what he considers to be the most vital issues, he may reason that there is nothing to summarize. Yet, *in all cases a final summary should be made.* The final statements may simply list the areas upon which there has been agreement and those where the group has failed to agree, but an impartial restatement of conclusions or final convictions (or perhaps a brief review) should be considered an indispensable part of any discussion.

Because interim summaries and the final summation are essential but frequently difficult to make, and because a chairman often finds all his mental faculties needed simply to guide the discussion, the use of a *recorder* is becoming increasingly popular. The *recorder's* one responsibility is to keep a record of what has happened and to be ready at any time upon request of the chairman or the group to summarize a part or the total discussion which has preceded. This eases the burden of the chairman, of course. It also provides a slightly different type of summary. *Good* chairmen assume greater prerogatives for interpreting and synthesizing in their summaries than do good recorders. The recorder is expected only to report back what the group has done.

Qualifications of the Chairman

In order to fulfill his responsibilities, a chairman needs certain qualities:

Ability to express himself clearly and concisely. The leader should talk no more than is absolutely necessary to accomplish his responsibilities. Chapters 5 and 6 concerning methods of developing and clarifying ideas can be of much help in this respect. In our observation the most effective discussion chairmen are almost always capable public speakers.

Sensitivity to the attitudes and reactions of his participants. He must have the ability to handle difficult situations with tact and diplomacy. Any subject worthy of a good discussion is apt to produce some crises among the discussants. The chairman must be alert to these situations and must be capable of handling them so as to preserve the ego or status of the participants and still keep them all at work.

A sense of humor. Many situations offer opportunities for humor. Good discussion requires concentrated and sustained intellectual effort, and persons will welcome an occasional easing of tension and effort. Obviously, humor can be overdone, but participants and chairmen alike should know that laughing together forms a bond among people. Most good conferences will admit occasions for gentle humor, but fun at the expense of some member can detract from rather than aid group solidarity.

Intelligence. Unless he has the ability to plan a discussion outline, to summarize accurately, and to sense at once whether a comment applies to the subject at hand or will lead the group onto some tangent, a person cannot fulfill his responsibilities as a chairman. Unquestionably, the abilities and the work of the group leader are tremendously important to the success of the discussion. Certainly, not everyone has sufficient inherent ability to do the task as well as it should be done. If an intelligent person is unsuccessful, however, the chances are not that he lacks the mental capacity, but rather that he is making insufficient use of his abilities.

Such a list of qualifications perhaps suggests that the ideal discussion leader is the embodiment of most of the social virtues—tact, fairness, tolerance, patience, broadmindedness, courtesy, a sense of humor, and quickness of wit. Unquestionably an effective leader of discussion should reveal these qualities, but the student eager to learn how to participate effectively in discussion need not despair if at first he falls short of the ideal. Such qualities, like most excellences of personality, can be fostered, and practice in discussion can help to develop them.

The Chairman in Action

A responsible, efficient chairman will behave in the following ways:

Respect the opinions of others. He will listen closely to what others say with the attitude that the other fellow may well be right, that he may have a good point or essential information to contribute. This is the beginning of tact and courtesy.

Let the participants do most of the talking. He will not monopolize the floor and the time, or enter the argument. It is the variety of opinion, fact, and argument that makes for thorough exploration of a problem and promotes the best possible decision.

Encourage everyone to participate without penalizing those who have more to say than others. The better-informed and the more alert participant has more to contribute than the ill-informed and the dull individual; some know more about some aspects of a question than they do about other phases of the problem, and it is unfair to them and the group to curb them unduly. Only when all the participants are eager to speak is it wise to adopt the rule that no person may speak a second time until all have had a chance to chime in.

In encouraging participation, a chairman will often encounter two extreme types of difficult members who will need special handling:

The long-winded speechmaker. With him the chairman may be forced to assert his authority. He can say, "Will the speaker please conclude his remarks?" or "We have time now only for a concluding sentence from you; will you summarize briefly?"

The silent, reluctant soul. He is somewhat more of a problem than the loquacious person. Sometimes he can be drawn out by a skillful question, but care must be taken not to embarrass him unduly. It is probably wise to avoid questions calling for specific information and definite knowledge, such as, "Can you supply further information on this point, Mr. X?" or "Does your experience suggest an illustration

on this point?" He may not have the information and can only say
no. Rather, prefer questions that call for his response to what has already been said, such as, "Will Mr. Y's proposal accomplish the goal
(or one of the goals) we have agreed upon?"

Keep the discussion as rational and as informative as possible. The
leader must train a sharp eye on argument and evidence. When the participants themselves overlook what seem to be poor reasoning and unsound evidence, the chairman should tactfully enter the discussion, not
as an advocate with an axe to grind, but as a friendly critic. The student
chairman in particular would do well to learn—if necessary, to memorize
—the chief rules that make for sound evidence and good reasoning (see
Chapter 11). He can then frame typical questions that will allow him
indirectly but positively to guide the group in weighing and considering
evidence and argument. For example:

When evidence is lacking, he can say:

You have heard Mr. X's point. Can anyone supply information (an example,
data, authoritative opinion) at this point?

When a participant offers an unsupported opinion, the leader may well
ask:

Mr. X, why do you hold that view? Can you give us the reasons for your
statement?

That kind of question is perhaps the most valuable single query a leader
can make, because it leads discussion onward and gives others a chance
to criticize and evaluate.

When evidence and reasoning seem weak, the leader might ask any
one of these questions:

Mr. X has offered a broad generalization. Do you think it is well founded?

Mr. X cited Professor Y in support of his point. How much reliance should
we put upon Professor Y's opinion (or data)?

Mr. X has drawn an analogy between so-and-so and so-and-so. Do you accept
the analogy as sound?

One cause giving rise to the problem before us has been stated. Are there
other causes? Mr. X has suggested in his argument that A causes B. Is the
connection sufficiently clear and direct?

Observe that in the examples above, each question is prefaced by a direct
reference to what has been said, and in actual discussion the reference
should specifically allude to the evidence or reasoning to be evaluated.
This practice contributes immeasurably to the *clarity* of discussion. The
only exception to this practice of direct reference comes when a partici-

pant's remarks have been so brief or so pointed and clear that direct reference is obviously superfluous. Then the chairman can use a question alone, such as, "Is Mr. X's example typical?"

Point up and emphasize areas of agreement. This is especially important during the earlier stages of discussion in seeking to establish the nature of the problem, the circumstances and causes giving rise to it, and the goals or principles that a good solution should be in harmony with. When a group can agree on these basic matters, its final decision as to what should be done comes easier than if differences are allowed to appear too large. The chair might ask:

Do we agree that our problem is essentially so-and-so?

Do we agree that the chief evils that give rise to the problem are so-and-so?

Prevent hasty decision, if necessary, by encouraging consideration of alternative solutions. Occasionally a group with a pressing problem will want to rush through to a decision that seems almost self-evident at the outset of a discussion.

The fraternity rushing rules have broken down because fraternities jump the gun by starting rushing before the date agreed upon. Obviously we could suspend or fine the offending fraternities.

Thus might an interfraternity council conclude after ten or fifteen minutes of discussion. In such cases, a chairman might delay formal approval of the easy and obvious decision by encouraging examination of the possible weaknesses of the solution. He might say:

We apparently approve of such-and-such a decision. But before we act finally, should we not look to the possible outcome of our decision? What are its weaknesses?

If he is fairly skillful he might lead the group to consider the weaknesses at a subsequent meeting and might even get one or two speakers to present the possible arguments against the decision. Such a procedure sometimes leads back to a reconsideration of the entire problem and to other solutions. It is the only means of testing a decision carefully before it meets the ultimate test of actual experience.

THE INFORMED AND SKILLFUL PARTICIPANT

Most of the suggestions which we have made to guide the chairman apply with equal force to an intelligent participant in discussion. Indeed, he can sometimes come to the aid of an inexpert chairman by tactful questions such as, "Mr. Chairman, are we ready to have an expression of opinion on such-and-such a proposal?" "Can we say that our principal goal is this; . . . ?" "Is this a fair definition of our problem? . . ." He may even summarize occasionally and thus aid in unifying discussion.

In order to function with the greatest efficiency, each member of a discussion group should try to act in the following ways:

Listen attentively. As in the impromptu speech, it is what others say that stimulates a member's thought and prompts him to speak. He must be willing to listen and give others a chance to make their contributions.

Enter the discussion whenever he has a relevant remark to make or a question to ask. Any member should follow the impulse to speak when an idea prompts him. If he hesitates and leans back, he will soon find that he is willing to do nothing but listen, and the chairman, if discussion is lively, may not try to draw him out. He then becomes a liability to the group rather than an asset. He should be *alert and active.*

Make a deliberate and persistent attempt always to relate his remarks to what has been said. He should open his contribution with specific reference to the point or argument or idea he wants to explain further, add to, criticize, question, or refute. This practice gives clarity to discussion. Examples of what he might say are:

Mr. X has said so-and-so. Another illustration of the same point is. . . . As to Mr. X's point that . . . , Senator Fulbright said. . . . What is the meaning of so-and-so? I don't understand. (This is better than, "I don't understand that," or "What do you mean?" Neither *what* nor *that* is sufficiently specific.)

The argument that foreign aid cements friendship seems doubtful, because. . . . (This is preferable to "That argument seems doubtful." Again the word *that* may not carry a specific reference to the hearers.)

I agree (or cannot agree) with Mr. X's statement that so-and-so is true. (This is better than "I cannot agree with Mr. X.")

We have said so-and-so and so-and-so. Now I'd like to raise a different question. (This is better than "I'd like to raise a different question.")

This habit of specifically relating what one has to say to what has gone before is invaluable.

Develop the ability to organize his remarks. The suggestions we have offered earlier (pages 155–156) for the patterning of impromptu speeches are as useful for discussion and conversation as for the impromptu speech. Discussion is marked by little speeches as well as by questions and one-sentence answers.

Avoid statements and references that cause clashes of personality and that provoke stubborn, unco-operative attitudes. Members must avoid name-calling and uncomplimentary references. If you tell a man he sounds like a reactionary, a radical, a Red, a stubborn fool, a liar, an ignoramus, or a hypocrite, he is likely to resent the label. He feels he must defend *himself* with a sharp rejoinder. When this happens, discussion is diverted from the critical examination of information, arguments, and evidence and descends to personalities. A red herring is drawn across the path of discussion; such remarks provoke antagonistic attitudes, setting a tone that increases the difficulty of reaching a decision acceptable to all.

If Mr. X makes an uncomplimentary reference to Mr. Y, Mr. Y has at least two courses. He may choose to ignore the reference, keep his temper and urbanity, and let discussion go on. If the reference cannot be overlooked, one device for softening antagonism is to address Mr. X through the chairman, "Mr. Chairman, will Mr. X explain why he thinks my position is reactionary?" X may at once see that his label was hastily or inadvisedly used and will move to soften it or withdraw it. In responding to the question, he too should address Y through the chairman. This convention preserves a civilized distance between personalities. (Some formal discussion groups, legislative bodies, and committees adopt the rule that all remarks must be made to the chairman.) Flat, dogmatic, contentious statements should be avoided—the "I'm-telling-you-that-I-know" statement. Examples occur all too frequently:

> I'm absolutely right.
>
> You're wrong and you should know it.
>
> Anybody with any sense knows that's so.
>
> That's utterly absurd.

More modest, tentative forms of statement are better, such as, "It seems to me that . . . ," "I think that . . . ," "My opinion is that. . . ." And, instead of flatly asserting that someone is wrong, one may say, "Can it be (it seems) that Mr. X's argument is weak in such-and-such respects."

Admit the truth of well-founded criticism. This is not easy for a young, sensitive person, for once he has publicly committed himself to a position or an argument, his tendency is to defend it. Pride rushes forward saying, "This is *my* argument and if I abandon it, I shall lose face."

Develop the willingness to see a good idea, originally his, become the property of some other person or of the group. He should not insist upon everyone's acknowledging his "copyright," nor should he insist that an idea, just because it is his, must be kept constantly before the group. There is no place for strong pride of paternity in *group* discussion.

Be willing to compromise but not eager to. When participants once learn that a spirit of co-operation is necessary to successful discussion, they are often too quick to compromise when they face the need of taking final decision on a proposal. The too-ready compromiser weakens the quality and progress of co-operative thinking just as surely as the stubborn die-hard. As we all know, it is easier to say "yes" than "no." The antidote to hasty compromise appears to be this: Let a member stick to his proposal or his argument until others present evidence and argument that leads him to abandon or modify it. If he believes his position is well grounded, then others can be led to accept it or will be stimulated to point out weaknesses he will admit. He might say something like this:

> Mr. Chairman, I cannot agree to the proposal before us until we have further examined such-and-such a point. It seems to me, as I have previously stated, that such-and-such is sound. Am I mistaken?

By preserving the integrity of his own convictions, a participant leads— even *forces*—a group to do a better job of thinking than if he acquiesces too readily in the belief that unanimity must be secured at all costs. Sincere belief in a rational position should not be confused with obstinacy.

PUBLIC AND PRIVATE DISCUSSIONS

So far we have considered the discussion in which only the participants are present. We now consider briefly the discussion which is carried on before an audience. Sometimes the audience merely listens in; sometimes it chimes in.

The circumstances under which a discussion is to be carried on before an audience will influence both the choice of subject and the conduct of the discussion. If, for example, the discussion is one of a radio or television series and is allotted only thirty minutes, the participants cannot expect to handle thoroughly all the implications of some national or international problem. Yet they will want their discussion to seem both important and interesting to listeners and viewers. Because of this difficulty, most successful radio and television discussions are rehearsed. Rehearsal helps members channel their remarks into the most productive areas. It tends to prevent going off on tangents where little is accomplished or where the group quibbles about relatively minor matters; since members know in advance the attitudes to be taken by other participants, they are able to think through their own positions and are prepared to state their convictions and proofs with a minimum of irrelevant detail. *This does not mean that participants should write out and rehearse their contributions word-for-word.* Memorizing is likely to injure both adaptability and spontaneity and to make the discussion even less stimulating than the typical memorized speech. It is all important that the discussion not be "canned"! Private discussions, on the contrary, should never be rehearsed. The group may gather at a planning meeting to determine their agenda or to clarify the views they *expect to take,* but they should not attempt to rehearse their processes of reflective thought!

As in a discussion on the air, so in any discussion for which there is to be an audience (which may or may not be privileged to ask questions or to contribute) the speakers must make concessions to that audience.

For example, the chairman's initial remarks to stimulate interest must not only put the group discussants on common ground but must bring the listeners onto that ground as well. Although in a public discussion, of course, participants address their comments to each other, they must be aware that they are addressing other listeners also, and that they should adapt their ideas and ways of stating their ideas accordingly.

In a public discussion, the general pace must be rapid enough for the audience to be kept interested and stimulated. In a private discussion the chairman may recognize a break or pause as desirable timeout for members to regroup their thoughts, following the introduction of some unexpected or extremely important point of view. Such dead time before an audience, however, would rarely be permitted by a capable chairman.

Many so-called public discussions are really debates, since it is obvious that the participants came with preconceived solutions and a determination to win others to their views. Group discussion does not require the abandonment of a participant's convictions, but it succeeds best with participants who are willing to pool their ideas and approach a group consensus.

TYPES AND STYLES OF DISCUSSION

Chiefly we have given our attention in this chapter to that form of joint, collaborative discourse called *group discussion*. Most of the principles and practices we have mentioned will serve as well in those other sorts of discussion whose chief concern is not strictly problem-solving and whose aim is not necessarily consensus. There is no special format which is clearly desirable under all or most circumstances for the activity of discussion. One need be no more than a mild addict to TV, for example, to realize that there are almost as many modifications of form as there are different programs, all of which serve more or less well the ends for which they are intended. Certain patterns, however, appear to be recognizable more often than others.

Informal Discussion

A gathering of fraternity brothers, club members, faculty personnel, business associates, or any other group orally considering a common goal or subject can be an informal discussion group. (*Committee discussion* may be of this type but is more likely to have the aims of *group discussion*.) In informal discussion a group of people meet together, as in a class without an audience or onlookers, for group consideration of some specific issue(s). No prepared speeches are given; the group simply converses together to reach common agreement.

Study-Group Discussion

Frequently a group will gather to discuss a subject or problem, the economics of state government, for example, realizing that group agreement is less important than the stimulation of individual members to think or study or do further reading on the issues raised. The *study group*, striving for common understanding of a novel or play, is fulfilling a parallel desire to open up the most significant implications and applications of the work.

Round Table

The *round table* adds an audience to an informal discussion, but members of the audience are not permitted to ask questions or otherwise to enter the discussion. The number of members participating in the *round table* may vary from three to fifteen or more. There are no set speeches by any of the participants, except for whatever introductory and concluding remarks the chairman may care to give.

Panel Discussion

A listening and participating audience makes the *informal* committee meeting into a *panel discussion*. Ordinarily the panel uses experts, four to eight in number, who may make initial statements and then discuss the subject informally before it is thrown open to questions and comments from the audience or other members.

Symposium

In a symposium each member presents a prepared talk on some phase of the subject. It should not be confused with the *panel*. Set talks (from five to fifteen minutes each) by a few people (three to eight, usually) followed by discussion and audience participation are the two requisites for the designation, *symposium*. Sometimes those who make the short talks will discuss among themselves before throwing the issue open to the others present. Or, the audience may be invited to participate immediately after the short speeches are given.

Case Conference (Or Problem Method)

Suppose a parent-teacher group is planning a public discussion. They might launch their discussion by presenting the following case study or problem:

James Hendricks is a rather frail eleventh grade student who until he entered high school had never liked school. He has considerable musical aptitude and started playing the trumpet while in the ninth grade. His general adjustment and over-all work have much improved, as a result apparently of his interest in music. During the last two weeks, however, he has been falling asleep in class and has shown almost no interest in his assignments. Investigation revealed that he has been playing in a dance band, but when confronted by the Principal with the fact that his studies were suffering badly, James' only reply was, "Aw, I never liked school anyway. The teacher's always been against me." What suggestions would you offer the Principal and the teachers working with James?

The consideration of this specific problem might well lead either a group of experts in front of the parent-teacher audience or the entire group in attendance (if it is not too large) into matters of general interest and importance. For example, much talk would probably concern the value of giving students opportunities to succeed or to develop their special aptitudes. The exact place of music, as well as other special activities, in the high school program would certainly be touched upon. The importance of counseling to establish rapport with students and to handle individual problems would probably be discussed.

The *Case Conference* or the *Problem Method* centers on a specific problem, the discussion of which will bring out general principles. It is widely used in adult education groups, military schools, and industry. The pitfalls of the method are many, for the group may easily become so embroiled in unimportant specifics that fundamental issues never emerge. The leader's task calls for even greater skill than in other discussions. But the method is invariably interesting and frequently highly productive.

Additional Types

One occasionally hears references to various other types of discussion; the list presented in this chapter is not intended to be exhaustive. The word *forum* is used in at least two different senses: (1) It frequently means audience participation. A *lecture-forum*, for example, provides both a speech and the opportunity for audience questions and contributions following the talk. A *debate-forum* simply combines formal debating (affirmative and negative sides) with audience participation inserted either before final rebuttals or after the regular debate. A *film-forum* includes a motion picture or film strip and a discussion period. (2) The term *forum* is sometimes used to signify a series of discussions: for example, a weekly television program or a particular discussion activity scheduled for perhaps every Wednesday evening.

A *colloquium* provides for the inclusion of one or a very few experts whose opinions or help will be utilized only when the group feels a particular desire for such assistance. Perhaps an Army general and an official of the State Department are available for a discussion of the ques-tion, "Should the United States continue compulsory military service during peace time?" We could reason that if we include these two ex-perts in a typical round table, panel, or symposium, they will so domi-nate the situation with the prestige of their backgrounds and the data available to them, that the ordinary citizens present will take little part. Yet we may feel that this is the sort of question of policy which should be decided not by the military or the State Department, but by the gen-eral public. Hence, we would call on the experts only when we feel the need of concrete data which they can supply in answer to direct ques-tions. Frequently, young people's discussion groups such as those spon-sored by the YMCA or YWCA will have a so-called *resource person* available in this same sort of expert capacity.

The term *parliamentary discussion* is applied to groups which provide for discussion within the framework of recognized principles of parlia-mentary law.

SEATING ARRANGEMENTS

Although the chairman must frequently go to some trouble to secure a desirable seating arrangement, this trouble is usually well worth the effort. If ten or fifteen people come together for an informal discussion, he should insist upon the group's getting into an orderly circle or fac-ing one another around a table (see Fig. 14). If a panel or symposium is planned for, one of the arrangements in Figure 15 will probably serve well.

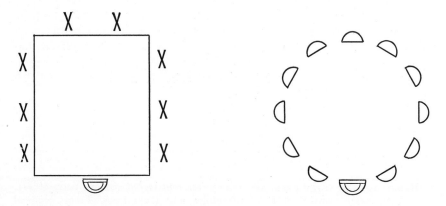

Fig. 14. Two Arrangements for Informal Group Discussion and Round Table

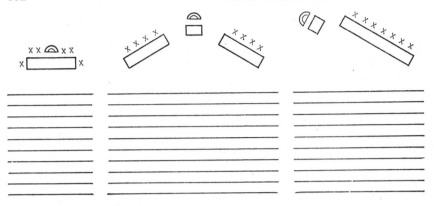

Fig. 15. Three Arrangements for Panel or Symposium

DISCUSSION AND THE PRINCIPLES OF SPEECH

As we remarked early in the chapter, the principles and methods of good speaking, whether expository or persuasive, will contribute as much to good group discussion as to good speechmaking. The knowledge and skill necessary for effective formulating and developing of statements and propositions, for amplifying and supporting ideas, for analyzing one's listeners and adapting one's material to them, for organizing and patterning one's discourse, for "adjusting people to ideas and ideas to people," will be as significant around the conference table as on the platform. The student should realize, therefore, that first of all he must develop as fully as possible his capacities for oral communication of all kinds. Then he will learn to make the special adaptations which the circumstances and purposes of discussion call for. Discussion and group methods, however, as we also remarked earlier, have become the subjects of extensive study in recent years. In some colleges and universities several courses are devoted to the problems and practices of group discussion alone. In this chapter, therefore, we have presented only a small beginning, largely in the form of do's and don't's. Interested students will wish to pursue the subject much further.

=== FURTHER READING ===

BAIRD, A. Craig, *Argumentation, Discussion, and Debate* (New York, 1950). A thorough consideration of principles and techniques. Treats "logical processes" in detail.

BRANDENBURG, Earnest S., and Waldo W. BRADEN, *Oral Decision-Making* (New York, 1955). An excellent comprehensive treatment of discussion and debate, with emphasis on the functional aspects of debate and on the ideal of consensus in discussion.

CHASE, Stuart, *Roads to Agreement* (New York, 1951). Interesting reading. Chapters 1, 8, 9, 10, and 11 will be particularly stimulating and useful for those interested in principles or theories underlying successful group activities.

CORTRIGHT, Rupert L., and George L. HINDS, *Creative Discussion* (New York, 1959). Up-to-date chapters on "Contemporary Methods of Discussion," "The Management of Meetings," and "Human Creativity." Presents discussion in terms of general application as well as classroom practice.

"The Dynamics of the Discussion Group," *Journal of Social Issues* (Spring 1948). The entire issue is devoted to this subject. Various articles describe concepts underlying the First National Training Laboratory in Group Development held in Bethel, Maine, during the summer of 1947, and report findings from experimentation there.

EWBANK, Henry Lee, and J. Jeffery AUER, *Discussion and Debate* (New York, 1951). Ch. 2, "Democracy, Discussion, and Debate," and Ch. 22, "Evaluating Discussion," will be of especial value to students in a general speech course who desire additional material on these subjects.

HAIMAN, Franklyn S., *Group Leadership and Democratic Action* (New York, 1951). Presents the "philosophical-scientific background and the practical techniques of democratic group leadership," drawing upon recent writings and theory in group dynamics as well as the traditional principles of discussion. Note the "Barnlund-Haiman Leader Rating Scale," pp. 237–243.

HOWELL, William S., and Donald K. SMITH, *Discussion* (New York, 1956). Useful section on "Critical Thinking in Discussion," containing three chapters on inductive analysis of evidence. Treats problems of ethics in section on "Discussion and Society."

McBURNEY, James H., and Kenneth G. HANCE, *Discussion in Human Affairs* (New York, 1950). Part IV, on "Types of Discussion," will be particularly helpful to those interested in various types of discussion and the relationships between discussion and other activities such as debating, parliamentary procedure, and classroom teaching.

SATTLER, William M., and N. E. MILLER, *Discussion and Conference* (New York, 1954). Good sections on leadership and participation. Presents chapters on interpersonal relations, methods of participation, and contributions and role patterns.

WAGNER, Russell H., and Carroll C. ARNOLD, *Handbook of Group Discussion* (New York, 1950). Excellent brief chapters on such important matters as "Leadership," "Participation," and "Subject-Problems."

APPENDIX

Speeches for Study
and Oral Practice

SIR JAMES JEANS

Why the Sky Looks Blue

The following explanation of a common phenomenon, by one of the world's greatest physicists, is about as perfect an example as one could find of the use of analogy in exposition, of relating the unfamiliar to the familiar. The selection expresses a single idea which is amplified through analogy.

IMAGINE that we stand on any ordinary seaside pier, and watch the waves rolling in and striking against the iron columns of the pier. Large waves pay little attention to the columns—they divide right and left and re-unite after passing each column, much as a regiment of soldiers would if a tree stood in their road; it is almost as though the columns had not been there. But the short waves and ripples find the columns of the pier a much more formidable obstacle. When the short waves impinge on the columns, they are reflected back and spread as new ripples in all directions. To use the technical term, they are "scattered." The obstacle provided by the iron columns hardly affects the long waves at all, but scatters the short ripples.

We have been watching a sort of working model of the way in which sunlight struggles through the earth's atmosphere. Between us on earth and outer space the atmosphere interposes innumerable obstacles in the form of molecules of air, tiny droplets of water, and small particles of dust. These are represented by the columns of the pier.

The waves of the sea represent the sunlight. We know that sunlight is a blend of lights of many colours—as we can prove for ourselves by passing it through a prism, or even through a jug of water, or as Nature demonstrates to us when she passes it through the raindrops of a summer shower and produces a rainbow. We also know that light consists of waves, and that the different colours of light are produced by waves of different lengths, red light by long waves and blue light by short waves. The mixture of waves which constitutes sunlight has to struggle through the obstacles it meets in the atmosphere, just as the mixture of waves at the seaside has to struggle past the columns of the pier. And these obstacles treat the light-waves much as the columns of the pier treat the sea-waves. The long waves which constitute red light are hardly affected, but the short waves which constitute blue light are scattered in all directions.

From Sir James Jeans, *The Stars in Their Courses* (Cambridge, 1931), pp. 23–24. By permission of the Cambridge University Press.

Thus, the different constituents of sunlight are treated in different ways as they struggle through the earth's atmosphere. A wave of blue light may be scattered by a dust particle, and turned out of its course. After a time a second dust particle again turns it out of its course, and so on, until finally it enters our eyes by a path as zigzag as that of a flash of lightning. Consequently the blue waves of the sunlight enter our eyes from all directions. And that is why the sky looks blue.

HOWARD E. SCHMITZ

The Old Crank Next Door

This speech was delivered by a young college graduate, a chemist, in an adult evening class in public speaking. His audience was composed of a variety of men and women from many businesses and professions, having in common chiefly their desire to improve their speaking. The speech was intended to fulfill a regular assignment of a 3- to 5-minute speech of simple structure and of expository purpose.

ALL OF US have a conscience and each of us has a pretty good idea of what a conscience is. I am not concerned, therefore, either with proving that you have a conscience or with explaining what I think a conscience is. What I want to do this evening is to point out three things which I think are important to keep in mind if we are to understand and get along with our consciences.

In the first place, the only thing that conscience does is to punish us. Its nature is clearly shown by the words used to describe it: "strict," "stern," "harsh," "pricking," "scolding," "nagging." Even "guilty," when used in this connection, refers not to the conscience itself, but to the way that it makes us feel. On the other hand, who ever heard of a "kind," "generous," or "forgiving" conscience?

Secondly, we can subdue our conscience but never escape from it, as evidenced by the story about Mr. —— which we all read in the papers two weeks ago. Here was a man who in a period of fifteen years embezzled something over $200,000 from the bank for which he worked. To me, the amazing thing about the story is not that he was able to embezzle so much money successfully, without even his wife's knowledge, but that he was caught by his own word. Not only did he admit his guilt without being accused, but he continued to volunteer a great deal of information about what he had done—information which might not have been found out even by close cross-questioning. I think it is plain that although his conscience had been by-passed for fifteen years, it finally caught up with him.

The last important thing to remember is that the punishments handed out by conscience are often much too severe for the crime committed. For example, think of the normally moderate drinker who goes to an especially good party one evening and has three or four too many drinks. He soon begins to feel pretty good and does and says things that he ordinarily would not, much to everyone's delight. But he finally goes home and goes to sleep, and by morning his drugged conscience will have regained full strength. You can rest assured that no one who was at the party will feel as ashamed of his behavior as he himself will, and it will probably be some time before he will be able to square himself with his precious conscience.

Thus we can see that although the conscience is often called "a little voice inside," it acts more like "the old crank next door." It never has a good word for us, is always looking for trouble, and when it finds it, often makes the punishment outweigh the crime. As with the crank next door, the best we can do is to understand its nasty disposition and try to give it few things to complain about.

BRUCE BARTON

Which Knew Not Joseph

Bruce Barton is Chairman of the Board of the advertising agency, Batten, Barton, Durstine and Osborn. He has been an editor of two magazines and an author of a number of books. For four years (1937–1941) he was a Republican member of Congress from the 17th New York District. Mr. Barton is regarded as one of the ablest business and political speakers of the last two decades.

This speech was delivered to the Public Relations Section of the National Electric Light Association at New York in 1923. The controlling idea of the speech may be phrased as "You must advertise persistently and wisely." To the audience this message was not exactly news. Accordingly, the speaker's task was to present the old idea in a fresh manner and to impart new life and strength to a credo his hearers already regarded with favor. The student should note the interest methods employed and observe how Mr. Barton handled his partisan audience.

THERE ARE two stories—and neither of them is new—which I desire to tell you, because they have a direct application to everyone's business. The first concerns a member of my profession, an advertising man, who was in the employ of a circus. It was his function to precede the circus into various communities, distribute tickets to the editor, put up on the barns pictures of the bearded lady and the man-eating snakes, and finally to get in touch with the proprietor of some store and persuade him to purchase the space on either side of the elephant for his advertisement in the parade.

Coming one day to a crossroads town our friend found that there was only one store. The proprietor did not receive him enthusiastically. "Why should I advertise?" he demanded. "I have been here for twenty years. There isn't a man, woman or child around these parts that doesn't know where I am and what I sell." The advertising man answered very promptly (because in our business if we hesitate we are lost), and he said to the proprietor, pointing across the street, "What is that building over there?" The proprietor answered, "That is the Methodist Episcopal Church." The advertising man said, "How long has that been there?" The proprietor said, "Oh, I don't know; seventy-five years probably." "And yet," exclaimed the advertising man, "they ring the church bell every Sunday morning."

By permission of the author. The text followed is that in *Modern Speeches*, rev. ed., comp. by Homer D. Lindgren (New York, 1930), pp. 358–364.

My second story has also a religious flavor. It relates to a gentleman named Joseph, who is now deceased.

Those of you who were brought up on the Bible may have found there some account of his very remarkable business career. Those of you who have not read that book may have heard of Joseph through the works of Rudyard Kipling.

Said Mr. Kipling:

> Who shall doubt the secret hid
> Under Cheops' pyramid
> Was that the contractor did
> Cheops out of several millions.
>
> And that Joseph's sudden rise
> To comptroller of supplies
> Was a graft of monstrous size
> Worked on Pharaoh's swart civilians.

The account of Joseph in the Old Testament is much more complete and to his credit. It tells how he left his country under difficulties and, coming into a strange country, he arose, through his diligence, to become the principal person in the state, second only to the King. Now, gentlemen, the Biblical narrative brings us to that point—the point where Joseph had public relations with all the best-paying jobs—it brings us up to the climax of his career and then it hands us an awful jolt. Without any words of preparation or explanation, it says bluntly:

"And Joseph died, and there arose a new king in Egypt which knew not Joseph."

I submit, gentlemen, that this is one of the most staggering lines which has ever been written in a business biography. Here was a man so famous that everybody knew him and presto, a few people die, a few new ones are born, and *nobody* knows him. The tide of human life has moved on; the king who exalted the friends of Joseph is followed by a king who makes them slaves; all the advertising that the name "Joseph" had enjoyed in one generation is futile and of no avail, because that generation has gone.

Now what has all that to do with you? Very much indeed. When we gathered in this room this afternoon, there were in this country, in bed, sick, several thousand old men. It perhaps is indelicate for me to refer to that fact, but it is a fact, and we are grown up and we have to face these things. On those old men you gentlemen collectively have spent a considerable amount of time and a considerable amount of money. It is to be supposed that you have made some impression upon them regarding your service and your purposes and your necessities. But in this interval, while we have been sitting here, those old men have died and all your time and all your money and whatever you have built up in the way of good will in their minds—*all* your labor and investment have passed out with them.

In the same brief interval, there have been born in this country several thousand lusty boys and girls to whom you gentlemen mean no more than the Einstein theory. They do not know the difference between a Mazda lamp and a stick of Wrigley's chewing gum. Nobody has ever told them that Ivory Soap floats or that children cry for Castoria, or what sort of soap you ought to use if you want to have a skin that people would like to touch. The whole job of giving them the information they are going to need in order to form an intelligent public opinion and to exercise an intelligent influence in the community has to be started from the beginning and done over again.

So the first very simple thing that I would say to you (and it is so simple that it seems to me it ought to be said at every convention of this kind) is that this business of public relations is a very constant business, that the fact that you told your story yesterday should not lead you into the delusion of supposing that you have ever told it. There is probably no fact in the United States that is easier to impress upon people's minds than that Ivory Soap floats, and yet the manufacturers of Ivory Soap think it is not inconsistent or wasteful to spend more than a million dollars a year in repeating that truth over and over again.

Cultivating good will is a day-by-day and hour-by-hour business, gentlemen. Every day and every hour the "king" dies and there arises a new "king" to whom you and all your works mean absolutely nothing.

Now the second very simple thing which I might say to you is that in your dealings with the public, in what you write and say, you must be genuine.

When I came to New York a great many years ago I had a lot of trouble with banks. It was very hard to find any bank that would be willing to accept the very paltry weekly deposit that I wanted to make. Finally I discovered one which was not as closely guarded as the others, and I succeeded for a period of three years in being insulted by the teller every Saturday. At the end of three years when I came to draw out my money I had an audience with the vice-president who wanted personally to insult me. I said to myself, if I live and grow old in this town, some day I think I would like to take a crack at this situation.

And so as the years passed (as they have the habit of doing), and I lived and grew old, one day a bank official came in to us and said he would like to have us do some advertising for him. I said to this banker, "Now you go back to your office and shave off all the side-whiskers that there are in your bank and you take all the high hats and carry them out into the back yard of the bank and put them in a pile and light a match to the pile and burn them up, because I am going to advertise to people that you're human, and it may be a shock to have them come in and find you as you are."

So he went back to his bank and I wrote an advertisement which said:

> There is a young man in this town who is looking for a friendly bank;
> a bank where the officers will remember his name and where some interest
> will be shown when he comes in, etc.

It was very successful. It was too successful. It was so successful that
we could not control it, and all over the country there broke out a perfect epidemic, a kind of measles, of "friendly banks." Bankers who had
not smiled since infancy and who never had or needed an electric fan in
their offices suddenly sat up and said, "Why, we are friendly."

Well, our bank dropped out. The competition was too keen. But it cul-
minated, I think, in a letter which I saw and which was mailed by the
president of a really very important bank in a large city. I won't attempt
to quote it verbatim, but it was to this effect:

> Dear Customer: As I sit here all alone in my office on Christmas Eve think-
> ing of you and how much we love you, I really wish that you and every other
> customer could come in here personally so I could give you a good sound kiss.

Well, that is a trifle exaggerated, but the fact is this—if you don't feel
these things you can't make other people feel them. Emerson said, as you
will remember, "What you are thunders so loud I cannot hear what you
say." Unless there is back of this desire for better public relations a real
conviction, a real genuine feeling that you are in business as a matter of
service, not merely as a matter of advertising service—unless there is that,
then it is very dangerous, indeed, to attempt to talk to the public. For as
sure as you live the public will find you out.

The third very simple thing, and the last thing that I suggest, is this: in
dealing with the public the great thing is to deal with them simply, briefly,
and in language that they can understand.

Two men delivered speeches about sixty years ago at Gettysburg. One
man was the greatest orator of his day, and he spoke for two hours and
a half, and probably nobody in the room can remember a single word
that he said. The other man spoke for considerably less than five minutes,
and every school child has at some time learned Lincoln's Gettysburg
Address, and remembers it more or less all his life. Many prayers have
been uttered in the world—many long, fine-sounding prayers—but the
only prayer that any large majority of people have ever learned is the
Lord's Prayer, and it is less than two hundred words long. The same
thing is true of the Twenty-third Psalm, and there is hardly a Latin word
in it. They are short, simple, easily understood words.

You electric light people have one difficulty. I was in Europe this
spring, and I rode a great deal in taxicabs. In England I sat in a taxicab
and watched the little clock go around in terms of shillings. Then I flew
over to Amsterdam and watched it go around in terms of guilders. Then
I went down to Brussels and it went around in terms of francs. Then I

went to France and it went around in terms of francs of a different value.

I would sit there trying to divide fifteen into one hundred and multiply it by seven, and wonder just where I was getting off, and I have no doubt now that really I was transported in Europe at a very reasonable cost, but because those meters talked to me in terms that were unfamiliar I never stepped out of a taxicab without having a haunting suspicion that probably I had been "gypped."

In a degree you suffer like those taxicab men. You come to Mrs. Barton and you say, "Buy this washing machine and it will do your washing for just a few cents an hour." She says, "Isn't that wonderful!" She buys it, and at the end of the month she sits with your bill in her hands and she says, "We have run this five hours and that will probably be so and so." Then she opens the bill and finds that she has not run it five hours; that she has run it 41 ks. and 11 amp. and 32 volts, and that amount is not so-and-so but it is $2.67.

Well, that is a matter that I suppose you will eventually straighten out.

Asking an advertising man to talk about advertising at a convention like this is a good deal like asking the doctor to talk about health. I have listened to many such addresses and they are all about the same. The eminent physician says, "Drink plenty of water. Stay outdoors as much as you can. Eat good food. Don't worry. Get eight hours' sleep. And if you have anything the matter with you, call a doctor."

So I say to you that there is a certain technique about this matter of dealing with the public, and if you have anything seriously the matter with you—whether it be a big advertising problem or merely a bad letterhead (and some of you have wretched letterheads)—there probably is some advertising doctor in your town who has made a business of the thing, and it may be worth your while to call him in. But in the meantime, and in this very informal and necessarily general talk, I say to you, "Be genuine, be simple, be brief; talk to people in language that they understand; and finally and most of all, be persistent." You can't expect to advertise in flush times and live on the memory of it when you are hard up. You can't expect to advertise when you are in trouble, or about to be in trouble, and expect to get anything in that direction. It is a day-by-day and hour-by-hour business. If the money that has been thrown away by people who advertised spasmodically was all gathered together it would found and endow the most wonderful home in the world for aged advertising men and their widows. Don't throw any more of that money away. If advertising is worth doing at all, it is worth doing all the time. For every day, gentlemen, the "king" dies, and there arises a new "king" who knows not Joseph.

NICHOLAS MURRAY BUTLER

Five Evidences of an Education

The following address before the Phi Beta Kappa Society of Vassar College,
June 10, 1901, was delivered by the youthful Professor of Philosophy of Columbia University, who was about to succeed to the presidency of Columbia
and to hold that position for more than forty years. Professor Butler (1862–
1947) became not only the president of a great university but one of the most
prominent internationalists and public men in this country in the first half
of the twentieth century. The persistent timeliness of the ideas of this speech,
and its organization and literary qualities, make it the subject of profitable
study by the college student of public speaking.

"IF YOU HAD had children, sir," said Boswell, "would you have
taught them anything?" "I hope," replied Doctor Johnson, "that I should
have willingly lived on bread and water to obtain instruction for them;
but I would not have set their future friendship to hazard, for the sake of
thrusting into their heads knowledge of things for which they might not
perhaps have either taste or necessity. You teach your daughters the di-
ameters of the planets, and wonder when you have done that they do not
delight in your company." From which it appears that Doctor Johnson,
by a sort of prolepsis, was moved to contribute to the discussion of one
of the vexed questions of our time. Who is the educated man? By what
signs shall we know him?

"In the first golden age of the world," Erasmus observes, in his *Praise
of Folly*, "there was no need of these perplexities. There was then no
other sort of learning but what was naturally collected from every man's
common sense, improved by an easy experience. What use could there
have been of grammar, when all men spoke the same mother tongue, and
aimed at no higher pitch of oratory than barely to be understood by each
other? What need of logic, when they were too wise to enter into any
dispute? Or what occasion for rhetoric, where no difference arose to
require any laborious decision?" Surely, in contrasting this picture of a
far-off golden age with our present-day strenuous age of steel, we must
be moved to say, with the preacher: "In much wisdom is much grief; and
he that increaseth knowledge increaseth sorrow."

It is only two hundred and fifty years ago that Comenius urged, with
ardent zeal, the establishment in London of a college of learned men who

should bring together in one book the sum total of human wisdom, so expressed as to meet the needs of both the present and all future generations. This scheme for a Pansophia, or repository of all learning, proved very attractive in the seventeenth century, for it easily adjusted itself to the notions of a period which looked upon learning as a substantial and measurable quantity, to be acquired and possessed. Unfortunately, this quantitative ideal of education, with its resultant processes and standards, is still widely influential, and it tempts us to seek the evidences of an education in the number of languages learned, in the variety of sciences studied, and generally in the quantity of facts held in the memory reserve. But, on the other hand, any serious attempt to apply quantitative standards to the determination of education quickly betrays their inadequacy and their false assumptions. If to be educated means to know nature in systematic fashion and to be able to interpret it, then nearly every man of letters, ancient or modern, must be classed with the uneducated. Or if to be educated means to have sympathetic, almost affectionate, insight into the great masterpieces of art and of literature, then innumerable great men of action, who have fully represented the ideals and the power of their time and who manifested most admirable qualities of mind and of character, were uneducated. The case is even worse to-day. A host of knowledges compass us about on every side and bewilder by their variety and their interest. We must exclude the many to choose the one. The penalty of choice is deprivation; the price of not choosing is shallowness and incapacity. The quantitative method of estimating education breaks down, then, of its own weight. A true standard is to be sought in some other direction.

A full analysis of the facts of life as they confront us to-day would show, I feel confident, that all knowledges and all influences are not on a single plane of indifference toward the human mind that would be educated. All parts of the spiritual machine are not mutually interchangeable. There are needs to be met and longings to be satisfied that will not accept any vicarious response to their demands. The scientific, the literary, the aesthetic, the institutional, and the religious aspects of life and of civilization, while interdependent, are yet independent of each other, in the sense that no one of them can be reduced to a function of another, or can be stated in terms of another. Therefore, each of these five aspects must, I think, be represented in some degree in every scheme of training which has education for its end. Nevertheless, this training when it arrives at education will not suffer itself to be measured and estimated quantitatively in terms either of science, of letters, of art, of institutions, or of religion. It will have produced certain traits of intellect and of character which find expression in ways open to the observation of all men, and it is toward these traits or habits, not toward external and substantial acquisition or accomplishment, that one must turn to find the true and sure evidences of an education, as education is conceived to-day.

First among the evidences of an education I name correctness and precision in the use of the mother tongue. Important as this power is, and is admitted to be, it is a comparatively new thing in education. The modern European languages took on educational significance only when the decentralization of culture began at the close of the Middle Ages. So late as 1549 Jacques du Bellay supported the study of French with the very mild assertion that it is "not so poor a tongue as many think it." Mulcaster, writing a little later, found it necessary to tell why his book on education was put in English rather than in Latin, and to defend the vernacular when he referred to its educational usefulness. Melanchthon put German in a class with Greek and Hebrew, and contrasted all three unfavorably with Latin. Indeed it was not until the present German Emperor plainly told the Berlin School Conference of 1890 that a national basis was lacking in German education; that the foundation of the gymnasium course of study must be German; that the duty of the schoolmasters was to train the young to become Germans, not Greeks and Romans; and that the German language must be made the centre around which all other subjects revolved, that a revision of the official school programme was brought about that made place for the really serious study of the German language and literature. And to-day, where the influence of the English universities and of not a few American Colleges is potent, the study of English is slight and insignificant indeed. The superstition that the best gate to English is through the Latin is anything but dead.

But for the great mass of the people the vernacular is not only the established medium of instruction, but fortunately also an important subject of study. A chief measure of educational accomplishment is the ease, the correctness, and the precision with which one uses this instrument.

It is no disrespect to the splendid literatures which are embodied in the French and the German tongues, and no lack of appreciation of the services of those great peoples to civilization and to culture, to point out that of modern languages the English is easily the first and the most powerful, for "it is the greatest instrument of communication that is now in use among men upon the earth." It is the speech of an active people among whom individual liberty and personal initiative are highly prized. It falls short, no doubt, of the philosophical pliability of the Greek and of the scientific ductility of the German; but what is there in the whole field of human passion and human action that it cannot express with freedom and with a power all its own? Turn *Othello* into German, or compare the verse of Shelley or of Keats with the graceful lines of some of their French contemporaries, and learn the peculiar power of the English speech. In simple word or sonorous phrase it is unequalled as a medium to reveal the thoughts, the feelings, and the ideals of humanity.

One's hold upon the English tongue is measured by his choice of words and by his use of idiom. The composite character of modern English offers a wide field for apt and happy choice of expression. The educated man, at home with his mother tongue, moves easily about in its Saxon, Romanic, and Latin elements, and has gained by long experience and wide reading a knowledge of the mental incidence of words as well as of their artistic effect. He is hampered by no set formulas, but manifests in his speech, spoken and written, the characteristic powers and appreciation of his nature. The educated man is of necessity, therefore, a constant reader of the best written English. He reads not for conscious imitation, but for unconscious absorption and reflection. He knows the wide distinction between correct English on the one hand, and pedantic, or, as it is sometimes called, "elegant," English on the other. He is more likely to "go to bed" than to "retire," to "get up" than to "arise," to have "legs" rather than "limbs," to "dress" than to "clothe himself," and to "make a speech" rather than to "deliver an oration." He knows that "if you hear poor English and read poor English, you will pretty surely speak poor English and write poor English," and governs himself accordingly. He realizes the power and place of idiom and its relation to grammar, and shows his skill by preserving a balance between the two in his style. He would follow with intelligent sympathy the scholarly discussions of idiom and of grammar by Professor Earle and would find therein the justification of much of his best practise. In short, in his use of his mother tongue he would give sure evidence of an education.

As a second evidence of an education I name those refined and gentle manners which are the expression of fixed habits of thought and of action. "Manners are behavior and good breeding," as Addison said, but they are more. It is not without significance that the Latin language has but a single word (*mores*) both for usages, habits, manners, and for morals. Real manners, the manners of a truly educated man or woman, are an outward expression of intellectual and moral conviction. Sham manners are a veneer which falls away at the dampening touch of the first selfish suggestion. Manners have a moral significance, and find their basis in that true and deepest self-respect which is built upon respect for others. An infallible test of character is to be found in one's manners toward those whom, for one reason or another, the world may deem his inferiors. A man's manners toward his equals or his superiors are shaped by too many motives to render their interpretation either easy or certain. Manners do not make the man, but manners reveal the man. It is by the amount of respect, deference, and courtesy shown to human personality as such that we judge whether one is on dress parade or whether he is so well-trained, well-educated, and so habitually ethical in thought and action that he realizes his proper relation to his fellows, and reveals his realization in his manners. As Kant insisted more than a century ago, a man exists as an end in himself, and not merely as a means to be arbitrarily used by this or that will; and in all his actions, whether they concern himself alone or other rational beings, he must always be regarded as an end. True manners are based upon a recognition of this fact, and that is a poor education indeed which fails to inculcate the ethical principle and the manners that embody it.

As a third evidence of an education I name the power and habit of reflection. It is a frequent charge against us moderns, particularly against Americans, that we are losing the habit of reflection, and the high qualities which depend upon it. We are told that this loss is a necessary result of our hurried and busy lives, of our diverse interests, and of the annihilation of space and time by steam and electricity. The whole world and its happenings are brought to our very doors by the daily newspaper. Our attention leaps from Manila to Pekin, from Pekin to the Transvaal, and from the Transvaal to Havana. We are torn by conflicting or unconnected emotions, and our minds are occupied by ideas following each other with such rapidity that we fail to get a firm and deep hold of any one of the great facts that come into our lives. This is the charge which even sympathetic critics bring against us.

If it be true—and there are some counts in the indictment which it is difficult to deny—then one of the most precious evidences of an education is slipping from us, and we must redouble our efforts to keep fast hold upon it. For an unexamined life, as Socrates unceasingly insisted, is not worth living. The life which asks no questions of itself, which traces events back to no causes and forward to no purposes, which raises no vital issues of principle, and which seeks no interpretation of what passes within and without, is not a human life at all; it is the life of an animal. The trained and the untrained mind are perhaps in sharpest contrast at this very point. An armory of insights and convictions always ready for applications to new conditions, and invincible save by deeper insights and more rational convictions, is a mark of a trained and educated mind. The educated man has standards of truth, of human experience, and of wisdom by which new proposals are judged. These standards can be gained only through reflection. The undisciplined mind is a prey to every passing fancy and the victim of every plausible doctrinaire. He has no permanent forms of judgment which give him character.

Renan was right when he held that the first condition for the development of the mind is that it shall have liberty; and liberty for the mind means freedom from the control of the unreasonable, and freedom to choose the reasonable in accordance with principle. A body of principles is a necessary possession of the educated man. His development is always with reference to his principles, and proceeds by evolution, not revolution.

Philosophy is, of course, the great single study by which the power of reflection is developed until it becomes a habit, but there is a philosophic study of literature, of politics, of natural science, which makes for the same end. The question how, whose answer is science, and the question why, whose answer is philosophy, are the beginnings of reflection. A truly educated man asks both questions continually, and as a result is habituated to reflection.

As a fourth evidence of an education I name the power of growth. There is a type of mind which, when trained to a certain point, crystallizes, as it were, and refuses to move forward thereafter. This type of mind fails to give one of the essential evidences of an education. It has perhaps acquired much and promised much; but somehow or other promise is not fulfilled. It is not dead, but in a trance. Only such functions are performed as serve to keep it where it is; there is no movement, no development, no new power or accomplishment. The impulse to continuous study, and to that self-education which are the conditions of permanent intellectual growth, is wanting. Education has so far failed of one of its chief purposes.

A human mind continuing to grow and to develop throughout a long life is a splendid and impressive sight. It was that characteristic in Mr. Gladstone which made his personality so attractive to young and ambitious men. They were fired by his zeal and inspired by his limitless intellectual energy. To have passed from being "the rising hope of the stern and unbending Tories" in 1838 to the unchallenged leadership of the anti-Tory party in Great Britain a generation later, and to have continued to grow throughout an exceptionally long life is no mean distinction; and it is an example of what, in less conspicuous ways, is the lot of every mind whose training is effective. Broadened views, widened sympathies, deepened insights are the accompaniments of growth.

For this growth a many-sided interest is necessary, and this is why growth and intellectual and moral narrowness are eternally at war. There is much in our modern education which is uneducational because it makes growth difficult, if not impossible. Early specialization, with its attendant limited range both of information and of interest, is an enemy of growth. Turning from the distasteful before it is understood is an enemy of growth. Failure to see the relation of the subject of one's special interest to other subjects is an enemy of growth. The pretense of investigation and discovery before mastering existent knowledge is an enemy of growth. The habit of cynical indifference toward men and things and of aloofness from them, sometimes supposed to be peculiarly academic, is an enemy of growth. These, then, are all to be shunned while formal education is going on, if it is to carry with it the priceless gift of an impulse to continuous growth. "Life," says Bishop Spalding in an eloquent passage, "is the unfolding of a mysterious power, which in man rises to self-consciousness, and through self-consciousness to the knowl-·edge of a world of truth and order and love, where action may no longer be left wholly to the sway of matter or to the impulse of instinct, but may and should be controlled by reason and conscience. To further this process by deliberate and intelligent effort is to educate"—and, I add, to educate so as to deliberately sow the seed of continuous growth, intellectual and moral.

And as a fifth evidence of an education I name efficiency—the power to do. The time has long since gone by, if it ever was, when contemplation pure and simple, withdrawal from the world and its activities, or intelligent incompetence was a defensible ideal of education. To-day the truly educated man must be, in some sense, efficient. With brain, tongue, or hand he must be able to express his knowledge, and so leave the world other than he found it. Mr. James is simply summing up what physiology and psychology both teach when he exclaims: "No reception without reaction, no impression without correlative expression—this is the great maxim which the teacher ought never to forget. An impression which simply flows in at the pupil's eyes or ears, and in no way modifies his active life, is an impression gone to waste. It is physiologically incomplete. It leaves no fruits behind it in the way of capacity acquired. Even as mere impression, it fails to produce its proper effect upon the memory; for, to remain fully among the acquisitions of the latter faculty, it must be wrought into the whole cycle of our operations. Its motor consequences are what clinch it." This is just as true of knowledge in general as of impressions. Indefinite absorption without production is fatal both to character and to the highest intellectual power. Do something and be able to do it well; express what you know in some helpful and substantial form; produce, and do not everlastingly feel only and revel in feelings— these are counsels which make for a real education and against that sham form of it which is easily recognized as well-informed incapacity. Our colleges and universities abound in false notions, notions as unscientific as they are unphilosophical, of the supposed value of knowledge, information, for its own sake. It has none. The date of the discovery of America is in itself as meaningless as the date of the birth of the youngest blade of grass in the neighboring field; it means something because it is part of a larger knowledge-whole, because it has relations, applications, uses; and for the student who sees none of these and knows none of them, America was discovered in 1249 quite as much as it was in 1492.

High efficiency is primarily an intellectual affair, and only *longo intervallo* does it take on anything approaching a mechanical form. Its mechanical form is always wholly subordinate to its springs in the intellect.

It is the outgrowth of an established and habitual relationship between intellect and will, by means of which knowledge is constantly made power. For knowledge is not power, Bacon to the contrary notwithstanding, unless it is made so, and it can be made so only by him who possesses the knowledge. The habit of making knowledge power is efficiency. Without it education is incomplete.

These five characteristics, then, I offer as evidences of an education— correctness and precision in the use of the mother tongue; refined and gentle manners, which are the expression of fixed habits of thought and action; the power and habit of reflection; the power of growth; and efficiency, or the power to do. On this plane the physicist may meet with the philologian, and the naturalist with the philosopher, and each recognize the fact that his fellow is an educated man, though the range of their information is widely different, and the centres of their highest interests are far apart. They are knit together in a brotherhood by the close tie of those traits which have sprung out of the reaction of their minds and wills upon that which has fed them and brought them strength. Without these traits men are not truly educated and their erudition, however vast, is of no avail; it furnishes a museum, not a developed human being.

It is these habits, of necessity made by ourselves alone, begun in the days of school and college, and strengthened with maturer years and broader experience, that serve to show to ourselves and to others that we have discovered the secret of gaining an education.

VIRGIL M. HANCHER

The State's Support of
Higher Education

In the following address, given in Iowa City on January 10, 1961, the President of the University of Iowa spoke to his neighbors and associates of the faculty and the city on two aspects of higher education—its central importance in the contemporary world and its cost. The first part of President Hancher's address came with special force because only the previous year he had served as a member of the United States delegation to the General Assembly of the United Nations. Though of course he spoke first of all to the audience before him at the luncheon tables, he had in mind also, especially in the second part, the Governor of the State and the legislature, who were then considering the biennial appropriation for the support of higher education in the state.

This speech seems especially worth study because of the realism and sobriety with which President Hancher faces the world-wide struggle for men's minds, and because of the clarity and force with which he brings complex factual materials to bear on the support of education.

EACH YEAR in January, for a number of years, I have been privileged to speak at a joint meeting of the Iowa City service clubs. This year I wish to express my appreciation to the host club, and to all the clubs which have joined together in providing me an opportunity to discuss the state of the University with you—my friends and neighbors. It is an annual event to which I look forward with pleasure. I rejoice in the fact that the differences which divide Town and Gown in some communities, and which once divided this community, are hardly present in Iowa City. There are notable exceptions, of course—persons who feel that the University was placed here in order that they might make money off the University and its students and patrons. This is regrettable, but, in an imperfect world, it must be expected that there will always be some people of limited vision and avaricious tendencies. Fortunately they are few.

The role of the University as a good neighbor is never an easy one. We, who teach in the University and administer it, must always remember that it is a State and not a municipal institution—and that our paramount obligation is to the people of the State. Within that limitation, however, we endeavor to be a good neighbor, and to be an intregal part of this delightful and enchanting city. Furthermore I have been astonished

Reprinted with the permission of President Hancher.

by, and wish to pay tribute to, the number of residents of this community who, in their dealings with the University, have been more than fair, who have often been generous to the point of sacrificing their interests and their properties in order to contribute to the advancement of this great institution. The names of Fuiks, Kessler, McGinnis, Brant and many others come to mind—and those names should be honored down the centuries as long as this University continues to serve generation after generation of students and citizens of this State and of this Republic.

You will note that I have written my remarks for this occasion—even though it meant extra effort for me to do so. This serves two purposes. It will conserve your time and mine. And it will provide me with a record of what I say. Occasionally my remarks on prior occasions have stirred discussion, and even controversy—sometimes when I least expected them. It is well, therefore, to have a document to which I can turn and say: "This is precisely what I said—now make the most of it."

As you know, I have been President of the University of Iowa for more than twenty years—longer than any other President—so that, if I have no other distinction, I do have one which cannot be taken away from me before 1981. Those years have witnessed such great changes in the University, in the nation, and in the world that I can echo the words of Robert Maynard Hutchins, paraphrasing one of the ancients, when he said that the words of the elders should be listened to, not because the elders are so wise, but because they have been through so much! The past twenty years have produced such catastrophic changes that, as Professor Ashley Montagu has pointed out, an optimist might be defined as *a man who believes that the future is uncertain.* More than a year ago, when Chairman Khrushchev made his first visit to this country, a quip ran around the U.N. Headquarters that an optimist is one who has his children learn Russian while a pessimist is one who has his children learn Chinese! I trust that no one who watched Chairman Khrushchev on TV last fall pound his desk with his shoes in the dignified and stately Hall of the General Assembly of the U.N. can doubt that his policy, and no doubt the policy of the USSR toward the U.N., was, and is, one of rule or ruin. Surely under such circumstances an optimist may be defined as one who *hopes* that the future is uncertain.

Someone else has defined the status quo as "the fix we are in." I do not wish to be an alarmist, and I recall my Mother often saying, "It is always darkest just before the dawn." Nevertheless, if we divorce ourselves from politics and partisanship and try to look at the world, as I have tried to do, without bias or emotion, I believe that we shall have to admit that the United States is in a far different position than it was in 1945.

Never had the United States stood at such a pinnacle of power and prestige and influence as it stood on September 1, 1945. Even President Wilson's triumphal tour of Europe in 1919 could not equal it. It was unnatural to hope that we could continue on such a pinnacle indefinitely. And we have not. Our relative power and prestige and influence have declined almost continuously over the last fifteen years. One needs only to review the last session of the U.N. General Assembly, or our international monetary situation, or the trouble in Laos or in Cuba or the Congo, or the ever-present pressure of Communism in many parts of the world, or the use of Communist science and armaments, to realize that we are in a new, dangerous and unprecedented situation.

It is not clear what we could have done to prevent this situation from arising. It is not clear what we should do now. It is easy enough to say "Do something." It is not so easy to know what to do or when or where to do it.

For most of its history our people have been engaged in conquering a continent and achieving a high degree of material prosperity. For the first time in our lives we face an external situation which we cannot resolve merely by energy, hard work, good will, and the accumulation of material resources—as we did in World Wars I and II. Something more is required. The fact is that the free nations, governed by representatives chosen in open elections, have not yet found a way both to preserve their freedoms and to cope with the insidious, creeping, conspiratorial tactics of international Communism.

We forget how new our institutions are. Universal suffrage is hardly more than a century old in the most advanced of the Western nations. Democratic institutions have prevailed in only a small segment of time or space from the beginning of recorded history. And we overlook the stubbornness with which we resist all efforts to make our governmental procedures adequate for a nuclear and a satellite age. It is nowhere written down, as far as I am aware, that in a contest between democratic and Communistic governments that the good Lord has decreed that democratic institutions shall prevail. They may—but again, they may not. And unless we succeed in making them work better than we have in the last fifteen years, we may, in the next fifteen, see all of Africa, South America, and Southeast Asia added to the Communist empire. It is sheer folly for us to close our eyes and hope that the Communists will go away. It is sheer folly—just as it was with Hitler—to believe that the Communists do not mean what they say. They believe in the ultimate triumph of their system—and they mean to achieve it by coexistence and subversion as long as coexistence achieves their ends; they mean to achieve it by force and subversion if coexistence does not achieve their ends. They mean to triumph over us—and no pretty words should deceive us as to their intent.

Once the common sense of the common man was adequate for our protection and our salvation. The Minute Man and his rifle were the symbols of a free and unconquerable people. This is the case no longer. It is in this setting that we must consider the state of the University. As we review it, we should remember the awesome and often quoted words of Alfred North Whitehead: [1]

> In the conditions of modern life the rule is absolute, *the race which does not value trained intelligence is doomed.* Not all your heroism, not all your social charm, not all your wit, not all your victories on land and sea, can move back the finger of fate. Today we maintain ourselves. Tomorrow science will have moved forward one more step, and there will be no appeal from the judgment which will then be pronounced on the uneducated.

If we in this country fail or falter now, historians of the twenty-first century may say that the United States had one of the shortest periods of greatness in the long history of mankind. Soon after Sharm Scheuerman was appointed head basketball coach, he gave a talk in which he said he had the opportunity before him of being the youngest ex-head basketball coach in the country. We want no such thing to happen in our beloved country.

And so when I report on the state of the University, I am reporting on Iowa's investment in the cultivation of that intelligence which is indispensable for the future of Iowa, the future of the United States, and the freedom of mankind.

Now we have the raw material which can make that investment worthwhile. Our Iowa youth are not lacking in intelligence, energy and character, and those who enter the University have been increasing in quality quite markedly in recent years. The percentage of entering freshmen in the upper 10 per cent of their high school classes increased by 6 per cent in the years 1956–1960; the percentage in the upper 20 per cent increased by more than 10 per cent in the same period; currently 86 per cent of the freshman class graduated in the top half of their high school classes—this percentage having increased from 71 per cent to 86 per cent in four years, while the class itself was increasing from 1,703 to 1,819. The picture of a state university—or this particular state university—as a refuge for intellectual derelicts was always false. From what I have just told you, you can see that it is a center for highly intelligent, energetic, and competent young people.

But these young people must not be expected to have the maturity of adults. They are young; they are inexperienced; they are gullible—and often they are victims—just as many adults are victims—of the pressure groups that know how to use them and maneuver them for their own purposes. And, if occasionally they are exuberant in their

[1] Alfred North Whitehead, *The Aims of Education* (Mentor Books: New York, New American Library of World Literature), p. 26.

moods and in their actions, do they not find plenty of precedents for their conduct among adults?

Not only have we a student body worthy of investment in higher education, but we have a faculty worthy of it also. Here again, as among students, the range is wide, but the great majority of the faculty are men and women of high achievement, and a considerable number are persons of international—one might almost say, interplanetary— eminence and reputation.

Finally, the State of Iowa has the resources to support this University and to support the institutions at Ames and Cedar Falls. According to the recently issued Gibson report on higher education in Iowa, the gross production from agriculture and industry in Iowa has increased from $4,600,000,000 in 1950 to $7,350,000,000 in 1959. Of that $7,350,000,000, $2,360,000,000 came from agricultural production and $4,960,000,000 —almost five billion dollars—came from industrial production. The over-all agricultural image of this State still hangs high in the public mind, although the dollar value of industrial production in 1959 was more than twice that of agricultural production; and while Iowa remains an unusual state in the quality of its soil and the value of its agricultural production, it is far more than just a state of farms and farm production.

It is said that the nation as a whole spends about 1 per cent of its gross national product for higher education. In Iowa this would mean an annual expenditure of $70,000,000. As a matter of fact, the State has a tradition of being above the national average in its per capita effort for the support of higher education. Consequently what the three institutions are now receiving and should receive in the future is in line with the growth in value of the State's industrial and agricultural production. If Iowa taxes are high—and this is an assertion often made— it is not so much because of the State sales tax and income tax as it is because of the multiplicity of district and local governments and the high per capita burden of local taxes. A few years ago there were in Iowa more than 7,000 units of government exclusive of the State and its agencies. This number is believed to have decreased substantially in recent years because of the consolidation of school districts, but even 5,000 units would seem excessive for the government of 2,700,000 essentially peace-loving and law-abiding citizens. In an editorial in the Marshalltown *Times Republican,* reprinted in the Iowa City *Press Citizen* on November 30, 1960, it was said that the tax load for local governments is above $9.00 per capita in Adams County and about $3.00 in Marshall County. This wide range has nothing to do with higher education. If the tax burden in this State is excessive, it is not excessive because of the costs of higher education.

This University is in a highly competitive situation. Both because of potential increases in enrollment and the vast increase in knowledge, the effort which we are currently making is not enough. To attain and hold third position in the eleven-state area for teaching salaries alone will call for an increased appropriation of $2,750,000 for the second year of the coming biennium, the year 1962–1963. The Gibson report recommends that the legislature appropriate enough money to increase the salaries of professors by $3,000, the salaries of associate professors by $2,000, and the salaries of assistant professors and instructors by $1,000 for the first year of the next biennium and that a further increase of 8 per cent be provided for the second year, the year 1962–1963. Other equitable adjustments need to be made in the salary and wage scales of the hospitals and other parts of the University.

Very few people have any clear notion of the complexity of this University. Far too many—and this includes students, faculty, Iowa Citians, and citizens generally—seem to think that if the University needs money in one spot all we have to do is to transfer it from some other spot. This is both inaccurate and misleading.

Actually we receive five major appropriations—one for teaching, research, and related services; one for the care of the indigent in the General Hospital; one for the Psychopathic Hospital; one for the Hospital School; and one for the Bacteriological Laboratory—and neither University officials nor the Regents are free to transfer funds from one appropriation to another. Each must be kept separately and be accounted for separately. Each of the first four appropriations is divided into two parts—one part for salaries and general support and the other part for repairs, replacements, and alterations—and no money for repairs, replacements, and alterations may be used for salaries or general support or for major capital construction.

Appropriations for buildings—the Chemistry wing, the Library addition, the Pharmacy building—come to us by yet other appropriations and must be handled and accounted for separately. In addition there are the self-supporting enterprises—such as the dormitories, intercollegiate athletics, the Iowa tests of educational development—each of which has its own funds; and they, in turn, must each be handled and accounted for separately.

Add to this the fact that the University is a community of 11,000 students, of 20,000 hospital bed patients and many thousands of ambulatory patients annually, of hundreds of teachers, and more hundreds of employees in offices, physical plant, hospitals, dormitories, the Memorial Union, and athletics, of some 16,000 people who come to the University annually for conferences and continuing education—a number which, with proper University facilities, could quickly rise to 22,000 and perhaps 30,000 annually—and you will get a clearer picture of this complex institution than you will get from the letters to the editor or from the over-simplified answers of those who have not yet learned what the questions are.

This institution is not easily presented in all of its ramifications to a Governor or to committees of the General Assembly or to the general public. Nor are its needs self-evident nor readily understood.

In an effort to make the presentataion of needs more realistic to the legislature, we have endeavored wherever possible during the last five or six years, to relate our needs to factual material which could be tested and verified. Instead of relying upon our opinions as to salary scales elsewhere, we have examined actual figures supplied us confidentially by other institutions and have sought as a goal the third highest position in the eleven-state area bounded on the east by Michigan and Indiana and on the west by Kansas, Nebraska, and the Dakotas. Instead of guessing what the trend in salaries may be to June 30, 1963, we have analyzed actual increases in past bienniums and have projected them at the same rate through the coming one. Instead of guessing about the cost of equipment and supplies, we have developed—through the College of Business Administration—a cost index based on the kind of things a university buys—and have projected future costs from that index. We have substituted fact for guess work wherever possible—so that we can assert with truth and confidence that these are honest figures honestly arrived at—and, although the totals seem large, there is no padding.

Consistently with all this, the University and four others in the Big Ten joined California and four other institutions outside of Iowa and the Big Ten some six years ago in what is now known as the California-Big Ten Study, designed to develop formulas for educational costs by levels of instruction. From this and other studies it became apparent that there were ratios of costs as well as sharp disparities in educational costs by levels of instruction—the lowest costs being in the first two years of college, the next two years being higher, and by far the heaviest costs being in professional education and graduate education in the fifth year and beyond. We then analyzed (1) our operating appropriations, excluding the hospitals and bacteriological laboratory, (2) ISU's (Ames) operating appropriations, excluding the Cooperative Extension Services, and (3) ISTC's (Cedar Falls) entire appropriations and subjected them to five tests:

1. an enrollment index weighted by cost levels,
2. a cost index from similar type institutions,
3. a straight head count,
4. the appropriation experience of other states, and
5. a weighted per student appropriation basis.

In all of this we assumed that the other two institutions needed and were using wisely all the money that they received. On that assumption we found that this University was undersupported, that it was receiving less in relation to its needs than were the other two institutions by amounts ranging between $1,960,000 and $2,300,000 annually. Averaging these five totals gave us a figure of slightly little more than $2,225,000 annually—and we presented that latter figure to the Regents as an amount that should be added to this University's starting base in preparing its requests to the General Assembly. This presented a new and novel question to the Regents, and they dealt with it with some caution. However, they did allow the request in the amount of $500,000 annually for the current General Assembly and undertook to study the amount beyond $500,000 and to reach a determination in time for the preparation of our requests to the 1963 General Assembly.

This allowance of $500,000 annually to us is a part of the Regents' program and is as binding on the other two institutions as are the Regents' decisions upon us with respect to the change of the names of the other two institutions and the decision to permit majors in English and Speech and Modern Foreign Languages at Iowa State and to permit the granting of the non-teaching B.A. at Iowa State Teachers College.

So far in these remarks I have not mentioned the rather appalling lag in capital construction on the three campuses, and particularly on our own. At the present time we are still using 51 barracks totaling 97,000 square feet for classrooms, faculty offices, storage rooms, etc. In addition we are using obsolete buildings, such as Old Dental and Electrical Engineering, totaling 145,000 square feet. This total of 242,000 square feet cannot be much reduced by any construction now in process, and any construction authorized in 1961 will hardly be completed before 1964. To meet this need alone would cost about $6,000,000. We expect only modest increases in enrollment up to the fall of 1965, but from then on the flood-tide will be upon us, and the question is how, then, the General Assembly will catch up so that we can wholly eliminate temporary and obsolete buildings on the one hand and meet the needs of rising enrollments on the other.

It seems clear, therefore, that 1961 will give the legislature its last chance to meet the need before the flood begins. And, if the need is not met in the 1961 session, the odds are two to one that some deserving Iowa youth will not be able to gain admission to any Iowa institution of higher learning—public or private—beginning in the years 1965 and 1966. Unfortunately for us, wherever you look, whether it be Minnesota, Illinois, Michigan, Wisconsin, Indiana, Missouri, Kansas or Nebraska, you will see how far the Iowa institutions—particularly Iowa and Iowa State—are behind the institutions of the states I have mentioned in capital construction. No wonder Iowans go to California. Thousands more may have to go—just to get their children educated.

Yet education is an investment—an investment in the future. Iowa can afford it. It affords good roads. It affords anything it wants. Of all that is good, Iowa can afford the best. But it may be required to make some hard and wise decisions in order to do so.

Indeed it can ill afford not to afford the best. Prior to the Civil War, the State of Mississippi had the highest per capita income in the United States and more millionaires than New York. But after the War it allowed conditions to arise which forced a high percentage of its best youth to emigrate. That erosion of its top intellectual soil cast a blight upon the State of Mississippi from which it has never recovered. Iowa should profit from her example.

Brains create wealth, and wealth, rightly used, can provide both civilization and culture. The natural richness of the Iowa soil and its potential productivity were as real when the Indians ranged the Iowa soil as they are today. What made the difference? Brains and purpose. They transformed Iowa into a rich and fertile land. What is there on the flinty soil of Manhattan Island to create wealth? Primarily the brains which New York has been able over a century and a half to attract to itself. Once Boston and Philadelphia were greater cities than New York. But New York gambled on brains, and the gamble paid off. Can Iowa do less and survive?

I repeat the awesome prophecy of Whitehead: "The race which does not value trained intelligence is doomed." So, too, is the nation and the State!

JOHN F. KENNEDY

Inaugural Address

President Kennedy's Inaugural Address, January 20, 1961, is one of the distinguished speeches of our time. "Its impact on Americans of both parties," wrote *Life* magazine, "and on people everywhere in the world was immediate and impressive." *The New Yorker* called it such a speech as an Athenian or a Roman of the great ages of Demosthenes and Cicero could not have listened to unmoved.

Although the Inaugural ceremony provides a formal occasion on which the American people expect the new President to set the tone for the incoming Administration, no fixed pattern for the Inaugural Address has emerged over the years. Some Presidents have undertaken in considerable detail and at length to outline programs and to elaborate positions to which they wished to commit themselves and their parties. Others, like Lincoln in his Second Inaugural, have sought primarily and briefly to enunciate ideals for the country and to move their fellow citizens to renewed commitment to worthy principles and courageous action. President Kennedy's address belongs among the latter. Its appropriateness to the temper of the times and to the mood and condition of the country and of the world can hardly be in doubt.

For these reasons the address is eminently worth study. We would direct the student's attention especially to the style—to the selection and management of the language. We recommend that he study it carefully for the qualities of clarity, simplicity, appropriateness, and impressiveness which we have discussed in Chapter 12.

MY FELLOW CITIZENS:

We observe today not a victory of party but a celebration of freedom —symbolizing an end as well as a beginning—signifying renewal as well as change. For I have sworn before you and Almighty God the same solemn oath our forebears prescribed nearly a century and three-quarters ago.

The world is very different now. For man holds in his mortal hands the power to abolish all form of human poverty and all form of human life. And yet the same revolutionary beliefs for which our forebears fought are still at issue around the globe—the belief that the rights of man come not from the generosity of the state but from the hand of God.

We dare not forget today that we are the heirs of that first revolution. Let the word go forth from this time and place, to friend and foe alike, that the torch has been passed to a new generation of Americans—born in this century, tempered by war, disciplined by a hard and bitter peace, proud of our ancient heritage—and unwilling to witness or permit the

Reprinted by permission of the White House.

slow undoing of those human rights to which this nation has always been committed, and to which we are committed today—at home and around the world.

Let every nation know, whether it wishes us well or ill, that we shall pay any price, bear any burden, meet any hardship, support any friend, oppose any foe to assure the survival and success of liberty.

This much we pledge—and more.

To those old allies whose cultural and spiritual origins we share, we pledge the loyalty of faithful friends. United, there is little we cannot do in a host of new co-operative ventures. Divided, there is little we can do—for we dare not meet a powerful challenge at odds and split asunder.

To those new states whom we welcome to the ranks of the free, we pledge our word that one form of colonial control shall not have passed away merely to be replaced by a far more iron tyranny. We shall not always expect to find them supporting our view. But we shall always hope to find them strongly supporting their own freedom—and to remember that, in the past, those who foolishly sought power by riding the back of the tiger ended up inside.

To those peoples in the huts and villages of half the globe struggling to break the bonds of mass misery, we pledge our best efforts to help them help themselves, for whatever period is required—not because the Communists may be doing it, not because we seek their votes, but because it is right. If a free society cannot help the many who are poor, it cannot save the few who are rich.

To our sister republics south of our border, we offer a special pledge —to convert our good words into good deeds—in a new alliance for progress—to assist free men and free governments in casting off the chains of poverty. But this peaceful revolution of hope cannot become the prey of hostile powers. Let all our neighbors know that we shall join with them to oppose aggression or subversion anywhere in the Americas. And let every other power know that this hemisphere intends to remain the master of its own house.

To that world assembly of sovereign states, the United Nations, our last best hope in an age where the instruments of war have far outpaced the instruments of peace, we renew our pledge of support—to prevent it from becoming merely a forum of invective—to strengthen its shield of the new and the weak—and to enlarge the area in which its writ may run.

Finally, to those nations who would make themselves our adversary, we offer not a pledge but a request: that both sides begin anew the quest for peace, before the dark powers of destruction unleashed by science engulf all humanity in planned or accidental self-destruction.

We dare not tempt them with weakness. For only when our arms are sufficient beyond doubt can we be certain beyond doubt that they will never be employed.

But neither can two great and powerful groups of nations take comfort from our present course—both sides overburdened by the cost of modern weapons, both rightly alarmed by the steady spread of the deadly atom, yet both racing to alter that uncertain balance of terror that stays the hand of mankind's final war.

So let us begin anew—remembering on both sides that civility is not a sign of weakness, and sincerity is always subject to proof. Let us never negotiate out of fear. But let us never fear to negotiate.

Let both sides explore what problems unite us instead of belaboring those problems which divide us.

Let both sides, for the first time, formulate serious and precise proposals for the inspection and control of arms—and bring the absolute power to destroy other nations under the absolute control of all nations.

Let both sides seek to invoke the wonders of science instead of its terrors. Together let us explore the stars, conquer the deserts, eradicate disease, tap the ocean depths and encourage the arts and commerce.

Let both sides unite to heed in all corners of the earth the command of Isaiah—to "undo the heavy burdens . . . [and] let the oppressed go free."

And if a beachhead of a co-operation may push back the jungles of suspicion, let both sides join in the next task: creating, not a new balance of power, but a new world of law, where the strong are just and the weak secure and the peace preserved.

All this will not be finished in the first one hundred days. Nor will it be finished in the first one thousand days, nor in the life of this Administration, nor even perhaps in our lifetime on this planet. But let us begin.

In your hands, my fellow citizens, more than mine, will rest the final success or failure of our course. Since this country was founded, each generation of Americans has been summoned to give testimony to its national loyalty. The graves of young Americans who answered the call to service surround the globe.

Now the trumpet summons us again—not as a call to bear arms, though arms we need—not as a call to battle, though embattled we are—but a call to bear the burden of a long twilight struggle, year in and year out, "rejoicing in hope, patient in tribulation"—a struggle against the common enemies of man: tyranny, poverty, disease, and war itself.

Can we forge against these enemies a grand and global alliance, north and south, east and west, that can assure a more fruitful life for all mankind? Will you join in that historic effort?

In the long history of the world, only a few generations have been granted the role of defending freedom in its hour of maximum danger.

I do not shrink from this responsibility—I welcome it. I do not believe that any of us would exchange places with any other people or any other generation. The energy, the faith, the devotion which we bring to this endeavor will light our country and all who serve it—and the glow from that fire can truly light the world.

And so, my fellow Americans: Ask not what your country can do for you—ask what you can do for your country.

My fellow citizens of the world: Ask not what America will do for you, but what together we can do for the freedom of man.

Finally, whether you are citizens of America or citizens of the world, ask of us here the same high standards of strength and sacrifice which we ask of you. With a good conscience our only sure reward, with history the final judge of our deeds, let us go forth to lead the land we love, asking His blessing and His help, but knowing that here on earth God's work must truly be our own.

BOOKER T. WASHINGTON

Atlanta Address

Booker T. Washington, principal of the Tuskegee Normal and Industrial Institute, Alabama, from 1881 until his death in 1915, was born a Negro slave and became the leading spokesman of the Negro cause in America. Because of his position and his high reputation, he was invited to speak at the Cotton States Exposition at Atlanta in 1896. His speech on that occasion is a distinguished example of successful adaptation to a very ticklish situation. He had to gain or hold the respect of the white men and avoid offending their prejudices at the same time that he asserted the dignity and humanity of the Negro. The speech is firm but not belligerent, self-respecting but not aggressive, modest but not fawning, warning but not threatening, fair alike to the white man and the Negro. The structure is marked by a refrain drawn from a highly effective but brief story. The student might consider what in the speech would be more appropriate or less appropriate today; and what in it might be received well or ill today by Negroes or by white men.

ONE-THIRD of the population of the South is of the Negro race. No enterprise seeking the material, civil, or moral welfare of this section can disregard this element of our population and reach the highest success. I but convey to you, Mr. President and Directors, the sentiment of the masses of my race when I say that in no way have the value and manhood of the American Negro been more fittingly and generously recognized than by the managers of this magnificent Exposition at every stage of its progress. It is a recognition that will do more to cement the friendship of the two races than any occurrence since the dawn of our freedom.

Not only this, but the opportunity here afforded will awaken among us a new era of industrial progress. Ignorant and inexperienced, it is not strange that in the first years of our new life we began at the top instead of at the bottom; that a seat in Congress or the state legislature was more sought than real estate or industrial skill; that the political convention or stump speaking had more attractions than starting a dairy farm or truck garden.

A ship lost at sea for many days suddenly sighted a friendly vessel. From the mast of the unfortunate vessel was seen a signal. "Water, water; we die of thirst!" The answer from the friendly vessel at once came back, "Cast down your bucket where you are." A second time the signal,

The text is from *The Negro and the Exposition*, by Alice M. Bacon, Occasional Papers of the Trustees of the John F. Slater Fund, No. 7 (Baltimore, 1896).

"Water, water; send us water!" ran up from the distressed vessel, and was answered, "Cast down your bucket where you are." And a third and fourth signal for water was answered, "Cast down your bucket where you are." The captain of the distressed vessel, at last heeding the injunction, cast down his bucket, and it came up full of fresh, sparkling water from the mouth of the Amazon River. To those of my race who depend on bettering their condition in a foreign land or who underestimate the importance of cultivating friendly relations with the Southern white man, who is their next-door neighbour, I would say: "Cast down your bucket where you are"—cast it down in making friends in every manly way of the people of all races by whom we are surrounded. Cast it down in agriculture, mechanics, in commerce, in domestic service, and in the professions. And in this connection it is well to bear in mind that whatever other sins the South may be called to bear, when it comes to business, pure and simple, it is in the South that the Negro is given a man's chance in the commercial world, and in nothing is this Exposition more eloquent than in emphasizing this chance. Our greatest danger is that in the great leap from slavery to freedom we may overlook the fact that the masses of us are to live by the productions of our hands, and fail to keep in mind that we shall prosper in proportion as we learn to dignify and glorify common labour and put brains and skill into the common occupations of life; shall prosper in proportion as we learn to draw the line between the superficial and the substantial, the ornamental gewgaws of life and the useful. No race can prosper till it learns that there is as much dignity in tilling a field as in writing a poem. It is at the bottom of life we must begin, and not at the top. Nor should we permit our grievances to overshadow our opportunities.

To those of the white race who look to the incoming of those of foreign birth and strange tongue and habits for the prosperity of the South, were I permitted, I would repeat what I say to my own race, "Cast down your bucket where you are." Cast it down among the eight millions of Negroes whose habits you know, whose fidelity and love you have tested in days when to have proved treacherous meant the ruin of your firesides. Cast down your bucket among these people who have, without strikes and labour wars, tilled your fields, cleared your forests, builded your railroads and cities, brought forth treasures from the bowels of the earth, and helped make possible this magnificent representation of the progress of the South. Casting down your bucket among my people, helping and encouraging them as you are doing on these grounds, and to education of head, hand, and heart, you will find that they will buy your surplus land, make blossom the waste places in your fields, and run your factories. While doing this, you can be sure in the future, as in the past, that you and your families will be surrounded by the most patient, faithful, law-abiding, and unresentful people that the world has seen. As we have proved our loyalty to you in the past, in nursing your children, watching by the sick-bed of your mothers and fathers, and often following them with tear-dimmed eyes to their graves, so in the future, in our humble way, we shall stand by you with a devotion that no foreigner can approach, ready to lay down our lives, if need be, in defence of yours, interlacing our industrial, commercial, civil, and religious life with yours in a way that shall make the interests of both races one. In all things that are purely social we can be as separate as the fingers, yet one as the hand in all things essential to mutual progress.

There is no defence or security for any of us except in the highest intelligence and development of all. If anywhere there are efforts tending to curtail the fullest growth of the Negro, let these efforts be turned into stimulating, encouraging, and making him the most useful and intelligent citizen. Effort or means so invested will pay a thousand per cent interest. These efforts will be twice blessed—"blessing him that gives and him that takes."

There is no escape, through law of man or God, from the inevitable:

> The laws of changeless justice bind
> Oppressor with oppressed;
> And close as sin and suffering joined
> We march to fate abreast.

Nearly sixteen millions of hands will aid you in pulling the load upward, or they will pull against you the load downward. We shall constitute one-third and more of the ignorance and crime of the South, or one-third its intelligence and progress; we shall contribute one-third to the business and industrial prosperity of the South, or we shall prove a veritable body of death, stagnating, depressing, retarding every effort to advance the body politic.

Gentlemen of the Exposition: As we present to you our humble effort at an exhibition of our progress, you must not expect overmuch. Starting thirty years ago with ownership here and there in a few quilts and pumpkins and chickens (gathered from miscellaneous sources), remember the path that has led from these to the inventions and production of agricultural implements, buggies, steam-engines, newspapers, books, statuary, carving, paintings, the management of drug-stores and banks, has not been trodden without contact with thorns and thistles. While we take pride in what we exhibit as a result of our independent efforts, we do not for a moment forget that our part in this exhibition would fall far short of your expectations but for the constant help that has come to our educational life, not only from the Southern states, but especially from Northern philanthropists who have made their gifts a constant stream of blessing and encouragement.

The wisest among my race understand that the agitation of questions of social equality is the extremest folly, and that progress in the enjoyment of all the privileges that will come to us must be the result of severe and constant struggle rather than of artificial forcing. No race that has anything to contribute to the markets of the world is long in any degree ostracized. It is important and right that all privileges of the law be ours, but it is vastly more important that we be prepared for the exercises of these privileges. The opportunity to earn a dollar in a factory just now is worth infinitely more than the opportunity to spend a dollar in an opera-house.

In conclusion, may I repeat that nothing in thirty years has given us more hope and encouragement, and drawn us so near to you of the white race, as the opportunity offered by this Exposition; and here bending, as it were, over the altar that represents the results of the struggles of your race and mine, both starting practically empty-handed three decades ago, I pledge that, in your effort to work out the great and intricate problem which God has laid at the doors of the South, you shall have at all times the patient, sympathetic help of my race. Only let this be constantly in mind, that while, from representations in these buildings of the product of field, of forest, of mine, of factory, letters, and art, much good will come—yet, far above and beyond material benefits will be that higher good, that let us pray God will come, in a blotting out of sectional differences and racial animosities and suspicions, in a determination, even in the remotest corner, to administer absolute justice; in a willing obedience among all classes to the mandates of law, and in a spirit that will tolerate nothing but the highest equity in the enforcement of law. This, this, coupled with our material prosperity, will bring into our beloved South a new heaven and a new earth.

Index